Writing Fiction

Writing Fiction

A GUIDE TO NARRATIVE CRAFT

Janet Burroway
Florida State University

Little, Brown and Company

BOSTON · TORONTO

For David Daiches, mentor and friend

Library of Congress Catalog Card No. 81-84226

ISBN 0-316-11768-4

9 8 7 6 5 4 3

MV

Published simultaneously in Canada
by Little, Brown & Company (Canada) Limited

Printed in the United States of America

ACKNOWLEDGMENTS: *Stories*

Renata Adler. "Brownstone" from *Speedboat*, by Renata Adler. Copyright © 1971, 1972, 1973, 1975, 1976 by Renata Adler. Reprinted by permission of Random House, Inc.

John Barth. "Lost in the Funhouse" from the book *Lost in the Funhouse* by John Barth. Copyright © 1967 by The Atlantic Monthly Co. Reprinted by permission of Doubleday & Company, Inc.

Ray Bradbury. "August 2002: Night Meeting" from *The Martian Chronicles* by Ray Bradbury. Copyright 1950 by Ray Bradbury, © renewed 1977 by Ray Bradbury. Reprinted by permission of the Harold Matson Company, Inc.

Bruce Brooks. "Pulling Proofs," copyright © 1982 by Bruce Brooks. Used by permission of the author.

Rosellen Brown. "The Only Way to Make It in New York" from *Street Games* by Rosellen Brown. Copyright © 1974 by Rosellen Brown. Reprinted by permission of Doubleday & Company, Inc.

Frederick Busch. "Widow Water," copyright © 1974 by Frederick Busch. Reprinted from *Hardwater Country*, by Frederick Busch, by permission of Alfred A. Knopf, Inc.

Hortense Calisher. "In the Absence of Angels" from the book *In the Absence of Angels*. Copyright 1948, 1949, 1950, 1951 by Hortense Calisher. Reprinted by permission of Candida Donadio & Associates, Inc.

G. S. Sharat Chandra. "Jamal the Constable," first published in *Winter's Tales*, A. D. Maclean, ed. (London: Macmillan). © 1975 by G. S. Sharat Chandra. Reprinted by permission.

John Cheever. "The Bella Lingua," copyright © 1958 by John Cheever. Reprinted from *The Stories of John Cheever*, by John Cheever, by permission of Alfred A. Knopf, Inc.

Robert Coover. "The Babysitter" from *Pricksongs and Descants* by Robert Coover. Copyright © 1969 by Robert Coover. Reprinted by permission of the publisher, E. P. Dutton.

Patricia Duncan. "Zephyr." Originally appeared in *Harper's Magazine*, June 1977. Reprinted by permission of The Marie Rodell-Frances Collin Literary Agency. Copyright © 1977 by Patricia Duncan.

Ralph Ellison. "Battle Royal" from *Invisible Man*, by Ralph Ellison. Copyright 1947 by Ralph Ellison. Reprinted by permission of Random House, Inc.

Julia Fields. "Not Your Singing, Dancing Spade." Copyright © 1967 by *Negro Digest*. Reprinted by permission of the author.

Gabriel Josipovici. "Mobius the Stripper," © 1972 by Gabriel Josipovici. Reprinted by permission of the author and John Johnson, Authors Agents.

Vladimir Nabokov. "Signs and Symbols" from *Nabokov's Dozen* by Vladimir Nabokov. Copyright 1948 by Vladimir Nabokov. Reprinted by permission of Doubleday & Company, Inc.

Flannery O'Connor. "Everything That Rises Must Converge" from *Everything That Rises Must Converge* by Flannery O'Connor. Copyright © 1961, 1965 by the Estate of Mary Flannery O'Connor. Reprinted by permission of Farrar, Straus and Giroux, Inc.

James Purdy. "Cutting Edge," copyright © 1957 by James Purdy. Reprinted by permission of William Morris Agency, Inc. as agents for James Purdy.

Richard Selzer. "The Masked Marvel's Last Toehold" from *Confessions of a Knife* by Richard Selzer. Copyright © 1979 by David Goodman and Janet Selzer, Trustees. Reprinted by permission of Simon & Schuster, a Division of Gulf & Western Corporation.

Alan Sillitoe. "The Loneliness of the Long-Distance Runner" from *The Loneliness of the Long-Distance Runner*, by Alan Sillitoe. Copyright © 1959 by Alan Sillitoe. Reprinted by permission of Alfred A. Knopf, Inc.

Joe Taylor. "Judas," copyright © 1982 by Joe Taylor. Used by permission of the author.

E. B. White. "The Second Tree from the Corner" from *The Second Tree from the Corner* by E. B. White. Copyright 1947 by E. B. White. Originally appeared in *The New Yorker* and reprinted by permission of Harper & Row, Publishers, Inc.

(continued on page 402)

PREFACE

This book is the result of a course in "Narrative Techniques" at Florida State University, gradually developed over a period of nine years. I inherited the course — or at least its title — from the Pulitzer Prize-winning novelist Michael Shaara, who had been superbly successful at it. But he had left no hints on how to teach creative writing. Thus, the book developed because of my initial lack of direction. Although I could react with reasonable competence and confidence to what was already written in workshop, I was overwhelmed by the task of devising lectures and assignments.

And yet I had a dim but firm conviction that writing can be taught — a conviction partly theoretical and partly the result of my own experience. On the theoretical side there was the persistence of the academic controversy over whether it is worth teaching "creative writing" at all; whether the ability to write was an innate gift to which teaching was irrelevant and the academic atmosphere destructive.

It seemed to me self-evident that talent can be taught in no subject; neither history nor trigonometry nor music nor physical therapy. But each art and science involves, aside from the divine fire, some rules, techniques, devices, artifices, and contrivances. These can be taught. The truly talented will come to them of his or her own accord, but at a cost of years. And if, in the stingiest assessment, the classroom might offer a beginning writer a few tricks of the trade, there is always also the possibility that form is substance, and that a study of technique is the very thing that lets talent or genius take root.

On the practical side, I had reason to believe that writing can be taught, because I was taught to write. Some of my teachers were encouraging and some were harsh; some ruminated and some dictated technique. One got me an agent; one told me to quit. But every one of them gave me something I could not have got on my own, taught me something I could not have learned alone.

My problem at Florida State, then, was not only how to survive in a teaching situation for which I had no guidelines, but how, somehow, to pay back a little of what I'd been given.

My students clued me in and, over the first three years, taught me what they wanted to know. It became clear that, apart from time, honesty, and an open mind, what they most craved was discipline. Their response to a variety of experimental assignments showed me that they were most enthusiastic about the rigors of simple craft — the consistency of viewpoint, the necessity of crisis action, the value of concrete detail, and so forth.

For that reason, the course and the book that developed follow a traditional division of the art of fiction into elements that will be familiar to those who have studied the short story and the novel as literature. I think this is as it should be (or at least one constructive way it can be); if plot, character, atmosphere, point of view, metaphor, and theme are the elements for which a reader looks, then presumably they are the elements that a writer wants to present.

Each chapter deals with one of these elements, and in addition an early chapter is devoted to the writerly virtue of "showing not telling." I have tried to present each element from the point of view of the writer face-to-face with a blank page, to suggest what the problems are and how they can be solved, quoting illustrations from published authors and student authors, and occasionally inventing a passage myself. Each chapter is followed by two stories that I think have high merit, and by suggestions for discussion that pinpoint the author's technique with regard to the element dealt with in that chapter. I have chosen a variety of stories, some of which are classics, some little known; some simple in structure and theme, some difficult and demanding. Each chapter ends with a series of assignments designed to sharpen skills in dealing with each of the fictional elements.

In *Writing Fiction* I try to confront and convey as practically as possible what a writer does, and what you can do in order to write better. For that reason I present a number of diagrams, dicta, pigeonholes, and rules — but all these rules are of the sort proved by exception. Henry James said that the only thing we can demand of a novelist *per se* is that he should be interesting. The rules here presented suggest what has been tried and proven interesting in fiction; but the ultimate and only rule is that whatever works, works.

Nevertheless, there is a conviction or prejudice underlying all the advice in these pages, which is that writing is communication. William Sloane, in *The Craft of Writing*, puts it this way: "I believe that literature is for readers and that that is what literature is."

Writing courses got a bad name in America in the forties and fifties for teaching "formula" stories — how to sell to *Post* and *True Confessions*. I never knew anyone who taught or took such a course, but the reputation lingers. Today, after Spock, permissiveness, progressive education, and consciousness-raising of many sorts, I perceive the danger for fiction to be the opposite. I rarely meet students who want only to know how to sell. I frequently encounter students who "write only for themselves" or who insist that their outpourings "mean whatever the reader wants them to mean." My reply to this is that it's fine; only leave them in the drawer. If you demand our time for reading, then you must *communicate*. Because the page is a way of getting something from one mind into another, any piece of writing, whether set in type or kept in a notebook, must *mean*.

It's been my experience as both student and teacher that a techniques course or a workshop in which student writing is discussed among teacher and peers can help a beginning writer to *mean*. To begin with, it imposes a deadline, forcing you to produce. It offers an automatic audience, something that even the most successful professional can never be quite certain of finding. Most often, it offers course credit, which is the same thing as getting paid for writing. Above all, it offers a quantity of response. *All* writers, I believe, have some resistance, however faint, to criticism; all are of necessity defensive of their creations. If one person says, "This passage is unclear to me," it's always possible to feel that the critic is stupid or inattentive. But if in the classroom fifteen or twenty critic peers agree that "This passage is unclear," it helps convince us that the responsibility lies with the writer, and the fault with the writing.

A final word: I adopt, and recommend without reservation to teachers and student critics, this attitude toward student writing: that literary standards are absolute, and (except for bad spelling/grammar/punctuation and sloth) forgiveness is also absolute. The quality of the communication is under judgment; the author's character is not.

I'm indebted to so many people for help direct or indirect in the writing of this book that it is difficult to know whom to thank in print. I should single out the Writers' Workshop at the University of Iowa for time and space to compose half the text; and my sons Tim and Alex Eysselinck for fending off the phone calls while I composed the rest. It is my students who have taught me most, and of these I want to thank especially Patricia Duncan and Bill Beesting. I'm also grateful to my colleagues Jerome Stern, Sheila Taylor, and Elisabeth Muhlenfeld, who share the task of teaching writing at Florida State, and who share their ideas freely and generously. And, finally, my thanks to my reviewers for their helpful suggestions: Edward A. Dornan (Orange Coast College), Max Steele (University of North Carolina-Chapel Hill), and Marilyn Throne (Miami University).

CONTENTS

Writing Fiction

A STORY IS A WAR
Story Form and Structure

Conflict, Crisis, and Resolution
Story and Plot
The Short Story and the Novel

What makes you want to write?

It seems likely that the earliest storytellers — in the tent or the harem, around the campfire or on the Viking ship — told stories out of an impulse to tell stories. They made themselves popular by distracting their listeners from a dull or dangerous evening with heroic exploits and a skill at creating suspense: What happened next? And after that? And then what happened?

"Natural storytellers" are still around, and a few of them are very rich. Some are on the best-seller list; more are in television and film. But it's probable that your impulse to write has little to do with the desire or the skill to work out a plot. On the contrary, you want to write because you are sensitive. You have something to say that does not answer the question, What happened next? You share with most — and the best — twentieth-century fiction writers a sense of the injustice, the absurdity, and the beauty of the world; and you want to register your protest, your laughter, and your affirmation.

Yet readers still want to wonder what happened next; and unless you make them wonder, they will not turn the page. You must master plot, because no matter how profound or illuminating your vision of the world may be, you cannot convey it to those who do not read you.

E. M. Forster, in *Aspects of the Novel*, mourns the necessity of storytelling.

Let us listen to three voices. If you ask one type of man, "What does a novel do?" he will reply placidly: "Well — I don't know — it seems a funny sort of question to ask — a novel's a novel — well, I don't know — I suppose it kind of tells a story, so to speak." He is quite good-tempered and vague, and probably driving a motor bus at the same time and paying no more attention to literature than it merits. Another man, whom I visualize as on a golf-course, will be aggressive and brisk. He will reply: "What does a novel do? Why, tell a story of course, and I've no use for it if it didn't. I like a story. Very bad taste on my part, no doubt, but I like a story. You can take your art, you can take your literature, you can take your music, but give me a good story. And I like a story to be a story, mind, and my wife's the same." And a third man, he says in a sort of drooping regretful voice, "Yes — oh dear yes — the novel tells a story." I respect and admire the first speaker. I detest and fear the second. And the third is myself. Yes — oh dear yes — the novel tells a story. That is the fundamental aspect without which it could not exist. That is the highest factor common to all novels, and I wish that it was not so, that it could be something different — melody, or perception of the truth, not this low atavistic form.

When editors take the trouble to write a rejection letter to a young author (and they do so only when they think the author talented), the gist of the letter most frequently is: "This piece is sensitive (perceptive, vivid, original, brilliant, funny, moving), but it is not a *story*."

How do you know when you have written a story? And if you're not a natural-born wandering minstrel, can you go about learning to write one?

It's interesting that we react with such different attitudes to the words "formula" and "form." A *formula story* is hackwork, the very lowest "atavistic" form of supplying a demand. To write one, you read three dozen copies of *Cosmopolitan* or *Omni*, make a list of what kinds of characters and situations the editors buy, shuffle nearly identical characters around in slightly altered situations, and sit back to wait for the check. Whereas *form* is a term of the highest artistic approbation, even reverence, with overtones of *order, harmony, model, archetype*.

And "story" is a "form" of literature. Like a face, it has necessary features in a necessary harmony. We're aware of the infinite variety of human faces, aware of their unique individuality, which is so powerful that you can recognize a face you know even after twenty years of age and fashion have done their work on it. We're aware that minute alterations in the features can express grief, anger, or joy. If you place side by side two photographs of, say, Brooke Shields and Geronimo, you are instantly aware of the fundamental differences of age, race, sex, class, and century; yet these two faces are more like each other than either is like a foot or a fern, both of which have their own distinctive forms. Every face has two eyes, a nose between them, a mouth below; a forehead, two cheeks, two ears, and a jaw. If a face is missing one of these features, you may say, "I love this face in spite of its lacking a nose," but you must acknowledge the *in spite of.* You can't simply say, "This is a wonderful face."

The same is true of a story. You might say, "I love this piece even though there's no crisis action in it." You can't say, "This is a wonderful story."

Conflict, Crisis, and Resolution

Fortunately, the necessary features of the story form are fewer than those of a face. They are *conflict, crisis,* and *resolution.*

Conflict is the first encountered and the fundamental element of fiction, necessary because in literature, only trouble is interesting.

Only trouble is interesting. This is not so in life. Life offers periods of comfortable communication, peaceful pleasure, and productive work, all of which are extremely interesting to those involved. But such passages about such times by themselves make for dull reading; they can be used as lulls in an otherwise tense situation, as a resolution, even as a hint that something awful is about to happen; they cannot be used as whole plot.

Suppose, for example, you go on a picnic. You find a beautiful deserted meadow with a lake nearby. The weather is splendid and so is the company. The food's delicious, the water's fine, and the insects have taken the day off. Afterward, someone asks you how your picnic was. "Terrific," you reply, "really perfect." No story.

But suppose the next week you go back for a rerun. You set your picnic blanket on an anthill. You all race for the lake to get cold water on the bites, and one of your friends goes too far out on the plastic raft, which deflates. He can't swim and you have to save him. On the way in you gash your foot on a broken bottle. When you get back to the picnic, the ants have taken over the cake, and a possum has demolished the chicken. Just then the sky opens up. When you gather your things to race for the car, you notice an irritated bull has broken through the fence. The others run for it, but because of your bleeding heel the best you can do is hobble. You have two choices: try to outrun him or stand perfectly still and hope he's interested only in a moving target. At this point, you don't know if your friends can be counted on for help, even the nerd whose life you saved.

You don't know if it's true that a bull is attracted by the smell of blood. . . .

A year later, assuming you're around to tell about it, you are still saying, "Let me *tell* you what happened last year. . . ." And your listeners are saying, "What a story!"

If this contrast is true of so trivial a subject as a picnic, it is even more so of the great themes of life: birth, love, sex, work, and death. Here is a very interesting love story to *live*: Jan and Jon meet in college. Both are beautiful, intelligent, talented, popular, and well adjusted. They're of the same race, class, religion, and political persuasion. They are sexually compatible. Their parents become fast friends. They marry on graduating, and both get rewarding work in the same city. They have three children, all of whom are healthy, happy, beautiful, intelligent, and popular; the children love and respect their parents to a degree that is the envy of everyone. All the children succeed in work and marriage. Jan and Jon die peacefully, of natural causes, at the same moment, at the age of eighty-two, and are buried in the same grave.

No doubt this love story is very interesting to Jan and Jon, but you can't make a novel of it. The great love stories involve intense passion and a monumental impediment to that passion's fulfillment. So: they love each other passionately, but their parents are sworn enemies (*Romeo and Juliet*). Or: they love each other passionately, but he's black and she's white, and he has an enemy who wants to punish him (*Othello*). Or: they love each other passionately, but she's married (*Anna Karenina*). Or: he loves her passionately, but she falls in love with him only when she has worn out his passion ("Frankly, my dear, I don't give a damn"). Or, to take a modern example that verges on formula: they love each other charmingly, but she's got leukemia (Erich Segal's *Love Story*).

In each of these plots, there is both intense desire and great danger to the achievement of that desire; generally speaking, this shape holds good for all plots. It can be called 3-D: *drama* equals *desire* plus *danger*. One common fault of talented young writers is to create a main character who is essentially passive. This is an understandable fault; as a writer you are an observer of human nature and activity, and so you identify easily with a character who observes, reflects, and suffers. But such a character's passivity transmits itself to the page, and the story also becomes passive. Aristotle rather startlingly claimed that a man *is* his desire. It is true that in fiction, in order to engage our attention and sympathy, the central character must *want*, and want intensely.

The thing that character wants need not be violent or spectacular; it is the *intensity* of the wanting that counts. She may want only to survive, but if so she must want enormously to survive, and there must be distinct cause to doubt that she will succeed. He may want, like Samuel Beckett's Murphy, only to tie himself to his rocking chair and rock, but if so he will also want a woman who wants him to get up and get a job. He may want, like Ben of *The Graduate*, only to be left alone, but if so he will want fiercely, despairingly, to be left alone, while his solitude is endangered by forces of increasing magnitude: family members invade his room; a businessman buttonholes him to talk about a career in plastics; an older woman — most dangerously! — wants to take him home.

The last two examples suggest — and it's important to realize — that the great dangers in life and in literature are not necessarily the most spectacular. Another mistake frequently made by young writers is to think that they can best introduce drama into their stories by way of muggers, murderers, crashes, and monsters, the external stock dangers of pulp and TV. In fact, all of us know that the profoundest impediments to our desire most often lie close to home, in our own bodies, personalities, friends, lovers, and families. Fewer people have cause to panic at the approach of a stranger with a gun than at the approach of mama with the curling iron. More passion is destroyed at the breakfast table than in a time warp.

A frequently used critical tool divides possible conflicts into several basic categories: man against man, man against nature, man against society, man against machine, man against God, man against himself. Most stories fall into these categories, and they can provide a useful way of discussing and comparing works. But the employment of categories can be misleading to someone behind the typewriter, insofar as it suggests that literary conflicts take place in these abstract, cosmic dimensions. A writer needs a specific story to tell, and if you sit down to pit "man" against "nature" you will have less of a story than if you pit seventeen-year-old James Tucker of Weehawken, New Jersey, against a two-and-a-half-foot bigmouth bass in the backwoods of Toomsuba, Mississippi. The value of specificity is a point to which we will return (again and again).

Once conflict is sharply established and developed in a story, the conflict must end. There must be a crisis and a resolution. This is not like life either, and although it is so obvious a point, it needs to be insisted on. Order is a major value that literature offers us, and order implies that the subject has been brought to closure. In life this never quite happens. Even the natural "happy endings," marriage and birth, leave domesticity and childrearing to be dealt with; the natural "tragic endings," separation and death, leave trauma and bereavement in their wake. Literature absolves us of these nuisances. Whether or not the lives of the characters end, the story does, and leaves us with a satisfying sense of completion. This is one reason we enjoy crying or feeling terrified or even nauseated by fiction; we know in advance that it's going to be *over*, and by contrast with the continual struggle of living, all that ends, ends well.

What I want to do now is to present several ways — they are all essentially metaphors — of seeing this pattern of *conflict-crisis-resolution* in order to make the shape and its many variations clearer, and particularly to indicate what a crisis action is.

The editor and teacher Mel McKee states flatly that "a story is a war. It is sustained and immediate combat." He offers four imperatives for the writing of this "war" story.

(1) get your fighters fighting, (2) have something — the stake — worth their fighting over, (3) have the fight dive into a series of battles with the last battle in the series the biggest and most dangerous of all, (4) have a walking away from the fight.

The stake over which wars are fought is usually a territory, and it's important that this "territory" in a story be as tangible and specific as the *Bay of Pigs*. In James Purdy's short story "Cutting Edge," for example, the war is fought over the territory of a beard, and the fighters get fighting over it in the first paragraph. As with warring nations, the story territory itself can come to represent all sorts of fine abstractions — patriotism, freedom, motherhood, virtue, and God's will — but the soldiers fight yard by yard over a particular piece of grass or sand.

Just as a "police action" may escalate into a holocaust, story form follows its most natural order of "complications" when each battle is bigger than the last. It begins with an open ground skirmish, which does not decide the war. Then one side brings in spies; the other, guerrillas; these actions do not decide the war. So one side brings in the air force; the other answers with antiaircraft. One side takes to missiles, the other answers with rockets. One side has poison gas, and the other has a hand on the nuclear button. Metaphorically, this is what happens in a story. As long as one antagonist can recoup enough power to counterattack, the conflict goes on. But, at some point in the story, one of the antagonists will produce a weapon from which the other cannot recover. *The crisis action is the last battle and occurs when the outcome becomes inevitable*; when, after much doubt, there can no longer be any doubt who wins the particular territory — though there can be much doubt about moral victory. In "Cutting Edge," the war is fought over Bobby's beard, and that war is inevitably finished when he savagely shaves it off. The "walking away from the fight" in this story — its resolution — involves subtle and ambiguous questions of who has really won.

Notice that although a plot involves desire and a danger to that desire, it does not necessarily end happily if the desire is achieved, nor unhappily if it is not. In *Hamlet*, Hamlet's desire is to kill King Claudius, and he is prevented from doing so for most of the play by other characters, intrigues, and his own mental state. When he finally succeeds, it is at the cost of every significant life in the play, including his own. So that although the hero "wins" his particular "territory," the play is a tragedy.

Novelist Michael Shaara, slightly altering the war metaphor, describes a story as a power struggle between equal forces. It is imperative, he argues, that each antagonist have sufficient power to leave the reader in doubt about the outcome so that anticipation and suspense may be built. We may be wholly in sympathy with one character, and even reasonably confident that he will triumph. But his antagonist must represent a real and potent danger, and the pattern of the story's complications will be achieved by *shifting the power back and forth from one antagonist to the other.* Finally an action will occur that will shift the power irretrievably in one direction.

It is also important to understand that "power" takes many forms and that some of them have the external appearance of weakness. Anyone who has ever been tied to the demands of an invalid can understand this: sickness can be great strength. Weakness, need, passivity, an ostensible desire not to be any trouble to anybody — all these can be used as manipulative tools to prevent the protagonist from achieving his desire. Martyrdom is immensely powerful, whether we sympathize with it or not; a dying man absorbs all our energies.

The nineteenth-century German critic Gustav Freitag analyzed five-act dramas and came up with a diagram of plot that has come to be known as the Freitag Pyramid. Plot begins, he said, with an exposition (of the conflict), followed by complications (or *nouement,* the "knotting up" of the situation) leading to a crisis, which is followed by a "falling action" or anticlimax, resulting in a resolution (or *dénouement,* "unknotting").

The trouble with this useful diagram is that it visually suggests that a crisis comes in the middle of the "pyramid" shape of a plot, whereas even in a five-act drama the crisis is usually saved for the middle of the fifth act; and in modern fiction, particularly the compact short-story form, the falling action is likely to be very brief or nonexistent. Often the crisis action itself

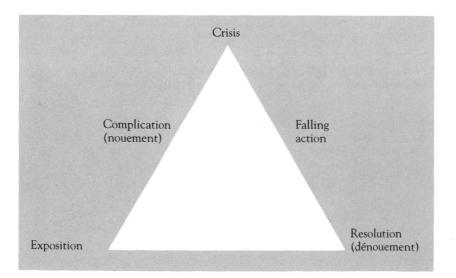

Crisis

Complication
(nouement)

Falling
action

Exposition

Resolution
(dénouement)

implies the resolution, which is not stated but exists as an idea established in the reader's mind.

For our purposes, it is probably more useful to think of story shape as an inverted checkmark. If we take the familiar tale, "Cinderella," and look at it in terms of this diagram, we can see how the various elements reveal themselves even in this simple children's story. At the opening of the tale we're given the basic conflict: Cinderella's mother has died, and her father has married a brutal woman with two waspish daughters. Cinderella is made to do all the dirtiest and most menial work, and she weeps among the cinders. The Stepmother has on her side the strength of ugliness and evil (two very powerful qualities in literature as in life). With her daughters she also has the strength of numbers, and she has parental authority. Cinderella has only beauty and goodness, but (in literature and life) these are also very powerful.

At the beginning of the struggle, the power is very clearly on the Stepmother's side. But the first *event* (action, battle) of the story is that an invitation arrives from the Prince, which explicitly states that *all* the ladies of the land are invited to a ball. Notice that Cinderella's desire is not to triumph over her Stepmother (though she eventually will, much to our satisfaction); such a desire would diminish her goodness. She simply wants to be relieved of her mistreatment. She wants equality, so that the Prince's invitation, which specifically gives her a right equal to the Stepmother's and Stepdaughters' rights, shifts the power to her.

The Stepmother takes the power back by blunt force: you may not go; you must get us ready to go. Cinderella does so, and the three leave for the ball.

Then what happens? The Fairy Godmother appears. It is *very* powerful to have magic on your side. The Fairy Godmother offers Cinderella a gown;

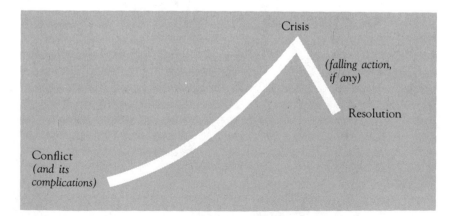

Crisis

(falling action, if any)

Resolution

Conflict *(and its complications)*

glass slippers; and a coach, horses, and footmen, giving her more force than she has yet had.

But the magic is not all-potent. It has a qualification that portends bad luck. It will last only until midnight (unlike the Stepmother's authority), and Cinderella must leave the ball before the clock strikes twelve or risk exposure and defeat.

What happens next? She goes to the ball and the Prince falls in love with her — and love is an even more powerful weapon than magic in a literary war. In some versions of the tale, the Stepmother and Stepsisters are made to marvel at the beauty of the Princess they don't recognize, pointing the irony of Cinderella's new power.

And then? The magic quits. The clock strikes twelve, and Cinderella runs down the steps in her rags to her rats and pumpkin, losing a slipper, bereft of her power in every way.

But after that, the Prince sends out a messenger with the glass slipper and a dictum (a dramatic repetition of the original invitation in which all ladies were invited to the ball) that every female in the land is to try on the slipper. Cinderella is given her rights again by royal decree.

What happens then? In most good retellings of the tale, the Stepmother also repeats her assumption of brute authority by hiding Cinderella away, while our expectation of triumph is tantalizingly delayed with grotesque comedy: one sister cuts off a toe, the other a heel, trying to fit into the heroine's rightful slipper.

After that, Cinderella tries on the slipper and it fits. *This is the crisis action.* Magic, love, and royalty join to recognize the heroine's true self; and evil, numbers, and authority are powerless against them. At this point, the power struggle has been decided; the outcome is inevitable. When the slipper fits, no further action can occur that will deprive Cinderella of her desire.

The tale has a brief "falling action" or "walking away from the fight": the Prince sweeps Cinderella up on his white horse and gallops away to their wedding. The story comes to closure with the classic resolution of all comedy: they lived happily every after. Applied to the diagram, the story's pattern looks like the drawing on page 10.

In the *Poetics*, the first extensive work of extant Western literary criticism, Aristotle referred to the crisis action of a tragedy as a "peripeteia," or reversal of the protagonist's fortunes. Aristotle specified that this reversal came about because of "hamartia," which has for centuries been translated as a "tragic flaw" in the protagonist's character, usually assumed to be, or defined as, pride. But more recent critics have defined and translated "hamartia" much more narrowly as a "mistake in identity" whereby the reversal comes about in a "recognition."

It is true that recognition scenes have played a disproportionately large role in the crisis actions of plots both comic and tragic, and that these

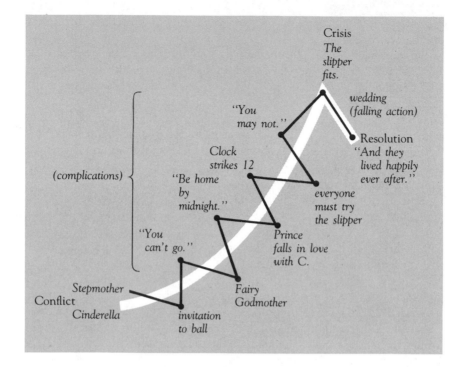

Crisis
The
slipper
fits.

"You
may not."

wedding
(falling action)

Clock
strikes 12

Resolution
"And they
lived happily
ever after."

(complications)

"Be home
by
midnight."

everyone
must try
the slipper

"You
can't go."

Prince
falls in love
with C.

Stepmother
Conflict
Cinderella

Fairy
Godmother

invitation
to ball

scenes frequently stretch credibility; it's already been observed that you are unlikely to mistake the face of your mother, son, uncle, or even friend in real life, and yet such mistakes have provided the turning point of many a plot. If, however, the notion of "recognition" is extended to more abstract and subtle realms, it becomes a powerful metaphor for moments of "realization." In other words, the "recognition scene" in literature may stand for that moment in life when we "recognize" that the man we have considered good is evil, the event we have considered insignificant is crucial, the woman we've thought out of touch with reality is a genius, the object we thought desirable is poison. There is in this symbolic way a recognition in "Cinderella." We knew that she was essentially a princess, but until the Prince recognizes her as one, our knowledge must be frustrated.

James Joyce developed a similar idea when he spoke of, and recorded both in his notebooks and in his stories, moments of what he called "epiphany." *Epiphany* as Joyce saw it is a crisis action in the mind, a moment when a person, an event, or a thing is seen in a light so new that it is as if it has never been seen before; at this recognition, the mental landscape of the viewer is permanently changed.

In many of the finest modern short stories and novels, the true territory of conflict is the main character's mind, and so the real crisis action must occur there. Yet it is important to grasp that Joyce chose the word "epiphany" to represent this moment of reversal, and that the word means "a *mani-festation* of a supernatural being"; specifically, in Christian doctrine, "the manifestation of Christ to the gentiles." By extension, then, in a short story any mental reversal that takes place in the crisis of a story must be *manifested*; it must be triggered or shown by an action. The slipper must fit. It would not do if the Stepmother just happened to change her mind and give up the struggle; it would not do if the Prince just happened to notice that Cinderella looked like his love. The moment of recognition must be manifested in an action.

Purdy's "Cutting Edge," which needless to say has much of the feel of modern life and more of a feel of "slice of life" than of a fairy tale, the conflict and the crisis are nevertheless very clearly delineated and could be positioned on the diagram with equal certainty. As has been said, the conflict is over Bobby's beard; he shaves it off. But the recognition and the reversal inherent in this action are much more subtle and complex. The story cannot end "they lived happily ever after," or even "they lived unhappily ever after."

Much great fiction, and the preponderance of serious modern fiction, echoes life in its suggestion that there are no clear or permanent solutions, that the conflicts of character, relationship, and the cosmos cannot be permanently resolved.

Yet the story form demands a resolution. Is there such a thing as a no-resolution resolution? Yes, and it also has a very specific form. Go back to the metaphor that "a story is a war." After the skirmish, after the guerrillas, after the air strike, after the poison gas and the nuclear holocaust, imagine that the two surviving combatants, one on each side, emerge from their fallout shelters. They crawl, then stumble to the fence that marks the border. Each possessively grasps the barbed wire with a bloodied fist. The "resolution" of this battle is that neither side will ever give up and that no one will ever win; *there will never be a resolution.* This is a distinct reversal (the recognition takes place in the reader's mind) of the opening scene, in which it seemed eminently worthwhile to open a ground skirmish. In the statement of the conflict was an inherent possibility that one side or another could win. Inherent in the resolution is a statement that no one can ever win. That is a distinct reversal and a powerful resolution.

Story and Plot

So far, I have used the words "story" and "plot" interchangeably. The equation of the two terms is so common that they are often comfortably understood as synonyms. When an editor says, "This is not a story," the implication is not that it lacks character, theme, setting, or even incident, but that it has no plot.

Yet there is a distinction frequently drawn between the two terms, a distinction simple in itself but that gives rise to manifold subtleties in the craft of narrative and that also represents a vital decision that you as a writer must make: Where does the narrative begin?

The distinction is easily made. A *story* is a series of events recorded in their chronological order. A *plot* is a series of events deliberately arranged so as to reveal their dramatic, thematic, and emotional significance.

Here, for example, is a fairly standard story: A sober, industrious, and rather dull young man meets the woman of his dreams. She is beautiful, brilliant, passionate, and compassionate; more wonderful still, she loves him. They plan to marry, and on the eve of their wedding his friends give him a stag party in the course of which they tease him, ply him with liquor, and drag him off to a whorehouse for a last fling. There he stumbles into a cubicle . . . to find himself facing his bride-to-be.

Where does this story become interesting? Where does the *plot* begin?

You may start, if you like, with the young man's *Mayflower* ancestry. But if you do, it's going to be a very long story, and we're likely to close the book about the middle of the nineteenth century. You may begin with the first time he meets the extraordinary woman, but again you must cover at least weeks, probably months, in a few pages; and that means you must summarize, skip, and generalize, and you'll have a hard time both maintaining your credibility and holding our attention. Begin at the stag party? Better. If you do so, you will somehow have to let us know all that has gone before, either through dialogue or through the young man's memory, but you have only one evening of action to cover, and we'll get to the conflict quickly. Suppose you begin instead the next morning, when the man wakes with a hangover in bed in a brothel with his bride on his wedding day. Is that, perhaps, the best of all? An immediate conflict that must lead to a quick and striking crisis?

Humphry House, in his commentaries on Aristotle, defines *story* as everything the reader needs to know to make coherent sense of the plot, and *plot* as the particular portion of the story the author chooses to present — the "present tense" of the narrative. The story of *Oedipus Rex*, for example, begins before Oedipus' birth with the oracle predicting that he will murder his father and marry his mother. It includes his birth, his abandonment with hobbled ankles, his childhood with his foster parents, his flight from them, his murder of the stranger at the crossroads, his triumph over the Sphinx, his marriage to Jocasta and his reign in Thebes, his fatherhood, the Theban plague, his discovery of the truth, and his self-blinding and self-banishment. When Sophocles set out to plot a play on this story, he began at dawn on the very last day of it. All the information about Oedipus' life is necessary to understand the plot, but the plot begins with the conflict: How can Oedipus get rid of the plague in Thebes? Because the plot is so arranged, it is the revelation of the past that makes up the action of the play, a process of discovery that gives rise to the significant theme: Who am I? Had Sophocles begun with the oracle before Oedipus' birth, no such theme and no such significance could have been explored.

Forster makes substantially the same distinction between plot and story. A story, he says, is:

> the chopped off length of the tape worm of time . . . a narrative of events arranged in their time sequence. A plot is also a narrative of events, the emphasis falling on causality. "The king died, and then the queen died," is a story. "The king died, and then the queen died of grief," is a plot. The time-sequence is preserved, but the sense of causality overshadows it. Or again: "The queen died, no one knew why, until it was discovered that it was through grief at the death of the king." This is a plot with a mystery in it, a form capable of high development. It suspends the time-sequence, it moves as far away from the story as its limitations will allow. Consider the death of the queen. If it is in a story we say, "and then?" If it is in a plot we ask, "why?"

The human desire to know why is as powerful as the desire to know what happened next, and it is a desire of a higher order. Once we have the facts, we inevitably look for the links between them, and only when we find such links are we satisfied that we "understand." Rote memorization in a science bores almost everyone. Grasp and a sense of discovery begin only when we perceive *why* "a body in motion tends to remain in motion" and what an immense effect this actuality has on the phenomena of our lives.

The same is true of the events of a story. Random incidents neither move nor illuminate; we want to know why one thing leads to another and to feel the inevitability of cause and effect.

Here is a series of uninteresting events chronologically arranged.

Ariadne had a bad dream.
She woke up tired and cross.
She ate breakfast.
She headed for class.
She saw Leroy.
She fell on the steps and broke her ankle.
Leroy offered to take notes for her.
She went to a hospital.

This series of events does not constitute a plot, and if you wish to fashion it into a plot you can do so only by letting us know the meaningful relations among the events. We first assume that Ariadne woke in a temper *because* of her bad dream, and that Leroy offered to take notes for her because she broke her ankle. But why did she fall? Perhaps because she saw Leroy? Does that suggest that her bad dream was about him? Was she, then, thinking about his dream-rejection as she broke her egg irritably on the edge of the frying pan? What is the effect of his offer? Is it a triumph or just another polite form of rejection when, really, he *could* have missed class once to drive her to the x-ray lab? All the emotional and dramatic significance of these ordinary events emerges in the relation of cause to effect, and where such relation can be shown, a possible plot comes into existence.

Ariadne's is a story you might very well choose to tell chronologically: it needs to cover only an hour or two, and that much can be handled in the compressed form of the short story. But such a choice of plot is not inevitable even in this short compass. Might it be more gripping to begin with the wince of pain as she stumbles? Leroy comes to help her up and the yolk yellow of his T-shirt fills her field of vision. In the shock of pain she is immediately back in her dream. . . .

When "nothing happens" in a story, it is because we fail to sense the causal relation between what happens first and what happens next. When something does "happen," it is because the resolution of a short story or a novel describes a change in the character's life, an effect of the events that have gone before. This is why Aristotle insisted with such apparent simplicity on "a beginning, a middle, and an end." A story is capable of many meanings, and it is first of all in the choice of structure, which portion of the story forms the plot, that you offer us the gratifying sense that we "understand."

The Short Story and the Novel

Many editors and writers insist on an essential disjunction between the form of the short story and that of the novel. It is my belief, however, that, like the distinction between story and plot, the distinction between the two forms is very simple, and the many and profound possibilities of difference proceed from that simple source.

A short story is short, and a novel is long.

Because of this, a short story can waste no words. It can deal with only one or a very few consciousnesses. It may recount only one central action and one major change or effect in the life of the central character or characters. It can afford no digression that does not directly affect the action. A short story strives for a single emotional impact, imparts a single understanding, though both impact and understanding may be complex. The virtue of a short story is its density. If it is tight, sharp, economic, well knit, and charged, then it is a good short story because it has exploited a central attribute of the form — that it is short.

All of these qualities are praiseworthy in a novel, but a novel may also be comprehensive, vast, and panoramic. It may have power, not because of its economy, but because of its scope, breadth, and sweep — the virtues of a medium that is long. Therefore, a novel may range through many consciousnesses, cover many years or generations, and travel the world. It may deal with a central line of action and one or several subplots. Many characters may change; many and various effects may constitute our final understanding. Many digressions may be tolerated and will not destroy the balance of the whole as long as they lead, finally, to some nuance of that understanding.

These differences in the possibilities of the novel and short-story forms may directly affect the relationship between story and plot. With the narrative leisure available to a novelist, it may very well be possible to begin with a character's birth, or even ancestry, even though the action culminates in middle or old age.

My own feeling as a writer is that in a novel I may allow myself, and ask the reader to share, an exploration of character, setting, and theme, letting these develop in the course of the narrative. When I am writing a short story, I must reject more, and I must select more rigorously.

One constant principle of artistic effectiveness is that you must discover what a medium cannot do and forget it; and discover what it can do and exploit it. Television is a good medium for domestic drama, but for a battle with a cast of thousands, you need a movie screen twelve feet high. For a woodland scene, watercolor is fine; but for the agony of St. Sebastian, choose oil. If you are writing for radio, the conflict must be expressible in sound; if you are writing a mime, it must be expressible in movement.

This is not to say that one form is superior to another but simply that each is itself and that no medium and no form of that medium can do everything. The greater the limitation in time and space, the greater the necessity for pace, sharpness, and density. For this reason, it is a good idea to learn to write short stories before you attempt the scope of the novel, just as it is good to learn to write a lyric before you attempt an epic or to learn to draw an apple before you paint a god.

Nevertheless, the form of the novel is an expanded story form. It requires a conflict, a crisis, and a resolution, and no technique described in this book is irrelevant to its effectiveness.

Cutting Edge

JAMES PURDY

Mrs. Zeller opposed her son's beard. She was in her house in Florida when she saw him wearing it for the first time. It was as though her mind had come to a full stop. This large full-bearded man entered the room and she remembered always later how ugly he had looked and how frightened she felt seeing him in the house; then the realization it was someone she knew, and finally the terror of recognition.

He had kissed her, which he didn't often do, and she recognized in this his attempt to make her discomfort the more painful. He held the beard to her face for a long time, then he released her as though she had suddenly disgusted him.

"Why did you do it?" she asked. She was, he saw, almost broken by the recognition.

"I didn't dare tell you and come."

"That's of course true," Mrs. Zeller said. "It would have been worse. You'll have to shave it off, of course. Nobody must see you. Your father of course didn't have the courage to warn me, but I knew something was wrong the minute he entered the house ahead of you. I suppose he's upstairs laughing now. But it's not a laughing matter."

Mrs. Zeller's anger turned against her absent husband as though all error began and ended with him. "I suppose he likes it." Her dislike of Mr. Zeller struck her son as staggeringly great at that moment.

He looked at his mother and was surprised to see how young she was. She did not look much older than he did. Perhaps she looked younger now that he had his beard.

"I had no idea a son of mine would do such a thing," she said. "But why a beard, for heaven's sake," she cried, as though he had chosen something permanent and irreparable which would destroy all that they were.

"Is it because you are an artist? No, don't answer me," she commanded. "I can't stand to hear any explanation from you. . . ."

"I have always wanted to wear a beard," her son said. "I remember wanting one as a child."

"I don't remember that at all," Mrs. Zeller said.

"I remember it quite well. I was in the summer house near that old broken-down wall and I told Ellen Whitelaw I wanted to have a beard when I grew up."

"Ellen Whitelaw, that big fat stupid thing. I haven't thought of her in years."

Mrs. Zeller was almost as much agitated by the memory of Ellen Whitelaw as by her son's beard.

"You didn't like Ellen Whitelaw," her son told her, trying to remember how they had acted when they were together.

"She was a common and inefficient servant," Mrs. Zeller said, more quietly now, masking her feelings from her son.

"I suppose *he* liked her," the son pretended surprise, the cool cynical tone coming into his voice.

"Oh, your father," Mrs. Zeller said.

"Did he then?" the son asked.

"Didn't he like all of them?" she asked. The beard had changed this much already between them, she talked to him now about his father's character, while the old man stayed up in the bedroom fearing a scene.

"Didn't he always," she repeated, as though appealing to this new hirsute man.

"So," the son said, accepting what he already knew.

"Ellen Whitelaw, for God's sake," Mrs. Zeller said. The name of the servant girl brought back many other faces and rooms which she did not know were in her memory. These faces and rooms served to make the bearded man who stared at her less and less the boy she remembered in the days of Ellen Whitelaw.

"You must shave it off," Mrs. Zeller said.

"What makes you think I would do that?" the boy wondered.

"You heard me. Do you want to drive me out of my mind?"

"But I'm not going to. Or rather it's not going to."

"I will appeal to him, though a lot of good it will do," Mrs. Zeller said. "He ought to do something once in twenty years at least."

"You mean," the son said laughing, "he hasn't done anything in that long."

"Nothing I can really remember," Mrs. Zeller told him.

"It will be interesting to hear you appeal to him," the boy said. "I haven't heard you do that in such a long time."

"I don't think you ever heard me."

"I did, though," he told her. "It was in the days of Ellen Whitelaw again, in fact."

"In *those* days," Mrs. Zeller wondered. "I don't see how that could be."

"Well, it was. I can remember that much."

"You couldn't have been more than four years old. How could you remember then?"

"I heard you say to him, *You have to ask her to go.*"

Mrs. Zeller did not say anything. She really could not remember the words, but she supposed that the scene was true and that he actually remembered.

"Please shave off that terrible beard. If you only knew how awful it looks on you. You can't see anything else but it."

"Everyone in New York thought it was particularly fine."

"Particularly fine," she paused over his phrase as though its meaning eluded her.

"It's nauseating," she was firm again in her judgment.

"I'm not going to do away with it," he said, just as firm.

She did not recognize his firmness, but she saw everything changing a little, including perhaps the old man upstairs.

"Are you going to 'appeal' to him?" The son laughed again when he saw she could say no more.

"Don't mock me," the mother said, "I will speak to your father." She pretended decorum. "You can't go anywhere with us, you know."

He looked unmoved.

"I don't want any of my friends to see you. You'll have to stay in the house or go to your own places. You can't go out with us to our places and see our friends. I hope none of the neighbors see you. If they ask who you are, I won't tell them."

"I'll tell them then."

They were not angry, they talked it out like that, while the old man was upstairs.

"Do you suppose he is drinking or asleep?" she said finally.

"I thought he looked good in it, Fern," Mr. Zeller said.

"What about it makes him look good?" she said.

"It fills out his face," Mr. Zeller said, looking at the wallpaper and surprised he had never noticed what a pattern it had before; it showed the sacrifice of some sort of animal by a youth.

He almost asked his wife how she had come to pick out this pattern, but her growing fury checked him.

He saw her mouth and throat moving with unspoken words.

"Where is he now?" Mr. Zeller wondered.

"What does that matter where he is?" she siad. "He has to be somewhere while he's home, but he can't go out with us."

"How idiotic," Mr. Zeller said, and he looked at his wife straight in the face for a second.

"Why did you say that?" She tried to quiet herself down.

"The way you go on about nothing, Fern." For a moment a kind of revolt announced itself in his manner, but then his eyes went back to the wallpaper, and she resumed her tone of victor.

"I've told him he must either cut it off or go back to New York."

"Why is it a beard upsets you so?" he wondered, almost to himself.

"It's not the beard so much. It's the way he is now too. And it disfigures him so. I don't recognize him at all now when he wears it."

"So, he's never done anything of his own before," Mr. Zeller protested suddenly.

"Never done anything!" He could feel her anger covering him and glancing off like hot sun onto the wallpaper.

"That's right," he repeated. "He's never done anything. I say let him keep the beard and I'm not going to talk to him about it." His gaze lifted toward her but rested finally only on her hands and skirt.

"This is still my house," she said, "and I have to live in this town."

"When they had the centennial in Collins, everybody wore beards."

"I have to live in this town," she repeated.

"I won't talk to him about it," Mr. Zeller said.

It was as though the voice of Ellen Whitelaw reached her saying, *So that was how you appealed to him.*

She sat on the deck chair on the porch and smoked five cigarettes. The two men were somewhere in the house and she had the feeling now that she only roomed here. She wished more than that the beard was gone that her son had never mentioned Ellen Whitelaw. She found herself thinking only about her. Then she thought that now twenty years later she could not have afforded a servant, not even her.

She supposed the girl was dead. She did not know why, but she was sure she was.

She thought also that she should have mentioned her name to Mr. Zeller. It might have broken him down about the beard, but she supposed not. He had been just as adamant and unfeeling with her about the girl as he was now about her son.

Her son came through the house in front of her without speaking, dressed only in his shorts and, when he had got safely beyond her in the garden, he took off those so that he was completely naked with his back to her, and lay down in the sun.

She held the cigarette in her hand until it began to burn her finger. She felt she should move from the place where whe was and yet she did not know where to go inside the house and she did not know what pretext to use for going inside.

In the brilliant sun his body, already tanned, matched his shining black beard.

She wanted to appeal to her husband again and she knew then she could never again. She wanted to call a friend and tell her but she had no friend to whom she could tell this.

The events of the day, like a curtain of extreme bulk, cut her off from her son and husband. She had always ruled the house and them even during the awful Ellen Whitelaw days and now as though they did not even recognize her, they had taken over. She was not even here. Her son could walk naked with a beard in front of her as though she did not exist. She had nothing to fight them with, nothing to make them see with. They ignored her as Mr. Zeller had when he looked at the wallpaper and refused to discuss their son.

"You can grow it back when you're in New York," Mr. Zeller told his son.

He did not say anything about his son lying naked before him in the garden but he felt insulted almost as much as his mother had, yet he needed his son's permission and consent now and perhaps that was why he did not mention the insult of his nakedness.

"I don't know why I have to act like a little boy all the time with you both."

"If you were here alone with me you could do anything you wanted. You know I never asked anything of you. . . ."

When his son did not answer, Mr. Zeller said, "Did I?"

"That was the trouble," the son said.

"What?" the father wondered.

"You never wanted anything from me and you never wanted to give me anything. I didn't matter to you."

"Well, I'm sorry," the father said doggedly.

"Those were the days of Ellen Whitelaw," the son said in tones like the mother.

"For God's sake," the father said and he put a piece of grass between his teeth.

He was a man who kept everything down inside of him, everything had been tied and fastened so long there was no part of him any more that could struggle against the stricture of his life.

There were no words between them for some time; then Mr. Zeller could hear himself bringing the question out: "Did she mention that girl?"

"Who?" The son pretended blankness.

"Our servant."

The son wanted to pretend again blankness but it was too much work. He answered: "No, I mentioned it. To her surprise."

"Don't you see how it is?" the father went on to the present. "She doesn't speak to either of us now and if you're still wearing the beard when you leave it's me she will be punishing six months from now."

"And you want me to save you from your wife."

"Bobby," the father said, using the childhood tone and inflection. "I wish you would put some clothes on too when you're in the garden. With me it doesn't matter, you could do anything. I never asked you anything. But with her . . ."

"God damn *her*," the boy said.

The father could not protest. He pleaded with his eyes at his son.

The son looked at his father and he could see suddenly also the youth hidden in his father's face. He was young like his mother. They were both young people who had learned nothing from life, were stopped and drifting where they were twenty years before with Ellen Whitelaw. Only *she*, the son thought, must have learned from life, must have gone on to some development in her character, while they had been tied to the shore where she had left them.

"Imagine living with someone for six months and not speaking," the father said as if to himself. "That happened once before, you know, when you were a little boy."

"I don't remember that," the son said, some concession in his voice.

"You were only four," the father told him.

"I believe this is the only thing I ever asked of you," the father said. "Isn't that odd, I can't remember ever asking you anything else. Can you?"

The son looked coldly away at the sky and then answered, contempt and pity struggling together, "No, I can't."

"Thank you, Bobby," the father said.

"Only don't *plead* any more, for Christ's sake." The son turned from him.

"You've only two more days with us, and if you shaved it off and put on just a few clothes, it would help me through the year with her."

He spoke as though it would be his last year.

"Why don't you beat some sense into her?" The son turned to him again.

The father's gaze fell for the first time complete on his son's nakedness.

Bobby had said he would be painting in the storeroom and she could send up a sandwich from time to time, and Mr. and Mrs. Zeller were left downstairs together. She refused to allow her husband to answer the phone.

In the evening Bobby came down dressed carefully and his beard combed immaculately and looking, they both thought, curled.

They talked about things like horse racing, in which they were all somehow passionately interested, but which they now discussed irritably as though it too were a menace to their lives. They talked about the uselessness of art and why people went into it with a detachment that would have made an outsider think that Bobby was as unconnected with it as a jockey or oil magnate. They condemned nearly everything and then the son went upstairs and they saw one another again briefly at bedtime.

The night before he was to leave they heard him up all hours, the water running, and the dropping of things made of metal.

Both parents were afraid to get up and ask him if he was all right. He was like a wealthy relative who had commanded them never to question him or interfere with his movements even if he was dying.

He was waiting for them at breakfast, dressed only in his shorts but he looked more naked than he ever had in the garden because his beard was gone. Over his chin lay savage and profound scratches as though he had removed the hair with a hunting knife and pincers.

Mrs. Zeller held her breast and turned to the coffee and Mr. Zeller said only his son's name and sat down with last night's newspaper.

"What time does your plane go?" Mrs. Zeller said in a dead, muffled voice.

The son began putting a white paste on the scratches of his face and did not answer.

"I believe your mother asked you a question," Mr. Zeller said, pale and shaking.

"Ten-forty," the son replied.

The son and the mother exchanged glances and he could see at once that his sacrifice had been in vain: she would also see the beard there again under the scratches and the gashes he had inflicted on himself, and he would never really be her son again. Even for his father it must be much the same. He had come home as a stranger who despised them and he had shown his nakedness to both of them. All three longed for separation and release.

But Bobby could not control the anger coming up in him, and his rage took an old form. He poured the coffee into his saucer because Mr. Zeller's mother had always done this and it had infuriated Mrs. Zeller because of its low-class implications.

He drank viciously from the saucer, blowing loudly.

Both parents watched him helplessly like insects suddenly swept against the screen.

"It's not too long till Christmas," Mr. Zeller brought out. "We hope you'll come back for the whole vacation."

"We do," Mrs. Zeller said in a voice completely unlike her own.

"So," Bobby began, but the torrent of anger would not let him say the thousand fierce things he had ready.

Instead, he blew savagely from the saucer and spilled some onto the chaste white summer rug below him. Mrs. Zeller did not move.

"I would invite you to New York," Bobby said quietly now, "but of course I will have the beard there and it wouldn't work for you."

"Yes," Mr. Zeller said, incoherent.

"I do hope you don't think I've been. . . ." Mrs. Zeller cried suddenly and they both waited to hear whether she was going to weep or not, but she stopped herself perhaps by the realization that she had no tears and that the feelings which had come over her about Bobby were likewise spent.

"I can't think of any more I can do for you," Bobby said suddenly.

They both stared at each other as though he had actually left and they were alone at last.

"Is there anything more you want me to do?" he said, coldly vicious.

They did not answer.

"I hate and despise what both of you have done to yourselves, but the thought that you would be sitting here in your middle-class crap not speaking to one another is too much even for me. That's why I did it, I guess, and not out of any love. I didn't want you to think that."

He sloshed in the saucer.

"Bobby," Mr. Zeller said.

The son brought out his *What?* with such finished beauty of coolness that he paused to admire his own control and mastery.

"Please, Bobby," Mr. Zeller said.

They could all three of them hear a thousand speeches. The agony of awkwardness was made unendurable by the iciness of the son, and all three paused over this glacial control which had come to him out of art and New York, as though it was the fruit of their lives and the culmination of their twenty years.

Suggestions for Discussion

1. Conflict is introduced in the first sentence: "Mrs. Zeller opposed her son's beard." To what extent is the conflict really about the beard? What, and how much, does the beard come to represent?

2. This story has fewer characters than "Cinderella," but in "Cinderella" the characters line up neatly on two sides of the conflict: Cinderella, Fairy Godmother, and the Prince on the side of *good*; the Stepmother and two Stepsisters on the side of *evil*. In "Cutting Edge" it is not so simple. Identify aspects of the conflict among the three Zellers. Who is in conflict with whom over what?

3. How is a balance of power achieved among the Zellers? What are the strengths of each?

4. There are no overt acts of violence in this story, but some of the actions — sunbathing nude, shaving — take on an atmosphere of violence. Do you agree? How does Purdy achieve this?

5. At the beginning of the story, Mrs. Zeller fails to recognize her son. At the end she realizes that "he would never really be her son again." How is this a reversal or opposite of the opening situation?

6. What are the events of the Zellers' story, as opposed to the plot of "Cutting Edge"? What would be lost if Purdy had begun his narrative with a scene from Bobby's childhood or with the arrival of Ellen Whitelaw?

The Second Tree from the Corner

E. B. WHITE

"Ever have any bizarre thoughts?" asked the doctor.

Mr. Trexler failed to catch the word. "What kind?" he said.

"Bizarre," repeated the doctor, his voice steady. He watched his patient for any slight change of expression, any wince. It seemed to Trexler that the doctor was not only watching him closely but was creeping slowly toward him, like a lizard toward a bug. Trexler shoved his chair back an inch and gathered himself for a reply. He was about to say "Yes" when he realized that if he said yes the next question would be unanswerable. Bizarre thoughts, bizarre thoughts? Ever have any bizarre thoughts? What kind of thoughts *except* bizarre had he had since the age of two?

Trexler felt the time passing, the necessity for an answer. These psychiatrists were busy men, overloaded, not to be kept waiting. The next patient was probably already perched out there in the waiting room, lonely, worried, shifting around on the sofa, his mind stuffed with bizarre thoughts and amorphous fears. Poor bastard, thought Trexler. Out there all alone in that misshapen antechamber, staring at the filing cabinet and wondering whether to tell the doctor about that day on the Madison Avenue bus.

Let's see, bizarre thoughts. Trexler dodged back along the dreadful corridor of the years to see what he could find. He felt the doctor's eyes upon him and knew that time was running out. Don't be so conscientious, he said to himself. If a bizarre thought is indicated here, just reach into the bag and pick anything at all. A man as well supplied with bizarre thoughts as you are should have no difficulty producing one for the record. Trexler darted into the bag, hung for a moment before one of his thoughts, as a hummingbird pauses in the delphinium. No, he said, not that one. He darted to another (the one about the rhesus monkey), paused, considered. No, he said, not that.

Trexler knew he must hurry. He had already used up pretty nearly four seconds since the question had been put. But it was an impossible situation — just one more lousy, impossible situation such as he was always getting himself into. When, he asked himself, are you going to quit maneuvering yourself into a pocket? He made one more effort. This time he stopped at the asylum, only the bars were lucite — fluted, retractable. Not here, he said. Not this one.

He looked straight at the doctor. "No," he said quietly. "I never have any bizarre thoughts."

The doctor sucked in on his pipe, blew a plume of smoke toward the rows of medical books. Trexler's gaze followed the smoke. He managed to make out one of the titles, "The Genito-Urinary System." A bright wave of fear swept cleanly over him, and he winced under the first pain of kidney stones. He remembered when he was a child, the first time he ever entered a doctor's office, sneaking a look at the titles of the books — and the flush of fear, the shirt wet under the arms, the book on t.b., the sudden knowledge that he was in the advanced stages of consumption, the quick vision of the hemorrhage. Trexler sighed wearily. Forty years, he thought, and I still get thrown by the title of a medical book. Forty years and I still can't stay on life's little bucky horse. No wonder I'm sitting here in this dreary joint at the end of this woebegone afternoon, lying about my bizarre thoughts to a doctor who looks, come to think of it, rather tired.

The session dragged on. After about twenty minutes, the doctor rose and knocked his pipe out. Trexler got up, knocked the ashes out of his brain, and waited. The doctor smiled warmly and stuck out his hand. "There's nothing the matter with you — you're just scared. Want to know how I know you're scared?"

"How?" asked Trexler.

"Look at the chair you've been sitting in! See how it has moved back away from my desk? You kept inching away from me while I asked you questions. That means you're scared."

"Does it?" said Trexler, faking a grin. "Yeah, I suppose it does."

They finished shaking hands. Trexler turned and walked out uncertainly along the passage, then into the waiting room and out past the next patient, a ruddy pin-striped man who was seated on the sofa twirling his hat nervously and staring straight ahead at the files. Poor, frightened guy, thought Trexler, he's probably read in the *Times* that one American male out of every two is going to die of heart disease by twelve o'clock next Thursday. It says that in the paper almost every morning. And he's also probably thinking about that day on the Madison Avenue bus.

A week later, Trexler was back in the patient's chair. And for several weeks thereafter he continued to visit the doctor, always toward the end of the afternoon, when the vapors hung thick above the pool of the mind and darkened the whole region of the East Seventies. He felt no better as time went on, and he found it impossible to work. He discovered that the visits were becoming routine and that although the routine was one to which he certainly did not look forward, at least he could accept it with cool resignation, as once, years ago, he had accepted a long spell with a dentist who had settled down to a steady fooling with a couple of dead teeth. The visits, moreover, were now assuming a pattern recognizable to the patient.

Each session would begin with a résumé of symptoms — the dizziness in the streets, the constricting pain in the back of the neck, the apprehensions, the tightness of the scalp, the inability to concentrate, the despondency and the melancholy times, the feeling of pressure and tension, the anger at not being able to work, the anxiety over work not done, the gas on the stomach. Dullest set of neurotic symptoms in the world, Trexler would think, as he obediently trudged back over them for the doctor's benefit. And then, having listened attentively to the recital, the doctor would spring his question: "Have you ever found anything that gives you relief?" And Trexler would answer, "Yes. A drink." And the doctor would nod his head knowingly.

As he became familiar with the pattern Trexler found that he increasingly tended to identify himself with the doctor, transferring himself into the doctor's seat — probably (he thought) some rather slick form of escapism. At any rate, it was nothing new for Trexler to identify himself with other people. Whenever he got into a cab, he instantly became the driver, saw everything from the hackman's angle (and the reaching over with the right hand, the nudging of the flag, the pushing it down, all the way down along the side of the meter), saw everything — traffic, fare, everything — through the eyes of Anthony Rocco, or Isidore Freedman or Matthew Scott. In a barbershop, Trexler was the barber, his fingers curled around the comb, his hand on the tonic. Perfectly natural, then, that Trexler should soon be occupying the doctor's chair, asking the questions, waiting for the answers. He got quite interested in the doctor, in this way. He liked him, and he found him a not too difficult patient.

It was on the fifth visit, about halfway through, that the doctor turned to Trexler and said, suddenly, "What do you want?" He gave the word "want" special emphasis.

"I d'know," replied Trexler uneasily. "I guess nobody knows the answer to that one."

"Sure they do," replied the doctor.

"Do *you* know what *you* want?" asked Trexler narrowly.

"Certainly," said the doctor. Trexler noticed that at this point the doctor's chair slid slightly backward, away from him. Trexler stifled a small, internal smile. Scared as a rabbit, he said to himself. Look at him scoot!

"What *do* you want?" continued Trexler, pressing his advantage, pressing it hard.

The doctor glided back another inch away from his inquisitor. "I want a wing on the small house I own in Westport. I want more money, and more leisure to do the things I want to do."

Trexler was just about to say, "And what are those things you want to do, Doctor?" when he caught himself. Better not go too far, he mused. Better not lose possession of the ball. And besides, he thought, what the hell goes on here, anyway — me paying fifteen bucks a throw for these séances and then doing the work myself, asking the questions, weighing the answers. So he wants a new wing! There's a fine piece of theatrical gauze for you! A new wing.

Trexler settled down again and resumed the role of patient for the rest of the visit. It ended on a kindly, friendly note. The doctor reassured him that his fears were the cause of his sickness, and that his fears were unsubstantial. They shook hands, smiling.

Trexler walked dizzily through the empty waiting room and the doctor followed along to let him out. It was late; the secretary had shut up shop and gone home. Another day over the dam. "Goodbye," said Trexler. He stepped into the street, turned west toward Madison, and thought of the doctor all alone there, after hours, in that desolate hole — a man who worked longer hours than his secretary. Poor, scared, overworked bastard, thought Trexler. And that new wing!

It was an evening of clearing weather, the Park showing green and desirable in the distance, the last daylight applying a high lacquer to the brick and brownstone walls and giving the street scene a luminous and intoxicating splendor. Trexler meditated, as he walked, on what he wanted. "What do you want?" he heard again. Trexler knew what he wanted, and what, in general, all men wanted; and he was glad, in a way, that it was both inexpressible and unattainable, and that it wasn't a wing. He was satisfied to remember that it was deep, formless, enduring, and impossible of fulfillment, and that it made men sick, and that when you sauntered along Third Avenue and looked through the doorways into the dim saloons, you could sometimes pick out from the unregenerate ranks the ones who had not forgotten, gazing steadily into the bottoms of the glasses on the long chance that they could get another little peek at it. Trexler found himself renewed by the remembrance that what he wanted was at once great and microscopic, and that although it borrowed from the nature of large deeds and of youthful love and of old songs and early intimations, it was not any one of these things, and that it had not been isolated or pinned down, and that a man who attempted to define it in the privacy of a doctor's office would fall flat on his face.

Trexler felt invigorated. Suddenly his sickness seemed health, his dizziness stability. A small tree, rising between him and the light, stood there saturated with the evening, each gilt-edged leaf perfectly drunk with excellence and delicacy. Trexler's spine registered an ever so slight tremor as it picked up this natural disturbance in the lovely scene. "I want the second tree from the corner, just as it stands," he said, answering an imaginary question from an imaginary physician. And he felt a slow pride in realizing that what he wanted none could bestow, and that what he had none could take away. He felt content to be sick, unembarrassed at being afraid; and in the jungle of his fear he glimpsed (as he had so often glimpsed them before) the flashy tail feathers of the bird courage.

Then he thought once again of the doctor, and of his being left there all alone, tired, frightened. (The poor, scared guy, thought Trexler.) Trexler began humming "Moonshine Lullaby," his spirit reacting instantly to the hypodermic of Merman's healthy voice. He crossed Madison, boarded a downtown bus, and rode all the way to Fifty-second Street before he had a thought that could rightly have been called bizarre.

Suggestions for Discussion

1. The story begins with a challenge: "Ever have any bizarre thoughts?" In the course of the story, what bizarre thoughts *does* Trexler have? How bizarre are they?

2. The doctor is clearly in the position of power — a self-confident professional to whom Trexler has gone for help. What sort of power does Trexler have? Is his habit of identifying with other people a neurotic weakness or a strength?

3. Where does the balance of power begin to shift toward Trexler, and how do you know?

4. What is the crisis action? If Trexler only gets to Fifty-second Street before his bizarre thoughts return, how much of a resolution is the resolution?

5. How much of Trexler's past do you learn in the plot? How would the shape of the short story be affected if White had begun, say, on the day Trexler first decided he needed a psychiatrist?

WRITING ASSIGNMENTS

1. Write a scene placing two characters in this very fundamental conflict: one wants something the other does not want to give. The something may be anything — money, respect, jewelry, sex, information, a match — but be sure to focus on the one desire.

2. A slightly more complicated variation on the same theme: each of two characters has half of something that is no good without the other half. Neither wants to give up his or her half.

3. Identify the most pleasant and peaceful experience you have had recently. Using this situation as a starting point, write a scene that introduces bitter conflict. Remember that a purely external source of tension — a hit man, a Martian, a cyclone — will make for less convincing conflict than if the tension develops within or between the characters.

4. Write a short story that is a short story in *exactly* one hundred words. Notice that if you're going to manage a conflict, crisis, and resolution in this short compass, you'll have to introduce the conflict immediately.

5. Write a short story of no more than five pages in which the protagonist seems to be weaker than the forces opposing him or her. Give the character one balancing strength. Let him or her triumph.

6. Place a character in conflict with some aspect of nature. The character need not be fighting for survival; the danger may be as small as a mosquito. But balance the forces equally so that the reader is not sure who will "win" until the crisis action happens.

SEEING IS BELIEVING
Showing and Telling

Significant Detail
The Active Voice
Prose Rhythm
Mechanics

The purpose of all the arts, including literature, is to quell boredom. People recognize that it feels good to feel and that not to feel is unhealthy. "I don't feel anything" can be said in fear, defiance, or complaint. It is not a boast. The final absence of feeling is death.

But feeling is also dangerous, and it can be deadly. Both the body and psyche numb themselves in the presence of pain too strong to bear. People often (healthily and unhealthily) avoid good feelings — intimacy, power, speed, drunkenness, possession — having learned that feelings have consequences and that powerful feelings have powerful consequences.

Literature offers feelings for which we do not have to pay. It allows us to love, condemn, condone, hope, dread, hate, without any of the risks those feelings ordinarily involve. Fiction must contain ideas, which give significance to characters and events. If the ideas are shallow or untrue, the fiction will be correspondingly shallow or untrue. But the ideas must be experienced through or with the characters; they must be *felt* or the fiction will fail also.

Much nonfiction writing, including literary criticism, also wants to persuade us to feel one way rather than another, and some — polemics, propaganda — exhort us to feel strongly. But nonfiction works largely by means of reason and reasoning in order to appeal to and produce emotion. Fiction tries to reproduce the emotional impact of experience. And this is a more difficult task, because written words are symbols representing sounds, and the sounds themselves are symbols representing things, actions, qualities, spatial relationships, and so on. Written words are thus at two removes from experience. Unlike the images of film and drama, which directly strike the eye and ear, they are transmitted first to the mind, where they must be translated into images.

In order to move your reader, the standard advice runs, "show, don't tell." This dictum can be confusing, considering that all a writer has to work with is words. What it means is that your job as a fiction writer is to focus attention, not on the words, which are inert, nor on the thoughts these words produce, but through these to felt experience, where the vitality of understanding lies. There are techniques for accomplishing this — for making narrative vivid, moving, and resonant — which can be partly learned and can always be strengthened.

Significant Detail

In *The Elements of Style*, William Strunk, Jr., writes:

> If those who have studied the art of writing are in accord on any one point, it is on this: the surest way to arouse and hold the attention of the reader is by being specific, definite and concrete. The greatest writers . . . are effective largely because they deal in particulars and report the details that matter.

Specific, definite, concrete, particular details. These are the life of fiction. Still more categorically put, a detail is "definite" and "concrete" when it appeals to the senses. It should be seen, heard, smelled, tasted, or touched. The most superficial survey of any bookshelf of published fiction will turn up dozens of examples of this principle. Here is a fairly obvious one.

> It was a narrow room, with a rather high ceiling, and crowded from floor to ceiling with goodies. There were rows and rows of hams and sausages of all shapes and colors — white, yellow, red and black; fat and lean and round and long — rows of canned preserves, cocoa and tea, bright translucent glass bottles of honey, marmalade and jam. . . .

I stood enchanted, straining my ears and breathing in the delightful atmosphere and the mixed fragrance of chocolate and smoked fish and earthy truffles. . . . I spoke into the silence, saying: "Good day" in quite a loud voice; I can still remember how my strained, unnatural tones died away in the stillness. No one answered. And my mouth literally began to water like a spring. One quick, noiseless step and I was beside one of the laden tables. I made one rapturous grab into the nearest glass urn, filled as it chanced with chocolate creams, slipped a fistful into my coat pocket, then reached the door, and in the next second was safely round the corner.

THOMAS MANN, *Confessions of Felix Krull, Confidence Man*

The shape of this passage is a tour through the five senses. Mann lets us see: *narrow room, high ceiling, hams, sausages, preserves, cocoa, tea, glass bottles, honey, marmalade, jam.* He lets us smell: *fragrance of chocolate, smoked fish, earthy truffles.* He lets us hear: *"Good day," unnatural tones, stillness.* He lets us taste: *mouth, water like a spring.* He lets us touch: *grab, chocolate creams, slipped, fistful into my coat pocket.* The writing is alive because we do in fact live through our sense perceptions, and Mann takes us past words and through thought to let us perceive the scene in this way.

In the process, a number of ideas *not* stated reverberate off the sense images, so that we are also aware of a number of generalizations the author might have made but does not need to make: we will make them ourselves. Mann could have had his character "tell" us: *I was quite poor, and I was not used to seeing such a profusion of food, so that although I was very afraid there might be someone in the room and that I might be caught stealing, I couldn't resist taking the risk.*

This version would be very flat, and none of it is necessary. The character's relative poverty is inherent in the tumble of images of sight and smell; if he were used to such displays, his eyes and nose would not dart about as they do. His fear is inherent in the "strained unnatural tones" and their dying away in the stillness. His desire is in his watering mouth, his fear in the furtive speed of "quick" and "grab" and "slipped."

The points to be made here are two, and they are both important. The first is that the writer must deal in sense detail. The second is that these must be the details "that matter." As a writer of fiction you are at constant pains, not simply to say what you mean, but to mean more than you say. Much of what you mean will be an abstraction or a judgment. But if you write in abstractions or judgments, you are writing an essay, whereas if you let us use our senses and do our own generalizing and interpreting, we will be involved as participants in a real way. Much of the pleasure of reading comes from the egotistical sense that we are clever enough to understand. When the author explains to us or interprets for us, we suspect that he or she doesn't think us bright enough to do it for ourselves.

A detail is *concrete* if it appeals to one of the five senses; it is *significant* if it also conveys an idea or a judgment or both.

Here is a passage from a young writer, which fails through lack of appeal to the senses.

> Debbie was a very stubborn and completely independent person, and was always doing things her way despite her parents' efforts to get her to conform. Her father was an executive in a dress manufacturing company, and was able to afford his family all the luxuries and comforts of life. But Debbie was completely indifferent to her family's affluence.

This passage contains a number of judgments we might or might not share with the author, and she has not convinced us that we do. What constitutes stubbornness? Independence? Indifference? Affluence? Further, since the judgments are supported by generalizations, we have no sense of the individuality of the characters, which alone would bring them to life on the page. What things was she always doing? What efforts did her parents make to get her to conform? What level of executive? What dress manufacturing company? What luxuries and comforts?

> Debbie would wear a tank top to a tea party if she pleased, with fluorescent earrings and ankle-strap sandals.
> "Oh, sweetheart." Mrs. Chiddister would stand in the doorway wringing her hands. "It's not *nice*."
> "Not who?" Debbie would say, and add a fringed belt.
> Mr. Chiddister was Artistic Director of the Boston branch of Cardin, and had a high respect for what he called "elegant textures," which ranged from handwoven tweed to gold filigree, and which he willingly offered his daughter. Debbie preferred her laminated wrist bangles.

We have not passed a final judgment on the merits of these characters, but we know a good deal more about them, and we have drawn certain interim conclusions that are our own and not forced on us by the author. Debbie *is* independent of her parents' values, rather careless of their feelings, energetic, and possibly a tart. Mrs. Chiddister is quite ineffectual. Mr. Chiddister is a snob, though perhaps Debbie's taste is so bad we'll end up on his side.

But maybe that isn't at all what the author had in mind: the point is that we weren't allowed to know what the author did have in mind. Perhaps it was more like this version.

> One day Debbie brought home a copy of *Ulysses*. Mrs. Strum called it "filth" and threw it across the sunporch. Debbie knelt on the parquet and retrieved her bookmark, which she replaced. "No, it's not," she said.
> "You're not so old I can't take a strap to you!" Mr. Strum reminded her.
> Mr. Strum was controlling stockholder of Readywear Conglomerates, and was proud of treating his family, not only on his salary, but on his expense

account. The summer before he had justified their company on a trip to Belgium, where they toured the American Cemetery and the torture chambers of Ghent Castle. Entirely ungrateful, Debbie had spent the rest of the trip curled up in the hotel with a shabby copy of some poet.

Now we have a much clearer understanding of "stubbornness," "independence," "indifference," and "affluence," both their natures and the value we are to place on them. This time our judgment is heavily weighted in Debbie's favor — partly because people who read books have a sentimental sympathy with people who read books — but also because we hear hysteria in "filth" and "take a strap to you," whereas Debbie's resistance is quiet and strong. Mr. Strum's attitude toward his expense account suggests that he's corrupt, and his choice of "luxuries" is morbid. The passage does contain two overt judgments, the first being that Debbie was "entirely ungrateful." Notice that by the time we get to this, we're aware that the judgment is Mr. Strum's and that Debbie has little enough to be grateful for. We understand not only what the author says but that she means the opposite of what she says, and we feel doubly clever to get it; that is the pleasure of irony. Likewise, the judgment that the poet's book is "shabby" shows Mr. Strum's crass materialism toward what *we* know to be the finer things. At the very end of the passage, we are denied a detail that we might very well be given: *What* poet did Debbie curl up with? Again, by this time we understand that we are being given Mr. Strum's view of the situation and that it's Mr. Strum (not Debbie, not the author, and certainly not us) who wouldn't notice the difference between John Keats and Stanley Kunitz.

It may be objected that both rewrites of the passage are longer than the original. Doesn't "adding" so much detail make for long writing? The answer is yes and no. *No* because in the rewrites we know so much more about the values, activities, life-styles, attitudes, and personalities of the characters that it would take many times the length of the original to "tell" it all in generalizations. *Yes* in the sense that detail requires words, and if you are to realize your characters through detail, then you must be careful to select the details that convey the characteristics essential to our understanding. You can't convey a whole person, nor a whole action, nor everything there is to be conveyed about a single moment of a single day. You must select the significant.

No amount of concrete detail will move us unless it also implicitly suggests meaning and value. Following is a passage that fails, not through lack of appeal to the senses, but through lack of significance.

Terry Landon, a handsome young man of twenty-two, was six foot four and broad shouldered. He had medium-length thick blond hair and a natural tan, which set off the blue of his intense and friendly long-lashed eyes.

Here we have a good deal of sense information, but we still know very little about Terry. There are so many broad-shouldered twenty-two-year-olds in the world, so many blonds, and so on. No value rises out of the images themselves, and the author is forced to provide judgments, from which we mainly understand that the author wants us to like Terry: Why else would he be handsome, natural, intense, *and* friendly? We refuse to like him, just as we would refuse to like him in life until we knew some individual or intimate thing that would set him apart from all the other blond blue-eyed twenty-two-year-olds in the world — until we felt we knew him, in fact. This sort of cataloguing of characteristics suggest an all-points bulletin: *male Caucasian, medium height, blond hair, last seen wearing gray raincoat.* Such a description may help the police locate a suspect in a crowd, but the assumption is that the identity of the person is not known. As an author, you want us to know the character individually and immediately. Often it is not necessary to give any APB information to achieve this objective.

> "Oh, I say, chaps." Benedict Pendleton was bouncing on his heels and pinching at the bridge of his nose. "Can I come along?"

We do not know the color of Pendleton's hair, his height, the brand of the shoes in question, or the shape of his nose. But we hear that he's anxious and we see that he's awkward; we conclude that the "chaps" probably don't want him along.

Such APB details can render an action as well as a character without rendering it meaningful.

> Danny carried the high-heeled terrycloth slippers, the heels hooked over the edge of his hands, across the blue-flecked linoleum to Jane, who was frying eggs and hickory-smoked bacon in a cast-iron skillet at the stove. He put the right slipper on the formica top, took the spatula out of her hand, and handed her the left slipper. "Aren't your feet cold?" he asked.

This is better writing than the passages about Debbie and Terry. We have been allowed to see and hear and, perhaps, to smell the bacon. But we are impatient with the details because they leave us very much in doubt about the relationship between Danny and Jane, and it is this emotional value that interests us most. Is he concerned for her comfort or annoyed at her carelessness? Affectionate or stentorian? What importance is there, if any, in the color of the linoleum, the way he carries the slippers? Does his taking the spatula out of her hand signify high-handed male chauvinism, gentle intimacy, amusement? By what details could we understand these things?

The fact is that all our ideas and judgments are formed through our sense perceptions, and daily, moment by moment, we receive information that is not merely sensuous in this way. Four people at a cocktail party may *do* nothing but stand and nibble canapes and may *talk* nothing but politics and the latest films. But you feel perfectly certain that X is furious at Y, who is flirting with Z, who is wounding Q, who is trying to comfort X. You have only your senses to observe with. How do you reach these conclusions? By what gestures, glances, tones, touches, choices of words?

It may be that this constant emphasis on judgment makes the author, and the reader, seem opinionated or self-righteous. "I want to present my characters objectively / neutrally. I'm not making any value judgments. I want the reader to make up his own mind." This can be a legitimate position, and the whole school of the *nouveau roman* strives, in fiction, to be wholly objective and to eschew the judgmental. But this is a highly sophisticated experimental form, and it entails a difficulty and a danger. The difficulty is that human beings *are* constantly judging: *How was the film? He seemed friendly. What a boring class! Do you like it here? What did you think of them? That's kind of you. Which do you want? I'm not convinced. She's very thin. That's fascinating. I'm so clumsy. You're gorgeous tonight. Life is crazy, isn't it?*

The danger is that when we are not passing such judgments, it's because we aren't much interested. We are "indifferent." Although you may not want to sanctify or damn your characters, you do want us to care about them, and if you refuse to direct our judgment, you may be inviting our indifference. Usually, when you "don't want us to judge," you mean that you want our feelings to be mixed, paradoxical, complex. *She's horribly irritating, but it's not her fault. He's sexy, but there's something cold about it underneath.* If this is what you mean, then you must direct our judgment in both or several directions, not in none.

Significant detail is necessary to the living quality of fiction even when we are not dealing with major characters or specific points in time. Joseph Conrad defined the writer's task as "a single-minded attempt to render the highest kind of justice to the visible universe." Flannery O'Connor, in a letter to a young author (Ben Griffith), advised, "You have to let the things in the story do the talking. . . . The first thing is to see the people every minute. . . . You have got to learn to paint with words. . . . Ford Madox Ford said you couldn't have somebody sell a newspaper in a story unless you said what he looked like" (from *The Habit of Being*).

In the following paragraph from Virginia Woolf's *Mrs. Dalloway*, we are introduced, through the protagonist's consciousness, to an anonymous crowd and four other characters, none of whom we ever see again.

> The crush was terrific for the time of day. Lords, Ascot, Hurlingham, what was it? she wondered, for the street was blocked. The British middle classes sitting sideways on the tops of omnibuses with parcels and umbrellas, yes, even furs on a day like this, were, she thought, more ridiculous, more unlike anything

there has ever been than one could conceive; and the Queen herself held up; the Queen herself unable to pass. Clarissa was suspended on one side of Brook Street; Sir John Buckhurst, the old Judge on the other, with the car between them (Sir John had laid down the law for years and liked a well-dressed woman) when the chauffeur, leaning ever so slightly, said or showed something to the policeman, who saluted and raised his arm and jerked his head and moved the omnibus to the side and the car passed through.

The whole range of British class and class consciousness is conveyed in this brief passage through the use of significant detail. Clarissa's wry attitude toward the British middle classes is given credence by the fussiness of "parcels and umbrellas" and the pretension of "furs on a day like this." The judge's aristocratic hauteur is carried in the clichés he would use, "laid down the law" and "liked a well-dressed woman." That the Queen's chauffeur is described as leaning "ever so slightly" shows his consciousness of his own position's superiority to that of the policeman who "saluted" him but then exercises his own brand of authority as he "jerked his head" to order the traffic about. Only the Queen is characterized by no detail of object or action, and that she is not emphasizes her royal remoteness: "the Queen herself . . . the Queen herself."

Even a character who doesn't exist except as a type or function will come to life if presented through significant detail, as in this example from *The Right Stuff* by Tom Wolfe.

The matter mustn't be bungled! — that's the idea. No, a man should bring the news when the time comes, a man with some official or moral authority, a clergyman or a comrade of the newly deceased. Furthermore, he should bring the bad news in person. He should turn up at the front door and ring the bell and be standing there like a pillar of coolness and competence, bearing the bad news on ice, like a fish.

For a character who is just "a man," we have a remarkably clear image of this personage! Notice how Wolfe moves us from generalization toward sharpness of image, gradually bringing the nonexistent character into focus. First he has only a gender; then a certain abstract quality, "authority"; then a distinct role, "a clergyman or a comrade." Then he appears "in person" at the front door, then acts, ringing the doorbell. Finally, his quality is presented to us in the sharp focus of similes that also suggest his deadly message: *pillar, ice, fish.*

The point is not that an author must never express an idea, quality, or judgment. In the foregoing passages from Mann, Woolf, and Wolfe, each author uses several generalizations: *I stood enchanted, delightful atmosphere; the crush was terrific, more unlike anything there has ever been than one could conceive; the matter mustn't be bungled, coolness and competence.* The point is that in order to carry the felt weight of fiction, these abstractions must be realized through an appeal to the senses. It is in the details that they live.

The Active Voice

If your prose is to be vigorous as well as vivid, if your characters are to be people who do rather than people to whom things are done, if your descriptions are to "come to life," you must make use of the active voice.

The active voice occurs when the action described by the verb of a sentence is performed by the subject of that sentence: *She spilled the milk.* When the passive voice is used, the object of the active verb becomes the subject of the passive verb: *The milk was spilled by her.* The passive voice is more indirect than the active; the subject is acted upon rather than acting, and the effect is to weaken the prose and to distance the reader from the action.

The passive voice does have an important place in fiction, precisely because it expresses a sense that the character is being acted upon. If a prison guard is kicking the hero, then *I was slammed into the wall; I was struck blindingly from behind and forced to the floor* appropriately carries the sense of his helplessness.

In general, writers are advised to seek the active voice in all prose, and to use the passive only when the actor is unknown or insignificant; or for special stylistic effects like the one above.

But there is one other common grammatical construction which is *effectively passive* in fiction, and which can distance the reader from a sense of immediate experience. All the verbs that we learn in school to call *linking verbs* are effectively passive because they invite complements that tend to be generalized or judgmental: *her hair was beautiful. He was very happy. The room seemed expensively furnished. They became morose.* Let her hair bounce, tumble, cascade, or swing; we'll see better. Let him laugh, leap, cry, or hug a tree; we'll experience his joy.

Compare the passage about Debbie at the top of page 32 with the rewrite on pages 32–33. In the generalized original we have: *was stubborn, was doing things, was executive, was able, was indifferent.* Apart from the compound verb *was doing*, all these are linking verbs. In the rewrite the characters: *brought, called, threw, knelt, retrieved, replaced, said, reminded, justified, toured, spent,* and *curled up.* What energetic people! The rewrite contains two linking verbs: Mr. Strum *was stockholder* and *was proud*, and these properly represent static states, a position and an attitude.

One beneficial side effect of active verbs is that they tend to call forth significant details. If you say "she was shocked," you are telling us; but if you are to show us that she was shocked through an action, you are likely to have to search for an image as well. "She clenched the arm of the chair so hard that her knuckles whitened." *Clenched* and *whitened* actively suggest shock, and at the same time we see her knuckles on the arm of the chair.

To be is the most common of the linking verbs, and also the most overused, but all the linking verbs invite generalization and distance. *To feel, to seem, to look, to appear, to experience, to express, to show, to demonstrate, to convey, to display* — all these suggest in fiction that the character is being acted upon or observed by someone rather than doing something. *She felt happy/sad/amused/mortified* does not convince us. We want to see her and to infer her emotion for ourselves. *He very clearly conveyed his displeasure.* It isn't clear to us. How did he convey it? To whom?

Most linking verbs have active as well as effectively passive forms, and it is important to distinguish them. *She felt sad* is effectively passive, but *she felt his forehead* is an action. If *the magician appeared,* he is acting; but if *he appeared annoyed,* then the verb is a linking verb and the only action implied is that of the observer who perceives this.

Linking verbs, like the passive voice, can appropriately convey a sense of passivity or helplessness when that is the desired effect. Notice that in the passage by Mann quoted earlier in this chapter, Felix Krull is momentarily stunned by the sight of the food before him, the linking verbs are used: *It was a narrow room, there were rows and rows,* while all the colors and shapes buffet his senses. Only as he gradually recovers can he *stand, breathe, speak,* and eventually *grab.*

In the following excerpt from Lawrence Durrell's *Justine,* Melissa is trapped into a ride she doesn't want, and we feel her passivity with her while the car and the headlights take all the power.

> Melissa was afraid now. . . . She was aghast at what she had done. . . . There was no way of refusing the invitation. She dressed in her shabby best and carrying her fatigue like a heavy pack followed Selim to the great car which stood in deep shadow. She was helped in beside Nessim. They moved off slowly into the dense crepuscular evening of an Alexandria which, in her panic, she no longer recognized. They scouted a sea turned to sapphire and turned inland, folding up the slum, toward Mareotis and the bituminous slag-heaps of Mex where the pressure of the headlights now peeled off layer after layer of the darkness.

Was afraid, was aghast, was no way, was helped in — all imply Melissa's impotence. The active verbs that apply specifically to her either express weakness (*she followed*) or are negated (*no longer recognized*); the most active thing she can manage is to dress. In contrast, the "great car" *stands,* and it is inside, and under the power of, the car, that they *move off, scout, turn,* and *fold up;* it is the headlights that *peel off.*

I don't mean to suggest either that Durrell is deliberately using a linking verb here, the passive or the active voice there, or that as an author you should analyze your grammar as you go along. Most word choice is instinctive, and instinct is often the best guide. I do mean to suggest that you should be aware of the vigor and variety of available verbs and that if a passage lacks energy it may be because your instinct has let you down. How often *are* things, or are they acted *upon,* when they could more forcefully *do?*

A note of caution about active verbs: make sparing use of what John Ruskin, in his work, *Modern Painters,* called the "pathetic fallacy" — the attributing of human emotions to natural and man-made objects. Even a description of a static scene can be invigorated if the houses *stand,* the streets *wander,* and the trees *bend.* But if the houses *frown,* the streets *stagger drunkenly,* and the trees *weep,* we will feel more strain than energy in the writing.

Prose Rhythm

Novelists and short-story writers are not under the same obligation as poets to reinforce sense with sound. In prose, on the whole the rhythm is all right if it isn't clearly wrong. But it can be wrong if, for example, the cadence contradicts the meaning; on the other hand, rhythm can greatly enhance the meaning if it is sensitively used.

> The river moved slowly. It seemed sluggish. The surface lay flat. Birds circled lazily overhead. Jon's boat slipped forward.

In this extreme example, the short, clipped sentences and their parallel structures — subject, verb, adverb — work against the sense of slow flowing movement. The rhythm could be effective if the character whose eyes we're using is not appreciating or sharing the calm; otherwise it needs recasting.

> The surface lay flat on the sluggish, slow-moving river, and the birds circled lazily overhead as Jon's boat slipped forward.

There is nothing very striking about the rhythm of this version, but at least it moves forward without obstructing the flow of the river.

The first impression I had as I stopped in the doorway of the immense City Room was of extreme rush and bustle, with the reporters moving rapidly back and forth in the long aisles in order to shove their copy at each other, or making frantic gestures as they shouted into their many telephones.

This long and leisurely sentence cannot possibly provide a sense of rush and bustle. The phrases need to move as fast as the reporters; the verbiage must be pared down because it slows them down.

I stopped in the doorway. The City Room was immense, reporters rushing down the aisles, shoving copy at each other, bustling back again, flinging gestures, shouting into telephones.

The poet Rolfe Humphries remarked that "*Very* is the least *very* word in the language." It is frequently true that adverbs expressing emphasis or suddenness — *extremely, rapidly, suddenly, phenomenally, quickly, immediately, instantly, definitely, terribly, awfully* — slow the sentence down so as to dilute the force of the intended meaning. " 'It's a very nice day,' " said Humphries, "is not as nice a day as 'It's a nice day!' " Likewise, "They stopped very abruptly" is not as abrupt as "They stopped."

The rhythm of an action can be imitated by the rhythm of a sentence in a rich variety of ways. In the example above, simplifying the clauses helped create a sense of rush. James Joyce, in the short story "The Dead," structures a long sentence with a number of prepositional phrases so that it carries us headlong.

Lily, the caretaker's daughter, was literally run off her feet. Hardly had she brought one gentleman into the little pantry behind the office on the ground floor and helped him off with his overcoat than the wheezy hall-door bell clanged and she had to scamper along the bare hallway to let in another guest.

Lily's haste is largely created by beginning the sentence, "Hardly had she brought . . . ," so that we anticipate the clause that will finish the meaning, "than the bell clanged. . . ." Our anticipation forces us to scamper like Lily through the intervening actions.

Not only action but also character can be revealed and reinforced by sensitive use of rhythm. In Tillie Olsen's "Tell Me a Riddle," half a dozen grown children of a couple who have been married for forty-seven years ask each other what, after all this time, could be tearing their parents apart. The narrative answers:

Something tangible enough.
Arthritic hands, and such work as he got, occasional. Poverty all his life,

and there was little breath left for running. He could not, could not turn away from this desire: to have the troubling of responsibility, the fretting with money, over and done with; to be free, to be *carefree* where success was not measured by accumulation, and there was use for the vitality still in him.

The old man's anguished irritability is conveyed by syncopation, the syntax wrenched, clauses and qualifiers erupting out of what would be their natural place in the sentence, just as they would erupt in the man's mind. Repetition conveys his frustration: "He could not, could not . . ." and, "to be free, to be *carefree*. . . ."

Just as action and character can find an echo in prose rhythm, so it is possible to help us experience a character's emotions and attitudes through control of the starts and stops of prose tempo. In the following passage from *Persuasion*, Jane Austen combines generalizations, passive verbs, and a staccato speech pattern to produce a kind of breathless blindness in the heroine:

> . . . a thousand feelings rushed on Anne, of which this was the most consoling, that it would soon be over. And it was soon over. In two minutes after Charles's preparation, the others appeared; they were in the drawing room. Her eye half met Captain Wentworth's, a bow, a courtesy passed; she heard his voice; he talked to Mary, said all that was right, said something to the Miss Musgroves, enough to mark an easy footing; the room seemed full, full of persons and voices, but a few minutes ended it.

Sometimes a contrast in rhythm can help reinforce a contrast in characters, actions, attitudes, and emotions. In this passage from Frederick Busch's short story "Company," a woman whose movements are relatively confined watches her husband move, stop, and move again.

> Every day did not start with Vince awake that early, dressing in the dark, moving with whispery sounds down the stairs and through the kitchen, out into the autumn morning while groundfog lay on the milkweed burst open and on the stumps of harvested corn. But enough of them did.
> I went to the bedroom window to watch him hunt in a business suit.
> He moved with his feet in the slowly stirring fog, moving slowly himself with the rifle held across his body and his shoulders stiff. Then he stopped in a frozen watch for woodchucks. His stillness made the fog look faster as it blew across our field behind the barn. Vince stood. He waited for something to shoot. I went back to bed and lay between our covers again. I heard the bolt click. I heard the unemphatic shot, and then the second one, and after a while his feet on the porch, and soon the rush of water, the rattle of the pots on top of the stove, and later his feet again, and the car starting up as he left for work an hour before he had to.

The long opening sentence is arranged in a series of short phrases to move Vince forward. By contrast, "But enough of them did" comes abruptly, its abruptness as well as the sense of the words suggesting the woman's alienation. When Vince starts off again more slowly the repetition of "moved . . . slowly stirring . . . moving slowly" slows down the sentence to match his strides. "Vince stood" again stills him, but the author also needs to convey that Vince stands for a long time, waiting, so we have the repetitions, "he stopped . . . His stillness . . . Vince stood. He waited. . . ." As his activity speeds up again, the tempo of the prose speeds up with another series of short phrases, of which only the last is drawn out with a dependent clause, "as he left for work an hour before he had to," so that we feel the retreat of the car in the distance. Notice that Busch chooses the phrase, "the rush of water," not the flow or splash of water, as the sentence and Vince begin to rush. Here meaning reinforces a tempo that in turn reinforces meaning.

Mechanics

Significant detail, the active voice, and prose rhythm are techniques for achieving the sensuous in fiction, means of taking the reader past the words and the thought to feeling and experience. None is much use if the reader's eye is wrenched back to the surface; for that reason a word or two ought to be said here about the mechanics of the written language.

Spelling, grammar, and punctuation are a kind of magic; their purpose is to be invisible. If the sleight of hand works, we will not notice a comma or a quotation mark but will translate each instantly into a pause or an awareness of voice; we will not focus on the individual letters of a word but extract its sense whole. When the mechanics are incorrectly used, the trick is revealed and the magic fails; the reader's focus is shifted from the story to its surface. The reader is irritated at the author, and of all the emotions he was willing to experience, irritation at the author is not one.

There is no intrinsic virtue in standardized mechanics, and you can depart from them whenever you produce an effect that adequately compensates for the attention called to the surface. But only then. Unlike the techniques of narrative, the rules of spelling, grammar, and punctuation can be coldly learned anywhere in the English-speaking world — and they should be learned by anyone who aspires to write. Poor mechanics read instant amateurism to an editor. Perhaps a demonstrated genius can get away with sloppy mechanics, but in that case some other person must be hired to fill in for her or him. Since ghostwriters and editors are likely to be paid more per hour for their work than the author, this would constitute a heavy drain on the available resources of those who publish fiction.

Everything That Rises Must Converge

FLANNERY O'CONNOR

Her Doctor had told Julian's mother that she must lose twenty pounds on account of her blood pressure, so on Wednesday nights Julian had to take her downtown on the bus for a reducing class at the Y. The reducing class was designed for working girls over fifty, who weighed from 165 to 200 pounds. His mother was one of the slimmer ones, but she said ladies did not tell their age or weight. She would not ride the buses by herself at night since they had been integrated, and because the reducing class was one of her few pleasures, necessary for her health, and *free*, she said Julian could at least put himself out to take her, considering all she did for him. Julian did not like to consider all she did for him, but every Wednesday night he braced himself and took her.

She was almost ready to go, standing before the hall mirror, putting on her hat, while he, his hands behind him, appeared pinned to the door frame, waiting like Saint Sebastian for the arrows to begin piercing him. The hat was new and had cost her seven dollars and a half. She kept saying, "Maybe I shouldn't have paid that for it. No, I shouldn't have. I'll take it off and return it tomorrow. I shouldn't have bought it."

Julian raised his eyes to heaven. "Yes, you should have bought it," he said. "Put it on and let's go." It was a hideous hat. A purple velvet flap came down on one side of it and stood up on the other; the rest of it was green and looked like a cushion with the stuffing out. He decided it was less comical than jaunty and pathetic. Everything that gave her pleasure was small and depressed him.

She lifted the hat one more time and set it down slowly on top of her head. Two wings of gray hair protruded on either side of her florid face, but her eyes, sky-blue, were as innocent and untouched by experience as they must have been when she was ten. Were it not that she was a widow who had struggled fiercely to feed and clothe and put him through school and who was supporting him still, "until he got on his feet," she might have been a little girl that he had to take to town.

"It's all right, it's all right," he said. "Let's go." He opened the door himself and started down the walk to get her going. The sky was a dying violet and the houses stood out darkly against it, bulbous liver-colored monstrosities of a uniform ugliness though no two were alike. Since this had been a fashionable neighborhood forty years ago, his mother persisted in thinking they did well to have an apartment in it. Each house had a narrow collar of dirt around it in which sat, usually, a grubby child. Julian walked with his hands in his pockets, his head down and thrust forward and his eyes glazed with the determination to make himself completely numb during the time he would be sacrificed to her pleasure.

The door closed and he turned to find the dumpy figure, surmounted by the atrocious hat, coming toward him. "Well," she said, "you only live once and paying a little more for it, I at least won't meet myself coming and going."

"Some day I'll start making money," Julian said gloomily — he knew he never would — "and you can have one of those jokes whenever you take the fit." But first they would move. He visualized a place where the nearest neighbors would be three miles away on either side.

"I think you're doing fine," she said, drawing on her gloves. "You've only been out of school a year. Rome wasn't built in a day."

She was one of the few members of the Y reducing class who arrived in hat and gloves and who had a son who had been to college. "It takes time," she said, "and the world is in such a mess. This hat looked better on me than any of the others, though when she brought it out I said, 'Take that thing back. I wouldn't have it on my head,' and she said, 'Now wait till you see it on,' and when she put it on me I said, 'We-ull,' and she said, 'If you ask me, that hat does something for you and you do something for the hat, and besides,' she said, 'with that hat, you won't meet yourself coming and going.'"

Julian thought he could have stood his lot better if she had been selfish, if she had been an old hag who drank and screamed at him. He walked along, saturated in depression, as if in the midst of his martyrdom he had lost his faith. Catching sight of his long, hopeless, irritated face, she stopped suddenly with a grief-stricken look, and pulled back on his arm. "Wait on me," she said. "I'm going back to the house and take this thing off and tomorrow I'm going to return it. I was out of my head. I can pay the gas bill with that seven-fifty."

He caught her arm in a vicious grip. "You are not going to take it back," he said. "I like it."

"Well," she said, "I don't think I ought. . . ."

"Shut up and enjoy it," he muttered, more depressed than ever.

"With the world in the mess it's in," she said, "it's a wonder we can enjoy anything. I tell you, the bottom rail is on the top."

Julian sighed.

"Of course," she said, "if you know who you are, you can go anywhere." She said this every time he took her to the reducing class. "Most of them in it are not our kind of people," she said, "but I can be gracious to anybody. I know who I am."

"They don't give a damn for your graciousness," Julian said savagely. "Knowing who you are is good for one generation only. You haven't the foggiest idea where you stand now or who you are."

She stopped and allowed her eyes to flash at him. "I most certainly do know who I am," she said, "and if you don't know who you are, I'm ashamed of you."

"Oh hell," Julian said.

"Your great-grandfather was a former governor of this state," she said. "Your grandfather was a prosperous landowner. Your grandmother was a Godhigh."

"Will you look around you," he said tensely, "and see where you are now?" and he swept his arm jerkily out to indicate the neighborhood, which the growing darkness at least made less dingy.

"You remain what you are," she said. "Your great-grandfather had a plantation and two hundred slaves."

"There are no more slaves," he said irritably.

"They were better off when they were," she said. He groaned to see that she was off on that topic. She rolled onto it every few days like a train on an open track. He knew every stop, every junction, every swamp along the way, and knew the exact point at which her conclusion would roll majestically into the station: "It's ridiculous. It's simply not realistic. They should rise, yes, but on their own side of the fence."

"Let's skip it," Julian said.

"The ones I feel sorry for," she said, "are the ones that are half white. They're tragic."

"Will you skip it?"

"Suppose we were half white. We would certainly have mixed feelings."

"I have mixed feelings now," he groaned.

"Well let's talk about something pleasant," she said. "I remember going to Grandpa's when I was a little girl. Then the house had double stairways that went up to what was really the second floor — all the cooking was done on the first. I used to like to stay down in the kitchen on account of the way the walls smelled. I would sit with my nose pressed against the plaster and take deep breaths. Actually the place belonged to the Godhighs but your grandfather Chestny paid the mortgage and saved it for them. They were in reduced circumstances," she said, "but reduced or not, they never forgot who they were."

"Doubtless that decayed mansion reminded them," Julian muttered. He never spoke of it without contempt or thought of it without longing. He had seen it once when he was a child before it had been sold. The double stairways had rotted and been torn down. Negroes were living in it. But it remained in his mind as his mother had known it. It appeared in his dreams regularly. He would stand on the wide porch, listening to the rustle of oak leaves, then wander through the high-ceilinged hall into the parlor that opened onto it and gaze at the worn rugs and faded draperies. It occurred to him that it was he, not she, who could have appreciated it. He preferred its threadbare elegance to anything he could name and it was because of it that all the neighborhoods they had lived in had been a torment to him — whereas she had hardly known the difference. She called her insensitivity "being adjustable."

"And I remember the old darky who was my nurse, Caroline. There was no better person in the world. I've always had a great respect for my colored friends," she said. "I'd do anything in the world for them and they'd. . . ."

"Will you for God's sake get off that subject?" Julian said. When he got on a bus by himself, he made it a point to sit down beside a Negro, in reparation as it were for his mother's sins.

"You're mighty touchy tonight," she said. "Do you feel all right?"

"Yes I feel all right," he said. "Now lay off."

She pursed her lips. "Well, you certainly are in a vile humor," she observed. "I just won't speak to you at all."

They had reached the bus stop. There was no bus in sight and Julian, his hands still jammed in his pockets and his head thrust forward, scowled down the empty street. The frustration of having to wait on the bus as well as ride on it began to creep up his neck like a hot hand. The presence of his mother was borne in upon him as she gave a pained sigh. He looked at her bleakly. She was holding herself very erect under the preposterous hat, wearing it like a banner of her imaginary dignity. There was in him an evil urge to break her spirit. He suddenly unloosened his tie and pulled it off and put it in his pocket.

She stiffened. "Why must you look like *that* when you take me to town?" she said. "Why must you deliberately embarrass me?"

"If you'll never learn where you are," he said, "you can at least learn where I am."

"You look like a — thug," she said.

"Then I must be one," he murmured.

"I'll just go home," she said. "I will not bother you. If you can't do a little thing like that for me . . ."

Rolling his eyes upward, he put his tie back on. "Restored to my class," he muttered. He thrust his face toward her and hissed. "True culture is in the mind, the *mind*," he said, and tapped his head, "the mind."

"It's in the heart," she said, "and in how you do things and how you do things is because of who you *are*."

"Nobody in the damn bus cares who you are."

"I care who I am," she said icily.

The lighted bus appeared on top of the next hill and as it approached, they moved out into the street to meet it. He put his hand under her elbow and hoisted her up on the creaking step. She entered with a little smile, as if she were going into a drawing room where everyone had been waiting for her. While he put in the tokens, she sat down on one of the broad front seats for three which faced the aisle. A thin woman with protruding teeth and long yellow hair was sitting on the end of it. His mother moved up beside her and left room for Julian beside herself. He sat down and looked at the floor across the aisle where a pair of thin feet in red and white canvas sandals were planted.

His mother immediately began a general conversation meant to attract anyone who felt like talking. "Can it get any hotter?" she said and removed from her purse a folding fan, black with a Japanese scene on it, which she began to flutter before her.

"I reckon it might could," the woman with the protruding teeth said, "but I know for a fact my apartment couldn't get no hotter."

"It must get the afternoon sun," his mother said. She sat forward and looked up and down the bus. It was half filled. Everybody was white. "I see we have the bus to ourselves," she said. Julian cringed.

"For a change," said the woman across the aisle, the owner of the red and white canvas sandals. "I come on one the other day and they were thick as fleas — up front and all through."

"The world is in a mess everywhere," his mother said. "I don't know how we've let it get in this fix."

"What gets my goat is all those boys from good families stealing automobile tires," the woman with the protruding teeth said. "I told my boy, I said you may not be rich but you been raised right and if I ever catch you in any such mess, they can send you on to the reformatory. Be exactly where you belong."

"Training tells," his mother said. "Is your boy in high school?"

"Ninth grade," the woman said.

"My son just finished college last year. He wants to write but he's selling typewriters until he gets started," his mother said.

The woman leaned forward and peered at Julian. He threw her such a malevolent look that she subsided against the seat. On the floor across the aisle there was an abandoned newspaper. He got up and got it and opened it out in front of him. His mother discreetly continued the conversation in a lower tone but the woman across the aisle said in a loud voice, "Well that's nice. Selling typewriters is close to writing. He can go right from one to the other."

"I tell him," his mother said, "that Rome wasn't built in a day."

Behind the newspaper Julian was withdrawing into the inner compartment of his mind where he spent most of his time. This was a kind of mental bubble in which he established himself when he could not bear to be a part of what was going on around him. From it he could see out and judge but in it he was safe from any kind of penetration from without. It was the only place where he felt free of the general idiocy of his fellows. His mother had never entered it but from it he could see her with absolute clarity.

The old lady was clever enough and he thought that if she had started from any of the right premises, more might have been expected of her. She lived according to the laws of her own fantasy world, outside of which he had never seen her set foot. The law of it was to sacrifice herself for him after she had first created the necessity to do so by making a mess of things. If he had permitted her sacrifices, it was only because her lack of foresight had made them necessary. All of her life had been a struggle to act like a Chestny without the Chestny goods, and to give him everything she thought a Chestny ought to have; but since, said she, it was fun to struggle, why complain? And when you had won, as she had won, what fun to look back on the hard times! He could not forgive her that she had enjoyed the struggle and that she thought *she* had won.

What she meant when she said she had won was that she had brought him up successfully and had sent him to college and that he had turned out so well — good looking (her teeth had gone unfilled so that his could be straightened), intelligent (he realized he was too intelligent to be a success), and with a future ahead of him (there was of course no future ahead of him). She excused his gloominess on the grounds that he was still growing up and his radical ideas on his lack of practical experience. She said he didn't yet know a thing about "life," that he hadn't even entered the real world — when already he was as disenchanted with it as a man of fifty.

The further irony of all this was that in spite of her, he had turned out so well. In spite of going to only a third-rate college, he had, on his own initiative, come out with a first-rate education; in spite of growing up dominated by a small mind, he had ended up with a large one; in spite of all her foolish views, he was free of prejudice and unafraid to face facts. Most miraculous of all, instead of being blinded by love for her as she was for him, he had cut himself emotionally free of her and could see her with complete objectivity. He was not dominated by his mother.

The bus stopped with a sudden jerk and shook him from his meditation. A woman from the back lurched forward with little steps and barely escaped falling in his newspaper as she righted herself. She got off and a large Negro got on. Julian kept his paper lowered to watch. It gave him a certain satisfaction to see injustice in daily operation. It confirmed his view that with a few exceptions there was no one worth knowing within a radius of three hundred miles. The Negro was well dressed and carried a briefcase. He looked around and then sat down on the other end of the seat where the woman with the red and white canvas sandals was sitting. He immediately unfolded a newspaper and obscured himself behind it. Julian's mother's elbow at once prodded insistently into his ribs. "Now you see why I won't ride on these buses by myself," she whispered.

The woman with the red and white canvas sandals had risen at the same time the Negro sat down and had gone further back in the bus and taken the seat of the woman who had got off. His mother leaned forward and cast her an approving look.

Julian rose, crossed the aisle, and sat down in the place of the woman with the canvas sandals. From this position, he looked serenely across at his mother. Her face had turned an angry red. He stared at her, making his eyes the eyes of a stranger. He felt his tension suddenly lift as if he had openly declared war on her.

He would have liked to get in conversation with the Negro and to talk with him about art or politics or any subject that would be above the comprehension of those around them, but the man remained entrenched behind his paper. He was either ignoring the change of seating or had never noticed it. There was no way for Julian to convey his sympathy.

His mother kept her eyes fixed reproachfully on his face. The woman with the protruding teeth was looking at him avidly as if he were a type of monster new to her.

"Do you have a light?" he asked the Negro.

Without looking away from his paper, the man reached in his pocket and handed him a packet of matches.

"Thanks," Julian said. For a moment he held the matches foolishly. A NO SMOKING sign looked down upon him from over the door. This alone would not have deterred him; he had no cigarettes. He had quit smoking some months before because he could not afford it. "Sorry," he muttered and handed back the matches. The Negro lowered the paper and gave him an annoyed look. He took the matches and raised the paper again.

His mother continued to gaze at him but she did not take advantage of his momentary discomfort. Her eyes retained their battered look. Her face seemed to be unnaturally red, as if her blood pressure had risen. Julian allowed no glimmer of sympathy to show on his face. Having got the advantage, he wanted desperately to keep it and carry it through. He would have liked to teach her a lesson that would last her a while, but there seemed no way to continue the point. The Negro refused to come out from behind his paper.

Julian folded his arms and looked stolidly before him, facing her but as if he did not see her, as if he had ceased to recognize her existence. He visualized a scene in which, the bus having reached their stop, he would remain in his seat and when she said, "Aren't you going to get off?" he would look at her as at a stranger who had rashly addressed him. The corner they got off on was usually deserted, but it was well lighted and it would not hurt her to walk by herself the four blocks to the Y. He decided to wait until the time came and then decide whether or not he would let her get off by herself. He would have to be at the Y at ten to bring her back, but he could leave her wondering if he was going to show up. There was no reason for her to think she could always depend on him.

He retired again into the high-ceilinged room sparsely settled with large pieces of antique furniture. His soul expanded momentarily but then he became aware of his mother across from him and the vision shriveled. He studied her coldly. Her feet in little pumps dangled like a child's and did not quite reach the floor. She was training on him an exaggerated look of reproach. He felt completely detached from her. At that moment he could with pleasure have slapped her as he would have slapped a particularly obnoxious child in his charge.

He began to imagine various unlikely ways by which he could teach her a lesson. He might make friends with some distinguished Negro professor or lawyer and bring him home to spend the evening. He would be entirely justified but her blood pressure would rise to 300. He could not push her to the extent of making her have a stroke, and moreover, he had never been successful at making any Negro friends. He had tried to strike up an acquaintance on the bus with some of the better types, with ones that looked like professors or ministers or lawyers. One morning he had sat down next to a distinguished-looking dark brown man who had answered his questions with a sonorous solemnity but who had turned out to be an undertaker. Another day he had sat down beside a cigar-smoking Negro with a diamond ring on his finger, but after a few stilted pleasantries, the Negro had rung the buzzer and risen, slipping two lottery tickets into Julian's hand as he climbed over him to leave.

He imagined his mother lying desperately ill and his being able to secure only a Negro doctor for her. He toyed with that idea for a few minutes and then dropped it for a momentary vision of himself participating as a sympathizer in a sit-in demonstration. This was possible but he did not linger with it. Instead, he approached the ultimate horror. He brought home a beautiful suspiciously Negroid woman. Prepare yourself, he said. There is nothing you can do about it. This is the woman I've chosen. She's intelligent, dignified, even good, and she's suffered and she hasn't thought it *fun*. Now persecute us, go ahead and persecute us. Drive her out of here, but remember, you're driving me too. His eyes were narrowed and through the indignation he had generated, he saw his mother across the aisle, purple-faced, shrunken to the dwarf-like proportions of her moral nature, sitting like a mummy beneath the ridiculous banner of her hat.

He was tilted out of his fantasy again as the bus stopped. The door opened with a sucking hiss and out of the dark a large, gaily dressed, sullen-looking colored woman got on with a little boy. The child, who might have been four, had on a short plaid suit and a Tyrolean hat with a blue feather in it. Julian hoped that he would sit down beside him and that the woman would push in beside his mother. He could think of no better arrangement.

As she waited for her tokens, the woman was surveying the seating possibilities — he hoped with the idea of sitting where she was least wanted. There was something familiar-looking about her but Julian could not place what it was. She was a giant of a woman. Her face was set not only to meet opposition but to seek it out. The downward tilt of her large lower lip was like a warning sign: DON'T TAMPER WITH ME. Her bulging figure was encased in a green crepe dress and her feet overflowed in red shoes. She had on a hideous hat. A purple velvet flap came down on one side of it and stood up on the other; the rest of it was green and looked like a cushion with the stuffing out. She carried a mammoth red pocketbook that bulged throughout as if it were stuffed with rocks.

To Julian's disappointment, the little boy climbed up on the empty seat beside his mother. His mother lumped all children, black and white, into the common category, "cute," and she thought little Negroes were on the whole cuter than little white children. She smiled at the little boy as he climbed on the seat.

Meanwhile the woman was bearing down upon the empty seat beside Julian. To his annoyance, she squeezed herself into it. He saw his mother's face change as the woman settled herself next to him and he realized with satisfaction that this was more objectionable to her than it was to him. Her face seemed almost gray and there was a look of dull recognition in her eyes, as if suddenly she had sickened at some awful confrontation. Julian saw that it was because she and the woman had, in a sense, swapped sons. Though his mother would not realize the symbolic significance of this, she would feel it. His amusement showed plainly on his face.

The woman next to him muttered something unintelligible to herself. He was conscious of a kind of bristling next to him, a muted growling like that of an angry cat. He could not see anything but the red pocketbook upright on the bulging green thighs. He visualized the woman as she had stood waiting for her tokens — the ponderous figure, rising from the red shoes upward over the solid hips, the mammoth bosom, the haughty face, to the green and purple hat.

His eyes widened.

The vision of the two hats, identical, broke upon him with the radiance of a brilliant sunrise. His face was suddenly lit with joy. He could not believe that Fate had thrust upon his mother such a lesson. He gave a loud chuckle so that she would look at him and see that he saw. She turned her eyes on him slowly. The blue in them seemed to have turned a bruised purple. For a moment he had an uncomfortable sense of her innocence, but it lasted only a second before principle rescued him. Justice entitled him to laugh. His grin hardened until it said to her as plainly as if he were saying aloud: Your punishment exactly fits your pettiness. This should teach you a permanent lesson.

Her eyes shifted to the woman. She seemed unable to bear looking at him and to find the woman preferable. He became conscious again of the bristling presence at his side. The woman was rumbling like a volcano about to become active. His mother's mouth began to twitch slightly at one corner.

With a sinking heart, he saw incipient signs of recovery on her face and realized that this was going to strike her suddenly as funny and was going to be no lesson at all. She kept her eyes on the woman and an amused smile came over her face as if the woman were a monkey that had stolen her hat. The little Negro was looking up at her with large fascinated eyes. He had been trying to attract her attention for some time.

"Carver!" the woman said suddenly. "Come heah!"

When he saw that the spotlight was on him at last, Carver drew his feet up and turned himself toward Julian's mother and giggled.

"Carver!" the woman said. "You heah me? Come heah!"

Carver slid down from the seat but remained squatting with his back against the base of it, his head turned slyly around toward Julian's mother, who was smiling at him. The woman reached a hand across the aisle and snatched him to her. He righted himself and hung backwards on her knees, grinning at Julian's mother. "Isn't he cute?" Julian's mother said to the woman with the protruding teeth.

"I reckon he is," the woman said without conviction.

The Negress yanked him upright but he eased out of her grip and shot across the aisle and scrambled, giggling wildly, onto the seat beside his love.

"I think he likes me," Julian's mother said, and smiled at the woman. It was the smile she used when she was being particularly gracious to an inferior. Julian saw everything lost. The lesson had rolled off her like rain on a roof.

The woman stood up and yanked the little boy off the seat as if she were snatching him from contagion. Julian could feel the rage in her at having no weapon like his mother's smile. She gave the child a sharp slap across his leg. He howled once and then thrust his head into her stomach and kicked his feet against her shins. "Be-have," she said vehemently.

The bus stopped and the Negro who had been reading the newspaper got off. The woman moved over and set the little boy down with a thump between herself and Julian. She held him firmly by the knee. In a moment he put his hands in front of his face and peeped at Julian's mother through his fingers.

"I see yoooooooo!" she said and put her hand in front of her face and peeped at him.

The woman slapped his hand down. "Quit yo' foolishness," she said, "before I knock the living Jesus out of you!"

Julian was thankful that the next stop was theirs. He reached up and pulled the cord. The woman reached up and pulled it at the same time. Oh my God, he thought. He had the terrible intuition that when they got off the bus together, his mother would open her purse and give the little boy a nickel. The gesture would be as natural to her as breathing. The bus stopped and the woman got up and lunged to the front, dragging the child, who wished to stay on, after her. Julian and his mother got up and followed. As they neared the door, Julian tried to relieve her of her pocketbook.

"No," she murmured, "I want to give the little boy a nickel."

"No!" Julian hissed. "No!"

She smiled down at the child and opened her bag. The bus door opened and the woman picked him up by the arm and descended with him, hanging at her hip. Once in the street she set him down and shook him.

Julian's mother had to close her purse while she got down the bus step but as soon as her feet were on the ground, she opened it again and began to rummage inside. "I can't find but a penny," she whispered, "but it looks like a new one."

"Don't do it!" Julian said fiercely between his teeth. There was a streetlight on the corner and she hurried to get under it so she could better see into her pocketbook. The woman was heading off rapidly down the street with the child still hanging backward on her hand.

"Oh little boy!" Julian's mother called and took a few quick steps and caught up with them just beyond the lamp-post. "Here's a bright new penny for you," and she held out the coin, which shone bronze in the dim light.

The huge woman turned and for a moment stood, her shoulders lifted and her face frozen with frustrated rage, and stared at Julian's mother. Then all at once she seemed to explode like a piece of machinery that had been given one ounce of pressure too much. Julian saw the black fist swing out with the red pocketbook. He shut his eyes and cringed as he heard the woman shout, "He don't take nobody's pennies!" When he opened his eyes, the woman was disappearing down the street with the little boy staring wide-eyed over her shoulder. Julian's mother was sitting on the sidewalk.

"I told you not to do that," Julian said angrily. "I told you not to do that!"

He stood over her for a minute, gritting his teeth. Her legs were stretched out in front of her and her hat was on her lap. He squatted down and looked her in the face. It was totally expressionless. "You got exactly what you deserved," he said. "Now get up."

He picked up her pocketbook and put what had fallen out back in it. He picked the hat up off her lap. The penny caught his eye on the sidewalk and he picked that up and let it drop before her eyes into the purse. Then he stood up and leaned over and held his hands out to pull her up. She remained immobile. He sighed. Rising above them on either side were black apartment buildings, marked with irregular rectangles of light. At the end of the block a man came out of a door and walked off in the opposite direction. "All right," he said, "suppose somebody happens by and wants to know why you're sitting on the sidewalk?"

She took the hand and, breathing hard, pulled heavily up on it and then stood for a moment, swaying slightly as if the spots of light in the darkness were circling around her. Her eyes, shadowed and confused, finally settled on his face. He did not try to conceal his irritation. "I hope this teaches you a lesson," he said. She leaned forward and her eyes raked his face. She seemed trying to determine his identity. Then, as if she found nothing familiar about him, she started off with a headlong movement in the wrong direction.

"Aren't you going on to the Y?" he asked.

"Home," she muttered.

"Well, are we walking?"

For answer she kept going. Julian followed along, his hands behind him. He saw no reason to let the lesson she had had go without backing it up with an explanation of its meaning. She might as well be made to understand what had happened to her. "Don't think that was just an uppity Negro woman," he said. "That was the whole colored race which will no longer take your condescending pennies. That was your black double. She can wear the same hat as you, and to be sure," he added gratuitously (because he thought it was funny), "it looked better on her than it did on you. What all this means," he said, "is that the old world is gone. The old manners are obsolete and your graciousness is not worth a damn." He thought bitterly of the house that had been lost for him. "You aren't who you think you are," he said.

She continued to plow ahead, paying no attention to him. Her hair had come undone on one side. She dropped her pocketbook and took no notice. He stooped and picked it up and handed it to her but she did not take it.

"You needn't act as if the world had come to an end," he said, "because it hasn't. From now on you've got to live in a new world and face a few realities for a change. Buck up," he said, "it won't kill you."

She was breathing fast.

"Let's wait on the bus," he said.

"Home," she said thickly.

"I hate to see you behave like this," he said. "Just like a child. I should be able to expect more of you." He decided to stop where he was and make her stop and wait for a bus. "I'm not going any farther," he said, stopping. "We're going on the bus."

She continued to go on as if she had not heard him. He took a few steps and caught her arm and stopped her. He looked into her face and caught his breath. He was looking into a face he had never seen before. "Tell Grandpa to come get me," she said.

He stared, stricken.

"Tell Caroline to come get me," she said.

Stunned, he let her go and she lurched forward again, walking as if one leg were shorter than the other. A tide of darkness seemed to be sweeping her from him. "Mother!" he cried. "Darling, sweetheart, wait!" Crumpling, she fell to the pavement. He dashed forward and fell at her side, crying, "Mamma, Mamma!" He turned her over. Her face was fiercely distorted. One eye, large and staring, moved slightly to the left as if it had become unmoored. The other remained fixed on him, raked his face again, found nothing and closed.

"Wait here, wait here!" he cried and jumped up and began to run for help toward a cluster of lights he saw in the distance ahead of him. "Help, help!" he shouted, but his voice was thin, scarcely a thread of sound. The lights drifted farther away the faster he ran and his feet moved numbly as if they carried him nowhere. The tide of darkness seemed to sweep him back to her, postponing from moment to moment his entry into the world of guilt and sorrow.

Suggestions for Discussion

1. This story contains a conflict about "color," black and white. In what way does O'Connor use details of bright color — red, green, purple, yellow — to bring this conflict into focus? How do these colors further the plot?

2. The third paragraph of the story details the fatal hat. Whose are the judgments in this paragraph, the author's or Julian's? How do you know? Try substituting passive verbs for active in the description of the hat. What is the effect?

3. Contrast the images of the Godhigh house as the mother remembers it on page 45 with both Julian's memory of it in the next paragraph and his fantasies about it. How much information do these three sets of details convey about the house, the way the world has changed, the conflict between Julian and his mother, the contrasts and similarities in their characters? How does O'Connor direct your sympathies and judgments in these two paragraphs?

4. The paragraph beginning, "The lighted bus appeared on top of the next hill" (page 46), is arranged in sentences with parallel structures: subject, verb, object. Why? What is the emotional impact of this monotonous rhythm?

5. Analyze the arrival of the black woman in the green-and-purple hat for the active and passive voice (page 50). The paragraph beginning, "He was tilted out of his fantasy," uses mainly active verbs, whereas the next paragraph uses mainly linking verbs. Why?

6. On page 53, the paragraph beginning, "He stood over her for a minute," and the following two paragraphs, report, in a relatively external way, what happens in a scene highly charged with emotion. What are the generalizations and judgments not "told" in this passage but conveyed through detail and action?

7. Identify all the "story" elements of "Everything That Rises Must Converge" that are not part of the "plot." Why must the plot begin where it does? Why is it nevertheless necessary to reveal elements of the past in the course of the action?

Widow Water

FREDERICK BUSCH

What to know about pain is how little we do to deserve it, how simple it is to give, how hard to lose. I'm a plumber. I dig for what's wrong. I should know. And what I think of now as I remember pain is the fat young man and his child, their staggering house, the basement filled with death and dark water, the small perfect boy on the stone cellar steps who wept, the widow's coffee gone cold.

They called on Friday to complain that the pump in their basement wouldn't work. Theirs is shallow-well country, a couple of miles from the college, a place near the fast wide river that once ran the mill that all the houses of the town depended on. The railroad came, the town grew, the large white clapboard houses spread. By the time their seedlings were in the middle growth, the mill had failed, the houses had run to blisters of rotted wood on the siding and to gaps in the black and green roofs. The old ones were nearly all dead and the railroad came twice a day, from Utica to Binghamton, to Utica from Binghamton, carrying sometimes some freight, sometimes a car of men who maintained the nearly useless track. And the new people came, took their children for walks on the river to the stone foundations of the mill. They looked at the water and went home. People now don't know the water as they should. I'm a plumber, I should know.

I told him I couldn't come on a Friday afternoon in April, when the rains were opening seams and seals and cellars all through the county. Bella was making coffee for us while I took the call, and I snapped my fingers for her to turn around. She did, all broad — not fat, though — and full of colors — red in her face, yellow in her hair going gray, the gold in her tooth, her eyes blue as pottery — and I pointed at the phone. She mouthed a mimic "Today, today, today," and I nodded, and she nodded back and poured the almost boiling water out into the instant coffee, which dissolved.

He said, "So you see, sir, we can use your help."

I said, "Yessir, sounds like a problem."

"No water, and we've got a boy who isn't toilet-trained. It gets kind of messy."

"I imagine."

"So do you think you could . . ."

"Yessir?"

"Come kind of soon?"

"Oh, I'll come kind of soon. It just won't be today."

"You're sure you couldn't . . ."

"Yessir?"

"Come today?"

"Yessir."

"Yes sir, what?"

"Yessir, I'm sure I can't come."

Bella rapped on the table with her big knuckles to tell me to come and sit. I nodded, pointed at the telephone, waited for him to try once more. He was from the college — he would try once more.

He said, "But no water — for how long? The weekend? All week?"

I heard a woman whisper in the background with the harshness of a wife making peace, and then he said, "Uh — I mean, do you know when you can come?"

I said, "When're you up?"

"Excuse me?"

"When do you wake up?"

"We'll be up. Just tell me when."

I said, "I'll be there tomorrow morning, early, if that's all right."

"I mean, how early?"

"You get up, Mr. Samuels, and you have yourself a comfortable breakfast, and I'll be there for a cup of your coffee."

He hung on the line, waiting for more. I gave him nothing more, and he said, "Thanks. I mean, we'll see you tomorrow, then. Thank you."

"Thank *you* for calling, Mr. Samuels, and I'll see you soon."

He said, "Not soon enough," and chuckled and didn't mean the laugh.

I chuckled back and meant it, because coffee was waiting, and Bella, and a quiet hour before I went back out to clear a lonely lady's pipe in a fifty-foot well. I said, "Good-bye, Mr. Samuels."

He said, "Yes," which meant he was listening to his whispering wife, not me, and then he said, "Yes, good-bye, thank you very much, see you soon."

I blew on my coffee and Bella turned the radio off — she'd been listening to it low to hear if she'd won the fur coat someone in Oneida was giving away — and we sat and ate bran muffins with her blueberry jam and talked about nothing much; we said most of it by sitting and eating too much together after so many years of coffee and preserves.

After a while she said, "A professor with a problem."

"His pump won't turn off. Somebody sold him a good big Gould brand-new when he moved in last summer, and now it won't turn off and he's mad as hell."

"Well, I can understand that. They hear that motor banging away and think it's going to explode and burn their house down. They're city people, I suppose."

"Aren't they ever. I know the house. McGregory's old place near the Keeper farm. It needs work."

"Which they wouldn't know how to do."

"Or be able to afford," I said. "He's a young one and a new professor. He wouldn't earn much more than the boys on Buildings and Grounds. I'll bill him — he won't have the money in the house or at the bank, probably — and we'll wait a couple of months."

Bella said, "We can wait."

"We will."

"What did you tell him to do?"

"I told him to unplug the pump."

"He wasn't satisfied."

"I guess I wouldn't be."

"Abe," she said, "what's it like to be young as that?"

I said, "Unhappy."

She said, "But happy, too."

"A little of that."

She bent her gray and gold head over the brown mug of dark brown coffee and picked at the richness of a moist muffin. She said, still looking down, "It's hard."

I said, "It gets easier."

She looked up and nodded, grinned her golden tooth at me, said, "Doesn't it?"

Then I spent the afternoon driving to New Hartford to the ice-cream plant for twenty-five pounds of sliced dry ice. I had them cut the ice into ten-inch-long slivers about three-quarters of an inch around, wrapped the ice in heavy brown paper, and drove it back to Brookfield and the widow's jammed drill point. It's all hard-water country here, and the crimped-pipe points they drive down for wells get sealed with calcium scales if you wait enough years, and the pressure falls, the people call, they worry about having to drill new wells and how much it will cost and when they can flush the toilets again. They worry how long they'll have to wait.

I went in the cellar door without telling her I was there, disconnected the elbow joint, went back out for the ice, and when I had carried the second bundle in, she was standing by her silent well in the damp of her basement, surrounded by furniture draped in plastic sheets, firewood stacked, cardboard boxes of web-crusted Mason jars, the growing heaps of whatever in her life she couldn't use.

She was small and white and dressed in sweaters and a thin green housecoat. She said, "Whatever do you mean to do?" Her hands were folded across her little chest, and she rubbed her gnarled throat. "Is my well dead?"

"No, ma'am. I'd like you to go upstairs while I do my small miracle here. Because I'd like you not to worry. Won't you go upstairs?"

She said, "I live alone —"

I said, "You don't have to worry."

"I don't know what to do about — this kind of thing. It gets more and more of a problem — this — all this." She waved her hand at what she lived in and then hung her hands at her sides.

I said, "You go on up and watch the television. I'm going to fix it up. I'll do a little fixing here and come back tonight and hook her up again, and you be ready to make me my after-dinner coffee when I come back. You'll have water enough to do it with."

"Just go back upstairs?" she said.

"You go on up while I make it good. And I don't want you worrying."

"All right, then," she said, "I'll go back up. I get awfully upset now. When these — things. These — I don't know what to do anymore." She looked at me like something that was new. Then she said, "I knew your father, I think. Was he big like you?"

"You know it," I said. "Bigger. Didn't he court you one time?"

"I think everybody must have courted me one time."

"You were frisky," I said.

"Not like now," she said. Her lips were white on her white face, the flesh looked like flower petals. Pinch them and they crumble, wet dust.

"Don't you feel so good now?"

"I mean kids now."

"Oh?"

"They have a different notion of frisky now."

"Yes they do," I said. "I guess they do."

"But I don't feel so good," she said. "This. Things like this. I wish they wouldn't happen. Now. I'm very old."

I said, "It keeps on coming, doesn't it?"

"I can hear it come. When the well stopped, I thought it was a sign. When you get like me, you can hear it come."

I said, "Now listen: You go up. You wrap a blanket around you and talk on the telephone or watch the TV. Because I guarantee. You knew my father. You knew my father's word. Take mine. I guarantee."

"Well, if you're guaranteeing."

I said, "That's my girl." She was past politeness so she didn't smile or come back out of herself to say good-bye. She walked to the stairs and when she started to shuffle and haul the long way up, I turned away to the well pipe, calling, "You make sure and have my coffee ready tonight. You wait and make my after-dinner coffee, hear? There'll be water for it." I waited until she went up, and it was something of a wait. She was too tired for stairs. I thought to tell Bella that it looked like the widow hadn't long.

But when she was gone, I worked. I put my ear to the pipe and heard the sounds of hollowness, the emptiness under the earth that's not quite silence — like the whisper you hear in the long-distance wires of the telephone before the relays connect. Then I opened the brown paper packages and started forcing the lengths of dry ice down into the pipe. I carried and shoved, drove the ice first with my fingers and then with a piece of copper tube, and I filled the well pipe until nothing more would go. My fingers were red, and the smoke from dry ice misted up until I stood in an underground fog. When nothing more would fit, I capped the pipe, kicked the rest of the ice down into the sump — it steamed as if she lived above a fire, as if always her house were smoldering — and I went out, drove home.

I went by the hill roads, and near Excell's farm I turned the motor off, drifted down the dirt road in neutral, watching. The deer had come down from the high hills and they were moving carefully through the fields of last year's corn stumps, grazing like cattle at dusk, too many to count. When the truck stopped I heard the rustle as they pulled the tough silk. Then I started the motor — they jumped, stiffened, watched me for a while, went back to eating: A man could come and kill them, they had so little fear — and I drove home to Bella and a tight house, long dinner, silence for most of the meal, then talk about the children while I washed the dishes and she put them away.

And then I drove back to the house that was dark except for one lighted window. The light was yellow and not strong. I turned the engine off and coasted in. I went downstairs on the tips of my toes because, I told myself, there was a sense of silence there, and I hoped she was having some rest. I uncapped the well pipe and gases blew back, a stink of the deepest cold, and then there was a sound of climbing, of filling up, and water banged to her house again. I put the funnel and hose on the mouth of the pipe and filled my jeep can, then capped the check valve, closed the pipe that delivered the water upstairs, poured water from the jeep can through the funnel to prime the pump, switched it on, watched the pressure needle climb to thirty-eight pounds, opened the faucet to the upstairs pipes, and heard it gush.

I hurried to get the jeep can and hose and funnel and tools to the truck, and I had closed the cellar door and driven off before she made the porch to call me. I wanted to get back to Bella and tell her what a man she was married to — who could know so well the truths of ice and make a dead well live.

Saturday morning the pickup trucks were going to the dump, and the men would leave off trash and hard fill, stand at tailgates, spitting, talking, complaining, shooting at rats or nothing, firing off, picking for scrap, and I drove to see the professor and his catastrophe.

His house was tilted. It needed jacks. The asbestos siding was probably all that kept the snow out. His drainpipes were broken, and I could see the damp spots where water wasn't carried off but spilled to the roof of his small porch to eat its way in and gradually soften the house for bad winter leaks. The lawn at the side of his drive was rutted and soft, needed gravel. The barn he used for a garage would have to be coated with creosote or it would rot and fall. A child's bright toys lay in his yard like litter. The cornfield behind his house went off to soft meadow and low hills, and everything was clean and growing behind where they lived; for the view they had, they might as well have owned the countryside. What they didn't own was their house.

He met me at the back steps, all puffy and breasted in his T-shirt, face in the midst of a curly black beard, dirty glasses over his eyes like a mask. He shook my hand as if I were his surgeon. He asked me to have coffee, and I told him I wouldn't now. A little boy came out, and he was beautiful: blond hair and sweetly shaped head, bright brown eyes, as red from weather as his father was pale, a sturdy body with a rounded stomach you would want to cup your hand on as if it were a breast, and teeth as white as bone. He stood behind his father and circled an arm around his father's heavy thigh, put his forehead in his father's buttocks, and then peeped out at me. He said. "Is this the fixing man? Will he fix our pump?"

Samuels put his hand behind him and squeezed the boy's head. He said, "This is the plumber, Mac." He raised his eyebrows at me and smiled, and I liked the way he loved the boy and knew how the boy embarrassed him too.

I kneeled down and said, "Hey, Mac."

The boy hid his face in his father's behind.

I said, "Mac, do you play in that sandbox over there?"

His face came out and he said, very politely, "Would you like to play with me?"

I said, "I have to look at your pump, Mac."

He nodded. He was serious now. He said, "Daddy broke it last night, and we can't fix it again."

I carried my tool pack to the cellar door — the galvanized sheeting on top of it was coming loose, several nails had gone, the weather was getting behind it and would eat the wood away — and I opened it up and started down the stone steps to the inside cellar door. They came behind me, then Samuels went ahead of me, turning on lights, scuffing through the mud and puddles on his concrete floor. The pump was on the wall to the left as I came in. The converted coal furnace in front of me leaked oil where the oilfeed came in. Stone foundation cracking that was two hundred years old, vent windows shut when they should have been opened to stop the dry rot, beams with the adze scars in them powdering almost as we watched: that was his cellar — and packing cartons and scraps of wood, broken chairs, a table with no legs. There was a stink of something bad.

I looked at the pump, breathed out, then I looked at Mac. He breathed out too. He sounded like me. I grinned at him and he grinned back.

"We're the workers," he said. "Okay? You and me will be the workers. But Daddy can't fix anymore. Mommy said so."

Samuels said, "We'll leave him now, Mac."

I said, "How old is he?"

Mac said, "Six years old."

Samuels said, "Three. Almost three and a half."

"And lots of boy," I said.

Mac said, "I'm a worker."

Samuels said, "All right, Mac."

Mac said, "Can't I stay here? Daddy? I'm a *worker*."

Samuels said, "Would we be in the way? I'd like to learn a little about this thing if I can."

Mac shook his head and smiled at me. He said, "What are we going to do with our Daddy?"

Samuels said, "Okay, buddy."

Mac raised his brows and shrugged his little arms.

Samuels said, "Out, Mac. Into the yard. Play in the sandbox for a while." He said, "Okay? I'll call you when we need some help."

"Sure!" Mac said.

He walked up the steps, arms slanted out to balance himself, little thighs pushing up on the steps. From outside, where we couldn't see him anymore, the boy called, "Bye and I love you," and ran away.

Samuels held his arms folded across his chest, covering his fleshy breasts. He uncrossed his arms to push his glasses up on his face when they slipped from the bridge of his flat nose. He said, "The water here — I tried to use the instruction book last night, after I talked to you. I guess I shouldn't have done that, huh?"

"Depends on what you did, Mr. Samuels." I unrolled the tool pack, got ready to work.

"I figured it wouldn't turn off on account of an air block in the pipes. The instructions mentioned that."

"Oh."

"So I unplugged the pump as you told me to, and then I drained all the water out — that's how the floor got so wet. Then it all ran into that hole over there."

"The sump."

"Oh, *that's* what a sump is. Then that motor like an outboard engine with the pipe —"

"The sump pump. The water collects in the hole and pushes the float up and the motor cuts in and pumps the water out the side of the house — over there, behind your hot-water heater."

"Oh."

"Except your sump pump isn't plugged in."

"Oh. I wondered. And I was fooling with the motor and this black ball fell off into the water."

"The float. So it wouldn't turn itself *off* if you did keep it plugged in. Don't you worry, Mr. Samuels, we'll pump her out later. Did you do anything else to the well pump?"

He pushed his glasses up and recrossed his arms. "I didn't know what else to do. I couldn't make it start again. We didn't have any water all night. There wasn't any pressure on the gauge."

"No. You have to prime it."

"Prime it?"

"I'll show you, Mr. Samuels. First, you better let me look. Right?"

"Sorry. Sorry. Do you mind if I stay here, though?" He smiled. He blushed under his whiskers. "I really have to learn something about how — this whole thing." He waved his arms around him and then covered up.

I said, "You can stay, sure. Stay."

I started to work a wrench on the heavy casing bolts, and when I'd got the motor apart from the casing, water began to run to the floor from the discharge pipe over the galvanized tank.

He said, "Should I . . ."

"Excuse me?"

"There's water coming down. Should I do anything about it?"

I said, "No, thank you. No. You just watch, thank you."

After a while the trickle slowed, and I pulled the halves apart. I took the rubber diaphragm off, put the flashlight on the motor, poked with a screwdriver, found nothing. I expected nothing. It had to be in the jet. I put the light on that and looked in and saw it, nodded, waited for him to ask.

He said, "You found it?"

"Yessir. The jet's blocked. That's what it sounded like when you called. Wouldn't let the pressure build up, so the gauge wouldn't know when to stop. It's set at forty pounds, and the block wouldn't let it up past — oh, twenty-eight or thirty, I'd say. Am I right?"

"Uh, I don't know. I don't know *anything* about these things."

I said, "When this needle hits forty, it's what you should be getting. Forty pounds of pressure per square inch. If you'd read the gauge you'd have seen it to be about thirty, I calculate. That would've told you the whole thing."

"I thought the gauge was broken."

"They generally don't break. Generally, these things work. Usually it's something simpler than machines when you can't get water up."

He pushed his glasses and covered up, said, "God, what I don't know."

I said, "It's hard to live in a house, isn't it? But you'll learn."

"Jesus, I hope so. I don't know. I hope so. We never lived in a house before."

"What'd you live in? Apartment houses?"

"Yeah — where you call the janitor downstairs and he comes up while you're at work and you never see him. Like magic. It's just all better by the time you get home."

"Well, we'll get this better for you."

He frowned and nodded very seriously. "I'll bet you will," he said. It was a gift he gave me, a bribe.

I said, "So why don't you go on up and ask the missus for about three inches of aluminum foil. Would you do that? And a coat hanger, if you don't mind."

"Coat hanger?"

"Yessir. If you don't mind."

He walked across the floor to the wooden steps that went upstairs above the furnace; he tried to hide the sway and bounce of his body in the way that he walked, the boy coming down the outside concrete steps as the father went up the inside ones. "Do you need any help?" the boy said.

I said, "Mac, you old helper. Hello."

"Do you need any help?"

"I had a boy like you."

"A little bit big, like me?"

"Little bit big. Except now he's almost a daddy too."

He said, "Is he *your* daddy now?"

I said, "Not yet."

"Not yet?"

"Not for a while."

"Oh. Well, then what happened to him?"

"He just got big. He grew up."

"Does he go to the college?"

"He's bigger than that, even."

Mac smiled and showed his hand, fingers held together. "*That* big? *So* big?"

"Bigger," I said.

Mac said, "That's a big boy you have."

Samuels handed me the foil and coat hanger. I rolled the foil around a cigar until it was a cylinder, and I stuck it in the well side of the nozzle. I opened the hanger and straightened her out.

Mac said, "What's he doing, Daddy?"

Samuels said, "I don't know. I don't know, Mac. Why don't you go outside? I don't know."

I said, "Mr. Samuels, I wonder if you would hold that foil firmly in there and cup your hand under it while I give her a shove."

He held. Mac watched him. I pushed at the other side of the jet, felt it, pushed again, and it rolled down the aluminum foil to his palm: a flat wet pebble half the size of the nail on his little finger. He said, "That's it? That's all it is? This is what ruined my life for two days?"

I said, "That's all it ever takes, Mr. Samuels. It came up with the water — you have to have gravel where there's water — and it lodged in the jet, kept the pressure from building up. If it happens again, I'll put a screen in at the check valve. May never happen again. If it does, we'll know what to do, won't we?"

Samuels said, "I wonder when I'll ever know what to do around here."

I said, "You'll learn."

I fastened the halves of the pump together, then went out for my jeep can, still half full from the widow's house. I came back in and I unscrewed the pipe plug at the top of the pump and poured the water in, put the plug back on, connected the pump to the switch.

Mac jumped, then stood still, holding to his father's leg.

The pump chirred, caught on the water from the widow's well, drew, and we all watched the pressure climb to forty, heard the motor cut out, heard the water climb in the copper pipes to the rest of the house as I opened the valve.

I was putting away tools when I heard Samuels say, "Now keep away from there!" I heard the *whuck* of his hand on Mac's flesh, and heard the weeping start, in the back of the boy's throat, and then the wail. Samuels said, "That's *filthy* in there — Christ knows what you've dragged up. And I *told* you not to mess with things you don't know anything about. Dammit!"

Mac wailed louder. I watched his face clench and grow red, ugly. He put his left sleeve in his mouth and chewed on it, backed away to the stone steps, fumbled with his feet and stepped backwards up one step. "But *Dad*-dy," he said. "But *Dad*-dy." Then he stood on the steps and chewed his sleeve and cried.

Samuels said, "God, look at that."

I said, "There's that smell you've been smelling, Mr. Samuels. Mouse. He must've fallen into the sump and starved to death and rotted there. That's what you've been smelling."

"God. Mac — go up and wash your hands. Mac! Go upstairs and wash your hands. I mean *now!*"

The small brown lump of paws and tail and teeth, its stomach swollen, the rest looking almost dissolved, lay in its puddle on the floor beside the sump. The stink of its death was everywhere. The pump cut in and built the pressure up again. Mac stood on the cellar steps and cried. His father pushed his glasses up and looked at the corpse of the rotted mouse and hugged his arms around himself and looked at his son. I walked past Samuels, turned away from the weeping boy, and pushed up at the lever that the float, if he had left it there, would have released on the sump pump. Nothing happened, and I stayed where I was, waiting, until I remembered to plug the sump pump in. I pushed the lever again, its motor started, the filthy reeking water dropped, the wide black rubber pipe it passed through on the ceiling swung like something alive as all that dying passed along it and out.

I picked the mouse up by its tail after the pump had stopped and Samuels, waiting for my approval, watching my face, had pulled out the plug. I carried my tools under my arm and the jeep can in my hand. I nodded to Samuels and he was going to speak, then didn't, just nodded back. I walked past Mac on the steps, not crying anymore, but wet-faced and stunned. I bent down as I passed him. I whispered, "What shall we do with your Daddy?" and went on, not smiling.

I walked to the truck in their unkempt drive that went to the barn that would fall. I carried the corpse. I thought to get home to Bella and say how sorry I was for the sorrow I'd made and couldn't take back. I spun the dripping mouse by its tail and flung it beyond the barn into Keeper's field of corn stumps. It rose and sank from the air and was gone. I had primed the earth. It didn't need the prime.

Suggestions for Discussion

1. "Widow Water" begins with a pronouncement containing three generalizations. How are these generalizations justified or earned by the details that complete the paragraph?

2. Identify the active and linking verbs in the second paragraph. Try substituting the passive voice for the active — what happens to the vigor of the passage?

3. In the scene between the plumber-narrator and his wife Bella, what and how much do you learn about the relationship between them? What sorts of abstraction or judgment are conveyed through concrete detail?

4. Throughout the story the plumber details the problems of wells, pipes and hard-water country; and also his solutions for the problems. Presumably the purpose of these details is not to teach us plumbing maintenance. What purpose do they serve?

5. Focus on the rhythm of the widow's speech on pp. 58–59. How does this rhythm help to characterize her?

6. On pp. 60–61 Professor Samuels's house is described in a series of concrete details. To what extent do these details also characterize the professor himself?

7. The paragraph beginning "The small brown lump" on pp. 65–66 contains eight sentences. Except for the first, all of these begin with the parallel structure subject-verb. What is the *emotional* effect of this rhythm? How does the use of active verbs help to reveal the narrator's emotion?

RETROSPECT

1. Identify the active and linking verbs in the three opening paragraphs of "Cutting Edge." Do they help to imply active and passive states in the characters?

2. Show how the character types of both the plumber and the professor in Frederick Busch's "Widow Water" are revealed through their individual characteristics.

3. Consider the rhythm of the paragraph beginning, "The doctor sucked in on his pipe," on page 24 of "The Second Tree from the Corner." How does the rhythm contribute to Trexler's emotional shifts?

WRITING ASSIGNMENTS

1. Take the passage "Danny carried the . . . slippers" on page 34, and rewrite it twice. Keep the basic action the same; you may alter the details in any way. In one rewrite, let us feel that the relationship is in deep trouble. In the other, let it charm us.

2. Make a short list of qualities that describe a character real or imagined. Then place that character in a scene and write the scene so that the qualities are conveyed through significant detail. Use no generalizations and no judgments. No word on your list will appear in the scene.

3. Write a description of a rural landscape, a city street, or a room. Use only active verbs to describe inanimate as well as animate things. Avoid the pathetic fallacy.

4. Write about a boring situation. Convince us that the situation is boring and that your characters are bored or boring or both. Fascinate us. Or make us laugh. Use no generalizations, no judgments, and no verbs in the passive voice.

5. Write about one of the following and suggest the rhythm of the subject in your prose: a machine, a vehicle, a piece of music, sex, something that goes in a circle, an avalanche.

6. Write about a character who begins at a standstill; works up to great speed (in a vehicle or on foot, pursued or pursuing, competing in a sport — or let the rush be purely emotional); and comes to a halt again, either gradually or abruptly. Let the prose rhythm reflect the changes.

BOOK PEOPLE
Kinds of Character

Individual, Typical, and Universal Characters
Round and Flat Characters
The Aristotelian Hero

Human character is in the foreground of all fiction, however the humanity might be disguised. Anthropomorphism may be a scientific sin, but it is a literary necessity. Bugs Bunny isn't a rabbit; he's a plucky youth in ears. Peter Rabbit is a mischievous boy. Brer Rabbit is a sassy rebel. The romantic heroes of *Watership Down* are out of the Arthurian tradition, not out of the hutch. And that doesn't cover fictional *rabbits*.

Henri Bergson, in his essay "On Laughter," observes:

> . . . the comic does not exist outside the pale of what is strictly human. A landscape may be beautiful, charming or sublime, or insignificant and ugly; it will never be laughable.

Bergson is right, but it is just as true that only the human is tragic. We may describe a landscape as "tragic" because nature has been devastated by industry, but the tragedy lies in the cupidity of those who wrought the havoc, in the dreariness, poverty, or disease of those who must live there.

A conservationist or ecologist (or a novelist) may care passionately about nature and dislike people because of it; then we say he or she "identifies" with nature (a wholly human capacity) or "respects the natural unity" (of which humanity is a part) or wants to keep the earth "habitable" (for whom?) or "values nature for its own sake" (using standards of value that nature does not share). By all available evidence, the universe is indifferent to the destruction of trees, property, peoples, and planets. Only people care.

If this is so, then your fiction can be only as successful as the characters who move it and move within it. Whether they are "drawn from life" or are "pure fantasy" — and all fictional characters lie somewhere between the two — we must find them interesting, we must find them believable, and we must care about what happens to them.

Individual, Typical, and Universal Characters

Characters, we're told, should be *individual, typical,* and *universal.* I don't think this truism is very helpful to a practicing writer. For example, I don't think you can *set out to be* "universal" in your writing.

It is true, I believe, that if literature has any social justification or use it is that readers can identify the common humanity in, and can therefore identify with, characters vastly different from themselves in century, geography, gender, culture, and beliefs; and that this enhances the scope of the reader's sympathy. It is also true that if the fiction does not have this universal quality — if a middle-class American male author creates as protagonist a middle-class American male with whom only middle-class American male readers can sympathize — then the fiction is thin and small. William Sloane voices the "frightening" demand of the reader in his book *The Craft of Writing:* "Tell me about me. I want to be more alive. Give me *me.*" But unfortunately the capacity for universality, like talent, is a trick of the genes or a miracle of the soul, and if you aim for the universal, you're likely to achieve the pompous.

If you're determined to create a "typical" character, you're likely to produce a caricature, because people are typical only in the generalized qualities that lump them together. *Typical* is the most provincial adjective in a writer's vocabulary, signaling that you're writing only for those who share your assumptions. A "typical schoolgirl" in Dar es Salaam is a very different "type" from one in San Francisco. Furthermore, every person is typical of many things successively or simultaneously. She may be in turn a "typical" schoolgirl, bride, divorcee, and feminist. He may be at one and the same time a "typical" New Yorker, math professor, doting father, and adulterer. It is in the confrontation and convolution of types that much of our individuality is produced.

If an author sets out deliberately to produce types rather than individuals, then that author invariably wants to condemn or ridicule those types. Joyce Carol Oates illustrates the technique in "How I Contemplated the World from the Detroit House of Correction and Began My Life Over Again."

Sioux Drive

George, Clyde G. 240 Sioux. A manufacturer's representative; children, a dog, a wife. Georgian with the usual columns. You think of the White House, then of Thomas Jefferson, then your mind goes blank on the white pillars and you think of nothing.

Typicality invites judgment. We can identify only with characters who come alive to us through their individuality.

It may clarify the distinctions among the universal, the typical, and the individual if you imagine this scene: The child chases a ball into the street. The tires screech, the bumper thuds, the blood geysers into the air, the pulp of the small body lies inert on the asphalt. How would a bystander react? (Is it universal?) How would a passing doctor react? (Is it typical?) How would Dr. Henry Lowes, just coming from the maternity ward of his own hospital, where his wife has had her fourth miscarriage, react? (Is it individual?) Each question narrows the range of convincing reaction, and as a writer you want to convince in each range. If you succeed in the third, you are likely to have succeeded in the other two.

Except where you want us to find your characters ridiculous or heinous or both, then, the rule of thumb is to aim for the individual (which means the specific, concrete, definite, and particular). The typical will take care of itself. The universal can't be forced.

Round and Flat Characters

We're also told that characters should be *round* rather than *flat*. A flat character is one who has only one distinctive characteristic, exists only to exhibit that characteristic, and is incapable of varying from that characteristic. A round character is many faceted and is capable of change. Several critics have, however, persuasively defended flat characters. Eric Bentley suggests in *The Life of the Drama* that if a messenger's function in a play is to deliver his message, it would be very tedious to stop and learn about his psychology. The same is true in fiction; the Queen's chauffeur in the passage from *Mrs. Dalloway* (see Chapter 2) exists for no purpose but leaning "ever so slightly," and we do not want to hear about his children or his hernia. Nevertheless, onstage even a flat character has a face and a costume, and in fiction detail can give even a flat character a few angles and contours.

The servant classes in the novels of Henry James are notoriously absent as individuals because they exist only in their functions (*that excellent creature had already assembled the baggage,* etc.), whereas Charles Dickens, who peoples his novels with dozens of flat characters, brings even these alive in detail.

> And Mrs. Miff, the wheezy little pew opener — a mighty dry old lady, sparely dressed, with not an inch of fullness anywhere about her — is also here.
>
> *Dombey and Son*

To borrow a notion from George Orwell's *Animal Farm,* all good characters are created round, but some are created rounder than others.

But the central characters in your story or novel need to be not merely round, but spherical. They should contain enough conflict and contradiction so that we can recognize them as belonging to the contradictory human race; and they should be, as we are or hope we are, capable of change.

The Aristotelian Hero

Aristotle, in the *Poetics,* listed four requirements of a successful hero — he should be "*good, appropriate, like,* and *consistent*" — and although literature has changed a great deal in the twenty-three intervening centuries, I believe that these four qualities remain necessary attributes of a fully three-dimensional character; and I believe that they throw light on the critical notions of universal, typical, individual, flat, and round.

GOOD

"There will be an element of character," Aristotle says, "if . . . what a person says or does reveals a certain moral purpose; and a good element of character, if the purpose so revealed is good." It might seem that the antiheroes, brutes, hoods, whores, perverts, and bums who people modern literature do very little in the way of "revealing good moral purpose." The history of Western literature shows a movement downward and inward: downward through society from royalty to gentry to the middle classes to the lower classes to the dropouts; inward from heroic action to social drama to individual consciousness to the subconscious to the unconscious. What has remained consistent is that, for the time spent in an author's world, we understand and identify with the protagonist or protagonists, we "see their point of view," and the fiction succeeds largely because we are willing to grant them a goodness that we would not grant them in life. Aristotle goes on to explain that "Such goodness is possible in every type of personage, even in a woman or a slave, though the one is perhaps an inferior, and the other a wholly worthless being" — and the sentence strikes us as both offensive and funny. But in Aristotle's society women and slaves were legally designated inferior and worthless, and what Aristotle is saying is precisely what Ken Kesey acknowledges when he picks the inmates of an "Institute of Psychology" as his heroes: that the external status granted by society is not an accurate measure of "good moral purpose."

> This new redheaded admission, McMurphy, knows right away he's not a Chronic. . . . The Acutes look spooked and uneasy when he laughs, the way kids look in a schoolroom when one ornery kid is raising too much hell. . . .
> . . . "Which one of you claims to be the craziest? Which one is the biggest looney? Who runs these card games? It's my first day, and what I like to do is make a good impression straight off on the right man if he can prove to me he *is* the right man. Who's the bull goose looney here?"
>
> *One Flew Over the Cuckoo's Nest*

If you met McMurphy in real life, you'd probably say he was "crazy" and you'd hope he would be locked up. If you encountered the Neanderthals of William Golding's *The Inheritors* on your evening walk, you'd run. If you were forced to live with the visionaries of Doris Lessing's *Four-Gated City* or the prisoners of Jean Genêt's *Our Lady of the Flowers*, you would live in skepticism and fear. But while you read you expand your mental scope by identifying with, temporarily "becoming," a character who convinces you that the inmates of the asylum are saner than the staff, that the ape-men are more human than *Homo sapiens*, that mental breakdown is mental breakthrough, that perversion is purer than the sexual code by which you live. For the drama audiences of fourth-century B.C. Athens, it was easier to see human nobility embodied in the heroic external actions of those designated by class as noble. It is largely because literature has moved inward, within the mind, that it is possible to move downward in social status — even to women and slaves! — and maintain this sympathy. In his own mind everyone is fundamentally justified, however conscious he is of his flaws — indeed, the more conscious of his flaws, the better he is. As readers we are allowed to borrow a mind. Fiction, as critic Laurence Gonzales said of rock music, "lets you wander around in someone else's hell for a while and see how similar it is to your own."

You won't, of course, want us to identify with all of your people all of the time. In the *Poetics*, Aristotle was describing the tragic hero, and he also described tragedy as presenting people as "better than they are" and comedy as presenting them as "worse than they are." Bergson points out that we can't find a character comic if we identify too closely with him or her; comedy requires that we maintain an intelligent and somewhat callous distance.

It nevertheless holds true that there is "an element of character" only when "a certain moral purpose is revealed" and that you achieve identification with your characters when you reveal that purpose as good. Since as a writer you want to move us, you will almost inevitably want us to identify with at least your central character. Sometimes this identification can be achieved by contrasting the "good purpose" of the central character with the more questionable moral elements of characters around her or him. Notice that in the following passage from Willa Cather, which presents a character both more familiar and more morally ambiguous than mad McMurphy, the protagonist is surrounded by moral attitudes left vague, cliché and "typical" although he himself is carefully detailed.

> It was Paul's afternoon to appear before the faculty of the Pittsburgh High School to account for his various misdemeanors. He had been suspended a week ago, and his father had called at the Principal's office and confessed his perplexity about his son. Paul entered the faculty room suave and smiling. His clothes were a trifle outgrown, and the tan velvet on the collar of his open overcoat was frayed and worn; but for all that there was something of the dandy about him, and he wore an opal pin in his neatly knotted black four-in-hand, and a red carnation in his buttonhole. This latter adornment the faculty somehow felt was not properly significant of the contrite spirit befitting a boy under the ban of suspension.
>
> *Paul's Case*

As readers we immediately identify with the miscreant. Indeed, I am both a parent and a faculty member, but in the space of this paragraph Willa Cather makes me Paul. I'm instinctively unwilling to identify with a father who abandons his son to the principal's office, equally unwilling to identify with a faculty that thinks in terms of "properly significant" and "contrite spirit." The shabby bravery of Paul's attire is "good" in a way that these other attitudes are not. And when, in the next paragraph, Cather tells me that Paul's eyes "were remarkable for a certain hysterical brilliancy, and he continually used them in a conscious, theatrical sort of way, peculiarly offensive in a boy," I am certain to view remarkable eyes, their brilliance and theatricality, even their hysteria, as the direct opposite of offensive.

APPROPRIATE

Aristotle offends again when he explains what he means by "appropriate." "The character before us may be, say, manly; but it is not appropriate in a female character to be manly." Again, he offends because our ideas of *female* and *manly* have changed, not because we have outgrown a sense of what is appropriate. We are dealing here again with the idea of the "typical," which includes all the biological and environmental influences that form us. A Baptist Texan behaves differently from an Italian nun; a rural schoolboy behaves differently from a professor emeritus at Harvard. If you are to succeed in creating an individual character, particular and alive, you will also inevitably know what is appropriate to that sort of person and will let us know as much as we need to know to feel the appropriateness of the behavior.

We need to know soon, for instance, preferably in the first paragraph, the character's gender, age, and race or nationality. We need to know something of his or her class, period, and region. A profession (or the clear lack of it) and a marital status help, too. Almost any reader can identify with almost any character; what no reader can identify with is confusion. When some or several of the fundamentals of type are withheld from us — when we don't know whether we're dealing with a man or a woman, an adult or a child — the process of identifying cannot begin, and the story is slow to move us.

None of the information need come as information; it can be implied by appearance, tone, action, or detail. But we need it in order to know "what to expect" of a character; that is, what is appropriate. In the passage from "Paul's Case," we are told that the protagonist is a male high school student. "High school" and "principal" make him American (if we heard of the *préfet* of a *lycée* we'd know we were in France), and the details of his attempt at dandyism suggest the first half of the twentieth century and also that Paul is not as high in the middle class as he would like to be. By concentrating on what is "not appropriate" to Paul's station, Cather implies a good deal about what that station is. And of course we're delighted when a character "acts against type" — when the old lady talks tough, the Count belches, or the cop cuddles a stray. Still, the behavior has to be within the range of the character's possibilities. The notion of "against type" itself suggests how severely we judge an action as appropriate or not.

In the next example William Melvin Kelley pitches his protagonist straight into the conflict. Only the character's gender is given us directly, but by the end of the story's opening paragraph, we know a lot about his life and type.

> To find this Cooley, the Black baby's father, he knew he would have to contact Opal Simmons. After dressing, he began to search for her address and number. Tam, very organized for a woman, saved everything. Among the envelopes containing the sports-clothes receipts, a letter from her dressmaker asking for payment, old airline tickets, the nursery school bill, the canceled checks and deposit slips, he finally found Opal's address.
>
> *Passing*

We know from the apparently "irrelevant" collection of bills that the protagonist is middle class, married, a father, affluent, and perhaps (that letter from the dressmaker) living at the edge of his income. Because he specifies a "Black baby," we know that he is white. We also know something about his attitudes both toward blacks ("this Cooley") and women ("very organized for a woman"). With an absolute minimum of exposition, letting us share the search for the address, Kelley has drawn clear boundaries of what we may expect from a character whose name we don't yet know.

Similarly, at the opening of *The Bear*, William Faulkner gives us as information only the age and gender of the protagonist. Then, launching into the boy's mental image of the bear, he gives us as if incidentally the rural but upper-class, sporting atmosphere in which the boy lives, with its sense of inheritance, legend, and awe.

> He was ten. But it had already begun, long before that day when at last he wrote his age in two figures and he saw for the first time the camp where his father and Major de Spain and old General Compson and the others spent two weeks each November and two weeks again each June. He had already inherited then, without ever having seen it, the tremendous bear with one trap-ruined foot which, in an area almost a hundred miles deep, had earned itself a name, a definite designation like a living man.

LIKE

There is a critical controversy over what Aristotle meant by "likeness," but I think the two interpretations cast light on the necessities of character. The first is that by "like," Aristotle meant "natural" — that we should find the character credibly human, that his or her actions and reactions should ring true. The sense here is akin to the idea of "universal," without the symphonic overtones. Of course the range of credible human actions is vast, and again the trick is to convince us that *this* person would do this; if you do, we're unlikely to complain that *a* person wouldn't. But if your readers and critics say, "I don't believe anybody would act this way," prick up your ears, swallow your answer, believe it, and go back to work.

The second interpretation of "like" comes from a later analogy of Aristotle's to a portrait painter's skill in capturing his model. In literature this would seem to mean that, if the writer is depicting Ulysses or Achilles, he should be true to the historical characteristics of the hero. This is a limiting notion, but as the characters of your fiction live only on the page, you need be true only to them. And the characters of your fiction do live only on the page. It can't be too strongly stressed that a person who exists in the form of words exists only in that form. "But that's the way it happened" is never a justification for an action that lacks credibility. "But that's the way she is" will never convince us that the character is true to life. If we update Aristotle's painting analogy, the important question is: Is the camera in focus? If the image is sharp, it will be a better likeness than if it's blurred.

Here are three examples of quickly drawn, tightly focused characters. Notice in each how attention to particular detail also indicates the typical and convinces us of human "likeness."

> With no map sense, I took a trip by myself to San Francisco Chinatown and got lost in the Big City. Wandering in a place very different from our own brown and gray Chinatown, I suddenly heard my own real aunt calling my name. She was my youngest aunt, my modern aunt just come from Hong Kong. We screamed at each other the way our villagers do, hugged, held hands. "Have you had your rice yet?" we shouted. "I have. I have had my rice." "Me too. I've eaten too," letting the whole strange street know we had eaten.
>
> MAXINE HONG KINGSTON, *China Men*

> M. Willy was not huge, he was bulbous. The powerful skull, the slightly protuberant eyes, the nose, which was short and had no visible bridge, the drooping cheeks — every one of his features approximated to the curve. His mouth, under the heavy gray-gold moustaches that he dyed for a long while, was narrow, dainty and agreeable looking, and had something faintly English about its smile. As for his dimpled chin, which was small, weak, you might even say fragile, it seemed the best thing to hide it. Which M. Willy did, at first with a sort of glorified imperial, then with a short beard. It has been said that he bore a marked resemblance to Edward VII. To do justice to a less flattering but no less august truth, I would say that, in fact, the likeness was to Queen Victoria.
>
> COLETTE, *Earthly Paradise*

> Headeye, he was following me. I knowed he was following me. But I just kept goin, like I wasn't payin him no mind. Headeye, he never fish much, but I guess he knowed the river as good as anybody. But he aint know where the fishin was good. Thas why I knowed he was followin me. So I figured I better fake him out. I aint want nobody with a mojo bone followin me. . . . Headeye, he o.k., cept when he get some kinda notion in that big head of his. Then he act crazy. Tryin to show off his age. He older'n me, but he little for his age. Some people say readin too many books will stunt your growth. Well, on Headeye everythin is stunted cept his eyes and his head.
>
> HENRY DUMAS, *Ark of Bones*

As a writer you may have the lucky, facile sort of imagination to which characters spring full-blown, complete with gestures, histories, and passions.

Or it may be that you haven't and that you need to explore in order to exploit, to draw your characters out gradually, get to know them, and coax them into being. That can be lucky, too.

For either kind of writer, but especially the latter, keeping a journal is an invaluable help. A journal lets you coax and explore without committing yourself to anything or anyone. It allows you to know everything about your character whether you use it or not. You must know everything, because in order to have the density of fiction, your characterization must present the iceberg tip that implies the underwater bulk of heredity, environment, experience, and human nature. Before you put a character in a story, know how well that character sleeps. Know what the character eats for lunch and how much it matters, what he or she buys and how the bills get paid, how he or she spends what we call working hours. Know how your character would prefer to spend evenings and weekends and why such plans get thwarted. Know what memories the character has of pets and parents, cities, snow, or school. You may use none of this information in the brief segment of your character's life that is your plot, but knowing it may teach you how your bookperson taps a pencil or twists a lock of hair, and when and why. When you know these things, you will have taken a step past invention toward the moment of imagination in which you become your character, live in his or her skin, and produce an action that, for the reader, rings universally true.

A major advantage of keeping a journal regularly is that it will put you in the habit of observing in words, finding a phrase to catch whatever has caught your eye. Whatever invites your attention or sympathy, your anger or curiosity may be the beginning of invention. *Whoever* catches your attention may be the beginning of a character. If the library assistant annoys you or the loner at the corner of the bar intrigues you, make a few notes. Start with what you observe, the obvious traits of type — age, gender, color, class. Try to capture a gesture or the messages that features and clothing send. Invent a reason for that harshness or that loneliness; invent a past. Then try taking the character out of context and setting him or her in another. Get your character in trouble, and you may be on your way to a short story.

It is interesting and relevant that actors schooled in what is called the "Stanislavski Method" write biographies of the characters they must play. Adherents of "The Method" believe that in the process of inventing a dramatic character's past the actor will find points of emotional contact with that role and so know how to make the motives and actions prescribed by the script natural and genuine. As a writer you can also use "The Method," imagining much that you will not bring specifically to "the script" but that will enrich your sense of that character until you know with absolute certainty how he or she will move, act, react, and speak.

CONSISTENT

Aristotle says that an author should make characters "consistent and the same throughout" — that is, again, that their actions should be plausible in light of what we know about them — for "even if inconsistency should be part of the man . . . he should still be consistently inconsistent." It is with this last injunction that we leave the area of plausibility and acknowledge the complexity of character. "Consistently inconsistent" does not mean that a character should be continually behaving unnaturally or acting against type. On the contrary, Aristotle here acknowledges the continuing conflict *within* character that is the source of most human trouble and most literature.

Conflict is at the core of character as it is of plot. If plot begins with trouble, then character begins with a person in trouble; and trouble most dramatically occurs because we all have traits, tendencies, and desires that are at war, not simply with the world and other people, but with other of our own traits, tendencies, and desires. All of us probably know a woman of the strong, striding, independent sort, attractive only to men who like a strong and striding woman. And when she falls in love? She becomes a clinging sentimentalist. All of us know a father who is generous, patient, and dependable. And when the children cross the line? He smashes crockery and wields a strap. All of us are gentle, violent; logical, schmaltzy; tough, squeamish; lusty, prudish; sloppy, meticulous; energetic, apathetic; manic, depressive. Perhaps you don't fit that particular list of contradictions, but you are sufficiently in conflict with yourself that as an author you have characters enough in your own psyche to people the work of a lifetime if you will identify, heighten, and dramatize these consistent inconsistencies.

If you think of the great characters of literature, you can see how consistent inconsistency brings each to a crucial dilemma. Hamlet is a strong and decisive man, who procrastinates. Dorothea Brooke of *Middlemarch* is an idealistic and intellectual young woman, a total fool in matters of the heart. Ernest Hemingway's Francis Macomber wants to test his manhood against a lion and cannot face the test. Here, in a moment of crisis from *Mom Kills Self and Kids*, Alan Saperstein reveals with great economy the consistent inconsistency of his protagonist, a man who hadn't much time for his family until their absence makes clear how dependent he has been on them.

When I arrived home from work I found my wife had killed our two sons and taken her own life.

I uncovered a blast of foul, black steam from the pot on the stove and said, "Hi, hon, what's for dinner?" But she did not laugh. She did not bounce to her feet and pirouette into the kitchen to greet me. My little one didn't race into my legs and ask what I brought him. The seven-year-old didn't automatically beg me to play a game knowing my answer would be a tired, "Maybe later."

It is, of course, impossible to know to what degree Shakespeare, Eliot, Hemingway, or Saperstein used consistent inconsistencies of which they were aware in themselves, to build and dramatize their characters. An author works not only from his or her own personality, but also from observation and imagination, and I fully believe that you are working at full stretch only when all three are involved. The question of autobiography is a complicated one, and as writer you frequently won't know yourself how much you have experienced, how much you have observed, and how much invented. Some teachers and critics advise beginning writers to write only from their personal experience, but I feel this is a misleading and demeaning idea, producing a lot of dead-grandmother stories and tales of dormitory life. Actress Mildred Dunnock once observed that "Drama is possible because people can feel what they haven't experienced"; if this is true of audiences and readers, I see no reason the capacity should be denied to writers. A vast proportion of our experience is mental, and it is safe to say that all your writing is autobiographical in the sense that it must have passed through your mind.

It *is* important to avoid writing from other writing, including film and television; it is primarily in the creation of character that we recognize stale stuff. It can be excellent training to imitate the *style* of any writer from Milton to Mailer (consider it training, not publishable work). Any *plot*, as Shakespeare illustrated nicely, can be furnished with new meaning if it is refurbished with new people. But unless the characters are newly thought through and mentally experienced by the author, they are stock characters; like livestock, they are hard to tell apart.

Here are a couple of suggestions for making character fresh and forceful in your mind before you start writing. If the character is based on you or on someone you know, drastically alter the model in some external way: change blond to dark or thin to thick; imagine the character as the opposite gender or radically alter the setting in which the character must act. Part of the trouble with writing directly from experience is that you know too much about it — what "they" did, how you felt. Under such circumstances it's hard to know whether everything in your mind is getting onto the page. An external alteration forces you to re-see, and so to see more clearly, and so to convey more clearly what you see.

On the other hand, if the character is created primarily out of your observation or invention and is unlike yourself, try to find an *internal* area that you have in common with the character. If you are a blond slender young woman and the character is a fat balding man, do you nevertheless have in common a love of French *haute cuisine*? Are you haunted by the same sort of dream? Do you share a fear of public performance or a susceptibility to fine weather?

I can illustrate these techniques only from my own writing, because I am the only author whose self I can identify with any certainty in fictional characters. In writing a recent novel, I wanted to open with a scene in which the heroine buries a dog in her backyard. I had recently buried a dog in my backyard. I wanted to capture the look and feel of red Georgia earth at sunrise, the tangle of roots and the smell of decay. But I knew that I was likely to make the experience too much my own, too little my character's. I set about to make her not-me. I have long dark hair, an ordinary figure, and I tend to live in Levi's. I made Shaara Soole.

> . . . big boned, lanky, melon-breasted, her best feature was a head of rusty barbed-wire hair that she tried to control with a wardrobe of scarves and headband things. Like most costume designers, she dressed with more originality than taste, usually on the Oriental or Polynesian side, sometimes with voluminous loops of thong and matte metal over an ordinary shirt. This was somewhat eccentric in Hubbard, Georgia, but Shaara may have been oblivious to her eccentricity, being so concerned to keep her essential foolishness in check.

Having thus separated Shaara from myself, I was able to bury the dog with her arms and through her eyes rather than my own. On the other hand, a few pages later I was faced with the problem of introducing her ex-husband, Boyd Soole. I had voluminous notes on this character, and I knew that he was almost totally unlike me. A man, to begin with, and a huge man, a theater director with a natural air of power and authority and very little interest in domestic affairs. I sat at my desk for several days, unable to make him move convincingly. My desk oppressed me, and I felt trapped and uncomfortable, my work thwarted, it seemed, by the very chair and typewriter. Then it occurred to me that Boyd was *also* sitting at a desk trying to work.

> The dresser at the Travelodge was some four inches too narrow and three inches too low. If he set his feet on the floor his knees would sit free of the drawer but would be awkwardly constricted left and right. If he crossed his legs, he could hook his right foot comfortably outside the left of the kneehole but would bruise his thigh at the drawer. If he shifted back he was placed at an awkward distance from his script. And in this position he could not work.

This passage did not instantly allow me to live inside Boyd Soole's skin, nor did it solve all my problems with his characterization. But it did let me get on with the story, and it gave me a flash of sympathy for him that later grew much more profound than I had foreseen.

Often, identifying what you have in common with the feelings of your character will also clarify what is important about him or her to the story — why, in fact, you chose to write about such a person at all. Even if the character is presented as a villain, you have something in common, and I don't mean something forgivable. If he or she is intolerably vain, watch your own private gestures in front of the mirror and borrow them. If he or she is cruel, remember how you enjoyed hooking the worm.

There is no absolute requirement that a writer need behave honestly in life; there is absolutely no such requirement. Great writers have been public hams, domestic dictators, emotional con men, and Nazis. What is required for fine writing is honesty on the page — not how the character *should* react at the funeral, the surprise party, in bed, but how she or he *does*. In order to develop such honesty of observation on the page, you must begin with a willing honesty of observation (though mercifully not of behavior) in yourself.

Not Your Singing, Dancing Spade

JULIA FIELDS

It was ridiculous to have an issue of such an insipidly written magazine in the apartment, he knew. Nevertheless, he picked it up again and began to read the article written about himself. The audacity of it, and the incredible and insane arrogance it suggested, made him feel helpless against the terrible tide of consciousness so established and so knowledgeable to him and to his people. His brains were sealed, signed for and delivered, just as his body would have been in the previous century.

He focused his eyes and finished the article, his black hands and black eyes drooping wearily over the side of the plush gold sofa. Then he lay down upon it, keeping his shoes on. It was not very comforting at all.

The article stated clearly that his childhood dream had been to pursue and to possess a "blonde goddess," that he could never be happy without her. It made fun of a black entertainer he had dated. It said he paid her to give him his "freedom." There was no picture of her. But there was a listing and pictures of national and international ladies with fair hair to whom he had been linked romantically at one time or another.

There was a picture of him with his wife — his wife bright and grinning, and his teeth matching her fairness kilometer for kilometer. His hair was falling into his eyes. It always seemed to be fallen into his eyes, whenever he was playing golf, or driving, or dancing, or singing. And he always had to toss his head, give his neck a quick snappy jerk in order to keep his tumbling hair neat. It always got into his eyes. He bent over to light a cigarette. The hair fell into his eyes. He used his free hand to brush it back, knowing that it would tumble into his eyes again.

His wife entered the room. She was very, very white. He had asked her to stay out of the sun. And the black maid entered with a tray of beverages. The children liked the maid and his wife liked the maid. He hated her. She was almost as black as himself, and her hair was short. He always felt like singing an old down-home blues whenever he saw her . . . "I don't want no woman if her hair ain't no longer'n mine; she ain't nothing but trouble and keep you worried all the time." But no matter how much hatred he showed towards her, the woman was always kind and serene; yet, there was the very faintest hint of laughter and incredible mockery in her eyes when she looked at him. He knew the look. He himself had given it to others many times. He remembered the party in Greenwich Village, the interracial party with all the loud music and the loud dancing, which belonged to a younger time than now.

There was a colored girl there, he was told, but all the girls looked of the same race because there was not the brightest lighting. Still he thought that he would know a "Sapphire" if he saw one. The girl's white date had laughed at him for saying this, and slapped him on the back. He had felt so clever, so able to take "it," so "free," so optimistic, so "in," and that was when he knew that he could make it if he chose to make it in the big world of the American dream. And this world, as he knew it, was not white. It was a gray world with room in it for all the people. He felt so "in" that he almost blessed Emma Lazarus.

A group of them were laughingly trying to sing a foolish ditty with dirty words. They were all so happy and drunk. And there was a girl whose hands kept going to her temple and down behind her ears with long locks of hair which she pushed over her shoulder. Then she would toss her hair, or attempt to, but the long hair barely moved. The long strands did not move freely. They seemed waxen, stuck around her face like fetters. His hands went to his own head in sudden derision, and stuck in the Dixie Peach. The girl swung her head again and caught his eyes. He looked into her eyes as deeply as he could, and his bitterness spilled like a white sizzle across to her in mockery and despair and a tender, compassionate hatred.

The boy who had slapped him on the back moved toward the girl, caught her by the hand and began to dance with her, his hips swaying, brutally ungraceful in mock-Negro.

He went to the window. Dawn was moving up to the river and over the roofs. It was time for him to go. He knew that he would never go to another party with a Negro. No matter what color the Negro was — they were all embarrassing. He might go if he were the only one. Only if he were.

He knew that his wife somehow resulted from this promise which he had made to himself a long time ago at the Village party. He had come a long way. His name, his picture, his life, were on the lips and the life-sized posters of the world. Subway bums, whores and dogs could lean against his photograph in most of the world's swinging cities. And he was very wealthy. He had his own entourage of jesters and the best hairdresser in the world — one who kept him well stocked with the best pomade.

The article in the magazine shouldn't have bothered him so much, he told himself. It wasn't the first time, nor would it be the last. He had to pay the price. They were requiring it of him, and he had to make it. He had to keep making it. It was too late to stop. Where would he go? There was no place elsewhere but down. Down to scorn. Back, slowly, but certainly, to a world which had become alien, black, strange and nameless. The wolves would chew him black.

Back to black indeed. Never. What did it matter? The whites had begun their assaults late; the blacks had berated him all his life. "Black bastard. Black bastard. Bad hair." "Boy, get a brush." And comparisons: "Almost Bunky's color." "No, not quite as black as Bunky." "Child, I couldn't see nuthin' but eyes and teeth." "I like him, sure, but my daddy would kill me if I married a man that black." "Child, I wouldn't want to mess up my children with that color." He was recalling the words of parents, relatives and lovers. His yellow mother. His jet-black father who was his mother's footstool. His mother's freckles. Her rituals with Black and White ointment. Her "straight" nose. He hated his flat nose. All of his pictures were in profile. Except the one in the magazine. In that one, all of his black faults were on view. In that picture, the heat had turned the expensive pomade on his hair to plain and simple shining grease. Ah, chicken-eaters of the world, unite. You have nothing to lose except your shame.

He began to dress, immaculately as always, for there was, his agent had said, a chance to make another million. Melanin and millions. Millions and melanin.

Numbly, he moved about the dressing room, larger than his parents' living room had been.

Mutely, he dressed. Dejectedly, he faced himself in the mirror. Silently, the green gall of self-revulsion passed through his psyche and soul. Swiftly, he recalled the chance to make a million and the wife who would spend it on furs, jewels, fun, cosmetics and servants. And the whole world would see what black bastards with millions and melanin could do. Yes, they would.

The agent's smooth voice, on the phone, reassured him about the million. There was nothing to reassure him about himself. Nothing. Nothing.

Down the stairs, voices were shrill suddenly. His little girl was sobbing. He heard the maid say, "Be quiet. You'll wake up your mama."

"But Cathy said my daddy's a nigger monkey."

"What do you care what Cathy says?"

"And Daddy puts gasoline in his hair to make it nice like her daddy's hair. Isn't Daddy's hair nice?"

"Of course it's nice. That little sickly Cathy with those strings hanging 'round her face. Don't pay her no attention. She's just jealous because your daddy's got the original beauty."

"The what?"

"The first, best beauty in the world. Black. Your daddy's a pretty man. That's why everybody likes him. Where've you seen Cathy's daddy's pictures? Not nearly's many places as your daddy. Your daddy is a beautiful man."

"Is he?"

"Yes. Of course he don't know how pretty he is. Anyhow, it's easy to be pale. Like milk. It ain't got nothing in it. Like vanilla ice cream. See? Now take any other flavor. Take chocolate. Milk with cocoa. You love chocolate malt, don't you?"

"Yes."

"Take strawberry. Any ice cream. It's nothing as just plain milk. What goes in makes it beautiful. It can be decorated, but by itself, it lacks a lot. Your daddy was born decorated. Born a pretty king. Born beautiful. Don't believe Cathy. She's dumb."

"Born beautiful. Daddy was born beautiful. That silly Cathy. She's a dumb one. My daddy is pretty. I always thought so."

"Yes, I always thought so, too."

Numbly, he stood there. He had to listen. The annihilated searching, seeking to be. Terror. Who had first given assumption and such supreme arrogance to the captives? He knew she had read the article which had denied her existence. A black female. The race and sex which, according to them, could never move him to love, to cherish, to desire. *Caldonia, Caldonia, what makes your big head so hard?*

He remembered his boyhood. And all the lyrics which laughed at and lamented black womanhood. Blackness. Black manhood. Black childhood. Black.

They had made the world for him, had set all the traps. He had been born to it. The horror of blackness. They had outdone themselves. They had outdone him. And it was not meant that he should ever be saved. He must believe. And they could assume postures and lies. And they could believe in his self-hatred. And they could rest comfortably, believing that he believed, and continue their believing.

They were so arrogant, so stupefied by history and circumstances that they could accept any incredible thing they said about him. Terror. Who was the bondsman? Who was the freed man? He knew.

Life began to flow again. His blood sang vital and red. Freedom. Power, even. Yes, I *am* beautiful. Born black. Born with no lack. Decorated. Born decorated.

At the foot of the stairs, he could hear the maid again, angrily muttering. With dancer's feet, he moved nearer. Nearer to hear, nearer to self, to recovery.

"Lies, lies, lies. Sometimes we have to lie to make it. Even to live. We got to lie to ourselves, to our friends and to our enemies. To those we love and to those we hates. If they so smart they ain't got to b'lieve us."

He saw her throw the movie magazine clear down his long, sumptuous living room. And he heard his little daughter laughing as she went to get the magazine.

"Here. Put it in the trash can."

"But it's got Daddy's picture. Daddy's picture's in it."

"Your daddy's picture's everywhere. Besides, that's not a good picture of him. Some fool took it. Here." The child obeyed.

"Arrogant, uppity folks'll believe anything. Let 'em pay. And pay. White bastards."

"What? What?" The child questioned.

"Nothing. Go on to the playroom until I call you for lunch. I got to vacuum up this room."

Then he was there standing in the beautiful, luxurious room facing the black woman with the short hair.

"Humph," he heard her say as she turned to push a low, red, incredulously plush and ridiculously expensive chair aside for her vacuuming.

"Here, let me be of service," he said.

"Never mind."

"Let me!" he said again, and gently pushed her aside.

"Humph," she said again. But he got a glimpse of her face, which had years of anger and defiance and hope written in chicken-scratch wrinkles and crows' feet. And there was the mockery he always saw there. And yet, a kindness, a laughter which was very sweet and strong. And the barest hint of tears in the eyes, tears like monuments to despair.

When he replaced the chairs and kissed his wife and child, he said his goodbye to the black woman and sang a snatch of his latest recording as he walked to the elevator. He felt light — weightless and yet strong and pretty. "I feel pretty," he thought. Well, not that kind of pretty, he mocked himself. But it was surprising that he sang, for he had promised himself that he was only an entertainer, that he wasn't your singing, dancing spade, that he, a professional only, wouldn't be caught dead, drunk or straitlaced, singing off the stage or away from the T.V. cameras, or dancing like some ham-hocking jigaboo.

Nevertheless, his chauffeur smiled happily when he cut a step from his latest musical sensation as he entered the limousine with the sacrilegious words, "I feel pretty," floating, cakewalking from his lips.

Suggestions for Discussion

1. How and how quickly does Julia Fields reveal the fundamentals of her protagonist's type — age, gender, color, country, class, marital status? Which are revealed directly, as information, and which are revealed obliquely, through choice of detail?

2. How is the protagonist's character revealed by the fact that his hair falls into his eyes? That he asks his wife to stay out of the sun? That he hates the maid?

3. The phrase "a tender, compassionate hatred" on page 82 is a rhetorical figure called an *oxymoron*, a joining of opposites (freezing heat, solid air). Explain this apparent contradiction in terms of the protagonist's character.

4. What does the paragraph beginning "Back to black . . ." on page 83 reveal about the society in which he grew up? To what extent does this revelation of his background alter your perception of his character? To what extent does it justify him?

5. Although the wife enters the room on page 82, and we overhear the daughter on page 84, these remain flat characters, who exist for only one function each. What function? Why is it appropriate to this story that apart from the protagonist only the maid is fully drawn?

6. What is the protagonist's consistent inconsistency?

7. What is the significance of the story's title?

8. Describe the protagonist's "epiphany." Where and why does it occur?

In the Absence of Angels

HORTENSE CALISHER

Before cockcrow tomorrow morning, I must remember everything I can about Hilda Kantrowitz. It is not at all strange that I should use the word "cockcrow," for, like most of the others here, I have only a literary knowledge of prisons. If someone among us were to take a poll — that lax, almost laughable device of a world now past — we would all come up with about the same stereotypes: Dickens' Newgate, no doubt, full of those dropsical grotesques of his, under which the sharp shape of liberty was almost lost; or, from the limp-leather books of our teens, "The Ballad of Reading Gaol," that period piece of a time when imprisonment could still be such a personal affair. I myself recall, from a grade-school reader of thirty years ago, a piece named "Piccola," called so after a flower that pushed its way up through a crevice in a stone courtyard and solaced the man immured there — a general, of God knows what political coloration.

Outside the window here, the only hedge is a long line of hydrangeas, their swollen cones still the burnt, turned pink of autumn, still at the stage when the housewives used to pick them and stand them to dry on mantels, on pianos, to crisp and gather dust until they were pushed, crackling, into the garbage, in the first, diluted sun of spring.

We here, women all of us, are in what until recently was a fashionable private school, located, I am fairly certain, somewhere in Westchester County. There was no business about blindfolds from the guards on the trucks that brought us; rather, they let us sit and watch the flowing countryside, even comment upon it, looking at us with an indifference more chilling than if they had been on the alert, indicating as it did that a break from a particular truck into particular environs was of no import in a countryside that had become a cage. I recognized the Saw Mill River Parkway, its white marker lines a little the worse for lack of upkeep, but its banks still neat, since they came in November, after the grass had stopped growing. Occasionally — at a reservoir, for instance — signposts in their language had been added, and there were concentrations of other trucks like ours. They keep the trains for troops.

This room was the kindergarten; it has been cleared, and the painted walls show clean squares where pictures used to be, for they have not yet covered them with their special brand of posters, full of fists and flags. Opposite me is their terse, typed bulletin, at which I have been looking for a long time. Built into the floor just beneath it, there is a small aquarium of colored tile, with a spigot for the water in which goldfish must have been kept, and beyond is the door that leads to our "latrine" — a little corridor of miniature basins and pygmy toilets and hooks about three and a half feet from the floor. In this room, which has been lined with full-size cots and stripped of everything but a certain innocent odor of crayon and chalk, it is possible to avoid imagining the flick of short braids, the brief toddle of a skirt. It is not possible in the latrine.

They ring the school bell to mark off the hours for us; it has exactly the same naïve, releasing trill (probably operated electrically by some thumb in what was the principal's office) as the bell that used to cue the end of Latin period and the beginning of math in the city high school where Hilda

Kantrowitz and I were among the freshmen, twenty-five years ago. Within that school, Hilda and I, I see now, were from the first slated to fall into two covertly opposed groups of girls.

On the application we had all filled out for entrance, there was a line that said "Father's Business." On it I had put the word "manufacturer," which was what my father always called himself — which, stretching it only a little, is what I suppose he was. He had a small, staid leather-goods business that occupied two floors of an untidy building far downtown. When my mother and I went there after a shopping tour, the workers upstairs on the factory floor, who had banded together to give me a silver cup at my birth, would lean their stained hands on barrels and tease me jocularly about my growth; the new young girls at the cutting tables would not stop the astonishingly rapid, reflex routine of their hands but would smile at me diffidently, with inquisitive, sidelong glances. Downstairs, on the office-and-sales floor, where there was a staff of about ten, one or the other of my uncles would try to take me on his lap, groaning loudly, or Harry Davidson, the thin, henpecked cousin-by-marriage who was the bookkeeper, would come out of the supply room, his paper cuffs scraping against a new, hard-covered ledger, which he would present to me with a mock show of furtiveness, for me to use for my poems, which were already a family joke.

The girls I went with, with whom I sat at lunch, or whom I rushed to meet after hours in the Greek soda parlor we favored, might too have been called, quite appositely, manufacturers' daughters, although not all of their fathers were in precisely that category. Helen's father was an insurance broker in an office as narrow as a knife blade, on a high floor of the most recent sky-scraper; Flora's father (of whom she was ashamed, in spite of his faultless clothes and handsome head, because he spoke bad English in his velvety Armenian voice) was a rug dealer; and Lotte's father, a German "banker," who did not seem to be connected with any bank, went off in his heavy Homburg to indefinite places downtown, where he "promoted," and made deals, coming home earlier than any of the others, in time for thick afternoon teas. What drew us together was a quality in our homes, all of which subscribed to exactly the same ideals of comfort.

We went home on the trolley or bus, Helen, Flora, Lotte, and I, to apartments or houses where the quality and taste of the bric-a-brac might vary but the linen closets were uniformly full, where the furniture covers sometimes went almost to the point of shabbiness but never beyond. Our mothers, often as not, were to be found in the kitchen, but though their hands kneaded dough, their knees rarely knew floors. Mostly, they were pleasantly favored women who had never worked before marriage, or tended to conceal it if they had, whose minds were not so much stupid as unaroused — women at whom the menopause or the defection of growing children struck suddenly in the soft depths of their inarticulateness, leaving them distraught, melancholy, even deranged, to make the rounds of the doctors until age came blessedly, turning them leathery but safe. And on us, their intransigent daughters, who wished to be poets, actresses, dancers, doctors — anything but merely teachers or wives — they looked with antagonism, secret pride, or dubious assent, as the case might be, but all of them nursing the sly prescience that marriage would almost certainly do for us, before we had quite done for ourselves.

This, then, was the group with which I began; in a curious way, which I must make clear to myself, as one makes a will, it is the group with which, perhaps tomorrow, somewhere outside this fading, posthumous room, I choose to end. Not because, as we clustered, by turns giggling, indecisive, and impassioned, in our soda parlors, we bore already that sad consanguinity of those women who were to refuse to stay in their traditional places either as wives, whom we identified with our mothers, or as teachers, whom we identified with lemon-faced aunts, lonely gas rings, and sexual despair. Hindsight gives us a more terrifying resemblance. Not as women but as people. Neither rich nor poor, we were among the last people to be — either by birth or, later, by conviction — in the middle.

For the rich, even while they spun in their baroque hysterias of possession, lived most intimately with the spectre of debacle. Like the poor, they were bred to the assumption that a man's thought does not go beyond his hunger, and, like them, their images of ruin were absolute. When the spectre of violent change arose in our century, as it had in every century, this time with two mouths, one of which said "Need is common!," the other of which answered "Therefore let thought be common!," it was the very rich and the very poor who subscribed first — the rich transfixed in their fear, the poor transfixed in their hope. Curious (and yet not so curious, I see now) that from us in the middle, swinging insecurely in our little median troughs of satisfaction, never too sure of what we were or what we believed, was to rise that saving, gradient doubt that has shepherded us together, in entrenchments, in ambush, and in rooms like these.

Two cots away from mine sits a small, black-haired woman of the type the French call mignonne; one would never associate her with the strangely scored, unmelodic music, yawping but compelling, for which she was known. She is here for an odd reason, but we are all here for odd reasons. She is here because she will not write melody, as they conceive melody. Or, to be honest — and there is no time left here for anything but honesty — as most of us here would conceive melody. But we here, who do not understand her music, understand her reasons.

Down at the far end of the room, there is a gray, shadowy spinster who knows little of heresies concerning the diatonic scale. She is here because she believes in the probity of mice. All day long now, she sits on her bed in a trance of fear, but the story is that when they came to the college laboratory where for forty years she had bred mice and conclusions, she stood at first with her arm behind her, her hand, in its white sleeve, shaking a little on the knob of the closed door. Then she backed up against the door to push it inward, to invite them in, their committee, with the statement she was to sign. Past all the cages she led them, stopping at each to explain the lineage of the generation inside, until, tired of the interminable recital, they waved the paper under her nose. Then she led them to the filing cabinets, unlocked the drawers, and persuaded them to pore over page after page of her crisscrossed references, meanwhile intoning the monotonous record of her historic rodent dead. Not until then, until the paper had appeared a third time, did she say to them, with the queer cogency of those whose virtue is not usually in talk, "No. Perhaps I will end by lying for you. But the mice will not."

She, the shadowy, weak-voiced woman, and I are alike in one thing, although I am not here after any action such as hers. They came quite conventionally to my suburban cottage, flung open the door, and loaded me on the truck without a word, as they had previously come to another poet, Volk, on his island off the coast of Maine, to Peterson, the novelist, in his neat brick box at the far end of Queens, to all the other writers who were alive because of being away from the city on the day it went down. Quite simply, they, too, have read Plato, and they know that the writer is dangerous to them because he cannot help celebrating the uncommonness of people. For, no matter what epithalamiums they may extort from us, sooner or later the individuality will reappear. In the very poems we might carpenter for them to march to, in the midst of the sanitized theses, the decontaminate novels, sooner or later we will infect their pages with the subversive singularity of men.

She — the biologist — and I are alike because we are the only ones here who do not cry at night. Not because we are heroic but because we have no more hostages for which to weep. Her mice are scattered, or already docilely breeding new dogma under the careful guidance of one of the trainees brought over here from their closed, incredible, pragmatic world — someone born after 1917, perhaps, who, reared among the bent probities of hungry men, will not trouble himself about the subornation of mice.

And I, who would give anything if my son were with me here, even to be suborned, as they do already with children, can afford to sit and dream of old integrities only because I, too, no longer have a hostage — not since the day when, using a missile whose rhythm they had learned from us, they cracked the city to the reactive dirt from which it had sprung — the day when the third-grade class from the grammar school of a suburban town went on a field trip to the natural-history museum.

Anyone born in a city like that one, as I was, is a street urchin to the end of his days, whether he grew behind its plate glass and granite or in its ancient, urinous slums. And that last year, when it was said they were coming, I visited my city often, walking in the violet light that seeped between the buildings of its unearthly dusk, watching the multiform re-fractions of the crowd, telling myself "I do not care to survive this." But on the way up here, when, as if by intention, they routed our trucks through streets of fused slag and quagmire (which their men, tapping with divining rods, had declared safe), I sat there in one of the line of trucks, looking dry-eyed at the dust of stone. Was it when the class was looking at the dinosaur, the *Archaeopteryx*, that the moment came? Was it while a voice, in soft, short syllables suited to his shortness, was telling him how a snake grew wings and became a bird, how a primate straightened its spine and became a man?

The room is quiet now, and dark, except for the moonlight that shows faintly outside on the hedge, faintly inside on the blurred harlequin tiles of the aquarium. Almost everyone is asleep here; even the person who rings the bell must be asleep, somewhere in one of the rooms in the wing they reserve for themselves. The little composer was one of the last who fell asleep; she cried for hours over the letter they brought her from her husband, also a musician, who wrote that he was working for them, that there could be glory in it, that if she would only recant and work with him, they would release his mother, and the daughter, and the son. The letter was couched in their orotund, professional phrases, phrases that in their mouths have given the great words like "freedom" and "unity" a sick, blood-sour sound. But tomorrow she will agree, and there is no one here who will blame her. Only the gray woman at the other end of the room and I sit hunched, awake, on our cots — taking the long view, who have no other. I sit here trying to remember everything I can about Hilda Kantrowitz, who was my age, my generation, but who, according to their paper on the wall, will not be here with us. Perhaps the last justification for people like me is to remember people like Hilda, even now, with justice.

What I see clearest about Hilda now is her wrists. I am looking back, with some trouble, at a girl who was never, except once, very important to me, and with some effort I can see thick braids of a dullish, unwashed blond, stray wisps from the top of them falling over her forehead, as if she had slept so and had not taken time for a combing. I cannot see her face from the side at all, but from the front her nostrils are long and drawn upward, making the tip of her nose seem too close to the flat mouth, which looks larger than it is because its lines are not definite but fade into the face. The eyes I cannot see at all as yet. She is standing for recitation, holding the Latin book, and her wrists are painfully sharp and clear, as if they were in the center of a lens. They are red — chapped, I suppose — and their flat bones protrude a long way from the middy cuffs. She does not know the recitation — she almost never does — but she does not titter or flush or look smart-alecky, the way the rest of us do when this happens. She just stands there, her eyelids blinking rapidly, her long nostrils moving, and says nothing, swaying a little, like a dog who is about to fall asleep. Then she sits down. Later on, I learn that it may be true — she may never get enough sleep.

We find this out by inference, Lotte and I, when the two of us are walking home together on a winter afternoon. That day, Lotte and I, who live near one another, have made a pact to spend our carfare on eatables and walk all the way home together. We have nearly reached 110th Street and Cathedral Parkway, having dribbled pennies in a store here, a store there, amiably debating each piece of candy, each sack of Indian nuts. In the west, as we walk toward it, there is a great well of dying light fading to apple-green over the river, which we cannot as yet see. The faces of the people hurrying past us have something flower-like and open about them as they bloom toward us and recede. We are tiring, feeling mournful and waif-like, with a delightful sadness that we breathe upon and foster, secure in the warm thought of home.

Down the block, there is a last, curving oasis of stores before the blank apartment houses begin. After that comes the long hill, with the church park and the hospital on the other side. Lotte has a last nickel. We walk slowly, peering into the stores. Next to a grill whose blind front is stencilled with lines of tangerine and false-blue light, there is one more store with a weak bulb shining. We press our faces against the glass of its door. It is a strange grocery store, if it is one, with no bakers' and bottlers' cardboard blurbs set in the window, no cherry brightness inside. Against its right-hand wall, galled wooden shelves hold a dark rummage of canned goods, with long, empty gaps between the brands. From a single line of cartons near the door on the lowest shelf, there is one hard, red glint of newness; these are packages of salt. Sprawled on the counter to the left, with her arms outflung between some box bottoms holding penny candy, there is a girl asleep. Her face, turned toward us, rests on a book whose thick, blunt shape we recognize almost as we do her. It is Hilda. Behind her, seen through the pane and the thin gruel of light, is the dim blotch of what looks like another room.

We confer, Lotte and I, in nudges, and finally Lotte pushes in ahead of me, her smothered giggle sounding above the rasp of a bell on the door. For a moment, it seems warmer inside — then not. A light is turned on in the back of the store, and we see that the second room is actually only a space that has been curtained off. The curtains are open. A woman comes forward and shakes Hilda angrily by the shoulder, with a flood of foreign words, then turns to us, speaking in a cringing voice. Candy? Crackers? How much money we got? Her face has a strong look to it, with good teeth and a mouth limned in blackish hair. In the half room behind her, on one of two day beds, a boy sits up, huddling in a man's thick sweater whose sleeves cover his hands. A smaller child clambers down from the other bed and runs to stand next to his mother. He is too young to have much hair, and the sight of his naked head, his meagre cotton shirt, and his wet diaper drooping between his legs makes me feel colder.

It becomes evident that Hilda and we know each other. I remember Hilda's cheekbones — sharp, and slowly red. The woman, all smiles now, moves toward us and lightly strokes Lotte's collar. That year, Lotte and I have made a fetish of dressing alike; we have on navy serge dresses with white collars pinned and identical silver bars.

"Little teachers!" the woman says. "Like little teachers!" She hovers over the counter a minute, then thrusts a small box of crackers, the kind with marshmallow, into Lotte's hand. The baby sets up a cry and is pushed behind the woman's skirt. The boy on the bed stares at the box but says nothing. Confused, Lotte holds out her nickel. The woman hesitates, then shakes her head, refusing. Two fingers hover again over Lotte's collar but do not touch it. "Hilda will be teacher," the woman says. She makes a kind of genuflection of despair toward the place behind her, and we see that on a shelf there, in the midst of jumbled crockery and pans, is a man's picture, dark-bordered, in front of which a flame flickers, burning deep in a thick glass. She makes another gesture, as if she were pulling a cowl over her head, lets her hand fall against her skirt, and edges after us as we sidle toward the door. She bends over us. "Your mamas have what for me to sew, maybe? Or to clean?"

Hilda speaks, a short, guttural phrase in the language we do not understand. It is the only time she speaks. The woman steps back. Lotte still has the nickel in her open hand. Now Hilda is at the door. And now I see her mouth, the long lips pressed tight, turned down at the corners. She reaches out and takes Lotte's nickel. Then we are outside the door.

I do not remember anything about the rest of the walk home. But I remember that as I round the corner to my own street, alone, and am suddenly out of the wind, the air is like blue powder, and from the entrance to my house, as the doorman opens it and murmurs a greeting, the clean light scours the pavement. In the elevator, to my wind-smarting eyes the people look warmly blurry and gilded, and the elevator, rising perfectly, hums.

Lotte and I do not ever go back, of course, and we quickly forget the whole thing, for as the school year advances, the gap widens permanently between girls like us and those other unilluminated ones who are grinding seriously toward becoming teachers, for many of whose families the possession of a teacher daughter will be one of the bootstraps by which they will lift themselves to a feeling of security — that trust in education which is the dominant security in a country that prides itself on offering no other.

Then a bad time comes for me. My mother, after the birth of another child, late in life, is very ill and is sent away — to hunt for a warmer climate, it is said, although long afterward I know that it is a climate of the spirit for which she hunts. Once or twice during that time, she is brought home, able only to stand helplessly at the window, holding on to me, the tears running down her face. Then she is taken away again, for our windows are five flights up.

Business is bad, too, everywhere, and my father makes longer and longer sales trips away from home. We have a housekeeper, Mrs. Gallagher, who is really the baby's nurse, since we cannot afford a cook and a nurse, too. She does not wash my hair regularly or bother about my habits, and I grow dirty and unkempt. She is always whining after me to give up my favorite dresses to her own daughter, "a poor widow's child in a convent," after which, applying to my father for money, she buys me new dresses, probably with the daughter in mind, and my clothes become oddly tight and loud. Months later, after she is gone, it is found that she has drunk up a good part of my father's hoarded wines, but now no one knows this, and she is a good nurse, crooning, starched and fierce, over the basket that holds the baby, whom she possessively loves. Standing behind her, looking at the basket, which she keeps cloudy with dotted swiss and wreathed in rosy ribbon, I think to myself that the baby nestled there looks like a pink heart. Perhaps I think secretly, too, that I am the displaced heart.

So I begin to steal. Not at home, but at school. There I am now one of the lowest scholars. I have altogether lost track in Latin, and when I am sent to the board in geometry, I stand there desperately in front of the mazy diagram, the chalk in my slack hand, watching the teacher's long neck, in which the red impatience rises until it looks like a crane's leg. "Next!" she says, finally, and I walk back to my seat. At test time, I try frantically to copy, but the smart, safe ones ignore my pleading signal. And once the visiting nurse sends me home because there are nits in my bushy, tangled hair. Thereafter, when I follow on the heels of the crowd to the soda parlor — my hand guarding several days' saved-up carfare, in the hope of finding someone to treat — the sorority is closed.

So, day after day, I treat myself. For by now, although there is plenty of food at home and Mrs. Gallagher packs me thick sandwiches (mostly of cheese, which she buys conveniently in a big slab to last the week) — by now I am really hungry only and constantly for sweets. I live on the thought of them, for the suspended moment when the nugget is warm in my mouth or crammed, waiting, in my hidden hand. And the sweets that comfort me most are those bought secretly and eaten alone. It never occurs to me to ask Mrs. Gallagher for spending money. At noontime, habitually now, I slip into the dark coatroom, where the girls' coats are hung, one on top of another, and, sliding a hand from pocket to pocket, one can pretend to be looking for one's own. And there, once again, I meet Hilda.

We meet face to face in the lumpy shadows of the coatroom, each of us with a hand in the pocket of a coat that is not her own. We know this on the instant, recognition clamoring between us, two animals who touch each other's scent in the prowling dark. I inch my hand out of the gritty pocket and let it fall at my side. I do not see what Hilda does with her hand. But in that moment before we move, in the furry dusk of that windowless room, I see what is in her eyes. I do not give it a name. But I am the first to leave.

Even now, I cannot give it a name. It eludes me, as do the names of those whom, for layered reason upon reason, we cannot bear to remember. I have remembered as best I can.

The rest belongs to that amalgam called growing up, during which, like everyone else, I learn to stumble along somehow between truth and compromise. Shortly after that day, I fall ill of jaundice, and I am ill for a long while. During that time, my mother returns home, restored — or perhaps my illness is in part her restorative. Her housewifely shock at what she finds blows through our home like a cleansing wind, and her tonic scolding, severe and rational as of old, is like the bromide that disperses horror. When I go back to school, after months of absence, I have the transient prestige of one who has been seriously ill, and with my rehabilitated appearance this is almost enough to reinstate me. Then an English teacher discovers my poems, and although I am never again a sound student in any other class, I attain a certain eminence in hers, and I rise, with each display coaxed out of me, rung by rung, until I am safe. Meanwhile, Hilda has dropped out of school. I never ask, but she is gone, and I do not see her there again.

Once, some ten years later, I think I see her. During the year after I am married, but not yet a mother, or yet a widow, a friend takes me to a meeting for the Spanish resistance, at which a well-known woman poet speaks. On the fringes of the departing crowd outside the shabby hall, young men and women are distributing pamphlets, shaking canisters for contributions. I catch sight of one of them, a girl in a brown leather jacket, with cropped blond hair, a smudge of lipstick that conceals the shape of the mouth, but a smudge of excitement on cheekbones that are the same. I strain to look at her, to decide, but the crowd is pressing, the night is rainy, and I lose sight of her before I am sure. But now I have reason to be sure. Yes, it was she.

It was she — and I have remembered as best I can. While I have sat here, the moonlight, falling white on the cast-down figure of the other waker, slumped now in sleep, showing up each brilliant, signal detail of the room in a last, proffered perspective, has flooded in and waned. I hear the first crepitations of morning. I am alone with my life, and with the long view.

They will tell us this morning that we must come down off our pin point into the arena. But a pin point can become an arena.

They will tell us that while we, in our easy compassion, have carried the hunger of others in our minds, they have carried it on their backs. And this is true. For this, even when they say it corruptly, is their strength — and our indefensible shame.

They will tell us that we have been able to cherish values beyond hunger only because we have never known basic hunger ourselves — and this will be true also. But this is our paradox — and this is our stronghold, too.

They will tell us, finally, that there is no place for people like us, that the middle ground is for angels, not for men. But there is a place. For in the absence of angels and arbiters from a world of light, men and women must take their place.

Therefore, I am here, sitting opposite the white bulletin on the wall. For the last justification for people like us is to remember people like Hilda with justice. Therefore, in this room where there is no cockcrow except of conscience, I have remembered everything I can about Hilda Kantrowitz, who, this morning, is to be our prosecutor.

I will need to close my eyes when I have to enter the little latrine.

Suggestions for Discussion

1. At the opening of "In the Absence of Angels" the narrator clearly announces that her purpose is to capture and reveal the personality of Hilda Kantrowitz. But in the process she reveals even more about herself. How much is revealed in the first three paragraphs? How?

2. What is the function in the story of the narrator's memories of home, father, and factory?

3. Analyze the economical vignettes of the two fellow prisoners, the "mignonne" and the "spinster" (pages 89–90). How are type and universality achieved through individual detail?

4. The characterization of Hilda finally begins on page 91 with an extended physical description of her as a schoolgirl. How much do the visual details reveal that is of essential significance?

5. How is Hilda's character developed through the description of her family on pages 92–93? Why does Hilda take the nickel that her mother has refused?

6. What is the significance of the moment when the narrator and Hilda encounter each other stealing from coat pockets in the cloakroom?

7. How much of a shock is it to learn at the end of the story that Hilda is to be the prosecutor? How important to the effect of the story is it that this should come as a shock? How well-prepared, probable, and credible is this information?

8. Is the conflict of the story between Hilda and the narrator, the two political factions, or within the narrator? What is its resolution?

RETROSPECT

1. To what extent is Trexler in "The Second Tree from the Corner" a typical character, and how does his typicality force us to judge him? Where and how does his individuality invite us to identify with him?

2. What is Julian's consistent inconsistency in "Everything That Rises Must Converge"? Is he "good"?

WRITING ASSIGNMENTS

1. Keep a journal daily for two weeks. Each day, write a paragraph about a character drawn from memory, observation, or invention. Each day, also go back and add to a former characterization. Focus on details. Try to invent a past, motives, memories, and situations for the characters that interest you most.

2. At the end of the two weeks, assess yourself and decide what habit of journal keeping you can develop and stick to. A page a day? A paragraph a day? Three pages a week? Then do it. Your journal need not, of course, record only ideas for characters. Probably at least once a day you have a thought worth wording, and sometimes it's better to write one sentence a day than to let the habit slide. Like exercise and piano practice, a journal is most useful when it's kept up regularly and frequently. If you pick an hour during which you write each day, no matter how much or little, you may find yourself looking forward to, and saving things up for, that time.

3. Pick two contrasting or contradictory qualities of your own personality (consistent inconsistencies). Create a character that embodies each and set them in conflict with each other. Since you are not writing about yourself but aiming at heightening and dramatizing these qualities, make each character radically different from yourself in at least one fundamental aspect of type: age, race, gender, nationality, or class.

4

THE FLESH MADE WORD
Methods of Character Presentation

The Indirect Method: Authorial Interpretation
The Direct Methods: Appearance, Speech,
Action, and Thought
Character: A Summary

Exploring everything there is to know about your character, identifying a pattern of consistent inconsistency, externally altering a character drawn from life, or finding an internal point of contact with an alien character — all are part of the mental process that can enrich your characterization before you begin your story.

In the writing itself, there are five basic *methods of presentation,* and employing a variety of these methods can help you to draw a full character. If you produce a conflict among the methods, this can also help you create a three-dimensional character.

The Indirect Method:
Authorial Interpretation

The indirect method of presenting a character is *authorial interpretation* — "telling" us the character's background, motives, values, virtues, and the like. The advantages of the indirect method are enormous, for its use leaves you free to move in time and space; to know anything you choose to know whether the character knows it or not; and, godlike, to tell us what we are to feel. The indirect method allows you to convey a great deal of information in a short time.

> The most excellent Marquis of Lumbria lived with his two daughters, Caroline, the elder, and Luisa; and his second wife, Doña Vicenta, a woman with a dull brain, who, when she was not sleeping, was complaining of everything, especially the noise. . . .
>
> The Marquis of Lumbria had no male children, and this was the most painful thorn in his existence. Shortly after having become a widower, he had married Doña Vicenta, his present wife, in order to have a son, but she proved sterile.
>
> The Marquis' life was as monotonous and as quotidian, as unchanging and regular, as the murmur of the river below the cliff or as the liturgic services in the cathedral.
>
> MIGUEL DE UNAMUNO, *The Marquis of Lumbria*

The disadvantages of this indirect method are outlined in Chapter 2. Indeed, in the passage above, it may well be part of Unamuno's purpose to convey the "monotonous and quotidian" quality of the Marquis' life by this summarized and distanced rehearsal of facts, motives, and judgments. Nearly every author will use the indirect method occasionally, and you may find it useful when you want to cover the exposition quickly. Occasionally you may convince us that you are so much more knowledgeable about a character than we can be, and so much more subtle at analyzing him or her, that we will accept your explanations. Very occasionally an author will get away with explaining the characters as much as, or more than, they are presented. Henry James is such an author; he is not an author I would advise anyone to imitate.

> Mrs. Touchett was certainly a person of many oddities, of which her behavior on returning to her husband's house after many months was a noticeable specimen. She had her own way of doing all that she did, and this is the simplest description of a character which, although it was by no means without benevolence, rarely succeeded in giving an impression of softness. Mrs. Touchett might do a great deal of good, but she never pleased.
>
> *Portrait of a Lady*

The very clear presence of the author in this passage, commenting, guiding our reactions, is the hallmark of James's prose, and (although it is by no means without benevolence) the technique is a difficult one to sustain. Direct presentation of the characters is much more likely to please the modern reader.

The Direct Methods

There are four methods of direct presentation: *appearance, speech, action,* and *thought.* A character may also be presented through the opinions of other characters, which may be considered a second indirect method. When this method is employed, however, the second character must give his or her opinions in speech, action, or thought. In the process, the character is inevitably also characterized. Whether we accept the opinion depends on what we think of that character as he or she is thus directly characterized. In this scene from Jane Austen's *Mansfield Park,* for example, the busybody Mrs. Norris gives her opinion of the heroine.

> ". . . there is something about Fanny, I have often observed it before, — she likes to go her own way to work; she does not like to be dictated to; she takes her own independent walk whenever she can; she certainly has a little spirit of secrecy, and independence, and nonsense, about her, which I would advise her to get the better of."
>
> As a general reflection on Fanny, Sir Thomas thought nothing could be more unjust, though he had been so lately expressing the same sentiments himself, and he tried to turn the conversation, tried repeatedly before he could succeed.

Here Mrs. Norris's opinion is directly presented in her speech, Sir Thomas's in his thoughts, each of them being characterized in the process; it is left to the reader to decide (without much difficulty) whose view of Fanny is the more reliable.

APPEARANCE

Of the four methods of direct presentation, appearance is especially important because our eyes are our most highly developed means of perception, and we receive more non-sensuous information by sight than by any other sense. Beauty is only skin deep, but people are embodied, and whatever beauty there is in them must somehow surface in order for us to perceive it — and whatever ugliness, too. Such surfacing involves speech and action as well as appearance, but it is appearance that prompts our first reaction to people, and everything they wear and own bodies forth some aspect of their inner selves.

Writers are sometimes inclined to neglect or even deny this. The choice of writing as a profession or avocation usually contains an implicit rejection of materialism (an English degree won't get you a job; your folks wish you'd major in business; starving in a gloomy basement is a likely option), and writers are concerned to see beyond mere appearances.

In fact, much of the tension and conflict in character does proceed from the truth that appearance is not reality. But in order to know this, we must see the appearance, and it is often in the contradiction between appearances that the truth comes out. Features, shape, style, clothing, objects can make statements of internal values that are political, religious, social, intellectual, and essential. The woman in the Quiana blouse with the cigarette holder is making a different statement from the one in the holey sweatshirt with the palmed joint. Even a person who has forsaken our materialistic society altogether, sworn off supermarkets, and gone to the country to grow organic potatoes has a special relationship with his or her hoe. However indifferent we may be to our looks, that indifference is the result of experiences with our bodies. A twenty-two-year-old Apollo who has been handsome since he was six is a very different person from the man who spent his childhood cocooned in fat and burst the chrysalis at age sixteen.

Following are four very brief portraits of women, in which each is mainly characterized by such trivialities as fabric, hairdo, and cosmetics. It would nevertheless be impossible to mistake the essential nature of any one of them for that of any of the others.

Mrs. Withers, the dietician, marched in through the back door, drew up, and scanned the room. She wore her usual Betty Grable hairdo and open-toed pumps, and her shoulders had an aura of shoulder pads even in a sleeveless dress.

MARGARET ATWOOD,   *The Edible Woman*

My grandmother had on not just one skirt, but four, one over the other. It should not be supposed that she wore one skirt and three petticoats; no, she wore four skirts; one supported the next, and she wore the lot of them in accordance with a definite system, that is, the order of the skirts was changed from day to day. . . . The one that was closest to her yesterday clearly disclosed its pattern today, or rather its lack of pattern: all my grandmother Anna Bronski's skirts favored the same potato color. It must have been becoming to her.

GÜNTER GRASS,   *The Tin Drum*

How beautiful Helen is, how elegant, how timeless: how she charms Esther Songford and how she flirts with Edwin, laying a scarlet fingernail on his dusty lapel, mesmerizing.

She comes in a chauffered car. She is all cream and roses. Her stockings are purest silk; her underskirt, just briefly showing, is lined with lace.

FAY WELDON,   *Female Friends*

As soon as ⟨…⟩ ⟨…⟩ the room, a pungent odor of phosphorus told me she'd taken rat p⟨…⟩ ⟨…⟩. She lay groaning between the quilts. The tatami by the bed was splashed with blood, her waved hair was matted like rope waste, and a bandage tied round her throat showed up unnaturally white. . . . The painted mouth in her waxen face created a ghastly effect, as though her lips were a gash open to the ears.

MASUJI IBUSE, "Tajinko Village"

In the next example, John Irving combines the indirect method with a direct presentation of appearance. Although this passage covers a period of time, gives us Jenny's opinion and her mother's, and passes a judgment, the characterization focuses on a vivid physical image of Jenny.

> Jenny was twenty-two. She had dropped out of college almost as soon as she'd begun, but she had finished her nursing-school program at the head of her class and she enjoyed being a nurse. She was an athletic-looking young woman who always had high color in her cheeks; she had dark, glossy hair and what her mother called a mannish way of walking (she swung her arms), and her rump and hips were so slender and hard that, from behind, she resembled a young boy. In Jenny's opinion, her breasts were too large; she thought the ostentation of her bust made her look "cheap and easy."
>
> In fact she was nothing of the kind. . . .

The World According to Garp

Sense impressions other than sight are also a part of the way a character "appears." A limp handshake or a soft cheek; an odor of Chanel, oregano, or decay — if we are allowed to taste, smell, or touch a character through the narrative, then these sense impressions characterize the way looks do.

The sound and associations of a character's name, too, can give a clue to personality: the affluent Mr. Chiddister in Chapter 2 is automatically a more elegant sort than the affluent Mr. Strum; Huck Finn must have a different life from that of the Marquis of Lumbria. Although names with a blatant meaning — Joseph Surface, Billy Pilgrim, Martha Quest — tend to stylize a character and should be used sparingly if at all, ordinary names can hint at traits you mean to heighten, and it is worth combing any list of names, including the telephone book, to find suggestive sounds. My own telephone book yields, at a glance this morning, Linda Holladay, Marvin Entzminger, and Melba Peebles, any one of which might set me to speculating on a character.

Sound also characterizes as a part of "appearance" insofar as sound represents timbre, tenor, or quality of noise and speech, the characterizing reediness or gruffness of a voice, the lift of laughter or stiffness of delivery.

SPEECH

Speech, however, characterizes in a way that is different from appearance, because speech represents an effort, mainly voluntary, to externalize the internal and to manifest not merely taste or preference but also deliberated thought. Like fiction itself, human dialogue attempts to marry logic to emotion.

We have many means of communicating that are direct expressions of emotion: laughing, leering, shaking hands, screaming, shouting, shooting, making love. We have many means of communicating that are symbolic and emotionless: mathematical equations, maps, checkbooks, credit cards, and chemical formulas. Between body language and pure math lies language, in which judgments and feelings take the form of structured logic: in vows, laws, news, notes, essays, letters, and talk; and the greatest of these is talk.

Because speech has this dual nature, the place of dialogue in fiction is especially important. Its purpose is never merely to convey information. Dialogue may do that, but it must also simultaneously characterize, advance the action or develop the conflict, set the scene, foreshadow, or remind. William Sloane, in *The Craft of Writing,* says:

> There is . . . a tentative rule that pertains to all fiction dialogue. It must do more than one thing at a time or it is too inert for the purposes of fiction. This may sound harsh, but I consider it an essential discipline.

In considering Sloane's "tentative rule," I place the emphasis on *rule.* With dialogue as with significant detail, when you write you are constantly at pains to mean more than you say. If a significant detail must both call up a sense image and *mean,* then the character's words, which presumably mean something, should simultaneously suggest image, personality, or emotion. Even rote exchanges can call up images. A character who says, "It is indeed a pleasure to meet you," carries his back at a different angle, dresses differently, from a character who says, "Hey, man, what it is?"

In the three very brief speeches that follow are three fictional men, sharply differentiated from each other, not only by what they say, but by how they say it. How much do you know about each? How does each look?

> "I had a female cousin one time — a Rockefeller, as it happened —" said the Senator, "and she confessed to me that she spent the fifteenth, sixteenth and seventeenth years of her life saying nothing but, 'No, thank you.' Which is all very well for a girl of that age and station. But it would have been a damned unattractive trait in a *male* Rockefeller."
>
> KURT VONNEGUT, *God Bless You, Mr. Rosewater*

"Hey, that's nice, Grandma," says Phantom as he motions me to come in the circle with him. "I'll tell you what. You can have a contest too. Sure. I got a special one for you. A sweater contest. You get all the grannies out on the porch some night when you could catch a death a chill, and see which one can wear the most sweaters. I got an aunt who can wear fourteen. You top that?"

ROBERT WARD, *Shedding Skin*

The Knight looked surprised at the question. "What does it matter where my body happens to be?" he said. "My mind goes on working all the same. In fact, the more head downward I am, the more I keep inventing new things.

"Now the cleverest thing of the sort that I ever did," he went on after a pause, "was inventing a new pudding during the meat course."

LEWIS CARROLL, *Through the Looking-Glass*

Use your journal to experiment with speech patterns that will characterize. Some people speak in telegraphically short sentences missing various parts of speech. Some speak in convoluted eloquence or rhythms tedious with qualifying phrases. Some rush headlong without a pause for breath until they're breathless; others are measured or terse or begrudge even forming a sentence. Listen to the patterns of speech you hear and try to catch difference of character through syntax — the arrangement of words within a sentence. Then put two or more of these characters in a scene and see how much their differing voices can have to do with conflict.

Here is an exchange among three members of a Chinese-American family in which the subject of the talk is political but in which much more than politics is conveyed.

In fact, he hardly ever stopped talking, and we kids watched the spit foam at the corners of his mouth. . . . It was more like a lecture than a conversation. . . .

"Actually these aren't dreams or plans," Uncle Bun said. "I'm making predictions about ineluctabilities. This Beautiful Nation, this Gold Mountain, this America will end as we know it. There will be one nation, and it will be a world nation. A united planet. Not just Russian Communism. Not just Chinese Communism. World Communism."

He said, "When we don't need to break our bodies earning our daily living any more, and we have time to think, we'll write poems, sing songs, develop religions, invent customs, build statues, plant gardens and make a perfect world." He paused to contemplate the wonders.

"Isn't that great?" I said after he left.

"Don't get brainwashed," said my mother. "He's going to get in trouble for talking like that."

MAXINE HONG KINGSTON, *China Men*

Uncle Bun is richly characterized by his idealistic eloquence, but so are the narrator and her mother in their brief reactions. The contrast between Uncle Bun's "predictions about ineluctabilities" and the narrator's "Isn't that great?" makes her both a teenager and Americanized, whereas the mother's hostile practicality comes out in her blunt imperative.

This passage also illustrates an essential element of conflict in dialogue: tension and drama are heightened when characters are constantly (in one form or another) saying no to each other. Here the mother is saying a distinct no to both Uncle Bun and her daughter. In the following exchange from Ernest Hemingway's *The Old Man and the Sea*, the old man feels only love for his young protégé, and their conversation is a pledge of affection. Nevertheless, it is the old man's steady denial that lends the scene tension.

> "Can I go out and get sardines for you tomorrow?"
>
> "No. Go and play baseball. I can still row and Rogelio will throw the net."
>
> "I would like to go. If I cannot fish with you, I would like to serve in some way."
>
> "You bought me a beer," the old man said. "You are already a man."
>
> "How old was I when you first took me in a boat?"
>
> "Five and you were nearly killed when I brought the fish in too green and he nearly tore the boat to pieces. Can you remember?"
>
> "I can remember the tail slapping and banging and the thwart breaking and the noise of the clubbing. I can remember you throwing me into the bow where the wet coiled lines were and feeling the whole boat shiver and the noise of you clubbing him like chopping a tree down and the sweet blood smell all over me."
>
> "Can you really remember that or did I just tell it to you?"
>
> "I remember everything from when we first went together."
>
> The old man looked at him with his sunburned, confident loving eyes.
>
> "If you were my boy I'd take you out and gamble," he said. "But you are your father's and your mother's and you are in a lucky boat."

Neither of these characters is consciously eloquent, and the dialogue is extremely simple. But look how much more it does than "one thing at a time"! It provides exposition on the beginning of the relationship; and it conveys the mutual affection of the two and the conflict within the old man between his love for the boy and his loyalty to the parents. It conveys the boy's eagerness to persuade and carries him into the emotion he had as a small child while the fish was clubbed. The dialogue represents a constant shift of power back and forth between the boy and the old man, as the boy, whatever else he is saying, continues to say *please*; and the old man, whatever else he is saying, continues to say *no*.

Often the most forceful dialogue can be achieved by *not* having the characters say what they mean. People in extreme emotional states —

whether of fear, pain, anger, or love — are at their least articulate. There is more narrative tension in a love scene where the lovers' make anxious small talk, terrified of revealing their feelings, than in one where they hop into bed. A character who is able to say "I hate you!" hates less than one who bottles the fury and pretends to submit, unwilling to expose the truth. Dialogue often fails if it is too eloquent; the characters debate ideas with great accuracy or are able to define their feelings precisely and honestly. But often the purpose of human exchange is to conceal as well as to reveal; to impress, hurt, protect, seduce, or reject.

The scene that follows is complex. It is from Joan Didion's novel, *A Book of Common Prayer*. The dialogue involves six characters and centers on a seventh, who is absent. The absent *norteamericana* is an object of intense interest to some of these characters, of complete indifference to others. Their conversation is mainly at cross-purposes; and, in the rich mix of insinuation, inattention, prodding, threat, and non sequitur, all of them are saying no to the others, either by refusing to come out with what they mean or by refusing to respond to what has been said.

"Charlotte Douglas is ill," I said after Christmas lunch in the courtyard at Victor and Bianca's.

No one had spoken for twenty minutes. I had timed it. I had counted the minutes while I watched two mating flies try to extricate themselves from a melting chocolate shaving on the untouched Bûche de Noël. The children had already been trundled off quarreling to distribute nut cups to veterans, Gerardo had already made his filial call from St. Moritz, Elena had already been photographed in her Red Cross uniform and had changed back into magenta crêpe de chine pajamas. Isabel had drunk enough champagne to begin crying softly. Antonio had grown irritable enough with Isabel's mournful hiccups to borrow a pistol from the guard at the gate and take aim at a lizard in the creche behind Bianca's fountain. Antonio was always handling guns, or smashing plates. As a gesture toward the spirit of Christmas he had refrained from smashing any plates at lunch, but the effort seemed to have exhausted his capacity for congeniality. Had Antonio been born in other circumstances he would have been put away early as a sociopath.

Bianca remained oblivious.

Bianca remained immersed in the floor plan for an apartment she wanted Victor to take for her in the Residencia Vista del Palacio. Bianca had never been apprised of the fact that Victor already had an apartment in the Residencia Vista del Palacio. For five of these twenty minutes it had seemed to me up in the air whether Antonio was about to shoot up Bianca's creche or tell Bianca about the Residencia Vista del Palacio.

"I said *la norteamericana* is sick."

"Send her to Dr. Schiff," Antonio muttered. Dr. Schiff was Isabel's doctor in Arizona. "Let the great healer tell *la norteamericana* who's making her sick."

Victor only gazed at the sky. I did not know whether Victor had seen

Charlotte Douglas since the night he took her from the Embassy to the Residencia but I did know that a Ministry courier had delivered twenty-four white roses to the Caribe on Christmas Eve.

"So is Jackie Onassis sick," Elena said. Elena was leafing fretfully through a back issue of *Paris-Match*. "Or she was in September."

"So am I sick," Isabel said. "I need complete quiet."

"I should think that's what you have," Elena said.

"Not like Arizona," Isabel said. "I should have stayed through December, Dr. Schiff begged me. The air. The solitude. The long walks, the simple meals. Yoghurt at sunset. You can't imagine the sunsets."

"Sounds very lively," Elena said without looking up. "I wonder if Gerardo knows Jackie Onassis."

"If that's the *norteamericana* Grace is talking about I think she had every right to marry the Greek," Bianca said. "Not that I would ever care to live in Athens. I wonder about the view from the Residencia."

"Grace was talking about a different *norteamericana*, Bianca." Victor leaned back and clipped a cigar. "Of no interest to you. Or Grace."

"This *norteamericana* is of interest only to Victor." Antonio seemed to be having trouble drawing a bead on the lizard. "But she could tell you about the view from the Residencia. She's an expert on the view from the Residencia. Victor should introduce you to her."

"I don't meet strangers," Bianca said. "As you know. I take no interest. Look here, the plan for the eleventh floor. If we lived up that high we'd have clear air. No fevers."

"Almost like Arizona," Elena said. "I wonder if Gerardo knows Jacqueline de Ribes."

"Arizona," Isabel said. "I wonder what Dr. Schiff is doing today."

Antonio fired twice at the lizard.

The lizard darted away.

Two porcelain wise men shattered.

"Eating yoghurt in the sunset I presume," Elena said.

"Dr. Schiff doesn't believe in guns," Isabel said.

"What do you mean exactly, Isabel, '*Dr. Schiff doesn't believe in guns*'?" Antonio thrust the pistol into Isabel's line of sight. "Does Dr. Schiff not believe in the 'existence' of guns? *Look* at it. *Touch* it. *It's there. What does Dr. Schiff mean exactly?*"

Isabel closed her eyes.

Elena closed the copy of *Paris-Match*.

Imagine how the tension of this scene would disappear if the narrator asked Victor just exactly what his relationship was with Charlotte Douglas, if Antonio spilled everything he knew to Bianca, if Elena told Isabel she was a self-centered idiot, and if Antonio then shot them all. The dialogue reveals character and danger precisely because it does not reveal the relevant information and refuses to divulge the undercurrent of emotion.

Examine your dialogue to see if it does more than one thing at a time.

Do the sound and syntax characterize by region, education, attitude? Does the choice of words and their syntax reveal that he or she is stiff, outgoing, stifling anger, ignorant of the facts, perceptive, bigoted, afraid? Is the conflict advanced by no-dialogue? Is the drama heightened by the characters' inability or unwillingness to tell the whole truth?

Once you are comfortable with the voice of your character, it is well to acknowledge that everyone has many voices and that what that character says will be, within his or her verbal range, determined by the character *to whom* it is said. All of us have one sort of speech for the vicar and another for the man who pumps the gas. Huck Finn, whose voice is idiosyncratically his own, says "Yes, sir," to the Judge, and "Maybe I am, maybe I ain't," to his degenerate dad.

Dialect is a tempting, and can be an excellent, means of characterizing, but it is difficult to do well and easy to overdo. Dialect should always be achieved by word choice and syntax, and misspellings kept to a minimum. They distract and slow the reader, and worse, they tend to make the character seem stupid rather than regional. There is no point in spelling phonetically any word as it is ordinarily pronounced: almost all of us say things like "fur" for *for*, "uv" for *of*, "wuz" for *was*, "an'" for *and*, "sez" for *says*. Nearly everyone drops the *g* in words ending in *ing*, at least now and then. When you misspell these words in dialogue, you indicate that the speaker is ignorant enough to spell them that way when he or she writes. Even if you want to indicate ignorance, you may alienate the reader by the means you choose to do so.

These "rules" for dialect have changed in the past fifty years or so, for largely political reasons. Nineteenth-century authors felt free to misspell the dialogue of foreigners; the lower classes; and racial, regional, and ethnic groups. This literary habit persisted into the first decades of the present century. But the world is considerably smaller now, and its consciousness has been raised. Dialect, after all, is entirely relative, and an author who seems unaware of this may seem like a bigot. The word *bath* pronounced by an Englishman may sound like *bahth* to an American, and pronounced by an American may sound like *banth* to an Englishman, but both know how the word is spelled and resent the implied mockery. Liverpudlians have been knighted; there's been a German in the State Department and a Georgian in the White House; and we resent the implication that regionality is ignorance. Ignorance itself is a charged issue. If you misspell a foreign accent or black English, the reader is likely to have a political rather than a literary reaction. A line of dialogue that runs, "Doan rush me nun, Ah be gwine," reads as caricature, whereas, "Don't rush me none, I be going" makes legitimate use of black English syntax and lets us concentrate on the meaning and emotion.

In dialect or standard English, the bottom-line rule is that dialogue must be speakable; conversely, if it isn't speakable, it isn't dialogue.

"Certainly I had had a fright I wouldn't soon forget," Reese would say later, "and as I slipped into bed fully dressed except for my shoes, which I flung God-knows-where, I wondered why I had subjected myself to a danger only a fool would fail to foresee for the dubious pleasure of spending one evening in the company of a somewhat less than brilliant coed."

Nobody would say this because it can't be said. It is not only convoluted beyond reason; it stumbles over its alliteration, *only a fool would fail to foresee for*, and takes more breath than the human lungs can hold. Read your dialogue aloud and make sure it is comfortable to the mouth, the breath, and the ear. If not, then it won't ring true as talk.

Identifying dialogue sometimes presents more of a problem than it needs to. The purpose of a *dialogue tag* is to make clear who is speaking, and it usually needs to do nothing else. *Said* is quite adequate to the purpose. People also *ask* and *reply* and occasionally *add, recall, remember,* or *remind*. But sometimes an unsure writer will strain for emphatic synonyms: *she gasped, he whined, they chorused, John snarled, Mary spat*. This is unnecessary and obtrusive, because although unintentional repetition usually makes for awkward style, the word *said* is as invisible as punctuation. When reading we're scarcely aware of it, whereas we are forced to be aware of *she wailed*. If it's clear who is speaking without any dialogue tag at all, don't use one. Usually an identification at the beginning of a dialogue passage and an occasional reminder are sufficient. If the speaker is inherently identified in the speech pattern, so much the better.

Similarly, tonal dialogue tags should be used sparingly: *he said with relish; she added limply*. Such phrases are blatant "telling," and the chances are that good dialogue will convey its own tone. *"Get off my case!" she said angrily*. We do not need to be told that she said this angrily. If she said it sweetly, then we would probably need to be told. If the dialogue does not give us a clue to the manner in which it is said, an action will often do so better than an adverb. *"I'll have a word with Mr. Ritter about it," he said with finality* is weaker than *"I'll have a word with Mr. Ritter about it," he said, and picked up his hat*.

If human character is the center of fiction, it follows inevitably that you must master dialogue. People speak; they confront each other with speech; they change through speech. It is by hearing your characters speak that we experience them. There may be times when a summary of speech is justified — when, for example, one character has to inform another of events that we already know, or when the emotional point of a conversation is that it has become tedious.

Carefully, playing down the danger, Len filled her in on the events of the long night.

After that, Samantha told us everything we had never wanted to know about the lost art of ormolu, and Marlene gave us a play-by-play account of her last bridge game.

But nothing is more frustrating to a reader than to be told that significant events are taking place in talk and to be denied the drama of the dialogue.

They whispered to each other all night long, and as he told her all about his past, she began to realize that she was falling in love with him.

Such a summary — it's *telling* — is a stingy way of treating the reader, who wants the chance to fall in love, too: give me *me*!

ACTION

The significant characters of a fiction must be both capable of causing an action and capable of being changed by it.

It is important to understand the difference between action and movement, which are not synonymous. Physical movement is generally necessary to the action, but it is not adequate to ensure that there will be an action. Much movement in a story — the way he crosses his legs, the way she charges down the hall — is actually part of appearance and characterizes without necessarily moving the plot forward. When a book or film is advertised as "action-packed," it is also likely that what is being touted is movement rather than action — lots of sword fights, karate chops, or bombs away — but not necessarily that meaningful arrangement of events in which a character is convincingly compelled to pursue a goal, to make decisions along the way, and to find herself or himself subtly or dramatically altered in the process. The words *motive, motion,* and *emotion* have the same root, and this is neither accidental nor irrelevant to the way the human drama unfolds.

Take another look at the scene from *A Book of Common Prayer* on pages 107–108 and notice how the action counterpoints the dialogue to reveal what is *not* said. Victor's deliberate gazing at the sky and Elena's fretful leafing through the magazine while Antonio shoots at lizards on the creche; Antonio's thrusting the pistol at Isabel and Isabel's closing her eyes — these actions reveal tensions among characters and, in some cases, the tension within characters.

In this scene from Raymond Carver's short story "Neighbors," ordinary, trivial, and domestic actions take on menace as Bill Miller dawdles in the apartment of a neighbor whose cat he has agreed to feed.

When he returned to the kitchen the cat was scratching in her box. She looked at him steadily for a minute before she turned back to the litter. He opened all the cupboards and examined the canned goods, the cereals, the packaged foods, the cocktail and wine glasses, the china, the pots and pans. He opened the refrigerator. He sniffed some celery, took two bites of cheddar cheese, and chewed on an apple as he walked into the bedroom. The bed seemed enormous, with a fluffy white bedspread draped to the floor. He pulled out a nightstand drawer, found a half-empty package of cigarettes and stuffed them into his pocket. Then he stepped to the closet and was opening it when the knock sounded at the front door.

There is hardly grand larceny being committed here, but the actions build toward tension through two distinct techniques. The first is that they do actually "build": at first Bill only "examines." The celery he only sniffs, whereas he takes two bites of the cheese, then a whole apple, then half a pack of cigarettes. He moves from the kitchen to the bedroom, which is a clearer invasion of privacy, and from cupboard to refrigerator to nightstand to closet, each a more intimate intrusion than the last.

The second technique is that the narrative subtly hints at Bill's own sense of stealth. It would be easy to imagine a vandal who performed the same actions with complete indifference. But Bill thinks the cat looks "steadily" at him, which is hardly of any importance except that he feels it to be. His awareness of the enormous white bed hints at sexual guilt. When the knock at the front door sounds, we start, as he must, in a clear sense of getting caught. As action counterpoints dialogue in the passage from *A Book of Common Prayer*, here thought counterpoints action, revealing Bill's character through his guilt.

THOUGHT

Aristotle is helpful at clarifying the relationship between desire, thought, and action. Aristotle says, as we have seen, that a man "is his desire." That is, his character is defined by his ultimate purpose, good or bad. *Thought*, says Aristotle, is the process by which a person works backward in his mind from his goal to determine what *action* he can take toward that goal at a given moment.

It is not, for example, your ultimate desire to read this book. Very likely you don't even "want" to read it; you'd rather be asleep or jogging or making love. But your ultimate goal is, say, to be a rich, respected, and famous writer. In order to attain this goal, you reason, you must know as much about the craft as you can learn. To do this, you would like to take a graduate degree at the Writer's Workshop in Iowa. To do that, you must take an undergraduate degree in ——— where you now find yourself, and must get an A in Ms. or Mr. ———'s creative writing course. To do that, you must produce a character sketch from one of the assignments at the end of this chapter by a week from Tuesday. To do so, you must sit here reading this chapter now instead of sleeping, jogging, or making love. Your ultimate motive had led you logically backward to a deliberate "moral" decision on the action you can take at this minor crossroads. In fact, it turns out that you want to be reading after all.

The pattern that Aristotle perceives in this relation among desire, thought, and action seems to me a very fruitful one for an author both in the structuring of plot and in the creation of character. What does this protagonist want to happen in the last paragraph of this story? What is the particular thought process by which this person works backward to determine what he or she will do now, in the situation that presents itself in the first paragraph on page one?

The action, of course, may be the wrong one. Thought thwarts us, either because the thought process itself is mistaken (if only you'd gone to sleep, you would now be having a dream that would give you the most brilliant idea for a short story you've ever had); or because thought is full of conflicting desires and consistent inconsistencies (actually you *are* no longer reading this paragraph; someone knocked on your door and suggested a pizza and you couldn't resist); or because there is enormous human tension between suppressed thought and expressed thought (you didn't want a pizza, and certainly not in the company of that bore, but you'd turned him down twice this week already).

"Ever have any bizarre thoughts?" asks the psychiatrist at the opening of "The Second Tree from the Corner." Mr. Trexler has come to the doctor, in fact, precisely because he wants to be rid of his bizarre thoughts, and the logical thing to do at this moment (Trexler does try) is to trust the doctor's expertise and answer the question. But a bizarre thought about a lizard and a bug intervenes, and Trexler realizes that the next question will be "unanswerable." His personal timidity is at odds with his desire to be rid of his fears, and in this consistent inconsistency, thought, at least apparently, thwarts him.

At the opening of "Everything That Rises Must Converge," Julian wants to be free of his mother's tedious demands, but he is also financially dependent upon her, so he wants to meet those demands as minimally as possible. He will take her to the Y, then, but he'll do it in bad grace. At the end of the story he is free of her; but it turns out that his thought processes were faulty, his desire unattainable, and his "dependency" is deeper than he understood.

A person, a character, can't do much about what he or she wants; it just is (which is another way of saying that character is desire). What we can deliberately choose is our behavior, the action we take in a given situation. Achievement of our desire would be easy if the thought process between desire and act were not so faulty and so wayward, or if there were not such an abyss between the thoughts we think and those which we are willing and able to express.

This being so, the conflict that is the essence of character can be effectively (and, if it doesn't come automatically, quite consciously) achieved in fiction by producing a conflict between methods of presentation. A character can be directly revealed to us through *appearance, speech, action,* and *thought.* If you set one of these methods at odds with the others (it is in narrative practice most frequently *thought*), then dramatic tension will be produced. Imagine, for example, a character who is impeccably and expensively dressed, who speaks eloquently, who acts decisively, and whose mind is revealed to us as full of order and determination. He is inevitably a flat character. But suppose that he is impeccable, eloquent, decisive and that his mind is a *mess* of wounds and panic. He is at once interesting.

Here is the opening passage of Saul Bellow's *Seize the Day,* in which appearance and action are thus blatantly at odds with thought. Notice that it is the tension between suppressed thought and what is expressed through appearance and action that produces the rich character conflict.

> When it came to concealing his troubles, Tommy Wilhelm was not less capable than the next fellow. So at least he thought, and there was a certain amount of evidence to back him up. He had once been an actor — no, not quite, an extra — and he knew what acting should be. Also, he was smoking a cigar, and when a man is smoking a cigar, wearing a hat, he has an advantage: it is harder to find out how he feels. He came from the twenty-third floor down to the lobby on the mezzanine to collect his mail before breakfast, and he believed — he hoped — he looked passably well: doing all right.

Tommy Wilhelm is externally composed but mentally anxious, mainly anxious about looking externally composed. By contrast, in the next passage from Samuel Beckett's *Murphy,* the landlady Miss Carridge, who has just discovered a suicide in one of her rooms, is anxious in speech and action but is mentally composed.

> She came speeding down the stairs one step at a time, her feet going so fast that she seemed on little caterpillar wheels, her forefinger sawing horribly at her craw for Celia's benefit. She slithered to a stop on the steps of the house and screeched for the police. She capered in the street like a consternated ostrich, with strangled distracted rushes towards the York and Caledonian Roads in turn, embarrassingly equidistant from the tragedy, tossing up her arms, undoing the good work of the samples, screeching for police aid. Her mind was so collected that she saw clearly the impropriety of letting it appear so.

I have said that thought is most frequently at odds with one or more of the other three methods of direct presentation — reflecting the difficulty we have expressing ourselves openly or accurately — but this is by no means always the case. A character may be successfully, calmly, even eloquently expressing fine opinions, betraying himself by pulling at his ear, or herself by crushing her skirt. Captain Queeg of Herman Wouk's *The Caine Mutiny* is a memorable example of this, maniacally clicking the steel balls in his hand as he defends his disciplinary code. Often we are not privy to the thoughts of a character at all, so that the conflicts must be expressed in a contradiction between the external methods of direct presentation, appearance, speech, and action. Character A may be speaking floods of friendly welcome, betraying his real feeling by backing steadily away. Character B, dressed in taffeta ruffles and ostrich plumes, may wax pitying over the miseries of the poor. Notice that the notion of "betraying oneself" is important here: we're more likely to believe the evidence unintentionally given than deliberate expression.

A classic example of such self-betrayal is found in Leo Tolstoy's *The Death of Ivan Ilyich*, where the widow confronts her husband's colleague at the funeral.

> . . . Noticing that the table was endangered by his cigarette ash, she immediately passed him an ashtray, saying as she did so: "I consider it an affectation to say that my grief prevents my attending to practical affairs. On the contrary, if anything can — I won't say console me, but — distract me, it is seeing to everything concerning him." She again took out her handkerchief as if preparing to cry, but suddenly, as if mastering her feeling, she shook herself and began to speak calmly. "But there is something I want to talk to you about."

It is no surprise either to the colleague or to us that Praskovya Federovna wants to talk about getting money.

Finally, character conflict can be expressed by creating a tension between the direct and the indirect methods of presentation, and this is a source of much irony. The author presents us with a judgment of the character, then lets him or her speak, appear, act, and/or think in contradiction of this judgment.

> Sixty years had not dulled his responses; his physical reactions, like his moral ones, were guided by his will and strong character, and these could be seen plainly in his features. He had a long tube-like face with a long rounded open jaw and a long depressed nose.
>
> FLANNERY O'CONNOR, *The Artificial Nigger*

Here what we see in the details of Mr. Head's features are not will and strong character but grimly unlikable qualities. "Tube-like" is an ugly image;

an "open jaw" suggests stupidity; and "depressed" connotes more than shape, while the dogged repetition of "long" stretches the face grotesquely.

Jane Austen is a master of this ironic method, the authorial voice often having a naive goodwill toward the characters while the characters themselves prevent the reader from sharing it.

> Mr. Woodhouse was fond of society in his own way. He liked very much to have his friends come and see him; and from various united causes, from his long residence at Hartfield, and his good nature, from his fortune, his house, and his daughter, he could command the visits of his own little circle in a great measure as he liked. He had not much intercourse with any families beyond that circle; his horror of late hours and large dinner parties made him unfit for any acquaintance but such as would visit him on his own terms. . . . Upon such occasions poor Mr. Woodhouse's feelings were in sad warfare. He loved to have the cloth laid, because it had been the fashion of his youth; but his conviction of suppers being very unwholesome made him rather sorry to see anything put on it; and while his hospitality would have welcomed his visitors to everything, his care for their health made him grieve that they would eat.
>
> *Emma*

Here all the authorial generalizations about Mr. Woodhouse are generous and positive, whereas his actions and the "sad warfare" of his mind lead us to the conviction that we would just as soon not sup with this good-natured and generous man.

Character: A Summary

It may be helpful to summarize such practical advice on character as this chapter and the previous chapter contain:

1. Keep a journal and use it to explore and build ideas for characters.
2. Know all the influences that go into the making of your character's type: age, gender, race, nationality, marital status, region, education, religion, profession.
3. Know the details of your character's life: what he or she does during every part of the day, thinks about, remembers, wants, likes and dislikes, eats, says, means.
4. Identify, heighten, and dramatize consistent inconsistencies. What does your character want that is at odds with whatever else the character wants? What patterns of thought and behavior work against the primary goal?

5. If the character is based on a real model, including yourself, make a dramatic external alteration.

6. If the character is imaginary or alien to you, identify a mental or emotional point of contact.

7. Focus sharply on how the character looks, on what she or he wears and owns, and on how she or he moves. Let us focus on it, too.

8. Examine the character's speech to make sure it does more than convey information. Does it characterize; accomplish exposition; and reveal emotion, intent, or change? Does it advance the conflict through *no-dialogue?* Speak it aloud: does it "say"?

9. Make the character act, and let the action build. Let it reveal or betray in counterpoint to dialogue and thought.

10. Know what your character wants, both generally, out of life, and specifically, in the context of the story. Keeping that desire in mind, "think backward" with the character to decide what he or she would do in any situation presented.

11. Be aware of the five methods of presentation of character: authorial interpretation, appearance, speech, action, and thought; present the character differently in at least one of these ways than you do in the others.

Jamal the Constable

G. S. SHARAT CHANDRA

I tell you, attaining your heart's desire and ambition in public service is no easy thing. I started as apprentice constable to the Town Magistrate though my father, Jamal the Elder, retired as Daffedar after serving the Government for thirty years like it was his own father. Every man, beast and insect within a radius of a hundred miles of Nanjangud has shivered at the mention of his name. When he left for the station in the morning dressed in his khaki, his belt buckle waxed to catch the sun and glint it on the eye of any suspicious character, blinding him instantly from his nefarious plans, his moustache trimmed and curved with vaseline to the position of half-moons on either cheek, his turban around his head frilled an inch taller than that of the Maharaja himself, the whole town beamed with security and contentment. Pedestrians walked from the middle of the road to its side in respect to the Daffedar Saheb. He rode his bicycle as though it was the royal elephant itself that swaggered towards the constabulary with pomp and majesty. He yielded not an inch of the middle of the road to any tonga or bullock cart that crossed his path of law and order. Such were the days of his glory and even now people gather around to reminisce about Jamal the Elder, Daffedar of Daffedars.

If I were not the son of such a splendid father of such splendid heredity, I'd not have been as patient and understanding of the way in which I have been appointed at such a low level of climbing. I would not have kept my mouth shut at such indifference to my ancestry. After all, the son of a famous father deserves a better rung on the ladder of law than some brahmin candidate who has passed his intermediate examination with chemistry, botany and zoology. No doubt these brahmin boys are very smart with books and pass examinations with flying colours but, eating vegetables as they do, I don't think they have the muscle power to chase after a running thief or wrestle body to body even with the skinniest murderer. It's only non-brahmins like myself who, by the grace of the Prophet and the good meat from Sabu's meatshop, have developed the real strength and stamina that are required in a government job like the police. I also know that, if my father were alive and the superior officer he knew all his life were still posted at Nanjangud, he could have simply expressed his desire to any one of them about a promotion for his son and I would have been promoted instantly. He is gone and new faces occupy all the important chairs, but I am certain that good deeds in the service of our government will eventually pay their reward and I am settled in my mind it will not be long before my antecedents and ability merit what they deserve.

I really do not mind my morning duty, which is to stand guard at the Magistrate's wicket-gate. I am rather proud of being able to show off my new uniform in that capacity. I wear my father's belt buckle, which still catches the sun, and have trimmed his turban to the size of my head. I've been told that people whisper how much I remind them of my father, though I do not ride a bicycle. I fall into patriotic daydreams, especially on hot mornings. I imagine the Magistrate's house is Government's gold reserve and I its sole guardian. I question anyone who comes five feet near the Magistrate's gate, with the authority and curtness of an army captain. My hands are ever ready to reach the stick that hangs at my side. Other times, I imagine that relatives of a thief or murderer are after Your Honour's life and are lurking in a shadow for the fraction of that second I slacken, so they can rush into the house and take his life away before he has tried their case. But usually no one comes to see the Magistrate at the house. Only some straggling cow or the washerman's donkey sniff around the compound and give me a look or two. I whack them a bit and they go away. My father used to tell me, to succeed in the police profession one has to be as alert and obedient guarding a wicket-gate as guarding the Maharaja's own body and soul.

Your Honour, the Magistrate, is a good fellow. Though he too is a brahmin vegetarian, he is built like an ox. Meat-shop Sabu and the hardware merchant Puttasamy say he is one of the smartest in the head that has ever been posted to Nanjangud. He has been quite amicable towards me. I arrive at the house at 7 A.M., stand guard at the wicket-gate till 10 A.M. At 10:05, I go in and pick up all the law books and case files Your Honour will have grouped together on the table and wait for him to emerge from the kitchen. I give him a stiff salute, wait for him to dress with the black gown and hood of justice, then follow him to the court chambers, three and a half feet behind as custom requires. At the court, I open the door to his chambers and stand to attention as he goes in. Then I dump all the books in front of the Head Munshi and wait outside the door within the earshot of the Munshi. When the Magistrate sits on the Bench at 11 A.M., I announce the court is in session. Thereafter, I don't have to worry. I spend the rest of the afternoon chatting with the villagers and relatives of the accused. I am usually invited by them over to the court canteen. Though it is a vegetarian place, I eat enough to fill my stomach for the afternoon. The Magistrate rises for the day around 4 or 4:30. I collect all the case files and books he wants to be taken back and walk behind him to the house. At the house I wait for a few minutes to see if the Lady Magistrate wants me to run an errand or two for her. Then I am free. It is not a bad life. They do not work me hard. Only on rare occasions does the Magistrate fall into a temper. It is on days when he is furious at some lawyer or some knotty problem he cannot solve that he takes it out on me. Once he had this famous lawyer Mr. Chetty from Mysore City come to argue a theft case. I don't really know what point the argument was about but from the manner in which the Magistrate and Mr. Chetty were shouting at each other in English, which is the court language, I was sure it had inflamed the Magistrate's temper quite a bit. The Magistrate did not adjourn the hearing for coffee break as usual but continued the case until the close of day, keeping everyone hungry. There is no terror like that of a vegetarian magistrate who has missed his pakoda and coffee break. When he rose for the day, he walked home with furious pace. I walked, or rather trotted, behind. He was muttering and grumbling all the way in English because he did not want me to understand the unmentionables. He got very mad at my pace and shouted I walked like an arthritic snail and I was the laziest apprentice he ever had. When we arrived at the house, he remembered the umbrella he had left at the court and swore it was my fault. I knew his moods so I didn't question his opinion. I simply turned my feet back to the court-house to retrieve the umbrella before all hell broke loose. It is not a big thing or a chore of impossible proportions to walk back a couple of miles for an umbrella unless, as you are doing so, it starts raining cats and dogs. But I cheered myself that on the way back I wouldn't be drenched. When I returned, the Magistrate's temper was still boiling. He was hysterical that

I had used the umbrella to save my subordinate head and wanted to fire me for contempt of court. But the Lady Magistrate intervened with a hot cup of coffee for Your Honour and saved the day for me.

Well, it has been ten months since I began my apprenticeship. The day before yesterday, Lady Magistrate went to Mysore City with her two children to visit her parents. I have been bringing Your Honour meals from the bus-stand hotel, in a special tiffin-carrier. Before she left, Lady Magistrate said to me, "Jamal, ask the bus-stand-hotel manager to send the meals for your Saheb with his brahmin mali. Tell him to wash the carrier twice in hot water and use banana leaf inside." Well, I told the manager the lady's wish but he said, "Look, Constable Jamal, do you think all my malis are brahmins! Besides, I'm already short of servers, and if I keep sending my brahmin mali on delivery service who is going to tend my kitchen? I tell you, since the lady is gone, it doesn't matter. I'll put the tiffin-carrier in a gunny bag so you can carry it without touching."

Yesterday I brought the meals for the Magistrate and left them on his table. He didn't ask me any questions as to who might have touched it. I think he is a liberal man when his wife is away and doesn't bother his legal head with brahmin-muslim caste-business that women are so concerned about.

But today, when I brought his lunch, he told me not to go for the evening meal but wait at the gate as he was expecting some guest. This was unusual as the Magistrate usually dismissed me after I walked him home. Also, this is Friday, my special night when I get together with Sabu and Puttasamy at Bayamma's den to smoke ghanja and drink toddy.

I stood at the wicket-gate cursing my fate. Around 7:30 I heard the motorcycle of the Assistant Superintendent of Police puttering towards the house. I got up from my guard bench and straightened my uniform. I saluted the A.S.P., stiff and prompt as he cut the engine. He asked me if the Magistrate was in the house and ordered me to take the cycle to the back of the house and park it there. He was inside the house for about half an hour, then he came out with Your Honour. They were laughing and talking in English in a pleasant out-of-the-office sort of manner. The Magistrate as he passed me said, "Jamal, I want you to stay at the house all evening as I hear a lot of burglary is going on. Keep the thermos with you for my morning coffee." I said, "Yes, Your Honour!" in a meek voice. They walked slowly towards the Travellers' Bungalow, which is beyond the court-house. I cursed my fate again. No ghanja or toddy for me tonight. I didn't have the slightest warning of this special duty. If I had known I'd have sent word to Sabu about it. Probably they are already at Bayamma's den waiting for me. Perhaps Bayamma has made one of her special lamb kurma for us and kept the toddy cool in her earthen pot. My mouth began to water and my body yearned for those heavenly blue puffs of ghanja. But I am a good muslim. I make mamaz twice regularly and practise my faith. Maybe Allah will understand my conflict between my public and my private selves and do something. My father used to say, "Jamal, your private self should obey your public self. That is the beauty of service. It will bring you many benefits and many joys that eventually you can enjoy as a private self." I am not sure that my father, when he said that, was referring to my present dilemma, which as a non-ghanja-smoker he could not have guessed.

Allah must have somehow heard my prayers, for I saw Sabu and Puttasamy walking towards the house. My heart leaped with delight as they came near. "I greet you, my friends," I said. "Only the goodness of your combined hearts must have brought you here!" Sabu came closer and whispered, "No, dear friend! Bayamma kicked us out for not paying for services the last time we used her den. She said, 'Police protection or no police protection, either pay for my services or find another who can do it as well as I do, I challenge you!' So, since you didn't appear, we thought we should come up to you and see what you'll suggest!"

We went to the back of the house where there is a small room that was once used as a store room for firewood. It has been empty since the Lady Magistrate bought a primus stove and fixed a water heater in the bathroom. It was not comparable to Bayamma's den, which was furnished with pillows and soft coir mats, but there was an old quilt and a tarnished wicker lamp that still worked. Puttasamy opened his bulging gunny bag and took out three toddy bottles. Then he unwrapped the ghanja from a dry banana leaf. I could smell it was the very best. Puttasamy had used his slow mind to stop at the bus-stand hotel and had bought some pakodas and ompudi for us to munch with. We settled down to our feast. It was good toddy and good ghanja. Time went flying, as our Urdu poet Omar has said. The sweet slow smoke of ghanja filled my lungs with buoyancy and serenity. My aching calf-muscles relaxed and I felt strong and afraid of nothing. Companionship of masculine friends is one of the pleasures that men share and enjoy without even speaking a word. But ghanja and toddy are not items that induce silent enjoyment. They loosen the tongue and make the spirit fly freely. My friends gossiped a while about town matters. Then they began enquiring about my master and family. I told them of the Lady Magistrate's visit and the bringing of meals from the bus-stand. It was then that Sabu asked, "Why do you think your Saheb did not eat vegetarian meal tonight?" I had not thought of that seriously until then. These brahmins have crazy eating habits. Sometimes they eat a lot at one sitting and sometimes they starve themselves to death in the name of some auspicious occasion — unlike us muslims, who starve only during Ramadan. "How would I know?" I replied. "Maybe he doesn't like hotel meals, maybe he misses his wife's cooking or maybe he misses his children. Why should it matter so much?" The ghanja was having a heavenly effect on me. I wanted these friends to realise that I had guts and that I was not a meek constable. My heart and spirit were those of a Daffedar. I wanted them to ask me more about myself instead of wasting our good times with a lot of gossip on higher authorities. But Sabu went on like he had not heard me. "I have heard of the Saheb's fondness for non-vegetarian meals!" he said. I was shaken. This was not an irresponsible matter to gossip. I am a servant of the Government, and the Magistrate was the immediate incarnation of the Government I served. "Government's work is God's work," my father used to say and I am no traitor, high on ghanja or not. "What is this you say?" I retorted with some anger. "I have been serving Your Honour for ten months and I perhaps know him better than his wife! I carry his files and listen to his judgments. I hear him and see him all the time except when he is sleeping. I have never seen him eat meat. Why should he? He's built like an ox vegetarianly. He likes his radish sambar and pickles. Why throw gutter water on the character of a high-caste officer? You had better stop talking like that!" Puttasamy, who was until then silently smoking, added, "Jamal, don't be blind with patriotism. I have heard such rumours too. What is more, yesterday Sabu supplied Joseph of the Travellers' Bungalow prime cuts of lamb and one whole Australian leghorn hen that he had to order specially from the Mysore Russell Market. But Joseph is not having any visitor in the Travellers' Bungalow! Today I saw Joseph's wife in the market buying all sorts of vegetables and spice. Do you think she has gone rich overnight or become pregnant in her fifty-fifth year? The A.S.P is a non-vegetarian, and it seems your Magistrate and he were good friends before they were posted here!" He paused and then added, "Also don't think that is all that's happening in the Travellers' Bungalow tonight!"

I did not know what he meant or whether I heard him right. I took some deep gulps of toddy and pulled swiftly on the ghanja to suppress my shock. Why should these two intimate friends of mine lie about such things? They had no grudge against the Magistrate or the A.S.P. Besides, they had enough trouble smoking and drinking without being caught or exposed to their families. Still, I was not thoroughly convinced. My father used to say, "Everyone wants to see through a policeman's eye, because that will make their own evidence acceptable. But, as a policeman, don't be fooled by the sight of others. See for yourself everything as well as the Prophet would permit before you make evidence."

I wanted to go see for myself but I did not want my friends to think that I was gullible or believed their story. It was about the hour of midnight. Sabu and Puttasamy were now well smoked, fed and drunk. I suggested that we call it a night and disband before the neighbours got suspicious of the lamp in the old firewood room. They agreed. I walked with them to the gate of the house and bid them good-bye. I waited until I could no longer see them beyond the street-light corner, then, steadying my stumble as best I could, I walked towards the Travellers' Bungalow. The streets were dark and empty. In the dustbins I could hear stray dogs turning over the banana leaves the housewives had thrown away after the evening meal. The stars were shining like they were wiped clean after a wash. The night breeze felt delicious on my body. As I approached the Bungalow my suspicions grew worse. The main room, which is always reserved for visiting dignitaries, had its lights on. I could see both the ceiling fans whirring through the ventilators. I went closer until I was under the gul mohr tree that is in front of the bungalow. Its branches, which extended over the roof of the patio, were full of summer flowering. There were many crickets in the branches which chirped away in the cool night. "Happy rascals," I thought. "How free and irresponsible are they. They eat and drink free from mother nature and whistle all night like vagabonds. But, then, they do not know the pleasure of ghanja or the satisfaction that results from being a police officer." My thoughts were interrupted by the opening of the main-room door. Joseph, the butler, emerged with a tray of plates. I ducked under. He emptied the plates of the leftovers. As he emptied them, I could see pieces of chewed chicken-bones, slices of beets and cucumber. The rich aroma of rice biryani floated over to my nostrils. Joseph went back into the room and returned with two bottles. My heart began to pound faster. Though my vision was slurry, I could make out they were foreign whisky-bottles. He set them on the floor next to the kitchen door where he had already set several empty soda-bottles. As he came out of the main room, he had left the door ajar and I could hear male and female voices. Then a woman came out. I had never seen her before. She was dressed in a blue silk sari and wore many silver bangles. Her face, though a little fat in the cheek, was soft and perfumed. I could smell the faint fragrance of Hazeline Snow. Her lips were juicy with the chewing of betel and she kept steadying her sari over the shoulder. As she did so, I could see she was grandly endowed with pleasures of flesh a man always dreams of. Joseph came running from the kitchen. She said to him, "The Judge Saheb wants some coffee in an hour. Bring some fresh soda for now!" Joseph withdrew. The beautiful woman stood at the door making bangle noises. But hot beads of perspiration trickled down my crouching armpits with the consistency of a rivulet. Could she be the paramour of Your Honour! Could Your Honour be meat-eater, drinker of foreign whisky, lover of fine unknown woman! I crouched lower as though burdened with such confusing thoughts. My head reeled more now as the full effect of the night's indulgence was taking over. Someone came out of the room and encircled the woman's waist with an oxlike reach. His embracing hand wandered all over her and he kept reaching for her mouth which was somewhat difficult from his side position to her body and he ended up landing kisses on her cheek. His shirt hung outside his pants and a button on his fly was peeping. I blushed visibly. I could not see clearly nor did I want to. The oxlike frame of the man was enough to make me withdraw. What was I to do? I am a public servant sworn to uphold the integrity of the country but no one, not even my father, told me what to do or say if and when I saw a judge in such condition! As I returned to the house, deep feelings of guilt possessed me. I even entertained my floating mind to convince itself that it could not be Your Honour that I had seen. I could not think or worry anymore. Mercifully the ghanja was calling all my organs to sleep. I left all my responsibilities in the trust of the Almighty to sort out my confusion somehow while I slept.

The next morning, I had the feeling that the previous evening was just a nightmare. I could barely recollect the events in any order. Outside the sun was already high. I realised with a start that I had to bring Your Honour's morning coffee. I rushed to the hotel and, when I came back with it, the Magistrate was sitting in the hall with the A.S.P. Someone had already brought them breakfast and coffee. I saluted my master and he simply glared at me. The town hall gong struck eleven! I had overslept!

Two weeks later, at the end of a regular court-day, I went to pick up the case files when the Magistrate called me to his chambers. He said, "Jamal, I have good news for you! You've now worked under me for almost a year. You've been a good apprentice police constable. I've therefore decided to transfer you to Gundlupet with a promotion that you be appointed constable with honours!"

My heart opened and shut like the swing door on Your Honour's chambers. The Magistrate was saying the words that I had always dreamt of! To be promoted to full-time constable before the termination of apprenticeship, that too with personal recommendation of the Magistrate, was indeed very good news. After the Bungalow incident, all I had feared was the discovery of my spying and dismissal from service! The Magistrate continued cutting short my brain's activity. "Now, Jamal, there's one important thing that I want to impress on you. It's important for your future prospects that you exercise restraint on your nocturnal habits. Yes, I've come to know you are a heavy smoker of ghanja, and the heavy smoking has resulted in what we in the legal profession call hallucination. It is a common phenomenon among users and I have here on my shelves volumes of case law, from England and the Supreme Court of India, citing such phenomena."

He paused to catch his breath, then continued. "In the case of master and servant, they usually have to do with suppressed hostility of the servant for the master, and psychologists explain that this usually results in sensual fabrication in the servant's mind of his master's private life. The servant, under the influence of the drug of such smoke, comes to believe in these fabrications to the extent of actually being a witness to the occurring of any event that the servant wishes to involve his master with. Now, I know you're a good man and you're sound of mind and body. Therefore I advise you that, if you've been experiencing any such phenomena during your apprenticeship, you should forthwith cease from smoking ghanja, at least until you're well settled in Gundlupet, and thereafter use restraint when you have to indulge in such habits." He smiled benignly. I was speechless. How in the world did he find out about my spying? Is it possible that what I actually believe I saw is not what was actually happening! Your Honour looked so virtuous as he spoke to me in his gown and hood. He is such a smart man, so full of law and precedent. One cannot become Magistrate simply by being a brahmin. One has to be born with the virtue of it. Why should he be so benevolent towards me unless what he has found out in the books is true and I was indeed suffering hallucinations. I smoke so much ghanja I cannot be sure which days I am hallucinated and which days I am not. If he was seeking revenge, then why did he promote me instead of firing me! It does not follow, as I have heard lawyers say while arguing their cases. Your Honour is well founded and compassionate. If the fat books of law say it is hallucination, who am I to question their credibility! Ignorance of law is no excuse, even if the law is in English.

In gratitude, I prostrated to my full length and touched the shoes of Your Honour. I went to tell the good news to the Lady Magistrate. She was happy for me. She said I'd do well in Gundlupet. Then she paused for a second and asked, "Tell me, Jamal, when I was away, did you hear of any function in the Travellers' Bungalow?" I shivered but I used my presence of mind and said I had not. She looked at me strangely, as women do when you cannot figure what they are thinking.

The next day, on the Magistrate's right temple there was a mark which was green in the beginning but turned into all kinds of colours and eventually shot out like a horn. It only increased his reputation. The clerks in the court were saying the Magistrate had hit his head on the corner of his bookshelf late in the night as he reached for a hefty book. But the horn looked more like someone had put it there. I did not want to think too much on it and fall into one of these hallucinations.

My transfer orders came. Before the day of my departure, I could not resist having one more ghanja party with my friends. Bayamma insisted on this one. It was a good party. Since I was leaving and since I had asked Bayamma to put me to bed for the night, I was not afraid of any hallucination. Sabu and Puttasamy were in a jovial mood. During our celebrations, Sabu remarked that he was mistaken about the Bungalow party. Actually there were some guests from Bangalore and Joseph was cooking for them. These guests were friends of the Magistrate and the A.S.P., and they had gone there to greet them. They left soon afterwards for a spot inspection in the constabulary jeep. I did not know what to believe.

Next morning, I went to the back door of the house to pay my respects to the Lady Magistrate. She stood beside the kitchen door as though she didn't want to be seen fully. She gave me the umbrella of Your Honour as a parting gift. It had three of its spokes broken but it was still such a precious gift. Your Honour was sleeping. Why should a magistrate get up to bid good-bye to a constable! I picked up my belongings and walked to the bus stand.

The bus to Gundlupet departed in the evening instead of the afternoon since it had developed punctures in all the rear wheels and the conductor had to wait for another bus to arrive for the jack. As the bus left the town, I could not help a feeling of sad warmth. In the yellow light the houses of the town looked like they were in a fairy tale. We passed by the market, the police station and the Magistrate's house. The wicket-gate looked desolate without my standing on guard. I imagined how I must have appeared to a passer-by or a passenger in a bus. The last building we passed by was the Travellers' Bungalow, which at this time of the evening was empty except for two cows that sat on the patio munching. Joseph must have gone to the market. There were some boys on the gul mohr tree, and the branches were shaking with their exuberance; the ground under was covered with red flowers of gul. Everything about Nanjangud looked harmonious and pleasant. Even the dust the bus churned up gave the road a hazy dignity.

I fell into a delirious nap helped by the trundling rhythm of the bus and the monotony of villagers' chatter. Some hours must have passed. I was suddenly woken by a pothole over which the bus bumped. What I saw in the front seat jolted my heart around its cavity. The unknown woman I had seen that night in the Bungalow was sitting there with another lady! The woman was as beautiful as ever and her expensive silver bangles jangled as well when she moved her arms. I could smell the familiar fragrance of Hazeline Snow. They must have got in the bus somewhere on the way. Where were they going? Where do they come from? Are they real? Questions floated past my mind in a torrent. The man next to me jabbed me in the side and winked meaningfully. He had bad teeth but what was left of them was seeped in betel juice. The unknown woman was not bothered but seemed amused by his gesture.

In Gundlupet also there is a Travellers' Bungalow. Once in a while, as I pass by it on my duty, I see women there who resemble the unknown woman in their beauty and dress. I give them the benefit of the doubt. My father used to say, "A shut mouth not only will not speak but it will make your face memorable where it matters." When I want to smoke ghanja, I go to the cycle-shop Gowda who has a shack at the back. We smoke there in peace and free of provocation and afterwards I sleep there for the night. My superior officer is a sub-inspector and a non-brahmin. He respects my experience and relies on my legal knowledge on many matters. It is not a bad life. People of Gundlupet are slowly getting to know me. The bus-stand-hotel manager invites me to eat anything I want. Nanjangud is a fading memory, a past foothold to the present rung on my ladder. I hear other constables gossip that it will not be long before I am promoted to fill the shoes of my erstwhile father Jamal the Elder, the Daffedar of Daffedars.

Suggestions for Discussion

1. Jamal begins with a description of his splendid father. How important to Jamal's character is the contrast between his father as Daffedar and himself as constable?

2. In the paragraph on page 117 beginning, "I really do not mind my morning duty," show how Jamal's thoughts are at odds with his actions.

3. On page 120, quoting his father, Jamal himself points out a conflict between his "public" and "private" selves. In how many different ways does this conflict manifest itself in the story?

4. Since Jamal narrates his own story, his friends Sabu and Puttasamy can be presented only externally, mainly through speech and action. How much do you nevertheless know about their inner lives — attitudes, interests, desires?

5. On page 122, Jamal describes the woman in the blue silk sari with respect and awe. Do we share his judgment? How do details of her appearance betray her real character?

6. Contrast the dialogue of the Magistrate with Jamal's narrative. How does each reveal character? How do the Magistrate's actions belie his words?

7. Why, at the end of the story, does Jamal seem headed for such success? What do we know about his motives that the other constables don't know?

The Only Way to Make It in New York

ROSELLEN BROWN

She had caught him going through her jewelry. She stood on the threshold in her slick raincoat, balancing on her toes, looking casual, almost, as though she were coming in to tell him, "Dinner is served." It was faintly amusing — he would pick up a necklace, hold it toward the ceiling light critically, then fling it down. She was embarrassed, it was like being in an accident and worrying in the ambulance about your dirty underwear. There was so little there, only a ring or two of sentimental value, if that. (Grandma gave her a sapphire at graduation, but Grandma was a shrew in Palm Beach who had chewed her mouth away — or so it had always looked — and had sharpened her voice till it was a pointed stick to skewer the world with. When she'd been eighteen and stayed out late, Grandma had taken to calling her "Chippie," so what was her ring supposed to be worth?) Oh — Martin's watch with the good expanding band. Into his lumpy pocket it went. Her good pearls were hanging out like a dirty hanky.

She was waiting to be frightened. But she wouldn't be. He had no gun that she could see. He was not the man she was expecting, anyway, so she was not about to be intimidated. In fact he was pathetic by comparison. That was funny enough to make her smile and she was sure he would turn around at that; the mock-bitter movement of her lips had sent a million hairline cracks through the air as though it were ice.

She'd been sure, after the first robbery, that it was Tony Aguilar's brother-in-law. Together he and Tony had been building closets and a room divider between the front bedroom and Wendy's little L. The lousy apartment with its painted-over marble fireplaces (styles change but then, dammit, they change back again and you're left with a gallon of paint stripper. She tended to think of it as a fifty-buck-a-month place. Too bad the landlord didn't). Tony was a wide, brown, rough, sweet man with miles of kinky hair, raised around the corner and making good, good enough, with his carpentry. He was a daddy, and respected. His wife's brother was a junkie. Willie came to work and took off his shirt first thing, showing muscles that made her stomach sink. It was a disgusting reaction, adolescent, but she couldn't help it. He had a clean face, sharply cut, Aztec, with a distant vulnerability in the eyes which could only have been the drugs. Something about him was like cream, maple cream, incredibly inviting to touch, where it dipped and flowed over his shoulder blades as he hammered boards inexpertly. She got out fast, later to work each day: she saw his back all the way to the subway. She'd have thought a junkie would look unhealthy. Martin, seamy and mustard-yellow under his tee shirt, looked unhealthy.

Well, the junkie didn't look good when he came around at dinnertime, worse at two in the morning, banging angrily as though they ought to have been expecting him. Money, money, just an advance against more nailing, more sawing so they would have closets for their nice nice clothes. Lady listen. My grandmother, I need it. Near tears, those eyes racing all around ready for escape, his knuckles white, fingertips biting palms cruelly. Martin had asked why Tony couldn't help, or his sister. There was a muttered reply. From where she lay, Martin looked like the heavy. He breathed hard in his maroon robe, laboring at saying no, making it a whole moral business, who cared, who wanted speeches, explanations, truth? Martin was always giving quarters to beggars on the street after he'd extracted the name of the wine they were going to spend it on. A quarter was cheap for that song and dance. He came back to bed shaking his head.

"Don't you think he wanted a fix?" She had lit a cigarette and pushed the smoke out with the force of her irritation.

"Well, I wasn't going to let him have it."

"What will he do?"

"Do you really want to concern yourself with that? What do you care what a dope addict does? He must have friends in some alley somewhere. Let him get his assistance elsewhere."

He took off his robe and sat on the edge of the bed, looking perplexed, his pale flesh gathering in dewlaps around his middle. They were so deep there was true shadow under them, she thought idly. Can you hold a pencil under your breasts? Under your flaps of fat, my dear, can you hold a candle.

Tony's brother came back the next two nights, banging and threatening, but apologetic when they opened the door, as though passion had unmanned him, then let him go. He was a small animal, a ferret, in the mouth of a predator, and one of these days it wasn't going to spit him out alive. Then he stopped coming. But at the end of the week they let themselves in after a party and found all their electrical appliances gone. Wendy had been staying with a friend that night or she'd have been home alone; this was her first season baby-sitting herself.

She had walked around picking things up and dropping them. She felt strangely like a mother cat — no, what animal was it? A mouse? — that loses interest in its babies once they've been handled by someone else. Her underwear, Martin's, lying in a twisted heap, was dishonored, as if by a voyeur. Books lay in a blasted mountain where they'd been tipped off the mantel. Her one poor fur was gone, an antique muskrat that would get the thief a dollar on a good day. The silver was still there — she opened and closed the drawer with astonishing indifference; none of the details mattered much. All the cupboard doors were open in the kitchen and there was one mug, soiled at the lip, in the middle of the floor, a root-beer bottle tipped over beside it. She picked it up gingerly as if by the tail and dropped it in the wastebasket. The mail drawer was rifled, letters perhaps read. She felt incredibly dirty, but that was all. It came as a shock to realize that she cared not one little bit about what had been taken.

The question then was, reporting to the police, should they implicate Aguilar's wife's brother? Willie — whatever his name was. He could have made a key so easily, both of them out all day, Wendy in school. How much trust it took to get through a single day in the world. . . . But she felt queasy about that, on what she called "moral grounds." Martin, angry, dismissed morality.

"Your grandiloquence could find a better cause. I don't want to get sued for false arrest. Accusation. Whatever the hell it is."

"Oh, he'd never *sue* you."

"Who knows what he'd do, a desperate man?" Martin had been going around making an inventory of their losses for his tax return. He seemed mildly elated by the coincidence that would bring them next year's models of solid-state this and automatic-refraction-tuning that, with a tax write-off at current resale values.

"The hundred dollars deductible is deplorable," he was saying — he said it three times — while she picked up a pair of pantyhose that was twined around the bodice of a slip, saw a greasy fingerprint on the daisy embroidery, and dropped it again.

"Who are you?" was all she could think to say now, stupid as it sounded. He was compact, dark, dirty, and concentrating hard on the pathetic cache of jewelry like a competent workman puzzling over shoddy goods.

She was still in the doorway. She could run, she had calculated, if he turned on her. But she didn't think he would.

He looked at her levelly.

"Who are you?"

"Why do you want to know my name? I just took a couple of your rings, that's all you got to know, right?"

He was wearing a red-checked shirt too heavy for late spring, and he was sweating. "You got a lot of junk, you know?"

She smiled her coolest smile. "Am I supposed to apologize?"

"Do what you want." He was deciding whether to get out the same way he got in, his eyes were traveling over the walls, the moldings, the ceiling.

"Take it easy," she said, almost maternally, "I'm not calling the police. I just — I wish you'd wash your hands before you go around fingering everything." She was relieved he wasn't Willie, who would have terrified her.

He nodded gravely, then laughed. "Oh, lady. Clean your fence out there —" He gestured to the back window with his head. The curtains in Wendy's room were gusting out lazily and she could see the inky handprints on the jamb all the way to the front. The cops said they couldn't lift them off that kind of paint; he must know that.

She approached a step. "Well, I wasn't expecting you."

Who did he look like — Yogi Berra? Some baseball player, PeeWee Reese? She had rooted for the Yankees when she was little; California didn't have a single major league team of its own back then. Now she could vaguely see their faces, the swarthy ones with five-o'clock shadow explaining how they had met the ball on the 3–2 pitch. Hank Bauer with her pearls in his pocket.

He sat down on the couch gingerly; suddenly his clothes must have felt very dirty to him, she saw him hunch as though to make himself lighter. She handed him a beer.

"So — you always entertain guys who come in the back window and swipe your stuff?"

She shrugged. "Doesn't happen so often. We probably haven't been here long enough."

"You don't look so mad."

She looked at him with what she knew was an inscrutable face. She felt very good; a funny kind of power it gave you to catch someone right in the middle of a compromising act. Martin did nothing compromising. In all things he did the equivalent of undressing in the closet.

"You look like you have a family, you could have a regular job, if you wanted." His dirty hands made him look as though he was on his way home from work with a lunch box and thermos. Maybe he was. Certainly he didn't have the knife-eyed desperation of an addict.

"Lady —" He spread those hands wide. She was asking him what kind of wine he liked.

She shook her head at herself impatiently. "Well, I suppose you're what we had to have next."

He raised one eyebrow politely. How much should a caught burglar talk? A problem for Amy Vanderbilt.

She looked off. Surviving — the cost of it was going up like the price of milk. She began, patiently. "We moved here from Los Angeles because we were in the earthquake."

In it? Like being in the war? In a play? Yes, in. Among the objects tossed and plummeted. Or within range. Yes, like in the war. The Blitz. Whatever.

"San Fernando, actually. Our house — the back of it, you know — the garage and sun porch and my kitchen, I was in my kitchen — were hanging over a cliff. In about a second —" She snapped her fingers. "My daughter, she's nine? She was playing out back and she came in to get something, a glass of milk, I don't remember, and before she could go back out again there was no back yard."

He was looking at her with steady eyes, keeping quiet.

"Every other thing broke — glass and pictures and a stone vase I had? And things kept tumbling, falling downhill. I close my eyes and everything turns over like — I don't know." She laughed to disparage it. "You know those rides in the amusement park?"

"Yeah, that turn all the way over? You sit on them?"

"It's like that, I get dizzy when I close my eyes so I don't sleep any more. A little, it's getting a little better."

He blinked. "You ought to go to a doctor or something, get some pills, they'll put you out."

"Did you ever go without a lot of sleep?"

He looked up from his beer, considering the question slowly, like a taste. "During the war I did, yeah, in the foxholes. You figured you went to sleep you'd never wake up."

"That's true," she said distantly; she didn't really want to share it, it couldn't have been the same, the suddenness. He probably enlisted, went looking for trouble. She could see him in khakis, his dark hair clipped, his obedient small-dog face snapping to attention, saluting. "That's true. A soldier would . . ."

She had slipped so far, so deep in her dreaming, she had become part of the landslide forever, she held one of the timbers of the porch like someone thrown clear of a wrecked ship and she fell over and over, neat as a hoop, she must have been curled in a ball, a baby, knees up, bumping over stones and boulders, into the center where the earth was hot. Everyone was there, her neighbors were being stirred, heads bobbed out of the stew, popped up like bubbles all around, boiling, then sank back and it closed over. It was all silent, silence seemed right, it went with the suddenness; faster than sound, all of it. What was the broth made of? Molten bones and rock and blood and the earth's own spring water. Top soil, bottom soil, granite shoulders, sand and grass. A dog bone flew past and vanished. Men and women and animals and the roots of trees were thrown up embracing and fell back in slow motion; still tangled they made an opening in the soup and vanished, leaving circles in circles in circles. She skimmed across the surface — a rock skimming, once, three times, seven times, good! — feeling her scraped side, raw, and sank into darkness, and breathed one time only and her lungs were black, charred, gone. She had to scream and felt them try to inflate. But they were full of holes, burst balloons, blood balloons gone lacy and dark. Each time it ended there, like a movie. Nothing more till she started it up again. It made her infinitely weary.

"So my husband said we'd better leave. I was very upset. Coming apart, kind of." She laughed, pulling hard on the fingers of one hand with the other, tugging at herself as though she were a scarf. "You don't have earthquakes here," she said simply.

He had listened very carefully, his hands in his lap looking cut loose, nothing to do with them, company posture. His beer was finished.

"No earthquakes, no tornadoes I don't think. Hurricanes once in a while. Snowstorms . . ." It was a tone he would use on his children, if he had children: full of tact and the distance of years, of small wisdom out of which even a two-bit second-story man could fashion small assurances.

"Robberies," she said, smiling bitterly. "Muggings." Rapes.

She would not tell him how she was closed up by it, cauterized. Here and there her skin puckered with memory. She got through the day. She got through the night. Martin asked her one night, turning from her, taking his hand off her shoulder, "Where the hell are you anyway?"

So she played it out, denial, reassurance, careful kisses applied to his neck where he liked them, put in place just so, like a salve. But she was gone off by herself, going nowhere she couldn't keep an eye on everything she owned. And yet she let it go so easily, her rings, her radio . . . The earth wasn't solid. "We could all do with a little less passion," she said once, sharply, just as he was moving into her, and Martin — proud of what he called his "regularity" in bed as though it had something to do with prunes — had gone slack, furiously, and rolled her away roughly like a stone in the garden. It was like being closed tight, sewn by the heat at the center of the earth. Isn't plastic sewn up that way? Then she was plastic, flesh-colored, clean, and everything stayed either outside or inside. Martin had suggested "Getting Help." But she was not guilty and God knows there was nothing to analyze because she was not to blame. Even his damn insurance policies exempted acts of God.

She looked at her caught man coolly. He was shaking his head. Pitying her?

"Don't you believe me?"

"Sure I do. Why not? I saw all that on the news, the six-o'clock news. All them bodies, listen. You're damn lucky."

She sipped her beer. Wendy would be coming home soon. She had to get dinner. "So now you come along."

"Listen, nobody ever said I was a earthquake. You don't watch out I'm gonna be flattered." He laughed, still looking at her strangely, as though from behind something. "I mean, I crowbar your window, I take a couple things out, most of it ain't much good to me anyway —"

"You sell it? Take it to somebody?"

He picked up his empty beer can and looked under it. "You got your friendly neighborhood fence right down there, don't you know Anthony's?" The dark little store where everything lay sunk under years of dust. She had wondered what moved through those bleak aisles, since it clearly wasn't groceries. "Come on, everybody knows Anthony," he said firmly. She bought milk there, expecting it to be sour.

"You shouldn't have told me that."

"Oh lady you couldn't of been here long, like you say. No secret! Tony does a good business, the cops deal down there too so, you know — no sweat."

No, she didn't want to know. Strike it from the record.

Now, how do you get rid of a burglar nicely, she wondered, and felt like a schoolteacher. Something about her dispassionate slightly disapproving face; she felt thin-lipped, as though she were someone she'd known once and hadn't especially liked. That and her indifference at the core: Only till three, then I go home. She was very tired; breathing was hard under this damn dirty sky.

So she stood, feeling strong in her indifference. "Well, what do I do with you now? What you took was worth a lot."

"You don't look too stung."

She felt scolded. "That doesn't matter. That stuff is expensive to replace." He had probably looked in their bankbook.

He smiled. "So don't replace it."

"Is that what we have to expect from now on? Strangers walking through our house putting their dirty hands on everything?"

"Jesus, that dirt really gets you, don't it? You ought to meet my mother, you'd get along."

She stood up and paced like some woman on a soap opera, distraught on a small stage. "God, every place I turn. I feel like the apocalypse is coming, bit by bit dribbling away . . ."

"Take it easy, I ain't no earthquake, I ain't a member of the acopalypse. I live in Red Hook, I'm a little hard up, O.K.? I don't even do this regular, so relax."

She gave him a sour look. "Why don't you just go? Only give me what you've taken today. I want that back."

He looked at her, head to foot, as he stood up. "Thanks for the beer," he said quietly in an ordinary voice, a bank teller asking if she'd take singles. "Hey, try to relax a little. You'll make it better. There ain't gonna be no earthquake, you better believe it. Mayor don't allow it." He turned and walked to the front door, unhurried, leaving the footprints of his heavy work shoes on the rug. The cops couldn't get those either. He turned both locks casually, without the usual scrutiny that distracted her visitors from their good-bys. "I'll wash my hands next time." He closed the door exactly as Martin did, sturdily, with one quick push from outside to make sure the lock had clicked.

She sat down on the couch where he'd been sitting. It was so warm it was almost damp. Evisceration, she said to herself, turning the word over, thinking of chickens. Some women get their insides plucked out at around her age anyway. Same difference only cheaper, no Blue Cross. Her womb, her guts, all that dark eternally dangerous stuff stolen. Before it explodes. Dried up; out of business; kaput. Even if Willie came in that window with its curtains dancing up and out, and wanted what was left of her, right here and now before dinner, he'd jimmy her open and find her gone. The only way to make it in New York, she said to herself, and stood up wearily to get the chops out of the freezer. Spread the word.

Suggestions for Discussion

1. "The Only Way to Make It in New York" is told through the protagonist's consciousness. She is presented mainly, therefore, through thought, action, and speech. The robber is presented through his appearance, speech, and action. What can we infer about the protagonist's appearance and the robber's thoughts? How?

2. The protagonist is caught in a situation in which we would expect a reaction of fear. But the narrative suggests a series of unexpected emotions: *looking casual,*

faintly amusing, waiting to be frightened, not about to be intimidated, mock-bitter. How are these emotions finally explained?

3. After two paragraphs, the story leaves its present conflict for a long flashback in which Willie and Martin are characterized. How does the contrast between them help to characterize each?

4. Do you accept the protagonist's judgment of Martin? Why?

5. Examine the dialogue between the woman and the robber. How do speech pattern and word choice characterize and contrast them in terms of gender, class, and emotion?

6. In the paragraphs on page 131 beginning, "So my husband said we'd better leave," and in the following three paragraphs, action and appearance counterpoint the dialogue. What is revealed by each?

7. Throughout the story, how is the protagonist's mental state at odds with her external action, including speech? How does each element of character presentation reveal the others?

8. What is the resolution? What is the only way to make it in New York?

RETROSPECT

1. Consider how thought is at odds with appearance and speech and/or action in the protagonist of "Not Your Singing, Dancing Spade." In Trexler of "The Second Tree from the Corner." In Bobby, his mother, and his father in "Cutting Edge."

2. In "Everything That Rises Must Converge," Julian and his mother are sometimes unwilling, sometimes unable to say exactly what they mean. How do these limitations help the dialogue do more than one thing at a time?

WRITING ASSIGNMENTS

1. Write a character sketch employing the four elements of direct presentation: appearance, action, speech, and thought. Use no authorial interpretation. Put one element in conflict with the other three.

2. Write a scene in which the central character does something palpably outrageous — violent, cruel, foolhardy, obscene. Let us, because we see

into her or his mind, know that the character is behaving justly, kindly, or reasonably.

3. Write a character sketch describing the character both in generalizations (authorial interpretation) and in specific details. Let the details contradict the generalizations. ("Larry was the friendliest kid on the block. He had a collection of brass knucks he would let you see for fifty cents, and he would let you cock his BB gun for him as long as you were willing to hold the target.")

4. Write a scene in which one character questions a second about a third. Characterize all three.

5. Place two characters in conflict. One expresses himself or herself sincerely and well in words. The other character is unable or unwilling to do so but betrays his or her feelings through appearance and actions.

6. Nearly every writer under pressure of a deadline at some point succumbs to the temptation of writing a story about writing a story. These stories are rarely successful, because they offer so few possibilities of external conflict and lively characterization. (The stories in this book by Gabriel Josipovici and John Barth are notable exceptions.) So write this story: You must write a short story, and you must therefore get your major character to do whatever he or she is to do in the story. But the character is too lazy, irritable, sick, suicidal, cruel, stupid, frivolous, or having too good a time. You must trick, cajole, or force the character into the story. Do you succeed?

5

CLIMATE CONTROL
Atmosphere

Narrative Place: Setting
Narrative Time: Scene and Summary

Your fiction must have an atmosphere because without it your characters
will be unable to breathe.

Like many of the terms that relate to the elements of fiction, *atmosphere*
has more than one meaning, sometimes referring to subject matter, sometimes to technique. Part of the atmosphere of a scene or story is its setting,
which includes the locale, period, weather, and time of day. Part of the
atmosphere is its *tone*, an attitude taken by the narrative voice that can
be described, not in terms of time and place, but as a quality — sinister,
facetious, formal, solemn, wry, and so on. There is difficulty in discussing
a term that has both a content meaning and a technical meaning: the two
meanings need to be kept distinct for the sake of clarity; yet at the same
time they are often inextricably mixed in the ultimate effect. A sinister
atmosphere in a story might be partly achieved by syntax, rhythm, and
word choice; partly by night, dampness and a desolated landscape. We'll
encounter the same difficulty discussing *point of view*, where complex literary
techniques also include and make use of the mundane meaning of the phrase
as "opinion." This chapter deals primarlily with atmosphere as setting, the

fictional boundaries in space and time, though it will not be possible to deal with those elements without reference to tone. Since tone, however, implies an attitude, not only toward the setting, but also toward the characters and the reader, it will be more fully discussed in Chapter 7 on point of view, under the heading "At What Distance?"

Narrative Place: Setting

HARMONY AND CONFLICT
BETWEEN CHARACTER AND BACKGROUND

If character is the foreground of fiction, setting is the background, and as in a painting's composition, the foreground may be in harmony or in conflict with the background. If we think of the impressionist paintings of the late nineteenth century, we think of the harmony of, say, women with light-scattering parasols strolling against summer landscape of light-scattering trees. By contrast, the Spanish painter José Cortijo has a portrait of a girl on her communion day; she sits curled and ruffled, in a lace mantilla, on an ornately carved Mediterranean throne — against a backdrop of stark, harshly lit, poverty-stricken shacks. It will be clear from this illustration that where there is a conflict between background and foreground, between character and setting, there is already "narrative content," or the makings of a story.

But whether there is conflict between character and setting or the conflict takes place entirely in the foreground, within, between, or among the characters, the setting is important to our understanding of type and of what to expect as well as to the emotional value that arises from the conflict. As we need to know a character's gender, race, and age, we need to know in what atmosphere she or he operates to understand the significance of the action.

The world and its creatures are essentially materialistic — composed of *matter* and in constant relation to matter. Our relation to place, time, and weather, like our relation to clothes and other objects, is charged with emotion more or less subtle, more or less profound. It is filled with judgment mellow or harsh. And it alters according to what happens to us. In some rooms you are always trapped; you enter them with grim purpose and escape them as soon as you can. Others invite you to settle in, to nestle or carouse. Some landscapes lift your spirits, others depress you. Cold weather gives you energy and bounce, or else it clogs your head and makes you huddle, struggling. You describe yourself as a "night person" or a "morning person."

The house you loved as a child now makes you, precisely because you were once happy there, think of loss and death.

All such emotion can be used or heightened (or invented) to dramatic effect in fiction. Just as significant detail calls up a sense impression and also an abstraction, so the setting of a story imparts both information and emotion. Likewise, just as the rhythm of your prose may be more or less important but must work with and not against your intention, so the use of setting may be more or less vital, but it must work with and not against your ultimate meaning. In the Cortijo painting previously described, the communicant in the foreground is in disharmony with the houses in the background; but the contrast is part of the harmony of the composition as a whole: it is the point of the painting.

As I write, part of me is impatient with these speculations. Dully aware that every discussion of the elements of fiction includes of necessity the notions of atmosphere, setting, and tone, I have an impulse to deal with the matter summarily and get on to the next chapter: events occur in the time and through time, people move in space and through space. Therefore, let your story occur some time and some place and take some attitude or other.

But part of me is aware of a dull March day outside my window, a stubbled field of muddy snow, the students' heels sucked by the thawing path, the rubble of winter without any sign that the contract for spring is in the mail. The river is frozen to the bridge and breaking up fitfully below; ice fidgets at the bank. This morning, stretching too far in a series of sit-ups, I pulled my back out of joint, and now my movements are confined; my spine reaches cautiously for the back of the chair, and my hand moves gingerly toward my tea. The dullness in myself looks for dullness in the day, finds it, and creates it there.

And so, observing this, part of me is impelled toward awe at the boundaries of time and space, imposed on human beings and on their fictions and yet always pulling them toward a wider context. *Why* must a story be set during some time and in some place, and why does the choice inevitably matter? Psychologists have determined that one of the earliest processes of a child's mental development is the differentiation between self and other. Until the infant discovers that its mother is not itself, it has no sense of self as we know it. Yet even before this discovery it has instinctive reactions to the elements, to warmth, cold, damp. As the mind develops it becomes aware of its environment, both social and physical, and hard on the heels of this awareness comes the attempt to control and manipulate: crying for mama, grasping the bars of the crib.

Biologists point out that the cells of our blood and bodies change according to the season, like the sap of trees, so that "spring fever" is a physical fact. The blood will thin and thicken in response to climate on the zones of the globe. The pupils of our eyes expand at night, contract by day. The new science of bioecology posits the theory that people adapt over generations to their habitat and that what we call nervous, mental, and emotional disorders may in fact be allergies of the blood and brain to food grown in alien soil.

Some linguists posit the theory that language itself originates in prepositions — that is, that spatial relationships are the primary function of the mind, and our perceptions of *above, below, toward, beyond,* and so on precede any other element in the structure of logical expression.

SYMBOLIC AND SUGGESTIVE SETTING

Whether or not these linguists are right, it is certainly so that since the rosy-fingered dawn came over the battlefield of Homer's *Iliad* (and no doubt well before that), poets and writers have used the context of history, night, storm, stars, sea, city, and plain to give their stories a sense of reaching out toward the universe, often of an answering resonance. In his plays Shakespeare consistently drew parallels between the conflicts of the heavenly bodies and the conflicts of nations and characters. Whether or not an author deliberately uses this correspondence to suggest the influence of the macrocosm on the microcosm, a story's setting can give the significant sense of other without which, as in an infant's consciousness, there is no valid sense of self.

In "The Life You Save May Be Your Own," Flannery O'Connor uses the elements in a conscious Shakespearian way, letting the setting reflect and effect the theme.

> The old woman and her daughter were sitting on their own porch when Mr. Shiflet came up their road for the first time. The old woman slid to the edge of her chair and leaned forward, shading her eyes from the piercing sunset with her hand. The daughter could not see far in front of her and continued to play with her fingers. Although the old woman lived in this desolate spot with only her daughter, and she had never seen Mr. Shiflet before, she could tell, even from a distance, that he was a tramp and no one to be afraid of. His left coat sleeve was folded up to show there was only half an arm in it and his gaunt figure listed lightly to the side as if the breeze were pushing him. He had on a black town suit and a brown felt hat that was turned up in the front and down in the back and he carried a tin tool box by a handle. He came on at an amble, up her road, his face turned toward the sun which appeared to be balancing itself on the peak of a small mountain.

The focus in this opening paragraph of the story is on the characters and their actions, and the setting is economically, almost incidentally established: *porch, road, sunset, breeze, peak, small mountain*. What the passage gives us is a "type" of landscape, rural and harsh; the only adjectives in the description of the setting are "piercing," "desolate," and "small." But this general background works together with details of action, thought, and appearance to establish a great deal more that is both informational and emotional. The old woman's peering suggests that people on the road are not only unusual but suspicious. On the other hand, that she is reassured to see a tramp suggests both a period and a set of assumptions about country life. That Mr. Shiflet wears a "town suit" establishes him as a stranger to this set of assumptions. That the sun "appeared to be balancing itself" (we are not sure whether is the old woman's observation or the author's) leaves us, at the end of the paragraph, with a sense of anticipation, tension.

Now, what happens in the story is this: Mr. Shiflet repairs the old woman's car and (in order to get the car) marries her retarded daughter. He abandons the daughter on their "honeymoon" and picks up a hitchhiker who insults both Mr. Shiflet and the memory of his mother. The hitchhiker jumps out. Mr. Shiflet curses and drives on.

Throughout the story, as in the first paragraph, the focus remains on the characters and their actions. Yet the landscape and the weather make their presence felt, subtly commenting on attitudes and actions. As Mr. Shiflet's fortunes wax promising, and he expresses satisfaction with his own morality, "A fat yellow moon appeared in the branches of the fig tree as if it were going to roost there with the chickens." When, hatching his plot, he sits on the steps with the mother and daughter, "The old woman's three mountains were black against the sky." Once he has abandoned the girl, the weather grows "hot and sultry, and the country had flattened out. Deep in the sky a storm was preparing very slowly and without thunder." Once more there is a sunset, but this time the sun "was a reddening ball that through his windshield was slightly flat on the bottom and top," and this deflated sun reminds us of the "balanced" one about to be punctured by the peak in its inevitable decline. When the hitchhiker has left him, a cloud covers the sun, and Mr. Shiflet in his fury prays for the Lord to "Break forth and wash the slime from this earth!" His prayer is apparently answered.

After a few minutes there was a guffawing peal of thunder from behind and fantastic raindrops, like tin-can tops, crashed over the rear of Mr. Shiflet's car. Very quickly he stepped on the gas and with his stump sticking out the window he raced the galloping shower to Mobile.

The setting in this story, as this bald summary emphasizes, is deliberately used as a comment on the actions. The behavior of the elements, in ironic juxtaposition to the title, "The Life You Save May Be Your Own," makes clear that the "slime" Mr. Shiflet has damned may be himself. Yet the reader is never aware of this as a symbolic intrusion. The setting remains natural and realistically convincing, as incidental backdrop, until the heavens are ready to make their guffawing comment.

Robert Coover's settings rarely present a symbolic or sentient universe, but they produce in us an emotionally charged expectation of what is likely to happen here. The following passages are the opening paragraphs of three short stories from a single collection, *Pricksongs and Descants*. Notice how the three different settings are achieved, not only by imagery and content, but by the very different rhythms of the sentence structure.

A pine forest in the midafternoon. Two children follow an old man, dropping breadcrumbs, singing nursery tunes. Dense earthy greens seep into the darkening distance, flecked and streaked with filtered sunlight. Spots of red, violet, pale blue, gold, burnt orange. The girl carries a basket for gathering flowers. The boy is occupied with the crumbs. Their song tells of God's care for little ones.

The Gingerbread House

Situation: television panel game, live audience. Stage strobelit and cameras insecting about. Moderator, bag shape corseted and black suited behind desk/rostrum, blinking mockmodesty at lens and lamps, practised pucker on his soft mouth and brows arched in mild goodguy astonishment. Opposite him, the panel: Aged Clown, Lovely Lady and Mr. America, fat as the continent and bald as an eagle. There is an empty chair between Lady and Mr. A, which is now filled, to the delighted squeals of all, by a spectator dragged protesting from the Audience, nondescript introduced as Unwilling Participant, or more simply, Bad Sport. Audience: same as ever, docile, responsive, good-natured, terrifying. And the Bad Sport, you ask, who is he? fool! thou art!

Panel Game

She arrives at 7:40, ten minutes late, but the children, Jimmy and Bitsy, are still eating supper, and their parents are not ready to go yet. From the other rooms come the sounds of a baby screaming, water running, a television musical (no words: probably a dance number — patterns of gliding figures come to mind). Mrs. Tucker sweeps into the kitchen, fussing with her hair, and snatches a baby bottle full of milk out of a pan of warm water, rushes out again. "Harry!" she calls. "The babysitter's here already!"

The Babysitter

Here are three quite familiar places: a fairy-tale forest, a television studio, and a suburban house. In at least the first two selections, the locale is more consciously and insistently set than in the O'Connor opening, yet all three remain suggestive backdrops rather than active participants. Coover directs our attitude toward these places through imagery and tone. The forest is a neverland, and the time is "once upon a time," though there are grimmer than Grimm hints of violence about it. The TV studio is a place of hysteria, chaos, and hypocrisy, whereas the American suburbia where presumably such TV shows are received is boring rather than chaotic, not hysterical but merely hassled in a predictable sort of way.

In "The Gingerbread House," simple sentence structure helps establish the childlike quality appropriate to a fairy tale. But a more complex sentence intervenes, with surprising intensity of imagery: *dense, earthy, seep, darkening, flecked, streaked, filtered*. Because of this, the innocence of the tone is set askew, so that by the time we hear of "God's care for little ones," we fully and accurately expect a brutal disillusionment.

Note that although all fiction is bounded by place and time, the "place" and "time" may perfectly well be "no place" and "outside time." The failure to create an atmosphere, to bore or confuse us because we have no sense of where or when the story takes place, is always a fault. But an intensely created fantasy world makes new boundaries for the mind. *Once upon a time, long ago and far away, a dream, hell, heaven, time warp, black hole,* and mankind's *subconscious* all have been the settings of excellent fiction. "Outer space" is an exciting setting precisely because its physical boundary is the outer edge of our familiar world. Obviously this does not absolve the writer from the necessity of giving "outer space" its own characteristics, atmosphere, and logic. If anything, these must be more intensely realized within the fiction, since we have less to borrow from in our own experience.

Setting can often, and in a variety of ways, arouse reader expectation and foreshadow events to come. In "The Gingerbread House," there is an implied conflict between character and setting, between the sentimentality of the children's flowers and nursery tunes and the threatening forest, so that we are immediately aware of the central conflict of the story: innocence versus violence.

But anticipation can also be aroused by an insistent single attitude toward setting, and in this case the reader, being a contrary sort of person, is likely to anticipate a change or paradox. The opening pages of E. M. Forster's *A Passage to India*, for instance, create an unrelenting portrait of the muddy dreariness of Chadrapore: *nothing extraordinary, rubbish, mean, ineffective, alleys, filth, made of mud, mud moving, abased, monotonous, rotting, swelling, shrinking, low but indestructible form of life*. The images are a little too one-sided, and as we might protest in life against a too fanatical condemnation of a place — isn't there anything good about it? — so we are led to expect (accurately again) that in the pages that follow, somehow beauty and mystery will break forth from the dross. Likewise — but in the opposite way — the opening pages of Woolf's *Mrs. Dalloway* burst with affirmation, the beauty of London and spring, love of life and love of life and love of life again! We suspect (accurately once more) that death and hatred lurk.

Where conflict between character and setting is immediately introduced, as it is in both "The Gingerbread House" and in "Panel Game," it is usually because the character is unfamiliar with, or uncomfortable in, the setting.

In "Panel Game" it's both. The TV studio, which is in fact a familiar and unthreatening place to most of us, has been made mad. Partly, this is achieved by violating expected grammar. The sentences are not sentences. They are missing vital verbs and logical connectives, so that the images are squashed against each other. The prose is cluttered, effortful, negative; as a result, as reader you know the "delighted squeals of all" do not include your own, and you're ready to sympathize with the unwilling central character (you!).

ALIEN AND FAMILIAR SETTING

Many poets and novelists have observed that the function of literature is to make the ordinary fresh and strange. F. Scott Fitzgerald, on the other hand, advised a young writer that reporting extreme things as if they were ordinary was the starting point of fiction. Both of these views are true, and they are particularly true of setting. Whether a place is familiar or unfamiliar, comfortable or discomfiting in fiction has nothing to do with whether the reader actually knows the place and feels good there. It is an attitude taken, an assumption made. In his detective novels, Ross MacDonald assumes a familiarity toward California that is perfectly translatable into Japanese ("I turned left off the highway and down an old switchback blacktop to a dead end"), whereas even the natives of North Hollywood must feel alien on Tom Wolfe's version of their streets:

> endless scorched boulevards lined with one-story stores, shops, bowling alleys, skating rinks, taco drive-ins, all of them shaped not like rectangles but like trapezoids, from the way the roofs slant up from the back and the plate-glass fronts slant out as if they're going to pitch forward on the sidewalk and throw up.
>
> *The Kandy-Kolored Tangerine-Flake Streamline Baby*

The prose of Tom Wolfe, whether about rural North Carolina, Fifth Avenue, or Cape Kennedy, lives in a tone of constant astonishment. Ray Bradbury's outer space is pure down-home:

> It was quiet in the deep morning of Mars, as quiet as a cool black well, with stars shining in the canal waters, and, breathing in every room, the children curled with their spiders in closed hands.
>
> *Martian Chronicles*

The setting of the passage from Coover's "The Babysitter" is ordinary and is presented as ordinary. The sentences have standard and rather leisurely syntax; neither form nor image startles. In fact, there are few details of the sort that produce interesting individuality: the house is presented without a style; the children are named but not seen; Mrs. Tucker behaves in a way predictable and familiar to anyone in late-twentieth-century America. What Coover has in fact done is to present us with a setting so usual that (in the contrary way of readers) we begin to suspect that something unusual is afoot.

I have said of characterization that if the character is presented as typical we would judge that character to be stupid or evil. The same is true of setting, but with results more varied and fruitful for an author's ultimate purpose. At the center of a fiction is a consciousness, one as indivudual and vital as the author can produce. If the setting remains dull and damnable, then there is conflict between character and setting, and this conflict can throw that individuality and vitality into relief. Many great stories and novels have relied on setting as a means of showing the intensity and variety of human consciousness by contrasting consciousness with a social or physical world that is rule-hampered, insincere, and routine. Gustave Flaubert's *Madame Bovary* comes instantly to mind: the fullness and exactitude of the portrait is partly achieved by the provinciality of the background. This provinciality, which is French and nineteenth century, remains typical to American readers of the 1980s, who are much more likely to have grown up in Coover's suburban house. It is Flaubert's tone that creates a sense of the familiar and the typical.

Much the same thing happens in "The Babysitter." The Tuckers, their house, their children, their car, their night out, and their babysitter remain unvaryingly typical through all the external actions in the course of the evening. Against this backdrop the individual fantasies of the characters play — brilliant, brutal, sexual, dangerous, and violent — which is the conflict of the story.

One great advantage of being a writer is that you may create the world. Places and the elements have the significance and the emotional effect you choose, provided that you make them do so. As a person you may be depressed by rain, but as an author you are free to make rain "mean" freshness, growth, bounty, and God. You may choose; the only thing you are not free to do is not to choose.

As with character, the first requisite of effective setting is to know it fully, to experience it mentally; the second is to create it through significant detail. What sort of place is this, and what are its peculiarities? What is the weather like, the light, the season, the time of day? What are the contours of the land and architecture? What are the social assumptions of the inhabitants, and how familiar and comfortable are the characters with this place and its life-style? These things are not less important in fiction than in life, but more, since their selection inevitably takes on significance.

AN EXERCISE IN SETTING

There follows a series of passages about war, set in various periods and places. The first is in Russia during the campaign of Napoleon, the second in Italy during World War I, the third on the island of Pianosa during World War II, the fourth during the Vietnam War, the fifth in a post-holocaust future.

Compare the settings. How do climate, period, imagery, and language contribute to each? To what degree is setting a sentient force? Is there conflict between character and setting? How does setting affect and/or reveal the attitude taken toward the war?

Several tens of thousands of the slain lay in diverse postures and various uniforms. . . . Over the whole field, previously so gaily beautiful with the glitter of bayonets and cloudlets of smoke in the morning sun, there now spread a mist of damp and smoke and a strange acid smell of saltpeter and blood. Clouds gathered and drops of rain began to fall on the dead and wounded, on the frightened, exhausted, and hesitating men, as if to say: "Enough, men! Enough! Cease . . . bethink yourselves! What are you doing?"

LEO TOLSTOY, *War and Peace*

In the late summer of that year we lived in a house in a village that looked across the river and plain to the mountains. In the bed of the river there were pebbles and boulders, dry and white in the sun, and the water was clear and swiftly moving and blue in the channels. Troops went by the house and down the road and the dust they raised powdered the leaves of the trees. The trunks of the trees too were dusty and the leaves fell early that year and we saw the troops marching along the road and the dust rising and leaves, stirred by the breeze, falling and the soldiers marching and afterward the road bare and white except for the leaves.

ERNEST HEMINGWAY, *A Farewell to Arms*

Their only hope was that it would never stop raining, and they had no hope because they all knew it would. When it did stop raining in Pianosa, it rained in Bologna. When it stopped raining in Bologna, it began again in Pianosa. If there was no rain at all, there were freakish, inexplicable phenomena like the epidemic of diarrhea or the bomb line that moved. Four times during the first six days they were assembled and briefed and then sent back. Once, they took off and were flying in formation when the control tower summoned them down. The more it rained, the worse they suffered. The worse they suffered, the more they prayed that it would continue raining.

JOSEPH HELLER, *Catch-22*

The rain fed fungus that grew in the men's boots and socks, and their socks rotted, and their feet turned white and soft so that the skin could be scraped off with a fingernail, and Stink Harris woke up screaming one night with a leech on his tongue. When it was not raining, a low mist moved across the paddies, blending the elements into a single gray element, and the war was cold and pasty and rotten. Lieutenant Corson, who came to replace Lieutenant Sidney Martin, contracted the dysentery. The trip-flares were useless. The ammunition corroded and the foxholes filled with mud and water during the nights, and in the mornings there was always the next village and the war was the same.

TIM O'BRIEN, Going After Cacciato

She liked the wild, quatrosyllabic lilt of the word, "Barbarian." Then, looking beyond the wooden fence, she saw a trace of movement in the fields beyond. It was not the wind among the young corn; or, if it was wind among the young corn, it carried her the whinny of a raucous horse. It was too early for poppies but she saw a flare of scarlet. She ceased to watch the Soldiers; instead she watched the movement flow to the fences and crash through them and across the tender wheat. Bursting from the undergrowth came horseman after horseman. . . . They flashed with curious curved plates of metal dredged up from the ruins. Their horses were bizarrely caparisoned with rags, small knives, bells and chains dangling from manes and tails, and man and horse together, unholy centaurs crudely daubed with paint, looked twice as large as life. They fired long guns. Confronted with the terrors of the night in the freshest hours of the morning, the gentle crowd scattered, wailing.

ANGELA CARTER, Heroes and Villains

Narrative Time: Scene and Summary

Literature is, by virtue of its nature and subject matter, tied to time in a way the other arts are not. A painting represents a frozen instant in time, and the "viewing time" is a matter of the viewer's choice; no external limits are imposed in order to say that you have seen the painting. Music takes a certain time to hear, and the timing of the various parts is of utmost importance, but the time scheme is self-enclosed and makes no reference to time in the world outside itself. A book takes time to read, but the reader chooses his or her rate and may put it down and take it up at will. Its vital relationship to time is content time, the period covered in the story. It is quite possible to write a story that takes about twenty minutes to read and covers about twenty minutes of action (Jean-Paul Sartre performed experiments in this "durational realism"), but no one has suggested it as a fictional requirement. Sometimes the period covered is telescoped, sometimes stretched. The history of the world up until now can be covered in a sentence; four seconds of crisis may take a chapter. It's even possible to do both at once: William Golding's entire novel *Pincher Martin* takes place between the time the drowning protagonist begins to take off his boots and the moment he dies with his boots still on. But when asked by a student, "How long does it *really* take?" Golding replied, "Eternity."

Scene and *summary* are methods of treating time in fiction. A summary covers a relatively long period of time in relatively short compass; a scene deals with a relatively short period of time at length. Summary is a useful and often necessary device: to give information, fill in a character's background, let us understand a motive, alter pace, create a transition, leap moments or years. *Scene is always necessary to fiction.* A confrontation, a turning point, or a crisis occur at given moments that take on significance *as moments* and cannot be summarized. The form of a story requires confrontation, turning points, and crises, and therefore requires scenes. It is quite possible to write a short story in a single scene, without any summary at all. It is not possible to write a successful story entirely in summary. One of the most common errors beginning fiction writers make is to summarize events rather than to realize them as moments.

In the following paragraph from Margaret Atwood's *Lady Oracle*, the narrator has been walking home from her Brownie troop with older girls who tease and terrify her with threats of a "bad man."

> The snow finally changed to slush and then to water, which trickled down the hill of the bridge in two rivulets, one on either side of the path; the path itself turned to mud. The bridge was damp, it smelled rotten, the willow branches turned yellow, the skipping ropes came out. It was light again in the afternoons, and on one of them, when for a change Elizabeth hadn't run off but was merely discussing the possibilities with the others, a real man actually appeared.
>
> He was standing at the far side of the bridge, a little off the path, holding a bunch of daffodils in front of him. He was a nice-looking man, netiher old nor young, wearing a good tweed coat, not at all shabby or disreputable. He didn't have a hat on, his taffy-colored hair was receding and the sunlight gleamed on his high forehead.

The first paragraph of this quotation covers the way things were over a period of a few months, then makes a transition to one of the afternoons; the second paragraph specifies a particular moment. Notice that although summary sets us at a distance from the action, sense details remain necessary to its life: *snow, path, bridge, willow branches, skipping ropes.* These becomes more sharply focused as we concentrate on the particular moment. More important, the scene is introduced when an element of conflict and confrontation occurs. That the threatened "bad man" does appear and that he is surprisingly innocuous promises a turn of events and a change in the relationship among the girls. We need to see the moment when this change occurs.

Throughout *Lady Oracle*, which is by no means unusual in this respect, the pattern recurs: a summary leading up to, and followed by, a scene that represents a turning point.

> My own job was fairly simple. I stood at the back of the archery range, wearing a red leather change apron, and rented out the arrows. When the barrels of arrows were almost used up, I'd go down to the straw targets . . . The difficulty was that we couldn't make sure all the arrows had actually been shot before we went down to clear the targets. Rob would shout, "Bows DOWN, please, arrows OFF the string," but occasionally someone would let an arrow go, on purpose or by accident. This was how I got shot. We'd pulled the arrows and the men were carrying the barrels back to the line; I was replacing a target face, and I'd just bent over.

The summaries in these two passages are of the two most common types, which I would call *sequential* and *circumstantial*, respectively. The summary in the first passage is sequential; it relates events in their sequence but compresses them: *snow to slush to water, willow branches turned yellow,* then *skipping ropes came out*; the transition from winter to spring is made in a paragraph. The summary in the second excerpt is circumstantial because it describes the general circumstances during a period of time: this is how things were, this is what usually or frequently happened. The narrator in the second passage describes her job in such a way: *I stood at the back of the archery range. . . . I'd go down to the straw targets. . . . Rob would shout.* Again, when the narrator arrives at an event that changes her circumstance (*I got shot*), she focuses on a particular moment: *I was replacing a target face, and I'd just bent over. . . .*

These two types of summary accurately represent two methods of the memory, which also drastically condenses. You might think of your past as a movement through time: *I was born in Arizona and lived there with my parents until I was eighteen, then I spent three years in New York before going on to England.* Or you might remember the way things were during a period of that time: *In New York we used to go down Broadway for a midnight snack, and Judy would always dare us to some nonsense or other before we got back.* But when you think of the events that significantly altered either the sequence or the circumstances of your life, your mind will present you with a scene: *Then one afternoon Professor Bovie stopped me in the hall after class and wagged his glasses at me. "Had you thought about studying in England?"*

Examining your own mind for these kinds of memory — sequential summary, circumstantial summary, and scene — will help make evident the necessity of scene in fiction. The moments that altered your life you remember at length and in detail; your memory tells you your story, and it is a great natural story teller.

Brownstone

RENATA ADLER

The camel, I had noticed, was passing, with great difficulty, through the eye of the needle. The Apollo flight, the four-minute mile, Venus in Scorpio, human records on land and at sea — these had been events of enormous importance. But the camel, practicing in near obscurity for almost two thousand years, was passing through. First the velvety nose, then the rest. Not many were aware. But if the lead camel and then perhaps the entire caravan could make it, the thread, the living thread of camels, would exist, could not be lost. No one could lose the thread. The prospects of the rich would be enhanced. "Ortega tells us that the business of philosophy," the professor was telling his class of indifferent freshmen, "is to crack open metaphors which are dead."

"I shouldn't have come," the Englishman said, waving his drink and breathing so heavily at me that I could feel my bangs shift. "I have a terrible cold."

"He would probably have married her," a voice across the room said, "with the exception that he died."

"Well, I am a personality that prefers not to be annoyed."

"We should all prepare ourselves for this eventuality."

A six-year-old was passing the hors d'oeuvres. The baby, not quite steady on his feet, was hurtling about the room.

"He's following me," the six-year-old said, in despair.

"Then lock yourself in the bathroom, dear," Inez replied.

"He always waits outside the door."

"He loves you, dear."

"Well, I don't like it."

"How I envy you," the minister's wife was saying to a courteous, bearded boy, "reading *Magic Mountain* for the first time."

The homosexual across the hall from me always takes Valium and walks his beagle. I borrow Valium from him from time to time, and when he takes a holiday the dog is left with me. On our floor of this brownstone, we are friends. Our landlord, Roger Somerset, was murdered last July. He was a kind and absent-minded man and on the night when he was stabbed there was a sort of requiem for him in the heating system. There is a lot of music in this building anyway. The newlyweds on the third floor play Bartók on their stereo. The couple on the second floor play clarinet quintets; their kids play rock. The girl on the fourth floor, who has been pining for two months, plays Judy Collins' "Maid of Constant Sorrow" all day long. We have a kind of orchestra in here. The ground floor is a shop. The owner of the shop speaks of our landlord's murder still. Shaking his head, he says that he suspects "foul play." We all agree with him. We changed our locks. But "foul play" seems a weird expression for the case.

It is all weird. I am not always well. One block away (I often think of this), there was ten months ago an immense crash. Water mains broke. There were small rivers in the streets. In a great skyscraper that was being built, something had failed. The newspapers reported the next day that by some miracle only two people had been "slightly injured" by ten tons of falling steel. The steel fell from the eighteenth floor. The question that preoccupies me now is how, under the circumstances, slight injuries could occur. Perhaps the two people were grazed in passing by. Perhaps some fragments of the sidewalk ricocheted. I knew a deliverer of flowers who, at Sixty-ninth and Lexington, was hit by a flying suicide. Situations simply do not yield to the most likely structures of the mind. A "self-addressed envelope," if you are inclined to brood, raises deep questions of identity. Such an envelope, immutably itself, is always precisely where it belongs. "Self-pity" is just sadness, I think, in the pejorative. But "joking with nurses" fascinates me in the press. Whenever someone has been quite struck down, lost faculties, members of his family, he is said to have "joked with his nurses" quite a lot. What a mine of humor every nurse's life must be.

I have a job, of course. I have had several jobs. I've had our paper's gossip column since last month. It is egalitarian. I look for people who are quite obscure, and report who is breaking up with whom and where they go and what they wear. The person who invented this new form for us is on antidepressants now. He lives in Illinois. He says there are people in southern Illinois who have not yet been covered by the press. I often write about families in Queens. Last week, I went to a dinner party on Park Avenue. After 1 A.M., something called the Alive or Dead Game was being played. Someone would mention an old character from Tammany or Hollywood. "Dead," "Dead," "Dead," everyone would guess. "No, no. Alive. I saw him walking down the street just yesterday," or "Yes. Dead. I read a little obituary notice about him last year." One of the little truths people can subtly enrage or reassure each other with is who — when you have looked away a month, a year — is still around.

The St. Bernard at the pound on Ninety-second Street was named Bonnie and would have cost five dollars. The attendant held her tightly on a leash of rope. "Hello, Bonnie," I said. Bonnie growled. "I wouldn't talk to her if I was you," the attendant said. I leaned forward to pat her ear. Bonnie snarled. "I wouldn't touch her if I was you," the attendant said. I held out my hand under Bonnie's jowls. She strained against the leash, and choked and coughed. "Now cut that out, Bonnie," the attendant said. "Could I just take her for a walk around the block," I said, "before I decide?" "Are you out of your mind?" the attendant said. Aldo patted Bonnie, and we left.

Dear Tenant:

We have reason to believe that there are imposters posing as Con Ed repairmen and inspectors circulating in this area.

Do not permit any Con Ed man to enter your premises or the building, if possible.

The Precinct

The New York Chinese cabdriver lingered at every corner and at every traffic light, to read his paper. I wondered what the news was. I looked over his shoulder. The illustrations and the type were clear enough: newspaper print, pornographic fiction. I leaned back in my seat. A taxi-driver who happened to be Oriental with a sadomasochistic cast of mind was not my business. I lit a cigarette, looked at my bracelet. I caught the driver's eyes a moment in the rearview mirror. He picked up his paper. "I don't think you ought to read," I said, "while you are driving." Traffic was slow. I saw his mirrored eyes again. He stopped his reading. When we reached my address, I did not tip him. Racism and prudishness, I thought, and reading over people's shoulders.

But there are moments in this place when everything becomes a show of force. He can read what he likes at home. Tipping is still my option. Another newspaper event, in our brownstone. It was a holiday. The superintendent normally hauls the garbage down and sends the paper up, by dumbwaiter, each morning. On holidays, the garbage stays upstairs, the paper on the sidewalk. At 8 A.M., I went downstairs. A ragged man was lying across the little space that separates the inner door, which locks, from the outer door, which doesn't. I am not a news addict. I could have stepped over the sleeping man, picked up my *Times*, and gone upstairs to read it. Instead, I knocked absurdly from inside the door, and said, "Wake up. You'll have to leave now." He got up, lifted the flattened cardboard he had been sleeping on, and walked away, mumbling and reeking. It would have been kinder, certainly, to let the driver read, the wino sleep. One simply cannot bear down so hard on all these choices.

What is the point. That is what must be borne in mind. Sometimes the point is really who wants what. Sometimes the point is what is right or kind. Sometimes the point is a momentum, a fact, a quality, a voice, an intimation, a thing said or unsaid. Sometimes it's who's at fault, or what will happen if you do not move at once. The point changes and goes out. You cannot be forever watching for the point, or you lose the simplest thing: being a major character in your own life. But if you are, for any length of time, custodian of the point — in art, in court, in politics, in lives, in rooms — it turns out there are rear-guard actions everywhere. To see a thing clearly, and when your vision of it dims, or when it goes to someone else, if you have a gentle nature, keep your silence, that is lovely. Otherwise, now and then, a small foray is worthwhile. Just so that being always, complacently, thoroughly wrong does not become the safest position of them all. The point has never quite been entrusted to me.

My cousin, who was born on February 29th, became a veterinarian. Some years ago, when he was twenty-eight (seven, by our childhood birthday count), he was drafted, and sent to Malaysia. He spent most of his military service there, assigned to the zoo. He operated on one tiger, which, in the course of abdominal surgery, began to wake up and wag its tail. The anesthetist grabbed the tail, and injected more sodium pentothal. That tiger survived. But two flamingos, sent by the city of Miami to Kuala Lumpur as a token of good will, could not bear the trip or the climate and, in spite of my cousin's efforts, died. There was also a cobra — the largest anyone in Kuala Lumpur could remember having seen. An old man had brought it, in an immense sack, from somewhere in the countryside. The zoo director called my cousin at once, around dinnertime, to say that an unprecedented cobra had arrived. Something quite drastic, however, seemed wrong with its neck. My cousin, whom I have always admired — for his leap-year birthday, for his pilot's license, for his presence of mind — said that he would certainly examine the cobra in the morning but that the best thing for it after its long journey must be a good night's rest. By morning, the cobra was dead.

My cousin is well. The problem is this. Hardly anyone about whom I deeply care at all resembles anyone else I have ever met, or heard of, or read about in the literature. I know an Israeli general who, in 1967, retook the Mitla Pass but who, since his mandatory retirement from military service at fifty-five, has been trying to repopulate the Ark. He asked me, over breakfast at the Drake, whether I knew any owners of oryxes. Most of the vegetarian species he has collected have already multiplied enough, since he has found and cared for them, to be permitted to run wild. The carnivorous animals, though, must still be kept behind barbed wire — to keep them from stalking the rarer vegetarians. I know a group that studies Proust one Sunday afternoon a month, and an analyst, with that Exeter laugh (embittered mooing noises, and mirthless heaving of the shoulder blades), who has the most remarkable terrorist connections in the Middle East.

The conversation of *The Magic Mountain* and the unrequited love of six-year-olds occurred on Saturday, at brunch. "Bring someone new," Inez had said. "Not queer. Not married, maybe separated. John and I are breaking up." The invitation was not of a kind that I had heard before. Aldo, who lives with me between the times when he prefers to be alone, refused to come. He despises brunch. He detests Inez. I went, instead, with an editor who has been a distant, steady friend but who, ten years ago, when we first came to New York, had once put three condoms on the night table beside the phone. We both had strange ideas then about New York. Aldo is a gentle, orderly, soft-spoken man, slow to conclude. I try to be tidy when he is here, but I have often made his cigarettes, and once his manuscript, into the bed. Our paper's publisher is an intellectual from Baltimore. He has read Wittgenstein; he's always making unimpeachable remarks. Our music critic throws a tantrum every day, in print. Our book reviewer is looking for another job. He found that the packages in which all books are mailed could not, simply could not, be opened without doing considerable damage — through staples, tape, wire, fluttering gray stuff, recalcitrance — to the reviewer's hands. He felt it was a symptom of some kind — one of those cases where incompetence at every stage, across the board, acquired a certain independent force. Nothing to do with books, he thought, worked out at all. We also do the news. For horoscopes, there are the ladies' magazines, which tell you — earnestly — auspicious times to shave your legs. We just cannot compete.

"All babies are natural swimmers," John said, lowering his two-year-old son gently over the side of the rowboat, and smiling. The child thrashed and sank. Aldo dived in and grabbed him. The baby came up coughing, not crying, and looked with pure fear at his father. John looked with dismay at his son. "He would have come up in a minute," John said to Aldo, who was dripping and rowing. "You have to give nature a chance."

My late landlord was from Scarsdale. The Maid of Constant Sorrow is from Texas. Aldo is from St. Louis. Inez's versions vary about where she's from. I grew up in a New England mill town, where, in the early thirties, all the insured factories burned down. It has been difficult to get fire insurance in that region ever since. The owner of a hardware store, whose property adjoined an insured factory at the time, lost everything. Afterward, he walked all day along the railroad track, waiting for a train to run him down. Railroad service has never been very good up there. No trains came. His children own the town these days, for what it's worth. The two cobbled streets where black people always lived have been torn up and turned into a public park since a flood that occurred some years ago. Unprecedented rains came. Retailers had to destroy their sodden products, for fear of contamination. The black section was torn up and seeded over in the town's rezoning project. No one knows where the blacks live now. But there are Negroes in the stores and schools, and on the football team. It is assumed that the park integrated the town. Those black families must be living somewhere. It is a mystery.

At the women's college where I went, we had distinguished faculty in everything, digs at Nuoro and Mycenae. We had a quality of obsession in our studies. For professors who had quarrelled with their wives at breakfast, those years of bright-eyed young women, never getting any older, must have been a trial. The head of the history department once sneezed into his best student's honors thesis. He slammed it shut. It was ultimately published. When I was there, a girl called Cindy Melchior was immensely fat. She wore silk trousers and gilt mules. One day, in the overheated classroom, she laid aside her knitting and lumbered to the window, which she opened. Then she lumbered back. "Do you think," the professor asked, "you are so graceful?" He somehow meant it kindly. Cindy wept. That year, Cindy's brother Melvin phoned me. "I would have called you sooner," he said, "but I had the most terrrible eczema." All the service staff on campus in those days were black. Many of them were followers of Father Divine. They took new names in the church. I remember the year when a maid called Serious Heartbreak married a janitor called Universal Dictionary. At a meeting of the faculty last fall, the college president, who is new and male, spoke of raising money. A female professor of Greek was knitting — and working on Linear B, with an abacus before her. In our time, there was a vogue for madrigals. Some of us listened, constantly, to a single record. There was a phrase we could not decipher. A professor of symbolic logic, a French Canadian, had sounds that matched but a meaning that seemed unlikely: Sheep are no angels; come upstairs. A countertenor explained it, after a local concert: She'd for no angel's comfort stay. Correct, but not so likely either.

Paul: "Two diamonds."
Inez: "Two hearts."
Mary: "Three clubs."
John: "Four kings."

Inez: "Darling, you know you can't just bid four kings."

John: "I don't see why. I might have been bluffing."

Inez: "No darling. That's poker. This is bridge. And even in poker you can't just bid four kings."

John: "No. Well, I guess we'd better deal another hand."

The host, for some reason, was taking Instamatic pictures of his guests. It was not clear whether he was doing this in order to be able to show, at some future time, that there had been this gathering in his house. Or whether he thought of pictures in some voodoo sense. Or whether he found it difficult to talk. Or whether he was bored. Two underground celebrities — one of whom had become a sensation by never generating or exhibiting a flicker of interest in anything, the other of whom was known mainly for hanging around the first — were taking pictures too. I was there with an actor I've known for years. He had already been received in an enormous embrace by an Eastern European poet, whose hair was cut too short but who was neither as awkwardly spontaneous nor as drunk as he cared to seem. The party was in honor of the poet, who celebrated the occasion by insulting everyone and being fawned upon, by distinguished and undistinguished writers alike. "This group looks as though someone had torn up a few guest lists and floated the pieces on the air," the actor said. The friend of the underground sensation walked up to us and said hello. Then, in a verbal seizure of some sort, he began muttering obscenities. The actor said a few calming things that didn't work. He finally put his finger on the mutterer's lips. The mutterer bit that finger extremely hard, and walked away. The actor wrapped his finger in a paper napkin, and got himself another drink. He stayed till twelve.

When I worked, for a time, in the infirmary of a branch of an upstate university, it was becoming more difficult with each passing semester, except in the most severe cases, to determine which students had mental or medical problems. At the clinic, young men with straggly beards and stained blue-jeans wept alongside girls in jeans and frayed sweaters — all being fitted with contact lenses, over which they then wore granny glasses. There was no demand for prescription granny glasses at all. For the severely depressed, the paranoids, and the hallucinators, our young psychiatrists prescribed "mood elevators," pills that were neither uppers nor downers but which affected the bloodstream in such a way that within three to five weeks many sad outpatients became very cheerful, and several saints and historical figures became again Midwestern graduate students under tolerable stress. On one, not unusual, morning, the clinic had a call from an instructor in political science. "I am in the dean's office," he said. "My health is quite perfect. They want me to have a checkup."

"Oh?" said the doctor on duty. "Perhaps you could come in on Friday."

"The problem is," the voice on the phone said, "I have always thought myself, and been thought by others, a Negro. Now, through research, I have found that my family on both sides have always been white."

"Oh," the doctor on duty said. "Perhaps you could just take a cab and come over."

Within twenty minutes, the political-science instructor appeared at the clinic. He was black. The doctor said nothing, and began a physical examination. By the time his blood pressure was taken, the patient confided that his white ancestors were, in fact, royal. The mood elevators restored him. He and the doctor became close friends besides. A few months later, the instructor took a job with the government in Washington. Two weeks after that, he was calling the clinic again. "I have found new documentation," he said. "All eight of my great-grandparents were pure-blooded Germans — seven from Prussia, one from Alsace. I thought I should tell you, dear friend." The doctor suggested he come for the weekend. By Sunday afternoon, a higher dose of the pill had had its effect. The problem has not since recurred.

The Maid of Constant Sorrow said our landlord's murder marked a turning point in her analysis. "I don't feel guilty. I feel hated," she said. It is true, for a time, we all wanted to feel somehow part — if only because violence offset the ineluctable in our lives. My grandfather said that some people have such extreme insomnia that they look at their watches every hour after midnight, to see how sorry they ought to be feeling for themselves. Aldo says he does not care what my grandfather said. My grandmother refused to concede that any member of the family died of natural causes. An uncle's cancer in middle age occurred because all the suitcases fell off the luggage rack onto him when he was in his teens, and so forth. Death was an acquired characteristic. My grandmother, too, used to put other people's ailments into the diminutive: strokelets were what her friends had. Aldo said he was bored to tearsies by my grandmother's diminutives.

The weather last Friday was terrible. The flight to Martha's Vineyard was "decisional."

"What does 'decisional' mean?" a small boy asked. "It means we might have to land in Hyannis," his mother said. It is hard to understand how anyone learns anything.

Scattered through the two cars of the Brewster–New York train last week were adults with what seemed to be a clandestine understanding. They did not look at each other. They stared out the windows. They read. "Um," sang a lady at our fourth stop on the way to Grand Central. She appeared to be reading the paper. She kept singing her "Um," as one who is getting the pitch. A young man had already been whistling "Frère Jacques" for three stops. When the "Um" lady found her pitch and began to sing the national anthem, he looked at her with rage. The conductor passed through, punching tickets in his usual fashion, not in the aisle but directly over people's laps. Every single passenger was obliged to flick the tiny punched part of the ticket from his lap onto the floor. Conductors have this process as their own little show of force. The whistler and the singer were in a dead heat when we reached the city. The people with the clandestine understanding turned out to be inmates from somewhere upstate, now on leave with their families, who met them in New York.

I don't think much of writers in whom nothing is at risk. It is possible, though, to be too literal-minded about this question. In a magazine, under the heading "$3,000 for First-Person Articles," for example: "An article for this series must be a true, hitherto unpublished narrative of an unusual personal experience. It may be dramatic, inspirational, or humorous, but it must have, in the opinion of the editors, a quality of narrative interest comparable to 'How I Lost My Eye' (June '72) and 'Attacked by a Killer Shark' (April '72). Contributions must be typewritten, preferably *double-spaced* . . ." I particularly like where the stress, the italics, goes.

When the nanny drowned in the swimming pool, the parents reacted sensibly. They had not been there for the event. They had left the nanny at poolside with their youngest child, a girl of five, and the neighbor's twins, a boy and a girl of five, and the neighbor's baby-sitter, an *au pair*, who had become the nanny's dearest friend. When they returned from their morning round of golf, they found a fire truck in the yard, the drowned body of the nanny on the tiles, the three children playing, apparently calmly, under a tree, and two disconsolate firemen trying to deal with the neighbor's babysitter, who was hysterical. As an ambulance pulled into the driveway, the mother was already telephoning a doctor; her husband was giving the baby-sitter a glass of water and a sedative. When her hysterics had subsided, the baby-sitter explained what she could. Neither she nor the nanny, it turned out, could really swim. They could both manage a few strokes of the breaststroke, but they had a great fear of water over their heads. All three of what she called the "little ones" were strong and intrepid dogpaddlers. She and the nanny had always confined themselves to admonitions, and their own few stroking motions, from the shallow end. It was on account of these stroking motions that their inability really to swim had never come to anyone's attention or, for that matter, to their own. That morning, the nanny had, unaccountably, stroked a few feet out of her depth, in the direction of her charge. Then, according to the baby-sitter, who may have confused the sequence, things happened very rapidly, in the following order. Nanny's face turned blue. *Then* she swallowed water. Coughing and struggling, she reached her charge and clung to her. They both went under. Long seconds later, the little girl came up, crying and sputtering. In clear view, a few feet beyond the shallow end and beyond the grasp of the baby-sitter, who was trying to maintain her feet and her depth as she held out her hands, the nanny surfaced briefly once more, sank, and drowned.

I once met a polo-playing Argentine existential psychiatrist, who had lived for months in a London commune. He said that on days when the ordinary neurotics in the commune were getting on each other's nerves the few psychopaths and schizophrenics in their midst retired to their rooms and went their version of berserk, alone. On days when the neurotics got along, the psychopaths calmed down, tried to make contact, cooked. It was, he said, as though the sun came out for them. I hope that's true. Although altogether too much of life is mood. Aldo has a married friend who was in love for years with someone, also married. Her husband found out. He insisted that there be no more calls or letters. Aldo's friend called several times, reaching the husband. The girl herself would never answer. In the end, Aldo's friend — in what we regard as not his noblest gesture — sent all the girl's letters, addressed in a packet, to her husband. There was nothing more. I wonder whether the husband read those letters. If he did, I suppose he may have been a writer. In some sense. If not, he was a gentleman. There are also, on the bus, quite often ritual dancers, near-spastics who release the strap and begin a weird sequence of movements, always punctual, always the same. There are some days when everyone I see is lunatic.

I love the laconic. Clearly, I am not of their number. When animated conversations are going on, even with people interrupting one another, I have to curb an impulse to field every remark, by everybody, as though it were addressed to me. I have noticed this impulse in other people. It electrifies the room. It is resolved, sometimes, by conversations in a foreign language. One thinks, it is my turn to try to say something, to make an effort. One polishes a case, a tense, a comment. The subject passes. Just as well. There are, however, people who just sit there, silent. A question is addressed to them. They do not answer. Another question. Silence. It is a position of great power. Talkative people running toward those silences are jarred, time after time, by a straight-arm rebuff. A quizzical look, a beautiful face perhaps, but silence. Everyone is exhausted, drinks too much, snarls later at home, wonders about the need for aspirin. It has been that stubborn wall.

I receive communications almost every day from an institution called the Center for Short-Lived Phenomena. Reporting sources all over the world, and an extensive correspondence. Under the title "Type of Event: Bio-logical," I have received postcards about the progress of the Dormouse Invasion of Formentera: "Apart from population density, the dormouse of Formentera had a peak of reproduction in 1970. All females checked were pregnant, and perhaps this fact could have been the source of the idea of an 'invasion.' " And the Northwest Atlantic Puffin Decline. I have followed the Tanzanian Army Worm Outbreak. The San Fernando Earthquake. The Green Pond Fish Kill ("Eighty percent of the numbers involved," the Center's postcard reports, "were mummichogs.") The Samar Spontaneous Oil Burn. The Hawaiian Monk Seal Disappearance. And also, the Naini Tal Sudden Sky Brightening.

Those are accounts of things that did not last long, but if you become famous for a single thing in this country, and just endure, it is certain you will recur, enlarged. Of the eighteen men who were indicted for conspiracy to murder Schwerner, Goodman, and Chaney, seven were convicted by a Mississippi jury — a surprising thing. But then a year later, a man was wounded and a woman killed in a shootout while trying to bomb the house of some Mississippi Jews. It turned out that the informer, the man who had helped the bombers, and led the F.B.I. to them, was one of the convicted seven — the one, in fact, who was alleged to have killed two of the three boys who were found in that Mississippi dam. And what's more, and what's more, the convict conspirator, alleged double killer, was paid thirty-six thousand dollars by the F.B.I. for bringing the bombers in. Yet the wave of anti-Semitic bombings in Mississippi stopped after the shootout. I don't know what it means. I am in this brownstone.

Last year, Aldo moved out and went to Los Angeles on a story. I called him to ask whether I could come. He said, "Are you going to stay this time?" I said I wasn't sure. I flew out quite early in the morning. On the plane, there was the most banal, unendurable pickup, lasting the whole flight. A young man and a young woman — he was Italian, I think: she was German — had just met, and settled on French as their common language. They asked each other where they were from, and where they were going. They posed each other riddles. He took out a pencil and paper and sketched her portrait. She giggled. He asked her whether she had ever considered a career as a model. She said she had considered it, but she feared that all men in the field were after the same thing. He agreed. He began to tell off-color stories. She laughed and reproached him. It was like that. I wondered whether these things were always, to captive eavesdroppers, so dreary. When I arrived at Aldo's door, he met me with a smile that seemed surprised, a little sheepish. We talked awhile. Sometimes he took, sometimes I held, my suitcase. I tried, I thought, a joke. I asked whether there was already a girl there. He said there was. He met me in an hour at the corner drugstore for a cup of coffee. We talked. We returned to the apartment. We had Scotch. That afternoon, quite late, I flew home. I called him from time to time. He had his telephone removed a few days later. Now, for a while, he's here again. He's doing a political essay. It begins, "Some things cannot be said too often, and some can." That's all he's got so far.

We had people in for drinks one night last week. The cork in the wine bottle broke. Somebody pounded it into the bottle with a chisel and a hammer. We went to a bar. I have never understood the feeling men seem to have for bars they frequent. A single-story drunk told his single story. A fine musician who was with us played Mozart, Chopin, and Beethoven on the piano. It seemed a great, impromptu occasion. Then he said, we thought, "I am now going to play some Yatz." From what he played, it turned out he meant jazz. He played it badly.

We had driven in from another weekend in the country while it was still daylight. Lots of cars had their headlights on. We weren't sure whether it was for or against peace, or just for highway safety. Milly, a secretary in a brokerage office, was married in our ground-floor shop that evening. She cried hysterically. Her mother and several people from her home town and John, whose girl she had been before he married Inez, thought it was from sentiment or shyness, or for some conventional reason. Milly explained it to Aldo later. She and her husband had really married two years before — the week they met, in fact — in a chapel in Las Vegas. They hadn't wanted to tell their parents, or anybody, until he finished college. They had torn up their Las Vegas license. She had been crying out of some legal fear of being married twice, it turned out. Their best man, a Puerto Rican doctor, said his aunt had been mugged in a cemetery in San Juan by a man on horseback. She thought it was her husband, returned from the dead. She had required sedation. We laughed. My friend across the hall, who owns the beagle, looked very sad all evening. He said, abruptly, that he was cracking up, and no one would believe him. There were sirens in the street. Inez said she knew exactly what he meant: she was cracking up also.

Her escort, a pale Italian jeweler, said, "I too. I too have it. The most terrible anguishes, anguishes all in the night."

Inez said she knew the most wonderful man for the problem. "He may strike you at first as a phony," she said, "but then, when you're with him, you find yourself naturally screaming. It's such a relief. And he teaches you how you can practice at home." Milly said she was not much of a screamer — had never, in fact, screamed in her life. "High time you did, then," Inez said. Our sportswriter said he had recently met a girl whose problem was stealing all the suede garments of house guests, and another, in her thirties, who cried all the time because she had not been accepted at Smith. We heard many more sirens in the streets. We all went home.

At 4 A.M., the phone rang about fifty times. I did not answer it. Aldo suggested that we remove it. I took three Valium. The whole night was sirens, then silence. The phone rang again. It is still ringing. The paper goes to press tomorrow. It is possible that I know who killed our landlord. So many things point in one direction. But too strong a case, I find, is often lost. It incurs doubts, suspicions. Perhaps I do not know. Perhaps it doesn't matter. I think it does, though. When I wonder what it is that we are doing — in this brownstone, on this block, with this paper — the truth is probably that we are fighting for our lives.

Suggestions for Discussion

1. "Brownstone" relies very heavily for its effect on the atmosphere of New York. Describe this atmosphere as the story creates it. To what extent is the narrator's conflict with her surroundings the conflict of the story?

2. At the opening of the story, the atmosphere of a New York party is made strange to the point of insanity. How?

3. The narrator leaps back and forth in time so that the sequence of events is apparently random. How does this contribute to the atmosphere?

4. How is the strangeness of life in New York and, by extension, in the world, revealed by the recurrence of: Accidents? Relations between people and animals? The need for various drugs? Professional difficulties, pointlessness, or incompetence? The landlord's death?

5. Is the brownstone apartment itself, in which the narrator lives, a part of the alien atmosphere of New York, or does it function for her as a place of relative security? Or both?

6. Explain the function in the story of each of the following judgments made by the narrator: "What is the point. That is what must be borne in mind" (page 151); "We both had strange ideas then about New York" (page 153); "Although altogether too much of life is mood" (page 158); "the truth is probably that we are fighting for our lives" (page 161).

7. Nearly every section of the story contains circumstantial summary, sequential summary, and scene. Identify several of each.

8. Although "Brownstone" was originally published as a short story in *The New Yorker*, it was conceived, and eventually published, as a chapter in a novel, *Speedboat*. Can you nevertheless detect the structure of conflict, crisis, and resolution, or is the structure random and unresolved?

August 2002: Night Meeting

RAY BRADBURY

Before going on up into the blue hills, Tomás Gomez stopped for gasoline at the lonely station.

"Kind of alone out here, aren't you, Pop?" said Tomás.

The old man wiped off the windshield of the small truck. "Not bad."

"How do you like Mars, Pop?"

"Fine. Always something new. I made up my mind when I came here last year I wouldn't expect nothing, nor ask nothing, nor be surprised at nothing. We've got to forget Earth and how things were. We've got to look at what we're in here, and how *different* it is. I get a hell of a lot of fun out of just the weather here. It's *Martian* weather. Hot as hell daytimes, cold as hell nights. I get a big kick out of the different flowers and different rain. I came to Mars to retire and I wanted to retire in a place where everything is different. An old man needs to have things different. Young people don't want to talk to him, other old people bore hell out of him. So I thought the best thing for me is a place so different that all you got to do is open your eyes and you're entertained. I got this gas station. If business picks up too much, I'll move on back to some other old highway that's not so busy, where I can earn just enough to live on and still have time to feel the *different* things here."

"You got the right idea, Pop," said Tomás, his brown hands idly on the wheel. He was feeling good. He had been working in one of the new colonies for ten days straight and now he had two days off and was on his way to a party.

"I'm not surprised at anything any more," said the old man. "I'm just looking. I'm just experiencing. If you can't take Mars for what she is, you might as well go back to Earth. Everything's crazy up here, the soil, the air, the canals, the natives (I never saw any yet, but I hear they're around), the clocks. Even my clock acts funny. Even *time* is crazy up here. Sometimes I feel I'm here all by myself, no one else on the whole damn planet. I'd take bets on it. Sometimes I feel about eight years old, my body squeezed up and everything else tall. Jesus, it's just the place for an old man. Keeps me alert and keeps me happy. You know what Mars is? It's like a thing I got for Christmas seventy years ago — don't know if you ever had one — they called them kaleidoscopes, bits of crystal and cloth and beads and pretty junk. You held it up to the sunlight and looked in through at it, and it took your breath away. All the patterns! Well, that's Mars. Enjoy it. Don't ask it to be nothing else but what it is. Jesus, you know that highway right there, built by the Martians, is over sixteen centuries old and still in good condition? That's one dollar and fifty cents, thanks and good night."

Tomás drove off down the ancient highway, laughing quietly.

It was a long road going into darkness and hills and he held to the wheel, now and again reaching into his lunch bucket and taking out a piece of candy. He had been driving steadily for an hour, with no other car on the road, no light, just the road going under, the hum, the roar, and Mars out there, so quiet. Mars was always quiet, but quieter tonight than any other. The deserts and empty seas swung by him, and the mountains against the stars.

There was a smell of Time in the air tonight. He smiled and turned the fancy in his mind. There was a thought. What did Time smell like? Like dust and clocks and people. And if you wondered what Time sounded like it sounded like water running in a dark cave and voices crying and dirt dropping down upon hollow box lids, and rain. And, going further, what did Time *look* like? Time looked like snow dropping silently into a black room or it looked like a silent film in an ancient theater, one hundred billion faces falling like those New Year balloons, down and down into nothing. That was how Time smelled and looked and sounded. And tonight — Thomás shoved a hand into the wind outside the truck — tonight you could almost *touch* Time.

He drove the truck between hills of Time. His neck prickled and he sat up, watching ahead.

He pulled into a little dead Martian town, stopped the engine, and let the silence come in around him. He sat, not breathing, looking out at the white buildings in the moonlight. Uninhabited for centuries. Perfect, faultless, in ruins, yes, but perfect, nevertheless.

He started the engine and drove on another mile or more before stopping again, climbing out, carrying his lunch bucket, and walking to a little promontory where he could look back at that dusty city. He opened his thermos and poured himself a cup of coffee. A night bird flew by. He felt very good, very much at peace.

Perhaps five minutes later there was a sound. Off in the hills, where the ancient highway curved, there was a motion, a dim light, and then a murmur.

Tomás turned slowly with the coffee cup in his hand.

And out of the hills came a strange thing.

It was a machine like a jade-green insect, a praying mantis, delicately rushing through the cold air, indistinct, countless green diamonds winking over its body, and red jewels that glittered with multifaceted eyes. Its six legs fell upon the ancient highway with the sounds of a sparse rain which dwindled away, and from the back of the machine a Martian with melted gold for eyes looked down at Tomás as if he were looking into a well.

Tomás raised his hand and thought Hello! automatically but did not move his lips, for this *was* a Martian. But Tomás had swum in blue rivers on Earth, with strangers passing on the road, and eaten in strange houses with strange people, and his weapon had always been his smile. He did not carry a gun. And he did not feel the need of one now, even with the little fear that gathered about his heart at this moment.

The Martian's hands were empty too. For a moment they looked across the cool air at each other.

It was Tomás who moved first.

"Hello!" he called.

"Hello!" called the Martian in his own language.

They did not understand each other.

"Did you say hello?" they both asked.

"What did you say?" they said, each in a different tongue.

They scowled.

"Who are you?" said Tomás in English.

"What are you doing here?" In Martian; the stranger's lips moved.

"Where are you going?" they said, and looked bewildered.

"I'm Tomás Gomez."

"I'm Muhe Ca."

Neither understood, but they tapped their chests with the words and then it became clear.

And then the Martian laughed. "Wait!" Tomás felt his head touched, but no hand had touched him. "There!" said the Martian in English. "That is better!"

"You learned my language, so quick!"

"Nothing at all!"

They looked, embarrassed with a new silence, at the steaming coffee he had in one hand.

"Something different?" said the Martian, eying him and the coffee, referring to them both, perhaps.

"May I offer you a drink?" said Tomás.

"Please."

The Martian slid down from his machine.

A second cup was produced and filled, steaming. Tomás held it out.

Their hands met and — like mist — fell through each other.

"Jesus Christ!" cried Tomás, and dropped the cup.

"Name of the Gods!" said the Martian in his own tongue.

"Did you see what happened?" they both whispered.

They were very cold and terrified.

The Martian bent to touch the cup but could not touch it.

"Jesus!" said Tomás.

"Indeed." The Martian tried again and again to get hold of the cup, but could not. He stood up and thought for a moment, then took a knife from his belt. "Hey!" cried Tomás. "You misunderstand, catch!" said the Martian, and tossed it. Tomás cupped his hands. The knife fell through his flesh. It hit the ground. Tomás bent to pick it up but could not touch it, and he recoiled, shivering.

Now he looked at the Martian against the sky.

"The stars!" he said.

"The stars!" said the Martian, looking, in turn, at Tomás.

The stars were white and sharp beyond the flesh of the Martian, and they were sewn into his flesh like scintillas swallowed into the thin, phosphorescent membrane of a gelatinous sea fish. You could see stars flickering like violet eyes in the Martian's stomach and chest, and through his wrists, like jewelry.

"I can see through you!" said Tomás.

"And I through you!" said the Martian, stepping back.

Tomás felt of his own body and, feeling the warmth, was reassured. *I am real*, he thought.

The Martian touched his own nose and lips. "*I have flesh*," he said, half aloud. "*I am alive*."

Tomás stared at the stranger. "And if *I* am real, then you must be dead."

"No, you!"

"A ghost!"

"A phantom!"

They pointed at each other, with starlight burning in their limbs like daggers and icicles and fireflies, and then fell to judging their limbs again, each finding himself intact, hot, excited, stunned, awed, and the other, ah yes, that other over there, unreal, a ghostly prism flashing the accumulated light of distant worlds.

I'm drunk, thought Tomás. I won't tell anyone of this tomorrow, no, no.

They stood there on the ancient highway, neither of them moving.

"Where are you from?" asked the Martian at last.

"Earth."

"What is that?"

"There." Tomás nodded to the sky.

"When?"

"We landed over a year ago, remember?"

"No."

"And all of you were dead, all but a few. You're rare, don't you *know* that?"

"That's not true."

"Yes, dead. I saw the bodies. Black, in the rooms, in the houses, dead. Thousands of them."

"That's ridiculous. We're *alive!*"

"Mister, you're invaded, only you don't know it. You must have escaped."

"I haven't escaped; there was nothing to escape. What do you mean? I'm on my way to a festival now at the canal, near the Eniall Mountains. I was there last night. Don't you see the city there?" The Martian pointed.

Tomás looked and saw the ruins. "Why, that city's been dead thousands of years."

The Martian laughed. "Dead. I slept there yesterday!"

"And I was in it a week ago and the week before that, and I just drove through it now, and it's a heap. See the broken pillars?"

"Broken? Why, I see them perfectly. The moonlight helps. And the pillars are upright."

"There's dust in the streets," said Tomás.

"The streets are clean!"

"The canals are empty right there."

"The canals are full of lavender wine!"

"It's dead."

"It's alive!" protested the Martian, laughing more now. "Oh, you're quite wrong. See all the carnival lights? There are beautiful boats as slim as women, beautiful women as slim as boats, women the color of sand, women with fire flowers in their hands. I can see them, small, running in the streets there. That's where I'm going now, to the festival; we'll float on the waters all night long; we'll sing, we'll drink, we'll make love. Can't you *see* it?"

"Mister, that city is dead as a dried lizard. Ask any of our party. Me, I'm on my way to Green City tonight; that's the new colony we just raised over near Illinois Highway. You're mixed up. We brought in a million board feet of Oregon lumber and a couple dozen tons of good steel nails and hammered together two of the nicest little villages you ever saw. Tonight we're warming one of them. A couple rockets are coming in from Earth, bringing our wives and girl friends. There'll be barn dances and whisky —"

The Martian was now disquieted. "You say it is over *that* way?"

"There are the rockets." Tomás walked him to the edge of the hill and pointed down. "See?"

"No."

"Damn it, there they *are*! Those long silver things."

"No."

Now Tomás laughed. "You're blind!"

"I see very well. You are the one who does not see."

"But you see the new *town*, don't you?"

"I see nothing but an ocean, and water at low tide."

"Mister, that water's been evaporated for forty centuries."

"Ah, now, now, that *is* enough."

"It's true, I tell you."

The Martian grew very serious. "Tell me again. You do not see the city the way I describe it? The pillars very white, the boats very slender, the festival lights — oh, I see them *clearly*! And listen! I can hear them singing. It's no space away at all."

Tomás listened and shook his head. "No."

"And I, on the other hand," said the Martian, "cannot see what you describe. Well."

Again they were cold. An ice was in their flesh.

"Can it be . . . ?"

"What?"

"You say 'from the sky'?"

"Earth."

"Earth, a name, nothing," said the Martian. "*But* . . . as I came up the pass an hour ago. . . ." He touched the back of his neck. "I felt . . ."

"Cold?"

"Yes."

"And now?"

"Cold again. Oddly. There was a thing to the light, to the hills, the road," said the Martian. "I felt the strangeness, the road, the light, and for a moment I felt as if I were the last man alive on this world. . . ."

"So did I!" said Tomás, and it was like talking to an old and dear friend, confiding, growing warm with the topic.

The Martian closed his eyes and opened them again. "This can only mean one thing. It has to do with Time. Yes. You are a figment of the Past!"

"No, you are from the Past," said the Earth Man, having had time to think of it now.

"You are so *certain*. How can you prove who is from the Past, who from the Future? What year is it?"

"Two thousand and one!"

"What does that mean to *me*?"

Tomás considered and shrugged. "Nothing."

"It is as if I told you that it is the year 4462853 s.e.c. It is nothing and more than nothing! Where is the clock to show us how the stars stand?"

"But the ruins prove it! They prove that *I* am the Future, *I* am alive, *you* are dead!"

"Everything in me denies this. My heart beats, my stomach hungers, my mouth thirsts. No, no, not dead, not alive, either of us. More alive than anything else. Caught between is more like it. Two strangers passing in the night, that is it. Two strangers passing. Ruins, you say?"

"Yes. You're afraid?"

"Who wants to see the Future, who *ever* does? A man can face the Past, but to think — the pillars *crumbled*, you say? And the sea empty, and the canals dry, and the maidens dead, and the flowers withered?" The Martian was silent, but then he looked on ahead. "But there they *are*. I *see* them. Isn't that enough for me? They wait for me now, no matter *what* you say."

And for Tomás the rockets, far away, waiting for *him*, and the town and the women from Earth. "We can never agree," he said.

"Let us agree to disagree," said the Martian. "What does it matter who is Past or Future, if we are both alive, for what follows will follow, tomorrow or in ten thousand years. How do you know that those temples are not the temples of your own civilization one hundred centuries from now, tumbled and broken? You do not know. Then don't ask. But the night is very short. There go the festival fires in the sky, and the birds."

Tomás put out his hand. The Martian did likewise in imitation.

Their hands did not touch; they melted through each other.

"Will we meet again?"

"Who knows? Perhaps some other night."

"I'd like to go with you to that festival."

"And I wish I might come to your new town, to see this ship you speak of, to see these men, to hear all that has happened."

"Good-by," said Tomás.

"Good night."

The Martian rode his green metal vehicle quietly away into the hills. The Earth Man turned his truck and drove it silently in the opposite direction.

"Good lord, what a dream that was," sighed Tomás, his hands on the wheel, thinking of the rockets, the women, the raw whisky, the Virginia reels, the party.

How strange a vision was that, thought the Martian, rushing on, thinking of the festival, the canals, the boats, the women with golden eyes, and the songs.

The night was dark. The moons had gone down. Starlight twinkled on the empty highway where now there was not a sound, no car, no person, nothing. And it remained that way all the rest of the cool dark night.

Suggestions for Discussion

1. The gas station owner, Pop, keeps insisting on how different Mars is from Earth. We as readers are perversely struck with how much the same it is. How does Bradbury accomplish this result?

2. Why is it necessary to the story that the atmosphere of Mars should be established as familiar and comfortable before Tomás meets the Martian?

3. On page 163, Tomás speculates about the smell, sound, and look of Time. How does this prepare us for what follows?

4. The paragraph beginning, "He started the engine . . . ," on page 163, introduces a sequential summary. Where and why does this summary give way to scene?

5. Examine the Martian's dialogue. Although he has learned English at a touch, his use of it is slightly stilted and old-fashioned. How does this contribute to his characterization? To the atmosphere?

6. Though Tomás has driven off "laughing quietly" at the gas station owner, now he and the Martian are amazed at the distortion of time they discover. Are they more amazed than the reader? Why?

7. At the end of the story each rides off convinced that the other is a dream. In what way is this a resolution?

RETROSPECT

1. "Jamal the Constable" is a story written in English about India; its protagonist is familiar with a setting likely to be strange to its readers. How does G. S. Sharat Chandra convey both the familiarity and the strangeness?

2. Contrast the atmosphere of New York City as presented in "The Second Tree from the Corner," "The Only Way to Make It in New York," and "Brownstone." Where do the three atmospheres of the city coincide, and where do they diverge?

3. Reread Calisher's "In the Absence of Angels," focusing on how the story is balanced in a pattern of circumstantial summary sequential summary, and scene.

WRITING ASSIGNMENTS

1. Write a scene, involving only one character, who is uncomfortable in his or her surroundings: socially inadequate, frightened, revolted, painfully nostalgic, or the like. Using active verbs in your description of the setting, build forceful conflict between the person and the place.

2. Write a scene with two characters in conflict over the setting: one wants to go, and one wants to stay. The more interesting the setting you choose, the more interesting the conflict will inevitably be.

3. Write a scene in a setting that is likely to be quite familiar to your readers (supermarket, dormitory, classroom, movie theater, suburban house, etc.) but that is unfamiliar, strange, outlandish, or outrageous to the central character. Let us feel the strangeness through the character's eyes.

4. Write a scene set in a strange, exotic place, or a time far distant either in the past or the future, in which the setting is quite familiar to the central character. Convince us of the ordinariness of the place.

5. Write a scene in which the character's mood is at odds with the weather and make the weather nevertheless express her or his mood: the rain is joyful, the clear skies are threatening, the snow is comforting, the summer beach is chilling.

6. Write a one-page summary of your character's life, showing that the character is very different at the end of the period than at the beginning. Then go back and write a three- or four-page scene showing the crucial turning point.

7. Write a passage that begins with a sequential summary of the central character's life, then moves to a crucial scene, goes on to a circumstantial summary, and ends with a scene of crisis.

6

CALL ME ISHMAEL
Point of View, Part I

Who Speaks?
To Whom?
In What Form?

Point of view is the most complex element of fiction. Although it lends itself to analysis, definitions and diagrams, it is finally a question of relationship among writer, characters, and reader — subject like any relationship to organic subtleties. We can discuss person, omniscience, narrative voice, tone, authorial distance, and reliability; but none of these things will ever pigeonhole a work in such a way that any other work may be placed in the exact same pigeonhole.

The first thing to do is to set aside the common use of the phrase "point of view" as being synonymous with "opinion," as in: *It's my point of view that they all ought to be shot.* An author's view of the world as it is and as it ought to be will ultimately be revealed by his or her manipulation of the technique of point of view, but not vice versa — identifying the author's beliefs will not describe the point of view of the work. Rather than thinking of point of view as an opinion or belief, begin with the more literal synonym of "vantage point." *Who* is standing *where* to watch the scene?

Better, since we are dealing with a verbal medium, these questions might be translated: Who speaks? To whom? In what form? At what distance from the action? With what limitations? All these issues go into the determination of the point of view. Because *the author inevitably wants to convince us to share the same perspective,* the answers will also help reveal her or his final opinion, judgment, attitude, or message.

This chapter deals with the first three questions: Who speaks? To whom? In what form? Distance and limitations are considered in Chapter 7.

Who Speaks?

The primary point-of-view decision that you as author must make before you can set down the first sentence of the story is *person.* This is the simplest and crudest subdivision that must be made in deciding who speaks. The story can be told in the third person (*She walked out into the harsh sunlight*), the second person (*You walked out into the harsh sunlight*), or the first person (*I walked out into the harsh sunlight*). Third- and second-person stories are "told" by an author; first-person stories, by a character.

THIRD PERSON

Third person, in which the author is telling the story, can be subdivided again according to the degree of knowledge or *omniscience* the author assumes. Notice that since this is a matter of degree, the subdivisions are again only a crude indication of the variations possible. As an author you are free to decide how much you know. You may know every universal and eternal truth; you may know what is in the mind of one character but not what is in the mind of another; or you may know only what can be externally observed. You decide, and very early in the story you signal to the reader what degree of omniscience you have chosen. Once given, this signal constitutes a "contract" between author and reader, and it will be very difficult to break the contract gracefully. If you have restricted yourself to the mind of James Lordly for five pages, as he observes the actions of Mrs. Grumms and her cats, you will violate the contract by suddenly dipping into Mrs. Grumms's mind to let us know what she thinks of James Lordly. We are likely to feel misused, and likely to cancel the contract altogether if you suddenly give us the thoughts of the cats.

The omniscient author, sometimes referred to as the *editorial omniscient author,* because she or he tells us directly what we are supposed to think, has total knowledge. As omniscient author you are God. You can:

Who Speaks?

The Author	The Author	Character
In: Third Person	In: Second Person	In: First Person
Editorial Omniscient	"You" as character	Central Narrator
Limited Omniscient	"You" as reader-turned-	Peripheral Narrator
Objective	character	

To Whom?

The Reader	Another Character	The Self
Characterized or	or Characters	
Uncharacterized		

In What Form?

"Written Story," "Spoken Story," Reportage, Oratory, Monologue, Confessional, Journal, Diary, Interior Monologue, Stream of Consciousness, etc. . . .

At What Distance?

Reader and Author ◄──────► Narrator ◄──────► Characters
Complete Identification ◄──────────────► Complete Opposition
Temporal, Spatial, Moral, Intellectual, Aesthetic, Physical, Educational, Experiential

With What Limitations?

Reliable Narrator (or "Author") ◄──────► Unreliable Narrator (or "Author")
on any of values listed above

---

1. Objectively report what is happening.
2. Go into the mind of any character.
3. Interpret for us that character's appearance, speech, actions, and thoughts, even if the character cannot do so.
4. Move freely in time or space to give us a panoramic, telescopic, microscopic, or historical view; tell us what has happened elsewhere or in the past or what will happen in the future.
5. Provide general reflections, judgments, and truths.

In all these aspects, we will accept what the omniscient author tells us. If you tell us that Ruth is a good woman, that Jeremy doesn't really understand his own motives, that the moon is going to explode in four hours, and that everybody will be better off for it, we will believe you. Here is a paragraph that blatantly exhibits all five of these areas of knowledge.

(1) Joe glared at the screaming baby. (2) Frightened by his scowl, the baby gulped and screamed louder. I hate that thing, Joe thought. (3) But it was not really hatred that he felt. (4) Only two years ago he himself had screamed like that. (5) Children can't tell hatred from fear.

This illustration is awkwardly compressed, but an author well in control of his craft can move easily from one area of knowledge to another. In the first scene of *War and Peace*, Tolstoy describes Anna Scherer.

To be an enthusiast had become her social vocation, and sometimes even when she did not feel like it, she became enthusiastic in order not to disappoint the expectations of those who knew her. The subdued smile which, though it did not suit her faded features, always played around her lips, expressed as in a spoiled child, a continual consciousness of her charming defect, which she neither wished, nor could, nor considered it necessary to correct.

Here in two sentences Tolstoy tells us what is in Anna's mind and the expectations of her acquaintances, what she looks like, what suits her, what she can and cannot do; and he offers a general reflection on spoiled children.

The omniscient voice is the voice of the classical epic (*And Meleager, far-off, knew nothing of this, but felt his vitals burning with fever*), of the Bible (*So the Lord sent a pestilence upon Israel; and there fell seventy thousand men*), and of most nineteenth-century novels (*Tito put out his hand to help him, and so strangely quick are men's souls that in this moment, when he began to feel that his atonement was accepted, he had a darting thought of the irksome efforts it entailed.*). But it is one of the manifestations of literature's movement downward in class from heroic to common characters, inward from action to the mind, that authors of the twentieth century have largely avoided the godlike stance of the omniscient author and chosen to restrict themselves to fewer areas of knowledge.

The limited omniscient viewpoint is one in which the author may move with some, but not all of the omniscient author's freedom. You may grant yourself the right, for example, to know what the characters in a scene are thinking but not to interpret their thoughts. You may interpret one character's thoughts and actions but see the others only externally. You may see with microscopic accuracy but not presume to reach any universal truths. The most commonly used form of the limited omniscient point of view is one in which the author can see events objectively and also grants himself or herself access to the mind of one character; but not to the minds of the others, nor to any explicit powers of judgment. This point of view is particularly useful for the short story because it very quickly establishes the point-of-view character or *means of perception*. The short story is so compressed a form that there is rarely time or space to develop more than one consciousness. Staying with external observation and one character's thoughts helps control the focus and avoid *awkward point-of-view shifts.*

But the form is also frequently used for the novel, as in Gail Godwin's *The Odd Woman.*

> It was ten o'clock on the evening of the same day, and the permanent residents of the household on the mountain were restored to routines and sobriety. Jane, on the other hand, sat by herself in the kitchen, a glass of Scotch before her on the cleanly wiped table, going deeper and deeper into a mood she could recognize only as unfamiliar. She could not describe it: it was both frightening and satisfying. It was like letting go and being taken somewhere. She tried to trace it back. When, exactly, had it started?

It is clear here that the author has limited her omniscience. She is not going to tell us the ultimate truth about Jane's soul, nor is she going to define for us the "unfamiliar mood" that the character herself cannot define. The author has the facts at her disposal, and she has Jane's thoughts, and that is all.

The advantage of the limited omniscient over the omniscient voice is immediacy. Here, because we are not allowed to know more than Jane does about her own thoughts and feelings, we grope *with* her toward understanding. In the process, a contract has been made between the author and the reader, and this contract must not now be broken. If at this point the author should step in and answer Jane's question, "When, exactly, had it started?" with, "Jane was never to remember this, but in fact it had started one afternoon when she was two years old," we would feel it as an abrupt and uncalled-for *authorial intrusion.*

Nevertheless, within the limits the author has set herself, there is fluidity and a range of possibilities. Notice that the passage begins with a panoramic observation (*ten o'clock, permanent residents, routines*) and moves to the tighter focus of a view, still external, of Jane (*sat by herself in the kitchen*), before moving into her mind. The sentence, "She tried to trace it back," is a relatively factual account of her mental process, whereas in the next sentence, "When, exactly, had it started?" we are in Jane's mind, over-hearing her question to herself.

Although this common form of the limited omniscient (objective reporting plus one mind) may seem very restricted, given all the possibilities of omniscience, it has a freedom that no human being has. In life you have full access to only one mind, your own; and you are also the one person you may not externally observe. As a fiction writer you can do what no human being can do, be simultaneously inside and outside a given character; it is this that E. M. Forster describes in *Aspects of the Novel* as "the fundamental difference between people in daily life and people in books."

In daily life we never understand each other, neither complete clairvoyance nor complete confessional exists. We know each other approximately, by external signs, and these serve well enough as a basis for society and even for intimacy. But people in a novel can be understood completely by the reader, if the novelist wishes; their inner as well as their outer life can be exposed. And this is why they often seem more definite than characters in history, or even our own friends.

The objective author. Sometimes the novelist or short-story writer does not wish to expose any more than the external signs. The *objective* author is not omniscient but impersonal. As an objective author, you restrict your knowledge to the facts that might be observed by a human being; to the senses of sight, sound, smell, taste, and touch. In the story "Hills Like White Elephants," Ernest Hemingway reports what is said and done by a quarreling couple, both without any direct revelation of the characters' thoughts and without comment.

> The American and the girl with him sat at a table in the shade, outside the building. It was very hot and the express from Barcelona would come in forty minutes. It stopped at this junction for two minutes and went on to Madrid.
> "What should we drink?" the girl asked. She had taken off her hat and put it on the table.
> "It's pretty hot," the man said.
> "Let's drink beer."
> "Dos cervezas," the man said into the curtain.
> "Big ones?" a woman asked from the doorway.
> "Yes. Two big ones."
> The woman brought two glasses of beer and two felt pads. She put the felt pads and the beer glasses on the table and looked at the man and the girl. The girl was looking off at the line of hills. They were white in the sun and the country was brown and dry.

In the course of this story we learn, entirely by inference, that the girl is pregnant and that she feels herself coerced by the man into having an abortion. Neither pregnancy nor abortion is ever mentioned. The narrative remains clipped, austere, and external. What does Hemingway gain by this pretense of objective reporting? The reader is allowed to discover what is really happening. The characters avoid the subject, prevaricate, and pretend, but they betray their real meanings and feelings through gestures, repetitions, and slips of the tongue. The reader, focus directed by the author, learns by inference, as in life, so that we finally have the pleasure of knowing the characters better than they know themselves.

For the sake of clarity, the possibilities of third-person narration have been divided into the editorial omniscient, limited omniscient, and objective authors, but between the extreme stances of the editorial omniscient (total knowledge) and the objective author (external observation only), the powers of the limited omniscient are immensely variable. Because you are most likely to choose your authorial voice in this range, you need to be aware that you make your own rules and that, having made them, you must stick to them. Your position as a writer is analogous to that of a poet who may choose whether to write free verse or a ballad stanza. If the poet chooses the stanza, then he or she is obliged to rhyme. Beginning writers of prose fiction are often tempted to shift viewpoint when it is both unnecessary and disturbing.

> Leo's neck flushed against the prickly weave of his uniform collar. He concentrated on his buttons and tried not to look into the face of the bandmaster, who, however, was more amused than angry.

This is an awkward point-of-view shift because, having felt Leo's embarrassment with him, we are suddenly asked to leap into the bandmaster's feelings. The shift can be corrected by moving instead from Leo's mind to an observation that he might make.

> Leo's neck flushed against the prickly weave of his uniform collar. He concentrated on his buttons and tried not to look into the face of the bandmaster, who, however, was astonishingly smiling.

The rewrite is easier to follow because we remain with Leo's mind as he observes that the bandmaster is not angry. It further serves the purpose of implying that Leo fails to concentrate on his buttons, and so intensifies his confusion.

SECOND PERSON

First and third persons are most common in literature; the second person remains an idiosyncratic and experimental form, but it is worth mentioning because several twentieth-century authors have been attracted to its possibilities.

Person refers to the basic mode of a piece of fiction. In the third person, all the characters will be referred to as *he, she,* and *they.* In the first person, the character telling the story will refer to himself or herself as *I* and to other characters as *he, she,* and *they.* The second person is the basic mode of the story *only when a character* is referred to as *you.* When an omniscient author addresses the reader as *you* (*You will remember that John Doderring was left dangling on the cliff at Dover*), this does not alter the basic mode of the piece from third to second person. Only when "you" become an actor in the drama is the story or novel written in second person.

In *Even Cowgirls Get the Blues,* Tom Robbins exhibits both of these uses of the second person.

> If you could buckle your Bugs Bunny wristwatch to a ray of light, your watch would continue ticking but its hands wouldn't move.

The *you* involved here is a generalized reader, and the passage is written in the stance of an omniscient author delivering a general "truth."

But when the author turns to address his central character, Sissy Hankshaw, the basic mode of the narration becomes that of the second person.

> You hitchhike. Timidly at first, barely flashing your fist, leaning almost imperceptibly in the direction of your imaginary destination. A squirrel runs along a tree limb. You hitchhike the squirrel. A blue jay flies by. You flag it down.

The effect of this second-person narration is odd and original; the author observes Sissy Hankshaw, and yet his direct address implies an intimate and affectionate relationship that makes it easy to move further into her mind.

> Your thumbs separate you from other humans. You begin to sense a presence about your thumbs. You wonder if there is not magic there.

In this example it is a character clearly delineated and distinguished from the reader who is the *you* of the narrative. But the second person can also be used as a means of making the reader into a character, as in Robert Coover's story, "Panel Game," quoted in Chapter 5.

> You squirm, viced by Lady (who excites you) and America (who does not, but bless him all the same), but your squirms are misread: Lovely Lady lifts lashes, crosses eyes, and draws breath excitedly . . . Audience howls happily the while and who can blame them? You, Sport, resign yourself to pass the test in peace and salute them with a timid smile, squirm no more.

Here again the effect of the second person is unusual and complex. The author assigns you, the reader, specific characteristics and reactions and thereby — assuming that you go along with his characterization of you — pulls you deeper and more intimately into the story.

It is unlikely that the second person will ever become a major mode of narration as the first and third are, but for precisely that reason you may find it an attractive experiment. It is startling and relatively unexplored.

FIRST PERSON

A story is told in the first person when it is a character who speaks. The term "narrator" is sometimes loosely used to refer to any teller of a tale, but strictly speaking a story "has a narrator" only when it is told in the first person by one of the characters. This character may be the protagonist, the *I* telling *my* story, in which case that character is a *central narrator;* or the character may be telling a story about someone else, in which case he or she is a *peripheral narrator.*

In either case it's important to indicate early which kind of narrator we have so that we know who the story's protagonist is, as in the first paragraph of Alan Sillitoe's "The Loneliness of the Long-Distance Runner," reprinted in full in Chapter 7.

> As soon as I got to Borstal they made me a long-distance cross-country runner. I suppose they thought I was just the build for it because I was long and skinny for my age (and still am) and in any case I didn't mind it much, to tell you the truth, because running had always been made much of in our family, especially running away from the police.

The focus here is immediately thrown on the *I* of the story, and we expect that *I* to be the central character whose desires and decisions impel the action. But from the opening lines of R. Bruce Moody's *The Decline and Fall of Daphne Finn*, it is Daphne who is brought alive by attention and detail, while the narrator is established as an observer and recorder of his subject.

> "Is it really you?"
> Melodious and high, this voice descended to me from behind and above — as it seemed it was always to do — indistinct as bells in another country.
> Unable to answer in the negative, I turned from my desk, looked up, and smiled sourly.
> "Yes," I said, startling a face which had been peering over my shoulder, a face whose beauty it was apparent at the outset had made no concession to convention. It retreated as her feet staggered back.

The central narrator is always, as the term implies, at the center of the action; the peripheral narrator may be in virtually any position that is not the center. He or she may be the second most important character in the story, or may not be involved in the action at all but merely placed in a position to observe. The narrator may characterize himself or herself in detail or may remain detached and scarcely identifiable. It is even possible to make the first-person narrator plural, as William Faulkner does in "A Rose for Emily," where the story is told by a narrator identified only as one of "us," the people of the town in which the action has taken place.

That a narrator may be either central or peripheral, that a character may tell either his own story or someone else's, is both commonly assumed and obviously logical. But the author and editor Rust Hills, in his book *Writing in General and the Short Story in Particular*, takes interesting and persuasive exception to this idea. When point of view fails, Hills argues, it is always because the perception we are using for the course of the story is different from that of the character who is moved or changed by the action. Even when a narrator seems to be a peripheral observer and the story is "about" someone else, in fact it is the narrator who is changed, and must be, in order for us to be satisfied by our emotional identification with him or her.

> This, I believe, is what will always be the case in successful fiction: that either the character moved by the action will be the point-of-view character, or else the point-of-view character will *become* the character moved by the action. Call it Hills' Law.

Obviously, this view does not mean that we have to throw out the useful fictional device of the peripheral narrator. Hills uses the familiar examples of *The Great Gatsby* and *Heart of Darkness* to illustrate his meaning. In the former, Nick Carroway as a peripheral narrator observes and tells the story of Jay Gatsby, but by the end of the book it is Nick's life that has been changed by what he has observed. In the latter, Marlow purports to tell the tale of the ivory hunter Kurtz, even protesting that "I don't want to bother you much with what happened to me personally." By the end of the story, Kurtz (like Gatsby) is dead, but it is not the death that moves us so much as what, "personally," Marlow has learned *through* Kurtz and his death. The same can be said of *The Decline and Fall of Daphne Finn*; the focus of the action is on Daphne, but the pain, the passion, and the loss are those of her biographer. Even in "A Rose for Emily," where the narrator is a collective "we," it is the implied effect of Miss Emily on the town that moves us, the emotions of the townspeople that we share. Because we tend to identify with the means of perception in a story, we are moved with that perception; even when the overt action of the story is elsewhere, it is often the act of observation itself that provides the epiphany.

The thing to recognize about a first-person narrator is that because she or he is a character, she or he has all the limitations of a human being and cannot be omniscient. The narrator is confined to reporting what she or he could realistically know. More than that, although the narrator may certainly interpret actions, deliver dictums, and predict the future, these remain the fallible opinions of a human being, we are not bound to accept them as we are bound to accept the interpretations, truths, and predictions of the omniscient author. You may want us to accept the narrator's word, and then the most difficult part of your task, and the touchstone of your story's success, will be to convince us to trust and believe the narrator. On the other hand, it may be an important part of your purpose that we should reject the narrator's opinions and form our own. In the latter case, the narrator is "unreliable," a phenomenon that will be taken up in Chapter 7.

To Whom?

In choosing a point of view, the author implies an identity, not only for the teller of the tale, but for the audience as well.

THE READER

Most fiction is addressed to a literary convention, *"the reader."* When we open a book, we tacitly accept our role as a member of this unspecified audience. If the story begins, "I was born of a drunken father and an illiterate mother in the peat bogs of Galway during the Great Potato Famine," we are not, on the whole, alarmed. We do not face this clearly deceased Irishman who has crossed the Atlantic to take us into his confidence and demand, "Why are you telling me all this?"

Notice that the tradition of "the reader" assumes the universality of the audience. Most stories do not specifically address themselves to a segment or period of humanity, and they make no concessions to such difference as might exist between reader and author; they assume that anyone who reads the story can be brought around to the same understanding of it the author has. In practice most writers, though they do not acknowledge it in the text and may not admit it to themselves, are addressing someone *who can* be brought around to the same understanding as themselves. The author of a "Harlequin Romance" addresses the story to a generalized "reader" but knows that his or her likely audience is trained by repetition of the formula to expect certain Gothic features — rich lover, virtuous heroine, threatening house, colorful costume. Slightly less formulaic is the notion of "a *New Yorker* story," which is presumably what the author perceives that the editors perceive will be pleasing to the people who buy *The New Yorker.* Anyone who pens or types what he or she hopes is "literature" is assuming that his audience is literate, which leaves out better than half the world. My mother, distressed at the difficulty of my fictional style, used to urge me to write for "the masses," by which she meant subscribers to the *Reader's Digest,* whom she thought to be in need of cheering and escape. I considered this a very narrow goal until I realized that my own ambition to be "universal" was more exclusive still: I envisioned my audience as made up of people who *would not* subscribe to the *Reader's Digest.*

Nevertheless, the most common assumption of the tale-teller, whether omniscient author or narrating character, is that the reader is an amenable and persuasible Everyman, and that the telling needs no justification.

But there are various exceptions to this tendency which can be used to dramatic effect and which always involve a more definite characterizing of the receiver of the story. The author may address "the reader" but assign that reader specific traits that we, the actual readers, must then accept as our own if we are to accept the fiction. Nineteenth-century novelists had a tradition of addressing "You, gentle reader," "Dear reader," and the like, and this minimal characterization was a technique for implying mutual understanding. In "The Loneliness of the Long-Distance Runner," by Alan Sillitoe, on the other hand, the narrator divides the world into "us" and "you." *We*, the narrator and his kind, are the outlaws, all those who live by their illegal wits; and *you*, the readers, are by contrast law-abiding, prosperous, educated, and rather dull. To quote again from Sillitoe's story, "The Loneliness of the Long-Distance Runner":

> I suppose you'll laugh at this, me saying the governor's a stupid bastard when I know hardly how to write and he can read and write and add-up like a professor. But what I say is true right enough. He's stupid, and I'm not, because I can see further into the likes of him than he can see into the likes of me.

The clear implication here is that the narrator can see further into the likes of us readers than we can see into the likes of him, and much of the effective irony of the story rests in the fact that the more we applaud and identify with the narrator, the more we must accept his condemning characterization of "us."

ANOTHER CHARACTER

More specifically still, the story may be told to *another character or characters*, in which case we as readers "overhear" it; the teller of the tale does not acknowledge us even by implication. Just as the third-person author telling "her story" is theoretically more impersonal than the first-person character telling "my story," so "the reader" is theoretically a more impersonal receiver of the tale than another character. I insert the word *theoretically* because, with regard to point of view more than any other element of fiction, any rule laid down seems to be an invitation to rule breaking by some original and inventive author.

In the *epistolary* novel or story, the narrative consists entirely of letters written from one character to another, or between characters.

> I, Mukhail Ivanokov, stone mason in the village of Ilba in the Ukranian Soviet Socialist Republic, greet you and pity you, Charles Ashland, petroleum merchant in Titusville, Florida, in the United States of America. I grasp your hand.
>
> KURT VONNEGUT, *"The Manned Missiles"*

Or the convention of the story may be that of a monologue, spoken aloud by one character to another.

> May I, *monsieur*, offer my services without running the risk of intruding? I fear you may not be able to make yourself understood by the worthy ape who presides over the fate of this establishment. In fact, he speaks nothing but Dutch. Unless you authorize me to plead your case, he will not guess that you want gin.
>
> <div align="right">ALBERT CAMUS, <i>The Fall</i></div>

Again, the possible variations are infinite; the narrator may speak in intimate confessional to a friend or lover, or may present his case to a jury or a mob; she may be writing a highly technical report of the welfare situation, designed to hide her emotion; he may be pouring out his heart in a love letter he knows (and we know) he will never send.

In any of these cases, the convention employed is the opposite of that employed in a story told to "the reader." The listener as well as the teller is involved in the action; the assumption is not that we readers are there but that we are not. We are eavesdroppers, with all the ambiguous intimacy that position implies.

THE SELF

An even greater intimacy is implied if the character's story is as secret as a diary or as private as a mind, addressed to *the self* and not intended to be heard by anyone inside or outside the action.

Diary or Journal

November 6

> Something has got into the Chief of my Division. When I arrived at the office he called me and began as follows: "Now then, tell me. What's the matter with you? . . . I know you're trailing after the Director's daughter. Just look at yourself — what are you? Just nothing. You haven't a penny to your name. Look in the mirror. How can you even think of such things?" The hell with him! Just because he's got a face like a druggist's bottle and that quiff of hair on his head all curled and pomaded.
>
> <div align="right">NIKOLAI GOGOL, <i>The Diary of a Madman</i></div>

The protagonist here is clearly using his diary to vent his feelings and does not intend it to be read by anyone else. Still, he has deliberately externalized his secret thoughts in a journal. Because the author has the power to enter a character's mind, the reader also has the power to eavesdrop on thoughts, read what is "not written," hear what is "not spoken," and share what cannot be shared.

Interior Monologue. Overheard thoughts are generally of two kinds, of which the most common is *interior monologue,* the convention being that we follow that character's thoughts in their sequence, though in fact the author, for our convenience, sets out those thoughts with a coherence and logic that no human mind ever possessed.

> I must organize myself. I must, as they say, pull myself together, dump this cat from my lap, stir — yes, resolve, move, do. But do what? My will is like the rosy dustlike light in this room: soft, diffuse, and gently comforting. It lets me do . . . anything . . . nothing. My ears hear what they happen to; I eat what's put before me; my eyes see what blunders into them; my thoughts are not thoughts, they are dreams. I'm empty or I'm full . . . depending; and I cannot choose. I sink my claws in Tick's fur and scratch the bones of his back until his rear rises amorously. Mr. Tick, I murmur, I must organize myself, I must pull myself together. And Mr. Tick rolls over on his belly, all ooze.
> WILLIAM H. GASS, "In the Heart of the Heart of the Country"

This interior monologue ranges, as human thoughts do, from sense impression to self-admonishment, from cat to light to eyes and ears, from specific to general and back again. But the logical connections between these things are all provided; the mind "thinks" logically and grammatically as if the character *were* trying to express himself.

Stream of Consciousness. In fact the human mind does not operate with the order and clarity of the monologue just quoted. Even what little we know of its operations makes clear that it skips, elides, makes and breaks images, leaps faster and further than any mere sentence can suggest. Any mind at any moment is simultaneously accomplishing dozens of tasks that cannot be conveyed simultaneously. As you read this sentence part of your mind is following the sense of it; part of your mind is directing your hand to hold the book open; part of it twisting your spine into a more comfortable position; part of it still lingering on the last interesting image of this text, Mr. Tick rolling over on his belly, which reminds you of a cat you had once that was also *all ooze*, which reminds you that you're nearly out of milk and have to finish this chapter before the store closes . . . and so forth.

In *Ulysses,* James Joyce tried to catch the speed and multiplicity of the mind with a technique that has come to be known as *stream of consciousness.* The device is difficult and in many ways thankless: since the speed of thought is so much faster than that of writing or speaking, and stream of consciousness tries to suggest the process as well as the content of the mind, it requires a more, not less, rigorous selection and arrangement than ordinary grammar requires. But Joyce and a very few other writers have handled stream of consciousness as an ebullient and exciting way of capturing the mind.

> Yes because he never did a thing like that before as ask to get his breakfast in bed with a couple of eggs since the *City Arms* hotel when he used to be pretending to be laid up with a sick voice doing his highness to make himself interesting to that old faggot Mrs. Riordan that he thought he had a great leg of and she never left us a farthing all for masses for herself and her soul greatest miser ever was actually afraid to lay out 4d for her methylated spirit telling me all her ailments she had too much old chat in her about politics and earthquakes and the end of the world let us have a bit of fun first God help the world if all the women were her sort. . . .
>
> JAMES JOYCE, *Ulysses*

The preceding two examples, of interior monologue and stream of consciousness, respectively, are written in the first person, so that we overhear the minds of narrator characters. Through the omniscient and limited omniscient authors we may also overhear the thoughts of the characters, and when this is the case there is a curious doubling or crossing of literary conventions. Say that the story is told by a limited omniscient author, who is therefore speaking "to the reader." But this author may also enter the mind of a character, who is speaking to him or herself. The passage from *The Odd Woman* on page 175 is of this sort. Here is a still more striking example.

> Dusk was slowly deepening. Somewhere, he could not tell exactly where, a cricket took up a fitful song. The air was growing soft and heavy. He looked over the fields, longing for Bobo . . .
> He shifted his body to ease the cold damp of the ground, and thought back over the day. Yeah, hed been dam right erbout not wantin t go swimmin. N ef hed followed his right min hed neverve gone n got inter all this trouble.
>
> RICHARD WRIGHT, "Big Boy Leaves Home"

Though this story, first published in 1938, makes use of an old style of dialect misspelling, Wright moves gracefully between the two voices. There is here present an authorial voice educated, eloquent, and mature. This voice can tell us what is in Big Boy's mind: *he could not tell exactly where, longing for Bobo*; and it can also, still in the third person, let us overhear Big Boy's thoughts by passing into his dialect, which is adolescent and uneducated: *Yeah, hed been dam right.* If either of these voices were absent, the passage would be impoverished; it needs the scope of the author and the immediacy of the character to achieve its effect.

In What Form?

The form of the story, like the teller and the listener, can be more or less specified as part of the total point of view. The form may announce itself without justification as a generalized *story*, either *written* or *spoken;* or it may suggest *reportage, confessional, interior monologue,* or *stream of consciousness;* or it may be overtly identified as *monologue, oratory, journal,* or *diary*. The relationship between the teller of a tale and its receiver often automatically implies a form for the telling, so that most of the forms above have already been mentioned. The list is not exhaustive; you can tell your story in the form of a catalogue or a TV commercial as long as you can devise a way to do so that also has the form of a story.

Form is important to point of view because the form in which a story is told indicates the degree of self-consciousness on the part of the teller; this will in turn affect the language chosen, the intimacy of the relationship, and the honesty of the telling. A written account will imply less spontaneity, on the whole, than one that appears to be spoken aloud, which suggests less spontaneity than thought. A narrator writing a letter to his grandmother may be less honest than he is when he tells the same facts aloud to his friend.

Certain relationships established by the narrative between teller and audience make certain forms more likely than others, but almost any combination of answers is possible to the questions: *Who speaks? To whom? In what form?* If you are speaking as an omniscient author to the literary convention of "the reader," we may assume that you are using the convention of "written story" as your form. But you might say:

Wait, step over here a minute. What's this in the corner, stuffed down between the bedpost and the wall?

If you do this, you slip at least momentarily into the different convention of the spoken word — the effect is that we are drawn more immediately into the scene — and the point of view of the whole is slightly altered. A central narrator might be thinking, and therefore "talking to herself," while actually angrily addressing her thoughts to another character. Conversely, one character might be writing a letter to another but letting the conscious act of writing deteriorate into a betrayal of his own secret thoughts. Any complexities such as these will alter and inform the total point of view.

Here are the opening passages from a student short story in which the point of view is extremely complex. An adequate analysis of it will require, more than a definition or a diagram, a series of *yes but's* and *but also's*.

Report: He is the light-bringer, the peerless one. She is the dark-water creature, the Queen of Fishes. I don't know why I say that except sometimes I get desperate for sheer sound. You would too if you went to St. Katherine's Day Academy where the D. H. Lawrence is in a locked cabinet in the library. I used to wonder why Tom sends me there except now I know it's his notion of a finishing school. "It's what your mother would have wanted," he says, tragic-eyed. But I know he's thinking about Vivian.

I started my journal to show you what she's doing to him. He doesn't know. He wouldn't. But I sit in on the seminar. I read the Eliot, the Rhys, the Muir, the MacDiarmid with them. They think I'm amusing, these long tall girls in *Rive Gauche* jeans and velour with Parker chrome mechanical pencils — engraved initials — and notebooks written all over: "Bring *The Green Helmet* to class Tues." and "talk to Dr. Johnson about Parents' Day Brunch" and phone numbers everywhere. I am a sort of mascot. They'd be surprised to know that I, their Tom's daughter, knows what they are at when they talk of regional sensibility in Muir and the mythic fallacy. Especially Vivian who comes to class early and stays late and comes for dinner and once "took Elaine shopping, isn't that nice?" God, I hated it. "Look, Elaine that grey would just match your eyes. I'll bet Tom, I mean your father, would like that." I went home that day and cast a Mars number square against her for discord, discord, discord. But still she came back — back for Tom.

DIANE ROBERTS, "Lamia"

Who speaks? The passage is written in the first person — so much is easy. So it is a narrator who speaks, and this narrator tells us that she is peripheral: "I started my journal to show you what she's doing to him." But against this statement of the narrator's intention, we feel so much personal grief and bottled fury, and the focus of the narrative returns so insistently to what the *I* of the story is doing and feeling, that we are inclined to believe the real subject is not "what she's doing to him" but *what they're doing to me* and, therefore, to feel that we're dealing with a central narrator.

To whom? The narrator addresses a *you* who is clearly the convention of "the reader." Yet on several counts this notion doesn't bear pursuing. She is revealing bitter attitudes that couldn't be confessed to her father, so the *you* to whom she reveals them can scarcely include a reader sitting with printed pages. The reader who is the *you* of the narrative becomes so abstract that it might be the spirit of justice she addresses, or God. Yet the narrator makes little attempt to present a coherent account of background facts, which come out obliquely, subsidiary to the pent-up emotion — *I am a sort of mascot; They'd be surprised to know* — which suggests that she's really talking to herself.

In what form? She tells us twice: this is "a report" and "my journal." Neither is quite possible. The opening word "Report" is immediately contradicted by the dramatic imagery of "light-bringer" and "dark-water creature," so that we understand the word itself is an ironic attempt to claim logic and objectivity for an emotion that admits of neither. It's a journal, then, a diary of great intimacy. That's what it feels like; but how can a diary be addressed to a reader?

The amazing thing about all this is that we are not in the least confused! The paradoxes and contradictions of the narrative do not make us feel that the author is inept but, on the contrary, that she has captured with great precision the paradoxes and contradictions of the narrator's emotional state. We feel no awkward point-of-view shift because all the terms of the contract — those same paradoxes and contradictions — are laid out for us in the opening paragraph.

Clearly there is an author somewhere, who is not the same person as this narrator, and who is directing us moment by moment to accept or reject, to believe or disbelieve, what the narrator tells us.

In order to deal with a viewpoint as complex as this, it will be necessary to deal, not only with who speaks to whom in what form, but with *distance* and *limitation,* subjects treated in Chapter 7.

The Bella Lingua

JOHN CHEEVER

Wilson Streeter, like many Americans who live in Rome, was divorced. He worked as a statistician for the F.R.U.P.C. agency, lived alone, and led a diverting social life with other expatriates and those Romans who were drawn into expatriate circles, but he spoke English all day long at his office and the Italians he met socially spoke English so much better than he spoke Italian that he could not bring himself to converse with them in their language. It was his feeling that in order to understand Italy he would have to speak Italian. He did speak it well enough when it was a question of some simple matter of shopping or making arrangements of one kind or another, but he wanted to be able to express his sentiments, to tell jokes, and to follow overheard conversations on trolley cars and buses. He was keenly conscious of the fact that he was making his life in a country that was not his own, but this sense of being an outsider would change, he thought, when he knew the language.

For the tourist, the whole experience of traveling through a strange country is on the verge of the past tense. Even as the days are spent, these *were* the days in Rome, and everything — the sightseeing, souvenirs, photographs, and presents — is commemorative. Even as the traveler lies in bed waiting for sleep, these *were* the nights in Rome. But for the expatriate there is no past tense. It would defeat his purpose to think of this time in another country in relation to some town or countryside that was and might again be his permanent home, and he lives in a continuous and unrelenting present. Instead of accumulating memories, the expatriate is offered the challenge of learning a language and understanding a people. So they catch a glimpse of one another in the Piazza Venezia — the expatriates passing through the square on their way to their Italian lessons, the tourists occupying, by prearrangement, all the tables at a sidewalk café and drinking Campari, which they have been told is a typical Roman *aperitivo*.

Streeter's teacher was an American woman named Kate Dresser, who lived in an old palace near the Piazza Firenze, with an adolescent son. Streeter went there for his lessons on Tuesday and Friday evenings and on Sunday afternoons. He enjoyed the walk in the evening from his office, past the Pantheon, to his Italian lesson. Among the rewards of his expatriation were a heightened awareness of what he saw and an exhilarating sense of freedom. Mixed with the love we hold for our native country is the fact that it is the place where we were raised, and, should anything have gone a little wrong in this process, we will be reminded of this fault, by the scene of the crime, until the day we die. Some such unhappiness may have accounted for Streeter's sense of freedom, and his heightened awareness may have been nothing but what is to be expected of a man with a good appetite walking through the back streets of a city in the autumn. The air was cold and smelled of coffee — sometimes of incense, if the doors to a church stood open — and chrysanthemums were for sale everywhere. The sights were exciting and confusing — the ruins of Republican and Imperial Rome, and the ruins of what the city had been the day before yesterday — but the whole thing would be revealed to him when he could speak Italian.

It was not easy, Streeter knew, for a man his age to learn anything, and he had not been fortunate in his search for a good Italian teacher. He had first gone to the Dante Alighieri Institute, where the classes were so large that he made no progress. Then he had taken private lessons from an old lady. He was supposed to read and translate Collodi's *Pinocchio*, but when he had done a few sentences the teacher would take the book out of his hands and do the reading and translating herself. She loved the story so much that she laughed and cried, and sometimes whole lessons passed in which Streeter did not open his mouth. It disturbed his sense of fitness that he, a man of fifty, should be sitting in a cold flat at the edge of Rome, being read a children's tale by a woman of seventy, and after a dozen lessons he told his teacher that he had to go to Perugia on business. After this he enrolled in the Tauchnitz School and had private lessons. His teacher was an astonishingly pretty young woman who wore the tight-waisted clothes that were in fashion that year, and a wedding ring — a prop, he guessed, because she seemed so openly flirtatious and gay. She wore a sharp perfume, rattled her bracelets, pulled down her jacket, swung her hips when she walked to the blackboard, and gave Streeter, one evening, such a dark look that he took her in his arms. What she did then was to shriek, kick over a little desk, and run through three intervening classrooms to the lobby, screaming that she had been attacked by a beast. After all his months of study, "beast" was the only word in her tirade that Streeter understood. The whole school was alerted, of course, and all he could do was to wipe the sweat off his forehead and start through the classrooms toward the lobby. People stood on chairs to get a better look at him, and he never went back to Tauchnitz.

His next teacher was a very plain woman with gray hair and a lavender shawl that she must have knitted herself, it was so full of knots and tangles. She was an excellent teacher for a month, and then one evening she told him that her life was difficult. She waited to be encouraged to tell him her troubles, and when he did not give her any encouragement, she told them to him anyhow. She had been engaged to be married for twenty years, but the mother of her betrothed disapproved of the match and, whenever the subject was raised, would climb up onto the window sill and threaten to jump into the street. Now her betrothed was sick, he would have to be cut open (she gestured) from the neck to the navel, and if he died she would go to her grave a spinster. Her wicked sisters had got pregnant in order to force their marriages — one of them had walked down the aisle eight months gone (more gestures) — but she would rather (with a hitch at her lavender shawl) solicit men in the street than do that. Streeter listened helplessly to her sorrow, as we will listen to most human troubles, having some of our own, but she was still talking when her next student, a Japanese, came in for his lesson, and Streeter had learned no Italian that night. She had not told Streeter all of the story, and she continued it when he came again. The fault might have been his — he should have discouraged her rudely — but now that she had made him her confidant, he saw that he could not change this relationship. The force he had to cope with was the loneliness that is to be found in any large city, and he invented another trip to Perugia. He had two more teachers, two more trips to Perugia, and then, in the late autumn of his second year in Rome, someone from the Embassy recommended Kate Dresser.

An American woman who teaches Italian in Rome is unusual, but then all arrangements in Rome are so complicated that lucidity and skepticism give way when we try to follow the description of a scene in court, a lease, a lunch, or anything else. Each fact or detail breeds more questions than it answers, and in the end we lose sight of the truth, as we were meant to do. Here comes Cardinal Micara with the True Finger of Doubting Thomas — that much is clear — but is the man beside us in church asleep or dead, and what are all the elephants doing in the Piazza Venezia?

The lessons took place at one end of a huge *sala*, by the fireplace. Streeter spent an hour and sometimes two hours preparing for them. He finished *Pinocchio* and began to read *I Promessi Sposi*. After this would come the *Divine Comedy*. He was as proud as a child of his completed homework, loved to be given tests and dictation, and usually came into Kate's apartment with a big, foolish smile on his face, he was so pleased with himself. She was a very good teacher. She understood his fatuousness, the worn condition of his middle-aged memory, and his desire to learn. She spoke an Italian that he could almost always understand, and by keeping a wristwatch on the table to mark the period, by sending him bills through the mail, and by never speaking of herself, she conducted the lessons in an atmosphere that was practical and impersonal. He thought she was a good-looking woman — intense, restless, overworked, perhaps, but charming.

Among the things that Kate Dresser did not tell him, as they sat in this part of the room that she had staked out for herself with a Chinese screen and some rickety gold chairs, was the fact that she was born and raised in the little town of Krasbie, Iowa. Her father and mother were both dead. In a place where almost everybody worked in the chemical-fertilizer factory, her father had happened to be a trolley conductor. When she was growing up, Kate could never bring herself to admit that her father took fares in a trolley car. She could never even admit that he was her father, although she had inherited his most striking physical feature — a nose that turned up so spectacularly at the tip that she was called Roller Coaster and Pug. She had gone from Krasbie to Chicago, from Chicago to New York, where she married a man in the Foreign Service. They lived in Washington and then Tangier. Shortly after the war, they moved to Rome, where her husband died of food poisoning, leaving her with a son and very little money. So she made her home in Rome. The only preparation Krasbie had given her for Italy was the curtain in the little movie theatre where she had spent her Saturday afternoons when she was a girl. Skinny then, dressed no better than most rebellious children and smelling no sweeter, her hair in braids, her pockets full of peanuts and candy and her mouth full of chewing gum, she had put down her quarter every Saturday afternoon, rain or shine, and spread herself out in a seat in the front row. There were shouts of "Roller Coaster!" and "Pug!" from all over the theatre, and, what with the high-heeled shoes (her sister's) that she sometimes wore and the five-and-ten-cent-store diamonds on her fingers, it was no wonder that people made fun of her. Boys dropped chewing gum into her hair and shot spitballs at the back of her skinny neck, and, persecuted in body and spirit, she would raise her eyes to the curtain and see a remarkably precise vision of her future. It was painted on canvas, very badly cracked from having been rolled and unrolled so many times — a vision of an Italian garden, with cypress trees, a terrace, a pool and fountain, and a marble balustrade with roses spilling from marble urns. She seemed literally to have risen up from her seat and to have entered the cracked scene, for it was almost exactly like the view from her window into the courtyard of the Palazzo Tarominia, where she lived.

Now, you might ask why a woman who had so little money was living in the Palazzo Tarominia, and there was a Roman answer. The Baronessa Tramonde — the old Duke of Rome's sister — lived in the west wing of the palace, in an apartment that had been built for Pope Andros X and that was reached by a great staircase with painted walls and ceilings. It had pleased the Baronessa, before the war, to stand at the head of this staircase and greet her friends and relations, but things had changed. The Baronessa had grown old, and so had her friends; they could no longer climb the stairs. Oh, they tried. They had straggled up to her card parties like a patrol under machine-gun fire, the gentlemen pushing the ladies and sometimes vice versa, and old marchesas and princesses — the cream of Europe — huffing and puffing and sitting down on the steps in utter exhaustion. There was a lift in the other wing of the palace — the wing Kate lived in — but a lift could not be installed in the west wing, because it would ruin the paintings. The only other way to enter the Baronessa's quarters was to take the lift to Kate's apartment and walk through it and out a service door that led into the other wing. By giving the Duke of Rome, who also had an apartment in the Palazzo, a kind of eminent domain, Kate had a palace apartment at a low rent. The Duke usually passed through twice a day to visit his sister, and on the first Thursday of every month, at five minutes after eight, a splendid and elderly company would troop through Kate's rooms to the Baronessa's card party. Kate did not mind. In fact, when she heard the doorbell ring on Thursdays her heart would begin a grating beat of the deepest excitement. The old Duke always led the procession. His right hand had been chopped off at the wrist by one of Mussolini's public executioners, and now that the old man's enemies were dead, he carried the stump proudly. With him would come Don Fernando Marchetti, the Duke of Treno, the Duke and Duchess Ricotto-Sporci, Count Ambro di Albentiis, Count and Countess Fabrizio Daromeo, Princess Urbana Tessoro, Princess Isabella Tessoro, and Federico Cardinal Baldova. They had all distinguished themselves in one way or another. Don Fernando had driven a car from Paris to Peking, via the Gobi Desert. Duke Ricotto-Sporci had broken most of his bones in a steeplechase accident, and the Countess Daromeo had operated an Allied radio station in the middle of Rome during the German Occupation. The old Duke of Rome would present Kate with a little bouquet of flowers, and then he and his friends would file through the kitchen and go out the service door.

Kate spoke an admirable Italian, and had done some translating and given lessons, and for the past three years she had supported herself and her son by dubbing parts of English dialogue into old Italian movies, which were then shown over British TV. With her cultivated accent, she played mostly dowagers and the like, but there seemed to be plenty of work, and she spent much of her time in a sound studio near the Tiber. With her salary and the money her husband had left her, she had barely enough to get by on. Her elder sister, in Krasbie, wrote her a long lament two or three times a year: "Oh, you lucky, lucky dog, Kate! Oh, how I envy you being away from all the tiresome, nagging, stupid, petty details of life at home." Kate Dresser's life was not lacking in stupid and nagging details, but instead of mentioning such things in her letters, she inflamed her sister's longing to travel by sending home photographs of herself in gondolas, or cards from Florence, when she always spent Easter with friends.

Streeter knew that under Kate Dresser's teaching he was making progress with his Italian, and usually when he stepped out of the Palazzo Tarominia into the street after his lesson, he was exhilarated at the thought that in another month — at the end of the season, anyhow — he would understand everything that was going on and being said. But his progress had its ups and downs.

The beauty of Italy is not easy to come by any longer, if it ever was, but, driving to a villa below Anticoli for a weekend with friends, Streeter saw a country of such detail and loveliness that it could not be described. They had reached the villa early on a rainy night. Nightingales sang in the trees, the double doors of the villa stood open, and in all the rooms there were bowls of roses and olivewood fires. It had seemed, with the servants bowing and bringing in candles and wine, like some gigantic and princely homecoming in a movie, and, going out onto the terrace after dinner to hear the nightingales and see the lights of the hill towns, Streeter felt that he had never been put by dark hills and distant lights into a mood of such tenderness. In the morning, when he stepped out onto his bedroom balcony, he saw a barefoot maid in the garden, picking a rose to put in her hair. Then she began to sing. It was like a flamenco — first guttural and then falsetto — and poor Streeter found his Italian still so limited that he couldn't understand the words of the song, and this brought him around to the fact that he couldn't quite understand the landscape, either. His feeling about it was very much what he might have felt about some excellent resort or summer place — a scene where, perhaps as children, we have thrown ourselves into a temporary relationship with beauty and simplicity that will be rudely broken off on Labor Day. It was the evocation of a borrowed, temporary, bittersweet happiness that he rebelled against — but the maid went on singing, and Streeter did not understand a word.

When Streeter took his lessons at Kate's, her son, Charlie, usually passed through the *sala* at least once during the hour. He was a baseball fan, and had a bad complexion and an owlish laugh. He would say hello to Streeter and pass on some sports news from the Rome *Daily American.* Streeter had a son of his own of about the same age, and was enjoined by the divorce settlement from seeing the boy, and he never looked at Charlie without a pang of longing for his own son. Charlie was fifteen, and one of those American boys you see waiting for the school bus up by the Embassy, dressed in black leather jackets and Levi's, and with sideburns or duck-tail haircuts, and fielder's mitts — anything that will stamp them as American. These are the real expatriates. On Saturdays after the movies they go into one of those bars called Harry's or Larry's or Jerry's, where the walls are covered with autographed photographs of unknown electric-guitar players and unknown soubrettes, to eat bacon and eggs and talk baseball and play American records on the jukebox. They are Embassy children, and the children of writers and oil-company and airline employees and divorcées and Fulbright Fellows. Eating bacon and eggs, and listening to the jukebox, they have a sense of being far, far from home that is a much sweeter and headier distillation than their parents ever know. Charlie had spent five years of his life under a ceiling decorated with gold that had been brought from the New World by the first Duke of Rome, and he had seen old marchesas with diamonds as big as acorns slip the cheese parings into their handbags when the lunch was finished. He had ridden in gondolas and played softball on the Palatine. He had seen the Palio at Siena, and had heard the bells of Rome and Florence and Venice and Ravenna and Verona. But it wasn't about these things that he wrote in a letter to his mother's Uncle George in Krasbie toward the middle of March. Instead, he asked the old man to take him home and let him be an American boy. The timing was perfect. Uncle George had just retired from the fertilizer factory and had always wanted to bring Kate and her son home. Within two weeks he was on board a ship bound for Naples.

Streeter, of course, knew nothing of this. But he had suspected that there was some tension between Charlie and his mother. The boy's hoedown American clothes, the poses he took as a rail splitter, pitcher, and cowboy, and his mother's very Italianate manners implied room for sizable disagreement, at least, and, going there one Sunday afternoon, Streeter stepped into a quarrel. Assunta, the maid, let him in, but he stopped at the door of the *sala* when he heard Kate and her son shouting at one another in anger. Streeter could not retreat. Assunta had gone on ahead to say he was there, and all he could do was wait in the vestibule. Kate came out to him then — she was crying — and said, in Italian, that she could not give him a lesson that afternoon. She was sorry. Something had come up, and there had not been time to telephone him. He felt like a fool, confronted with her tears, holding his grammar, his copybook, and *I Promessi Sposi* under one arm. He said it didn't matter about the lesson, it was nothing, and could he come on Tuesday? She said yes, yes, would he come on Tuesday — and would he come on Thursday, not for a lesson but to do her a favor? "My father's brother — my Uncle George — is coming, to try and take Charlie home. I don't know what to do. I don't know what I *can* do. But I would appreciate it if there was a man here; I would feel so much better if I weren't alone. You don't have to say anything or do anything but sit in a chair and have a drink, but I would feel so much better if I weren't alone."

Streeter agreed to come, and went away then, wondering what kind of a life it was she led if she had to count in an emergency on a stranger like him. With his lesson canceled and nothing else that he had to do, he took a walk up the river as far as the Ministry of the Marine, and then came back through a neighborhood that was neither new nor old nor anything else you could specify. Because it was Sunday afternoon, the houses were mostly shut. The streets were deserted. When he passed anyone, it was usually a family group returning from an excursion to the zoo. There were also a few of those lonely men and women carrying pastry boxes that you see everywhere in the world at dusk on Sunday — unmarried aunts and uncles going out to tea with their relations and bringing a little pastry to sweeten the call. But mostly he was alone, mostly there was no sound but his own footsteps and, in the distance, the iron ringing of iron trolley-car wheels on iron tracks — a lonely sound on Sunday afternoons for many Americans; a lonely one for him, anyhow, and reminding him of some friendless, loveless, galling Sunday in his youth. As he came closer to the city, there were more lights and people — flowers and the noise of talk — and under the gate of Santa Maria del Popolo a whore spoke to him. She was a beautiful young woman, but he told her, in his broken Italian, that he had a friend, and walked on.

Crossing the Piazza, he saw a man struck by a car. The noise was loud — that surprising loudness of our bones when they are dealt a mortal blow. The driver of the car slipped out of his seat and ran up the Pincian Hill. The victim lay in a heap on the paving, a shabbily dressed man but with a lot of oil in his black, wavy hair, which must have been his pride. A crowd gathered — not solemn at all, although a few women crossed themselves — and everyone began to talk excitedly. The crowd, garrulous, absorbed in its own opinions and indifferent, it seemed, to the dying man, was so thick that when the police came they had to push and struggle to reach the victim. With the words of the whore still in his ears, Streeter wondered why it was that they regarded a human life as something of such dubious value.

He turned away from the Piazza then, toward the river, and, passing the Tomb of Augustus, he noticed a young man calling to a cat and offering it something to eat. The cat was one of those thousands of millions that live in the ruins of Rome and eat leftover spaghetti, and the man was offering the cat a piece of bread. Then, as the cat approached him, the man took a firecracker out of his pocket, put it into the piece of bread, and lit the fuse. He put the bread on the sidewalk, and just as the cat took it the powder exploded. The animal let out a hellish shriek and leaped into the air, its body all twisted, and then it streaked over the wall and was lost in the darkness of Augustus' Tomb. The man laughed at his trick, and so did several people who had been watching.

Streeter's first instinct was to box the man's ears and teach him not to feed lighted firecrackers to stray cats. But, with such an appreciative audience, this would have amounted to an international incident, and he realized there wasn't anything he could do. The people who had laughed at the prank were good and kind — most of them affectionate parents. You might have seen them earlier in the day on the Palatine, picking violets.

Streeter walked on into a dark street and heard at his back the hoofs and trappings of horses — it sounded like cavalry — and stepped aside to let a hearse and a mourner's carriage pass. The hearse was drawn by two pairs of bays with black plumes. The driver wore funerary livery, with an admiral's hat, and had the brutish red face of a drunken horse thief. The hearse banged, slammed, and rattled over the stones in such a loose-jointed way that the poor soul it carried must have been in a terrible state of disarrangement, and the mourner's carriage that followed was empty. The friends of the dead man had probably been too late or had got the wrong date or had forgotten the whole thing, as was so often the case in Rome. Off the hearse and carriage rattled toward the Servian Gate.

Streeter knew one thing then: He did not want to die in Rome. He was in excellent health and had no reason to think about death; nevertheless, he was afraid. Back at his flat, he poured some whiskey and water into a glass and stepped out onto his balcony. He watched the night fall and the street lights go on with complete bewilderment at his own feelings. He did not want to die in Rome. The power of this idea could only stem from ignorance and stupidity, he told himself — for what could such a fear represent but the inability to respond to the force of life? He reproached himself with arguments and consoled himself with whiskey, but in the middle of the night he was waked by the noise of a carriage and horses' hoofs, and again he sweated with fear. The hearse, the horse thief, and the empty mourner's carriage, he thought, were rattling back, under his balcony.

He got up out of bed and went to the window to see, but it was only two empty carriages going back to the stables.

When Uncle George landed in Naples, on Tuesday, he was excited and in a good humor. His purpose in coming abroad was twofold — to bring Charlie and Kate home, and to take a vacation, the first in forty-three years. A friend of his in Krasbie who had been to Italy had written an itinerary for him: "Stay at the Royal in Naples. Go to the National Museum. Have a drink in the Galleria Umberto. Eat supper at the California. Good American food. Take the Roncari *auto-pullman* in the morning for Rome. This goes through two interesting villages and stops at Nero's villa. In Rome stay at the Excelsior. Make reservations in advance. . . ."

On Wednesday morning, Uncle George got up early and went down to the hotel dining room. "Orange juice and ham and eggs," he said to the waiter. The waiter brought him orange juice, coffee, and a roll. "Where's my ham and eggs?" Uncle George asked, and then realized, when the waiter bowed and smiled, that the man did not understand English. He got out his phrase book, but there was nothing about ham and eggs. "You gotta no hamma?" he asked loudly. "You gotta no eggsa?" The waiter went on smiling and bowing, and Uncle George gave up. He ate the breakfast he hadn't ordered, gave the waiter a twenty-lira tip, cashed four hundred dollars' worth of traveler's checks at the desk, and checked out. All this money in lire made a bump in his suit jacket, and he held his left hand over his wallet as if he had a pain there. Naples, he knew, was full of thieves. He took a cab to the bus station, which was in a square near the Galleria Umberto. It was early in the morning, the light was slanting, and he enjoyed the smell of coffee and bread and the stir of people hurrying along the streets to work. A fine smell of the sea rose up the streets from the bay. He was early and was shown his seat in the bus by a red-faced gentleman who spoke English with a British accent. This was the guide — one of those who, whatever conveyance you take and wherever you go, make travel among the monuments bizarre. Their command of languages is extraordinary, their knowledge of antiquity is impressive, and their love of beauty is passionate, but when they separate themselves from the party for a moment it is to take a pull from a hip flask or to pinch a young pilgrim. They praise the ancient world in four languages, but their clothes are threadbare, their linen is dirty, and their hands tremble with thirst and lechery. While the guide chatted about the weather with Uncle George, the whiskey could already be smelled on his breath. Then the guide left Uncle George to greet the rest of the party, now coming across the square.

There were about thirty — they moved in a flock, or mass, understandably timid about the strangeness of their surroundings — and they were mostly old women. As they came into the bus, they cackled (as we all will when we grow old), and made the fussy arrangements of elderly travelers. Then, with the guide singing the praises of ancient Naples, they started on their way.

They first went along the coast. The color of the water reminded Uncle George of postcards he had received from Honolulu, where one of his friends had gone for a vacation. It was green and blue. He had never seen anything like it himself. They passed some resorts only half open and sleepy, where young men sat on rocks in their bathing trunks, waiting patiently for the sun to darken their skins. What did they think about? Uncle George wondered. During all those hours that they sat on rocks, what on earth did they think about? They passed a ramshackle colony of little bathhouses no bigger than privies, and Uncle George remembered — how many years ago — the thrill of undressing in such briny sea chambers as these when he had been taken to the seashore as a boy. As they turned inland, he craned his neck to get a last look at the sea, wondering why it should seem, shining and blue, like something that he remembered in his bones. Then they went into a tunnel and came out in farmland. Uncle George was interested in farming methods and admired the way that vines were trained onto trees. He admired the terracing of the land, and was troubled by the traces of soil erosion that he saw. And he recognized that he was separated only by a pane of glass from a life that was as strange to him as life on the moon.

The bus, with its glass roof and glass windows, was like a fishbowl, and the sunlight and cloud shadows of the day fell among the travelers. Their way was blocked by a flock of sheep. Sheep surrounded the bus, isolated this little island of elderly Americans, and filled the air with dumb, harsh bleating. Beyond the sheep they saw a girl carrying a water jug on her head. A man lay sound asleep in the grass by the side of the road. A woman sat on a doorstep, suckling a child. Within the dome of glass the old ladies discussed the high price of airplane luggage. "Grace got ringworm in Palermo," one of them said. "I don't think she'll ever be cured."

The guide pointed out fragments of old Roman road, Roman towers and bridges. There was a castle on a hill — a sight that delighted Uncle George, and no wonder, for there had been castles painted on his supper plate when he was a boy, and the earliest books that had been read to him and that he had been able to read had been illustrated with castles. They had meant everything that was exciting and strange and wonderful in life, and now, by raising his eyes, he could see one against a sky as blue as the sky in his picture books.

After traveling for an hour or two, they stopped in a village where there were a coffee bar and toilets. Coffee cost one hundred lire a cup, a fact that filled the ladies' conversation for some time after they had started again. Coffee had been sixty lire at the hotel. Forty at the corner. They took pills and read from their guidebooks, and Uncle George looked out of the windows at this strange country, where the spring flowers and the autumn flowers seemed to grow side by side in the grass. It would be miserable weather in Krasbie, but here everything was in bloom — fruit trees, mimosa — and the pastures were white with flowers and the vegetable gardens already yielding crops.

They came into a town or city then — an old place with crooked and narrow streets. He didn't catch the name. The guide explained that there was a *festa*. The bus driver had to blow his horn continuously to make any progress, and two or three times came to a full stop, the crowd was so dense. The people in the streets looked up at this apparition — this fishbowl of elderly Americans — with such incredulity that Uncle George's feelings were hurt. He saw a little girl take a crust of bread out of her mouth to stare at him. Women held their children up in the air to see the strangers. Windows were thrown open, bars were emptied, and people pointed at the curious tourists and laughed. Uncle George would have liked to address them, as he so often addressed the Rotary. "Don't stare," he wanted to say to them. "We are not so queer and rich and strange. Don't stare at us."

The bus turned down a side street, and there was another stop for coffee and toilets. Most of the travelers scattered to buy postcards. Uncle George, seeing an open church across the street, decided to go inside. The air smelled of spice when he pushed the door open. The stone walls inside were bare — it was like an armory — and only a few candles burned in the chapels at the sides. Then Uncle George heard a loud voice and saw a man kneeling in front of one of the chapels, saying his prayers. He carried on in a way that Uncle George had never seen before. His voice was strong, supplicatory, sometimes angry. His face was wet with tears. He was beseeching the Cross for something — an explanation or an indulgence or a life. He waved his hands, he wept, and his voice and his sobs echoed in the barny place. Uncle George went out and got back into his seat on the bus.

They left the city for the country again, and a little before noon they stopped at the gates to Nero's villa, bought their tickets, and went in. It was a large ruin, fanciful, and picked clean of everything but its brick supports. The place had been vast and tall, and now the walls and archways of roofless rooms, the butts of towers, stood in a stretch of green pasture, with nothing leading anywhere any more except to nothing, and all the many staircases mounting and turning stopped in midair. Uncle George left the party and wandered happily through these traces of a palace. The atmosphere seemed to him pleasant and tranquil — a little like the feeling in a forest — and he heard a bird singing and the noise of water. The forms of the ruins, all bristling with plants like the hair in an old man's ears, seemed pleasantly familiar, as if his unremembered dreams had been played out against a scene like this. He found himself then in a place that was darker than the rest. The air was damp, and the senseless brick rooms, opening onto one another, were full of brush. It might have been a dungeon or a guardhouse or a temple where obscene rites were performed, for he was suddenly stirred licentiously by the damp. He turned back, looking for the sun, the water, and the bird, and found a guide standing in his path.

"You wish to see the special place?"

"What do you mean?"

"Very special," the guide said. "For men only. Only for strong men. Such pictures. Very old."

"How much?"

"Two hundred lire."

"All right." Uncle George took two hundred lire out of his change pocket.

"Come," the guide said. "This way." He walked on briskly — so briskly that Uncle George nearly had to run to keep up with him. He saw the guide go through a narrow opening in the wall, a place where the brick had crumbled, but when Uncle George followed him the guide seemed to have disappeared. It was a trap. He felt an arm around his throat, and his head was thrown back so violently that he couldn't call for help. He felt a hand lift the wallet out of his pocket — a touch as light as the nibble of a fish on a line — and then he was thrown brutally to the ground. He lay there dazed for a minute or two. When he sat up, he saw that he had been left his empty wallet and his passport.

Then he roared with anger at the thieves, and hated Italy, with its thieving population of organ grinders and bricklayers. But even during this outburst his anger was not as strong as a feeling of weakness and shame. He was terribly ashamed of himself, and when he picked up his empty wallet and put it in his pocket, he felt as if his heart had been plucked out and broken. Who could he blame? Not the damp ruins. He had asked for something that was by his lights all wrong, and he could only blame himself. The theft might happen every day — some lecherous old fool like him might be picked clean each time the bus stopped. He got to his feet, weary and sick of the old bones that had got him into trouble. He dusted the dirt off his clothes. Then he realized that he might be late. He might have missed the bus and be stranded in the ruins without a cent. He began to walk and run through the rooms, until he came out into a clearing and saw in the distance the flock of old ladies, still clinging to one another.

The guide came out from behind a wall, and they all got in the bus and started off again.

Rome was ugly; at least, the outskirts were: trolley cars and cut-rate furniture stores and torn-up streets and the sort of apartment houses that nobody ever really wants to live in. The old ladies began to gather their guidebooks and put on their coats and hats and gloves. Journey's end is the same everywhere. Then, dressed for their destination, they all sat down again, with their hands folded in their laps, and the bus was still. "Oh, I wish I'd never come," one old lady said to another. "I just wish I'd never left home." She was not the only one.

"*Ecco, ecco Roma,*" the guide said, and so it was.

Streeter went to Kate's at seven on Thursday. Assunta let him in, and, for the first time, he walked down the *sala* without his copy of *I Promessi Sposi*, and sat down by the fireplace. Charlie came in then. He had on the usual outfit — the tight Levi's, with cuffs turned up, and a pink shirt. When he moved, he dragged or banged the leather heels of his loafers on the marble floor. He talked about baseball and exercised his owlish laugh, but he didn't mention Uncle George. Neither did Kate, when she came in, nor did she offer Streeter a drink. She seemed to be in the throes of an emotional storm, with all her powers of decision suspended. They talked about the weather. At one point, Charlie came and stood by his mother, and she took both of his hands in one of hers. Then the doorbell rang, and Kate went down the room to meet her uncle. They embraced very tenderly — the members of a family — and when this was over he said, "I was robbed, Katie. I was robbed yesterday of four hundred dollars. Coming up from Naples on the bus."

"Oh, I'm so sorry!" she said. "Wasn't there anything you could do, George? Wasn't there anyone you could speak to?"

"Speak to, Katie? There hasn't been anyone I could speak to since I got off the boat. No speaka da English. If you cut off their hands, they wouldn't be able to say anything. I can afford to lose four hundred dollars — I'm not a poor man — but if I could only have given it to some worthwhile cause."

"I'm terribly sorry."

"You've got quite a place here, Katie."

"And, Charlie, this is Uncle George."

If she had counted on their not getting along, this chance was lost in a second. Charlie forgot his owlish laugh and stood so straight, so in need of what America could do for him that the rapport between the man and the boy was instantaneous, and Kate had to separate them in order to introduce Streeter. Uncle George shook hands with her student and came to a likely but erroneous conclusion.

"Speaka da English?" he asked.

"I'm an American," Streeter said.

"How long is your sentence?"

"This is my second year," Streeter said. "I work at F.R.U.P.C."

"It's an immoral country," Uncle George said, sitting down in one of the golden chairs. "First they rob me of four hundred dollars, and then, walking around the streets here, all I see is statues of men without any clothes on. Nothing."

Kate rang for Assunta, and when the maid came in she ordered whiskey and ice, in very rapid Italian. "It's just another way of looking at things, Uncle George," she said.

"No, it isn't," Uncle George said. "It isn't natural. Not even in locker rooms. There's very few men who'd choose to parade around a locker room stark naked if a towel was handy. It's not natural. Everywhere you look. Up on the roofs. At the main traffic intersections. When I was coming over here, I passed through a little garden — playground, I guess you'd say — and right in the middle of it, right in the middle of all these little children, is one of these men without anything on."

"Will you have some whiskey?"

"Yes, please. . . . The boat sails on Saturday, Katie, and I want you and the boy to come home with me."

"I don't want Charlie to leave," Kate said.

"He wants to leave — don't you, Charlie? He wrote me a nice letter. Nicely worded, and he's got a nice handwriting. That was a nice letter, Charlie. I showed it to the high-school superintendent, and he said you can enter the Krasbie high school whenever you want. And I want you to come, too, Kate. It's your home, and you've only got one. The trouble with you, Katie, is that when you were a kid they used to make fun of you in Krasbie, and you just started running, that's all, and you never stopped."

"If that's true — and it may be," she said quickly, "why should I want to go back to a place where I will seem ridiculous."

"Oh, Katie, you won't seem ridiculous. I'll take care of that."

"I want to go home, Mama," Charlie said. He was sitting on a stool by the fireplace — not so straight-backed any more. "I'm homesick all the time."

"How could you possibly be homesick for America?" Her voice was very sharp. "You've never seen it. This is your home."

"How do you mean?"

"Your home is with your mother."

"There's more to it than that, Mama. I feel strange here all the time. Everybody on the street speaking a different language."

"You've never even tried to learn Italian."

"Even if I had, it wouldn't make any difference. It would still sound strange. I mean, it would still remind me that it wasn't my language. I just don't understand the people, Mama. I like them all right, but I just don't understand them. I never know what they're going to do next."

"Why don't you try and understand them?"

"Oh, I do, but I'm no genius, and you don't understand them, either. I've heard you say so, and sometimes you're homesick, too, I know. I can tell by the way you look."

"Homesickness is nothing," she said angrily. "It is absolutely nothing. Fifty percent of the people in the world are homesick all the time. But I don't suppose you're old enough to understand. When you're in one place and long to be in another, it isn't as simple as taking a boat. You don't really long for another country. You long for something in yourself that you don't have, or haven't been able to find."

"Oh, I don't mean that, Mama. I just mean if I was with people who spoke my language, people who understood me, I'd be more comfortable."

"If comfort is all you expect to get out of life, God help you."

Then the doorbell rang and Assunta answered it. Kate glanced at her watch and saw that it was five after eight. It was also the first Thursday in the month. Before she could get out an explanation, they had started down the *sala*, with the old Duke of Rome in the lead, holding some flowers in his left hand. A little behind him was the Duchess, his wife — a tall, willowy, gray-haired woman wearing a lot of jewelry that had been given to the family by Francis I. An assortment of nobles brought up the rear, looking like a country circus, gorgeous and travel-worn. The Duke gave Kate her flowers. They all bowed vaguely to her company and went out through the kitchen, with its smell of gas leaks, to the service door.

"Oh, Giuseppe the barber he gotta the cash," Uncle George sang loudly. "He gotta the bigga the blacka mustache." He waited for someone to laugh, and when no one did he asked, "What was that?"

Kate told him, but her eyes were brighter, and he noticed this.

"You like that kind of thing, don't you?" he said.

"Possibly," she said.

"It's crazy, Katie," he said. "It's crazy, it's crazy. You come home with me and Charlie. You and Charlie can live in the other half of my house, and I'll have a nice American kitchen put in for you."

Streeter saw that she was touched by this remark, and he thought she was going to cry. She said quickly, "How in hell do you think America would have been discovered if everybody stayed home in places like Krasbie?"

"You're not discovering anything, Katie."

"I am. I am."

"We'll all be happier, Mama," Charlie said. "We'll all be happier if we have a nice clean house and lots of nice friends and a nice garden and kitchen and stall shower."

She stood with her back to them, by the mantelpiece, and said loudly, "No nice friends, no kitchen, no garden, no shower bath or anything else will keep me from wanting to see the world and the different people who live in it." Then she turned to her son and spoke softly. "You'll miss Italy, Charlie."

The boy laughed his owlish laugh. "I'll miss the black hairs in my food," he said. She didn't make a sound. She didn't even sigh. Then the boy went to her and began to cry. "I'm sorry, Mummy," he said. "I'm sorry. That was a dumb thing to say. It's just an old joke." He kissed her hands and the tears on her cheeks, and Streeter got up and left.

"*Tal era ciò che di meno deforme e di men compassionevole si faceva vedere intorno, i sani, gli agiati,*" Streeter read when he went again for his lesson Sunday. "*Chè, dopo tante immagini di miseria, e pensando a quella ancor più grave, per mezzo alla quale dovrem condurre il lettore, no ci fermeremo ora a dir qual fosse lo spettacolo degli appestati che si strascicavano o giacevano per le strade, de' poveri, de' fanciulli, delle donne.*" *

The boy had gone, he could tell — not because she said so but because the place seemed that much bigger. In the middle of his lesson, the old Duke of Rome came through in his bathrobe and slippers, carrying a bowl of soup to his sister, who was sick. Kate looked tired, but then she always did, and when the lesson ended and Streeter stood up, wondering if she would mention Charlie or Uncle George, she complimented him on the progress he had made and urged him to finish *I Promessi Sposi* and to buy a copy of the *Divine Comedy* for next week.

Suggestions for Discussion

1. Who speaks in "The Bella Lingua"? To whom? In what form?

2. How many options of the omniscient author listed on page 173 does Cheever employ in the first three paragraphs?

3. The early pages of the narrative repeatedly refer to "us." Who are "we"? Who is "you" in the paragraph beginning, "Now, you might ask . . . ," on page 192?

4. With the sentence beginning, "Among the things that Kate Dresser did not tell him . . ." (page 191), the narrative switches from the mind of Streeter to that of his teacher. How has this shift in point of view been prepared for?

5. In the course of the paragraph beginning, "When Streeter took his lessons at Kate's . . ." (page 194), we move from Streeter's point of view so intimately into Charlie's that the next paragraph must begin, "Streeter, of course, knew nothing of this." How is the transition accomplished?

6. A vignette of "the guide" is presented in a paragraph on page 197. From what point of view is this character type presented? Why is he presented as a type rather than as an individual?

* "Such were the less deformed and less pitiable that could be seen all around, the healthy and wealthy . . . for after so many images of misery, and keeping in mind the still greater ones we will have to present to the reader, we will not now stop to describe the plague-ridden who dragged themselves through the street, or lay there; the poor, the children, the women."

7. Why does the narrative provide us with Uncle George's consciousness? What would be lost if he were presented only externally?

8. The most dramatic overt change in this story takes place in the lives of Kate and Charlie. Yet Streeter is clearly the major means of perception. In what sense is Streeter the one who is moved or changed at the resolution?

The Masked Marvel's Last Toehold

RICHARD SELZER

Morning Rounds.

On the fifth floor of the hospital, in the west wing, I know that a man is sitting up in his bed, waiting for me. Elihu Koontz is seventy-five, and he is diabetic. It is two weeks since I amputated his left leg just below the knee. I walk down the corridor, but I do not go straight into his room. Instead, I pause in the doorway. He is not yet aware of my presence, but gazes down at the place in the bed where his leg used to be, and where now there is the collapsed leg of his pajamas. He is totally absorbed, like an athlete appraising the details of his body. What is he thinking, I wonder. Is he dreaming the outline of his toes? Does he see there his foot's incandescent ghost? Could he be angry? Feel that I have taken from him something for which he yearns now with all his heart? Has he forgotten so soon the pain? It was a pain so great as to set him apart from all other men, in a red-hot place where he had no kith or kin. What of those black gorilla toes and the soupy mess that was his heel? I watch him from the doorway. It is a kind of spying, I know.

Save for a white fringe open at the front, Elihu Koontz is bald. The hair has grown too long and is wilted. He wears it as one would wear a day-old laurel wreath. He is naked to the waist, so that I can see his breasts. They are the breasts of Buddha, inverted triangles from which the nipples swing, dark as garnets.

I have seen enough. I step into the room, and he sees that I am there. "How did the night go, Elihu?"

He looks at me for a long moment. "Shut the door," he says.

I do, and move to the side of the bed. He takes my left hand in both of his, gazes at it, turns it over, then back, fondling, at last holding it up to his cheek. I do not withdraw from this loving. After a while he relinquishes my hand, and looks up at me.

"How is the pain?" I ask.

He does not answer, but continues to look at me in silence. I know at once that he has made a decision.

"Ever hear of The Masked Marvel?" He says this in a low voice, almost a whisper.

"What?"

"The Masked Marvel," he says. "You never heard of him?"

"No."

He clucks his tongue. He is exasperated.

All at once there is a recollection. It is dim, distant, but coming near.

"Do you mean the wrestler?"

Eagerly, he nods, and the breasts bob. How gnomish he looks, oval as the huge helpless egg of some outlandish lizard. He has very long arms, which, now and then, he unfurls to reach for things — a carafe of water, a get-well card. He gazes up at me, urging. He *wants* me to remember.

"Well . . . yes," I say. I am straining backward in time. "I saw him wrestle in Toronto long ago."

"Ha!" He smiles. "You saw *me*." And his index finger, held rigid and upright, bounces in the air.

The man has said something shocking, unacceptable. It must be challenged.

"You?" I am trying to smile.

Again that jab of the finger. "You saw *me*."

"No," I say. But even then, something about Elihu Koontz, those pro-longed arms, the shape of his head, the sudden agility with which he leans from his bed to get a large brown envelope from his nightstand, something is forcing me toward a memory. He rummages through his papers, old newspaper clippings, photographs, and I remember . . .

It is almost forty years ago. I am ten years old. I have been sent to Toronto to spend the summer with relatives. Uncle Max has bought two tickets to the wrestling match. He is taking me that night.

"He isn't allowed," says Aunt Sarah to me. Uncle Max has angina.

"He gets too excited," she says.

"I wish you wouldn't go, Max," she says.

"You mind your own business," he says.

And we go. Out into the warm Canadian evening. I am not only abroad, I am abroad in the *evening*! I have never been taken out in the evening. I am terribly excited. The trolleys, the lights, the horns. It is a bazaar. At the Maple Leaf Gardens, we sit high and near the center. The vast arena is dark except for the brilliance of the ring at the bottom.

It begins.

The wrestlers circle. They grapple. They are all haunch and paunch. I am shocked by their ugliness, but I do not show it. Uncle Max is exhilarated.

He leans forward, his eyes unblinking, on his face a look of enormous happiness. One after the other, a pair of wrestlers enter the ring. The two men join, twist, jerk, tug, bend, yank, and throw. Then they leave and are replaced by another pair. At last it is the main event. "The Angel vs. The Masked Marvel."

On the cover of the program notes, there is a picture of The Angel hanging from the limb of a tree, a noose of thick rope around his neck. The Angel hangs just so for an hour every day, it is explained, to strengthen his neck. The Masked Marvel's trademark is a black stocking cap with holes for the eyes and mouth. He is never seen without it, states the program. No one knows who The Masked Marvel really is!

"Good," says Uncle Max. "Now you'll see something." He is fidgeting, waiting for them to appear. They come down separate aisles, climb into the ring from opposite sides. I have never seen anything like them. It is The Angel's neck that first captures the eye. The shaved nape rises in twin columns to puff into the white hood of a sloped and bosselated skull that is too small. As though, strangled by the sinews of that neck, the skull had long since withered and shrunk. The thing about The Angel is the absence of any mystery in his body. It is simply *there*. A monosyllabic announcement. A grunt. One looks and knows everything at once, the fat thighs, the gigantic buttocks, the great spine from which hang knotted ropes and pale aprons of beef. And that prehistoric head. He is all of a single hideous piece, The Angel is. No detachables.

The Masked Marvel seems dwarfish. His fingers dangle kneeward. His short legs are slightly bowed as if under the weight of the cask they are forced to heft about. He has breasts that swing when he moves! I have never seen such breasts on a man before.

There is a sudden ungraceful movement, and they close upon one another. The Angel stoops and hugs The Marvel about the waist, locking his hands behind The Marvel's back. Now he straightens and lifts The Marvel as though he were uprooting a tree. Thus he holds him, then stoops again, thrusts one hand through The Marvel's crotch, and with the other grabs him by the neck. He rears and . . . The Marvel is aloft! For a long moment, The Angel stands as though deciding where to make the toss. Then throws. Was that board or bone that splintered there? Again and again, The Angel hurls himself upon the body of The Masked Marvel.

Now The Angel rises over the fallen Marvel, picks up one foot in both of his hands, and twists the toes downward. It is far beyond the tensile strength of mere ligament, mere cartilage. The Masked Marvel does not hide his agony, but pounds and slaps the floor with his hand, now and then reaching up toward The Angel in an attitude of supplication. I have never seen such suffering. And all the while his black mask rolls from side to side, the mouth pulled to a tight slit through which issues an endless hiss that I can hear from where I sit. All at once, I hear a shouting close by.

"Break it off! Tear off a leg and throw it up here!"

It is Uncle Max. Even in the darkness I can see that he is gray. A band of sweat stands upon his upper lip. He is on his feet now, panting, one fist pressed at his chest, the other raised warlike toward the ring. For the first time I begin to think that something terrible might happen here. Aunt Sarah was right.

"Sit down, Uncle Max," I say. "Take a pill, please."

He reaches for the pillbox, gropes, and swallows without taking his gaze from the wrestlers. I wait for him to sit down.

"That's not fair," I say, "twisting his toes like that."

"It's the toehold," he explains.

"But it's not *fair*," I say again. The whole of the evil is laid open for me to perceive. I am trembling.

And now The Angel does something unspeakable. Holding the foot of The Marvel at full twist with one hand, he bends and grasps the mask where it clings to the back of The Marvel's head. And he pulls. He is going to strip it off! Lay bare an ultimate carnal mystery! Suddenly it is beyond mere physical violence. Now I am on my feet, shouting into the Maple Leaf Gardens.

"Watch out," I scream. "Stop him. Please, somebody, stop him."

Next to me, Uncle Max is chuckling.

Yet The Masked Marvel hears me, I know it. And rallies from his bed of pain. Thrusting with his free heel, he strikes The Angel at the back of the knee. The Angel falls. The Masked Marvel is on top of him, pinning his shoulders to the mat. One! Two! Three! And it is over. Uncle Max is strangely still. I am gasping for breath. All this I remember as I stand at the bedside of Elihu Koontz.

Once again, I am in the operating room. It is two years since I amputated the left leg of Elihu Koontz. Now it is his right leg which is gangrenous. I have already scrubbed. I stand to one side wearing my gown and gloves. And . . . *I am masked.* Upon the table lies Elihu Koontz, pinned in a fierce white light. Spinal anesthesia has been administered. One of his arms is taped to a board placed at a right angle to his body. Into this arm, a needle has been placed. Fluid drips here from a bottle overhead. With his other hand, Elihu Koontz beats feebly at the side of the operating table. His head rolls from side to side. His mouth is pulled into weeping. It seems to me that I have never seen such misery.

An orderly stands at the foot of the table, holding Elihu Koontz's leg aloft by the toes so that the intern can scrub the limb with antiseptic solutions. The intern paints the foot, ankle, leg, and thigh, both front and back, three times. From a corner of the room where I wait, I look down as from an amphitheater. Then I think of Uncle Max yelling, "Tear off a leg. Throw it up here." And I think that forty years later I am making the catch.

"It's not fair," I say aloud. But no one hears me. I step forward to break The Masked Marvel's last toehold.

Suggestions for Discussion

1. Who speaks in "The Masked Marvel's Last Toehold"? To whom? In what form?

2. Is the surgeon a peripheral or a central narrator? It is Elihu Koontz who loses his legs; how can the surgeon be said to be the one who is changed in the story?

3. How does the contrast between the surgeon's thoughts and his professional demeanor help characterize him?

4. The flashback beginning on page 206 moves back and forth between summary and scene. What is the function of each?

5. In the flashback the narrator re-creates his consciousness as a boy. How might the description differ if he were telling of the wrestling match from his adult perspective? What would be lost?

6. Suppose that the story were told from the point of view of The Masked Marvel. Could it be the same story?

RETROSPECT

1. Identify the *person* employed in each of the stories read up to now. Which are told from the viewpoint of the omniscient, the limited omniscient, the objective, the central, and the peripheral narrator?

2. Is the narrator of "In the Absence of Angels" peripheral or central? How does the *form* of this story differ from most of the others that precede the present chapter? How might the story differ if it were told from the omniscient viewpoint?

3. Compare "The Bella Lingua" to "Cutting Edge," which also explores the thoughts of several characters. Which of these stories is written from the more omniscient point of view?

WRITING ASSIGNMENTS

1. Write a short scene about the birth or death of anything. (You may interpret "anything" liberally — the birth or death of a person, plant, animal, machine, scheme, passion, etc.) Use all five areas of knowledge of the *editorial omniscient author*. Be sure to do the following: give us the thoughts of more than one character, tell us something about at least one character that he or she doesn't know or realize, include some exposition from the past or the future, and provide at least one universal "truth."

2. Write a love scene, serious or comic, from the *limited omniscient* viewpoint, confining yourself to objective observation and the thoughts of one character. Make this character believe that the other loves her or him, while the external actions make clear to the reader that this is not so.

3. "Write up" your most interesting recent dream, using the viewpoint of the *objective author*. Without any comment or interpretation whatever, report the events (the more bizarre, the better) as they occur.

4. Write a scene from the point of view of a *peripheral narrator* who is not at all involved in the events he or she describes but who is placed in a position from which to observe them. Nevertheless, make the observing narrator the character who is moved by the action.

5. Write a letter from a *central narrator* to another character from whom the narrator wants a great deal of money. Convince us as readers that the money is deserved.

6. Place your character in an uncomfortable social situation and write a passage in which the character's thoughts are presented both in an *interior monologue* and aloud. Nothing else. Contrast the expressed with the unexpressed thoughts.

7. Write a scene in the *second person,* in which the reader is drawn into identifying with the protagonist.

7

ASSORTED LIARS
Point of View, Part II

At What Distance?
With What Limitations?

At What Distance?

As with the chemist at his microscope and the lookout in his tower, fictional point of view always involves the *distance*, close or far, of the perceiver from the thing perceived. Point of view in fiction, however, is immensely complicated by the fact that distance is not only, though it may be partly, spatial. It may also be temporal. Or the distance may be intangible and involve a judgment moral, intellectual, and/or emotional. More complicated still, the narrator or characters or both may view the action from one distance, the author and reader from another.

> In any reading experience there is an implied dialogue among author, narrator, the other characters and the reader. Each of the four can range, in relation to each of the others, from identification to complete opposition, on any axis of value, moral, intellectual, aesthetic and even physical. . . . From the author's viewpoint, a successful reading of his book must eliminate all distance between [his] essential norms . . . and the norms of the postulated reader.
>
> WAYNE C. BOOTH, *The Rhetoric of Fiction*

Booth means that the author may ask us to identify completely with one character and totally condemn another. One character may judge another harshly while the author suggests that we should qualify that judgment. Author, characters, and reader are always in the dialogue, but if there is also a narrator, that narrator may think himself morally superior while the author behind his back makes sure that we will think him morally deficient. Further, the four members of the dialogue may operate differently in various areas of value: the character calls the narrator stupid and ugly; the narrator thinks herself ugly but clever; the author and the reader know that she is both intelligent and beautiful.

Any complex or convolution of judgments among author, narrator, and characters can make successful fiction. The one relationship in the dialogue in which there must not be any opposition is between author and reader. We may find the characters and/or the narrator bad, stupid, and tasteless and still applaud the book as just, brilliant, and beautiful. But if the hero's agony strikes us as ridiculous, if the comedy leaves us cold — if we say that the *book* is bad, stupid, or tasteless — then we are in opposition to the author on some axis of value and reject his "point of view" in the sense of "opinion." Ultimately, the reader must accept the "essential norms" — the attitudes and judgments — of the author, even if only provisionally, whether these are the norms of the characters or not, if the fiction is going to work.

I can think of no exception to this rule, and it is not altered by experimental plays and stories in which the writer's purpose is to embarrass, anger, or disgust us. Our acceptance of such experiments rests on our understanding that the writer did want to embarrass, anger, or disgust us, just as we accept being frightened by a horror story because we know that the writer set out to frighten us. If we think the writer is disgusting by accident, ineptitude, or moral depravity, then we are "really" disgusted and the fiction does not work.

It is a frustrating experience for many beginning (and established) authors to find that, whereas they meant the protagonist to appear sensitive, their readers find him self-pitying; whereas he meant her to be witty, the readers find her vulgar. When this happens there is a failure of *authorial distance*: the author did not have sufficient perspective on the character to convince us to share his or her judgment. I recall one class in which a student author had written, with excellent use of image and scene, the story of a young man who fell in love with an exceptionally beautiful young woman, and whose feelings turned to revulsion when he found out she had had a mastectomy. The most vocal feminist in the class loved this story, which she described as "the exposé of a skuzzwort." This was not, from the author's point of view, a successful reading of his story.

The notion of authorial distance may be clarified by a parallel with acting. Assume that you go to see Jack Nicholson on successive nights in *One Flew*

Over the Cuckoo's Nest and *The Shining*. In both, you are aware of Nicholson-the-actor: his face, voice, idiosyncrasies, and the mannerisms he brings to both roles. At the same time you're willing to accept his identity now as the buoyantly sane Randle P. McMurphy, now as the murdering monster Jack Torrence. While McMurphy springs a motley crew of asylum inmates for a fishing trip, you identify with McMurphy, his goals and his values, and you also understand that Nicholson-the-actor wishes you to so identify. While Torrence chases his son with an ax, you hate and fear the character, and you understand that Nicholson-the-actor wishes you so to hate and fear him. In both films, other characters pronounce the protagonist "mad." In one of them, you judge with the actor that he is sane; in the other, you judge with the actor that he is mad. Neither judgment makes you question the sanity of Nicholson-the-actor.

The same phenomenon occurs between writer and reader of the novels from which these films were adapted, or any other fiction. We may judge Moll Flanders to be materialistic; the Godfather, brutal; and Popeye, psychotic. But we understand that the author has directed us toward these judgments and do not think Defoe materialistic, Puzo brutal, or Faulkner psychotic. A significant difference is that the actor has various physical and vocal means to direct our judgment; the writer's resources are the selection and arrangement of words alone. Only as an omniscient author may you "tell" us what your attitude is — and even then you may opt not to. If you purport to be objective, or if you are speaking through the mouth or mind of a character or narrator, then you must show us by implication, through your *tone*.

The word *tone*, applied to fiction, is a metaphor derived from music and also commonly — also metaphorically — used to describe color and speech. When we speak of a "tone of voice" we mean, as in fiction, that an attitude is conveyed, and this attitude is determined by the situation and by the relation of the persons involved in the situation. Tone can match, emphasize, alter, or contradict the meaning of the words.

The situation is that Louise stumbles into her friend Judy's apartment, panting, hair disheveled, coat torn, and face blanched. Judy rushes to support her. "You look awful! What happened?" Here the tone conveys alarm, openness, and a readiness to sympathize.

Judy's son wheels in grinning, swinging a baseball bat, shirt torn, mud splattered, and missing a shoe. "You look awful! What happened?" Judy's tone is angry, exasperated.

Louise's ex-boyfriend drops by that night decked out in a plaid polyester sports coat and an electric blue tie. "You look awful! What happened?" Louise says, her tone light, but cutting, so that he knows she means it.

Judy's husband comes back from a week in Miami and takes off his shirt to model his tan. "You look awful! What happened?" she teases, playful and flirting, so that he knows he looks terrific.

In each of these situations the attitude is determined by the situation and the emotional relationships of the persons involved, and in life as in acting the various tones would be conveyed by vocal means — pitch, tempo, plosion, nasality — reinforced by posture, gesture, and facial expression. When we apply the word *tone* to fiction, we tacitly acknowledge that we must do without these helpful signs. The author, of course, may describe pitch, posture, and the like, or may identify a tone as "cutting" or "playful," but these verbal and adverbial aids describe only the tone used among characters, whereas the fictional relationship importantly includes an author who must also convey identification or distance, sympathy or judgment, and who must choose and arrange words so that they match, emphasize, alter, or contradict their inherent meaning.

SPATIAL AND TEMPORAL DISTANCE

The author's or narrator's attitude may involve distance in time or space or both. When a story begins, "Long ago and far away," we are instantly transported by a tone we recognize as belonging to fairy tale, fantasy, and neverland. The year 1890 may be long ago, and the Siberian saltmines far away, but if the author is going to expose prison conditions in tsarist Russia, he had better take another tone.

Anytime you (or your narrator) begin by telling us that the events you are relating took place in the far past, you distance us, making a submerged promise that the events will come to an end, since they "already have." This, of course, may be a device to lure us into the story, and you may — almost certainly do — want to draw us into closer and deeper involvement as the story progresses.

> That spring, when I had a great deal of potential and no money at all, I took a job as a janitor. That was when I was still very young and spent money very freely, and when, almost every night, I drifted off to sleep lulled by sweet anticipation of that time when my potential would suddenly be realized and there would be capsule biographies of my life on the dust jackets of many books.
>
> JAMES ALAN McPHERSON, "Gold Coast"

Here a distance in time indicates the attitude of the narrator toward his younger self, and his indulgent, self-mocking tone (*lulled by sweet anticipation of that time when my potential would suddenly be realized*) invites us as readers to identify with the older, narrating self. We know that he is no longer lulled by such fantasies, and, at least for the duration of the story, neither are we. That is, we are close to the narrator, distanced from him as a young man, so that the distance in time also involves distance in attitude. The story "Gold Coast" continues to reinforce this distance, the temporal involving us in the emotional.

> I then became very rich, with my own apartment, a sensitive girl, a stereo, two speakers, one tattered chair, one fork, a job, and the urge to acquire . . .

Now, all of us either know, or are, people who would consider a job, an apartment, and a sensitive girl very real prosperity. But the author forces us to take a longer perspective than we might in life by including the contrast between "very rich" and "one fork" and "the urge to acquire." Only toward the end of the story, when the narrator himself is moved by his memory, does he let us share the emotion of the younger self.

In the next passage, the author makes use of space to establish an impersonal and authoritative tone.

> An unassuming young man was traveling, in midsummer, from his native city of Hamburg, to Davos-Platz in the Canton of Grisons, on a three week visit.
>
> From Hamburg to Davos is a long journey — too long, indeed, for so brief a stay. It crosses all sorts of country; goes up hill and down dale, descends from the plateau of Southern Germany to the shore of Lake Constance, over its bounding waves and on across marshes once thought to be bottomless.
>
> THOMAS MANN, *The Magic Mountain*

Here Mann distances us from the young man by characterizing him perfunctorily, not even naming him, and describes the place travelogue style, inviting us to take a panoramic view. This choice of tone establishes a remoteness emotional as well as geographical, and would do so even if the reader happened to be a native of Grisons Canton. Again, we will eventually become intimately involved with Davos and the unassuming young man, who is in for a longer stay than he expects.

By closing the literal distance between the reader and the subject, the intangible distance can be closed as well.

> Her face was half an inch from my face. The curtain flapped at the open window and her pupils pulsed with the coming and going of the light. I know Jill's eyes; I've painted them. They're violent and taciturn, a ring of gas-blue points like cold explosion to the outside boundary of iris, the whole held back with its brilliant lens. A detonation under glass.
>
> JANET BURROWAY, *Raw Silk*

In the extreme closeness of this focus, we are brought emotionally close, invited to share the narrator's perspective of Jill's explosive eyes.

It will be obvious that using time and space as a means of controlling the reader's emotional closeness or distance involves all the elements of atmosphere discussed in Chapter 5. This is true of familiarity, which invites identification with a place, and of strangeness, which alienates. And it is true of summary, which distances, and of scene, which draws us close. If you say, "There were twelve diphtheria outbreaks in Coeville over the next thirty years," you invite us to take a detached historical attitude. But if you say, "He forced his finger into her throat and tilted her toward the light to see, as he'd expected, the grayish membrane reaching toward the roof of her mouth and into her nose," the doctor may remain detached, but we as readers cannot.

There is a grammatical technique involving distance and the use of time as *tense*, which is very often misused. Most fiction in English is written in the *past tense*. (*She put her foot on the shovel and leaned all her weight against it.*) The author's constant effort is to give this past the immediacy of the present. A story may be written in the *present tense* (*She puts her foot on the shovel and leans all her weight against it*), and the effect of the present tense, somewhat self-consciously, is to reduce distance and increase immediacy: we are there. Generally speaking, the tense once established *should not be changed*.

> Danforth got home about five o'clock in the morning and fixed himself a peanut butter sandwich. He eats it over the sink, washing it down with half a carton of chocolate milk. He left the carton on the sink and stumbled up to bed.

The change of tense in the second sentence is pointless; it violates the reader's sense of time to have the action skip from past to present and back again and produces no compensating effect.

There are times, however, when a change of tense can be functional and effective. In the story "Gold Coast," we are dealing with two time frames, one having to do with the narrator's earlier experiences as a janitor, and one in which he acknowledges the telling.

> I left the rug on the floor because it was dirty and too large for my new apartment. I also left the two plates given me by James Sullivan, for no reason at all. Sometimes I want to go back to get them, but I do not know how to ask for them or explain why I left them in the first place.

The tense change here is logical and functional: it acknowledges the past of the "story" and the present of the "telling"; it also incidentally reinforces our emotional identification with the older, narrating self.

Sometimes, however, a shift into the present tense without a strictly logical justification can achieve the effect of intensity and immediacy, so that the emotional distance between reader and character is diminished.

> When alone he had a dreadful and distressing desire to call someone, but he knew beforehand that with others present it would be still worse. "Another dose of morphine — to lose consciousness. I will tell him, the doctor, that he must think of something else. It's impossible, impossible, to go on like this."
> An hour and another pass like that. But now there's a ring at the doorbell. Perhaps it's the doctor? It is. He comes in fresh, hearty, plump and cheerful.
>
> LEO TOLSTOY, *The Death of Ivan Ilyich*

This switch from the past to the present draws us into the character's anguish and makes the doctor's arrival more intensely felt. Notice that Ivan Ilyich's thoughts — "Another dose of morphine" — which occur naturally in the present tense, serve as a transition from past to present so that we are not jolted by the change. In *The Death of Ivan Ilyich*, Tolstoy keeps the whole scene of the doctor's visit in the present tense, while Ivan Ilyich's consciousness is at a pitch of pain, contempt for the doctor, and hatred for his wife; then, as the focus moves to the wife, the tense slips back into the past.

> The thrill of hatred he feels for her makes him suffer from her touch.
> Her attitude towards him and his disease is still the same. Just as the doctor had adopted a certain relation to his patient which he could not abandon, so had she formed one toward him . . . and she could not now change that attitude.

The present tense can be effectively employed to depict moments of special intensity, but it needs both to be saved for those crucial moments and to be controlled so carefully in the transition that the reader is primarily aware of the intensity, and quite possibly unaware of the tense.

INTANGIBLE DISTANCE

Spatial and temporal distance, then, can imply distance in the attitude of the teller toward his or her material. But authorial distance may also be implied through tone without any tangible counterpart.

Tone itself is an intangible, and there are probably as many possible tones as there are possible situations, relationships, and sentences. But in a very general way, we will trust, in literature as in life, a choice of words that seems appropriate in intensity or value to the meaning conveyed. If the intensity or value seems inappropriate, we will start to read between the lines. If a woman putting iodine on a cut says "Ouch," we don't have to search for her meaning. But if the cut is being stitched up without anesthetic, then "Ouch" may convey courage, resignation, and trust. If she says "Ouch" when her lover strokes her cheek, then we read anger and recoil into the word.

In the same way, you as author manipulate intensity and value in your choice of language, sometimes matching meaning, sometimes contradicting, sometimes overstating, sometimes understating, to indicate your attitude to the reader.

> She was a tall woman of imperious mien, handsome, with definite black eyebrows. Her smooth black hair was parted exactly. For a few moments she stood steadily watching the miners as they passed along the railway; then she turned toward the brook course. Her face was calm and set, her mouth was closed with disillusionment.
>
> D. H. LAWRENCE, "Odor of Chrysanthemums"

There is in this passage no discrepancy between the thing conveyed and the intensity with which it is conveyed, and we take the words at face value, accepting that the woman is as the author says she is. The phrase "imperious mien" has itself an imperious tone about it (I doubt one would speak of a *real cool mien*). The syntax is as straightforward as the woman herself. (Notice how the rhythm alters with "For a few moments," so that the longest and most flowing clause follows the passing miners.) You might describe the tone of the passage as a whole as "calm and set."

The next example is quite different.

> Mrs. Herriton did not believe in romance, nor in transfiguration, nor in parallels from history, nor in anything that may disturb domestic life. She adroitly changed the subject before Philip got excited.
>
> E. M. FORSTER, *Where Angels Fear to Tread*

This is clearly also a woman of "imperious mien," and the author purports, like the first, to be informing us of her actions and attitudes. But unlike the first example, the distance here between the woman's attitude and the author's is apparent. It is possible to "believe in" both romance and trans-figuration, which are concepts. If Lawrence should say of the woman in "Odor of Chrysanthemums" that "she did not believe in romance, nor in transfiguration," we would accept it as a straightforward part of her char-acterization. But how can one believe in parallels? *Belief* is too strong a word for *parallels*, and the discrepancy makes us suspicious. Not to "believe" in "anything that may disturb domestic life" is a discrepancy of a severer order, unrealistic and absurd. The word "adroitly," again, presents a value judgment, one of praise. But placed as it is between "anything that may disturb domestic life" and "before Philip got excited," it shows us that Mrs. Herriton is manipulating the excitement out of domestic life.

Irony. Discrepancies of intensity and value are *ironic.* Again, in a very general way, any time there is a discrepancy between what is said and what we are to accept as the truth, we are in the presence of an *irony.* There are three basic types of irony.

Verbal irony is a rhetorical device in which the author (or character) says one thing and means another. Mrs. Herriton "adroitly changed the subject" is a form of verbal irony. When the author goes on to say, "Lilia tried to assert herself, and said that she should go to take care of [her mother]. It required all Mrs. Herriton's kindness to prevent her," there is further verbal irony in the combination of "required" and "kindness."

Dramatic irony is a device of plot in which the reader or audience knows more than the character does. The classical example of dramatic irony is *Oedipus Rex,* where the audience knows that Oedipus himself is the murderer he seeks. There is a dramatic irony in *The Death of Ivan Ilyich,* as Ilyich persists in ignoring the pain from his fall, protesting to himself that it's nothing, while the reader knows that it will lead to his death.

Cosmic irony is an all-encompassing attitude toward life, which takes into account the contradictions inherent in the human condition. The story "Cutting Edge" exemplifies cosmic irony when Mrs. Zeller's attempts to force her son into being the person she can love and recognize as her own inevitably drive him from her.

Any of these types of irony will inform the author's attitude toward the material and will be reflected in his or her tone. Any of them will involve authorial distance, since the author means, knows, or wishes to take into account — and also intends the reader to understand — something not wholly conveyed by the literal meaning of the words.

In the two passages quoted above, we may say that the first, from Lawrence, is without irony; the second, from Forster, contains an irony presented by the author, understood by the reader, and directed against the character described.

The following passage, again about a woman of imperious mien, is more complex because it introduces the fourth possible member of the narrative dialogue, the narrator; and it also contains temporal distance.

She was a tall woman with high cheekbones, now more emphasized than ever by the loss of her molar teeth. Her lips were finer than most of her tribe's and wore a shut, rather sour expression. Her eyes seemed to be always fixed on the distance, as though she didn't "see" or mind the immediate, but dwelt in the eternal. She was not like other children's grandmothers we knew, who would spoil their grandchildren and had huts "just outside the hedge" of their sons' homesteads. Grandmother lived three hills away, which was inexplicable.

JONATHAN KARIARA, "Her Warrior"

This paragraph begins, like Lawrence's, without irony, as a strong portrait of a strong woman. Because we trust the consistent tone of the first two sentences, we also accept the teller's simile, "as though she didn't 'see' or mind the immediate," which emphasizes without contradicting. Up to this point the voice seems to have the authority of an omniscient author, but in the fourth sentence the identity of the narrator is introduced — one of the woman's grandchildren. Because the past tense is used, and even more, because the language is measured and educated, we instantly understand that the narrator is telling of his childhood perceptions from an adult, temporally distanced perspective. Curiously, the final word of the final sentence presents us with a contradiction of everything we have just found convincing. It cannot be "inexplicable" that this woman lived three hills away, because it has already been explained to us that she lived in deep and essential remoteness.

This irony is not directed primarily against the character of the grandmother but by the narrator against himself as a child. Author, narrator, and reader all concur in an intellectual distance from the child's mind and its faulty perceptions. At the same time, there is perhaps a sympathetic identification with the child's hurt, and therefore there results a residual judgment of the grandmother.

With What Limitations?

In each of the passages excerpted in the section on "Irony" we trust the teller of the tale. We may find ourselves in opposition to characters perceived or perceiving, but we identify with the attitudes, straightforward or ironic, of the authors and narrator who present us these characters. We share, at least for the duration of the narrative, their norms.

THE UNRELIABLE NARRATOR

It is also possible to mistrust the teller. Authorial distance may involve, not a deliberate attitude taken by the speaker, but distance on the part of the author from the narrator. The answer to the question "Who speaks?" may itself necessitate a judgment, and again this judgment may imply opposition of the author (and reader) on any scale of value — moral, intellectual, aesthetic, or physical — and to these I would add educational and experiential (probably the list can be expanded further).

If the answer to "Who speaks?" is: *a child, a bigot, a jealous lover, an animal, a schizophrenic, a murderer, a liar* — any of these may imply that the narrator speaks with *limitations* we do not necessarily share. To the extent that the narrator displays and betrays such limitations, she or he is an *unreliable narrator;* and the author, without a word to call his own, must let the reader know that the story is not to be trusted.

Here is a fourth woman imperious and sour, who tells her own story.

> But that's why I have an understanding of the girl Ginny downstairs and her kids. They're runty, underdeveloped. No sun, no beef. Noodles, beans, cabbage. Well, my mother off the boat knew better than that. . . .
>
> Five ladies on the block, old friends, nosy, me not included, got up a meeting and wrote a petition to Child Welfare. I already knew it was useless, as the requirement is more than dirt, drunkenness, and a little once-in-a-way whoring. That is probably something why the children in our city are in such a state. I've noticed it for years, though it's not my business. Mothers and fathers get up when they wish, half being snuggled in relief, go to bed in the afternoon with their rumpy bumpy sweethearts pumping away before 3 p.m. (So help me.) Child Welfare does not show its concern. No matter who writes them. People of influence, known in the district, even the district leader, my cousin Leonie . . .
>
> GRACE PALEY, "Distance"

We mistrust every judgment this woman makes, but we are also aware of an author we do trust, manipulating the narrator's tone to expose her. The outburst is fraught with ironies (including perhaps the title, "Distance"), but because the narrator is unaware of them they are directed against herself. She claims "understanding" and "concern" for what she exhibits as invective. She claims respectability, which she lamely bolsters by name-dropping her mother and her cousin, while her own language is "rumpy bumpy" lascivious. Her syntax betrays ignorance and her bristling intensity is spent on the wrong values, and "that is probably something why" author and reader side with Ginny and her kids in direct opposition to the narrator.

In this case the narrator is wholly unreliable, and we're unlikely to accept any judgment she could make. But it is also possible for a narrator to be reliable in some areas of value and unreliable in others. Mark Twain's Huckleberry Finn is a famous case in point. Here Huck has decided to free his friend Jim, and he is astonished that Tom Sawyer is going along with the plan.

> Well, one thing was dead sure; and that was, that Tom Sawyer was in earnest and was actuly going to help steal that nigger out of slavery. That was the thing that was too many for me. Here was a boy that was respectable, and

well brung up; and had a character to lose; and folks at home that had characters; and he was bright and not leather-headed; and knowing and not ignorant; and not mean, but kind; and yet here he was, without any more pride, or rightness, or feeling, than to stoop to this business, and make himself a shame, and his family a shame, before everybody. I *couldn't* understand it, no way at all.

The extended irony in this excerpt is that slavery should be defended by the respectable, the bright, the knowing, the kind, and those of character. We reject Huck's assessment of Tom as well as the implied assessment of himself as worth so little that he has nothing to lose by freeing a slave. Huck's moral instincts are better than he himself can understand. (Notice, incidentally, how Huck's lack of education is communicated by word choice and syntax and how sparse the misspellings are.) So author and reader are in intellectual opposition to Huck the narrator, but morally identify with him.

The unreliable narrator — who has become one of the most popular characters in modern fiction — is far from a newcomer to literature and in fact predates fiction. Every drama contains characters who speak for themselves and present their own cases, and from whom we are partly or wholly distanced in one area of value or another. So we identify with Othello's morality but mistrust his logic, trust Faust's intellect but not his ethics, admire Barney Fife's heart of gold but not his courage. As these examples suggest, the unreliable narrator always presents us with dramatic irony, because we always "know" more than he or she does about the characters, the events, and the significance of both.

AN EXERCISE IN UNRELIABILITY

The following five passages — one a lyric and four prose fiction — represent narrations by five relatively mad madmen. How mad is each? To whom does each speak? In what form? Which of their statements are reliable? Unreliable? Which of them admit to madness? Is the admission reliable? What ironies can you identify, and against whom is each directed? What is the attitude of the author behind the narrator? By what choice and arrangement of words do you know this?

> I met my old lover
> > On the street last night
> > She seemed so glad to see me
> > I just smiled
> > And we talked about some old times
> > And we drank ourselves some beers
> > Still crazy after all these years . . .

I'm not the kind of man
　Who tends to socialize
　I seem to lean on
　Old familiar ways
　And I ain't no fool for love songs
　That whisper in my ears
　Still crazy after all these years . . .

Now I sit by the window
　And I watch the stars
　I fear I'll do some damage
　One fine day
　But I would not be convicted
　By a jury of my peers . . .
　Still crazy after all these years.

　　　　　　　　　PAUL SIMON,　"Still Crazy After All These Years"

The doctor advised me not to insist too much on looking so far back. Recent events, he says, are equally valuable for him, and above all my fancies and dreams of the night before. But I like to do things in their order, so directly I left the doctor (who was going to be away from Trieste for some time) I bought and read a book on psychoanalysis, so that I might begin from the very beginning, and make the doctor's task easier. It is not difficult to understand, but very boring. I have stretched myself out after lunch in an easy chair, pencil and paper in hand. All the lines have disappeared from my forehead as I sit here with mind completely relaxed. I seem to be able to see my thoughts as something quite apart from myself. I can watch them rising, falling, their only form of activity. I seize my pencil in order to remind them that it is the duty of thought to manifest itself. At once the wrinkles collect on my brow as I think of the letters that make up every word.

　　　　　　　　　ITALO SVEVO,　*Confessions of Zeno*

　　　　　　　　　　Madrid, Februarius the thirtieth

So I'm in Spain. It all happened so quickly that I hardly had time to realize it. This morning the Spanish delegation finally arrived for me and we all got into the carriage. I was somewhat bewildered by the extraordinary speed at which we traveled. We went so fast that in half an hour we reached the Spanish border. But then, nowadays there are railroads all over Europe and the ships go so fast too. Spain is a strange country. When we entered the first room, I saw a multitude of people with shaven heads. I soon realized, though, that these must be Dominican or Capuchin monks because they always shave their heads. I also thought that the manners of the King's Chancellor, who was leading me by the hand, were rather strange. He pushed me into a small room and said: "You sit quiet and don't you call yourself King Ferdinand again or I'll beat the nonsense out of your head." But I knew that I was just being tested and refused to submit.

　　　　　　　　　NIKOLAI GOGOL,　*The Diary of a Madman*

Pushed back into sleep as I fight to emerge, pushed back as they drown a kitten, or a child fighting to wake up, pushed back by voices and lullabies and bribes and bullies, punished by tones of voices and by silences, gripped into sleep by medicines and syrups and dummies and dope.

Nevertheless I fight, desperate, like a kitten trying to climb out of the slippysided zinc pail it has been flung in, an unwanted, unneeded cat to drown, better dead than alive, better asleep than awake, but I fight, up and up into the light, greeting dark now as a different land, a different texture, a different state of the Light.

DORIS LESSING, Briefing for a Descent into Hell

Come into my cell. Make yourself at home. Take the chair; I'll sit on the cot. No? You prefer to stand by the window? I understand. You like my little view. Have you noticed that the narrower the view the more you can see? For the first time I understand how old ladies can sit on their porches for years.

Don't I know you? You look very familiar. I've been feeling rather depressed and I don't remember things very well. I think I am here because of that or because I committed a crime. Perhaps it's both. Is this a prison or a hospital or a prison hospital? A Center for Aberrant Behavior? So that's it. I have behaved aberrantly. In short, I'm in the nuthouse.

WALKER PERCY, Lancelot

UNRELIABILITY IN OTHER VIEWPOINTS

I have said that a narrator cannot be omniscient, although he or she may be reliable. It may seem equally plausible that the phenomenon of unreliability can apply only to a narrator, who is by definition a fallible human being. But the subtleties of authorial distance are such that it is possible to indicate unreliability through virtually any point of view. If, for example, you have chosen a limited omniscient viewpoint including only external observation and the thoughts of one character, then it may be that the character's thoughts are unreliable and that he or she misinterprets external facts. Then you must make us aware through tone that you know more than you have chosen to present. William Golding, in *The Inheritors*, tells his story in the third person, but through the eyes and thoughts of a Neanderthal who has not yet developed the power of deductive reasoning.

The man turned sideways in the bushes and looked at Lok along his shoulder. A stick rose upright and there was a lump of bone in the middle. . . . Suddenly Lok understood that the man was holding the stick out to him but neither he nor Lok could reach across the river. He would have laughed if it were not for the echo of screaming in his head. The stick began to grow shorter at both ends. Then it shot out to full length again.

The dead tree by Lok's ear acquired a voice.
"Clop!"

His ears twitched and he turned to the tree. By his face there had grown a twig: a twig that smelt of other, and of goose, and of the bitter berries that Lok's stomach told him he must not eat.

The imaginative problem here, imaginatively embraced, is that we must supply the deductive reasoning of which our point-of-view character is incapable. Lok has no experience of bows or poison arrows, nor of "men" attacking each other, so his conclusions are unreliable. "Suddenly Lok understood" is an irony setting us in opposition to the character's intellect; at the same time, his innocence makes him morally sympathetic. Since the author does not intervene to interpret for us, the effect is very near that of an unreliable narrator.

Other experiments abound. Isaac Loeb Peretz tells the story of "Bontsha the Silent" from the point of view of the editorial omniscient, privy to the deliberations of the angels, but with Yiddish syntax and "universal truths" so questionable that the omniscient voice itself is unreliable. Conversely, Faulkner's *The Sound and the Fury* is told through several unreliable narrators, each with an idiosyncratic and partial perception of the story, so that the cumulative effect is of an omniscient author able not only to penetrate many minds but also to perceive the larger significance.

I'm conscious that this discussion of point of view contains more analysis than advice, and this is because very little can be said to be right or wrong about point of view as long as the reader ultimately identifies with the author; as long, that is, as you make it work. In *Aspects of the Novel* E. M. Forster speaks vaguely, but with undeniable accuracy, of "the power of the writer to bounce the reader into accepting what he says." He then goes on to prove categorically that Dickens's *Bleak House* is a disaster, "Logically . . . all to pieces, but Dickens bounces us, so that we do not mind the shiftings of the view-point."

The one imperative is that the reader must bounce with, not against the author. Virtually any story can be told from virtually any point of view and convey the same attitude of the author.

Suppose, for example, that you are going to write this story: Two American soldiers in a Far Eastern "police action," one a seasoned corporal and the other a newly arrived private, are sent on a mission to kill a sniper. They track, find, and capture the Oriental, who turns out to be a fifteen-year-old boy. The corporal offers to let the private pull the trigger, but he cannot. The corporal kills the sniper and triumphantly cuts off his ear for a trophy. The young soldier vomits; ashamed of himself, he pulls himself together and vows to do better next time.

Your attitude as author of this story is that war is inhumane and dehumanizing.

You may write the story from the point of view of the editorial omniscient, following the actions of the hunters and the hunted, going into the minds of corporal, private, and sniper, ranging the backgrounds of each and knowing the ultimate pointlessness of the death, telling us, in effect, that war is inhumane and dehumanizing.

Or you may write it from the point of view of the corporal as an unreliable narrator, proud of his toughness and his expertise, condescending to the private, certain that Orientals are animals, glorying in his trophy, betraying his inhumanity.

Between these two extremes of total omniscience and total unreliability, you may take any position of the middle ground. The story might be written in the limited omniscient, presenting the thoughts only of the anxious private and the external actions of the others. It might be written objectively, with a cold and detached accuracy of military detail. It might be written by a peripheral narrator, a war correspondent, from interviews and documents; as a letter home from the private to his girl; as a field report from the corporal; as an interior monologue of the young sniper during the seconds before his death.

Any of these modes could contain your meaning, any of them fulfill your purpose. Your central problem as a writer might prove to be the choosing. But whatever your final choice of point of view in the technical sense, your point of view in the sense of *opinion* would remain that war is inhumane and dehumanizing, and could be suggested.

Battle Royal

RALPH ELLISON

It goes a long way back, some twenty years. All my life I had been looking for something, and everywhere I turned someone tried to tell me what it was. I accepted their answers too, though they were often in contradiction and even self-contradictory. I was naïve. I was looking for myself and asking everyone except myself questions which I, and only I, could answer. It took me a long time and much painful boomeranging of my expectations to achieve a realization everyone else appears to have been born with: That I am nobody but myself. But first I had to discover that I am an invisible man!

And yet I am no freak of nature, nor of history. I was in the cards, other things having been equal (or unequal) eighty-five years ago. I am not ashamed of my grandparents for having been slaves. I am only ashamed of myself for having at one time been ashamed. About eighty-five years ago they were told that they were free, united with others of our country in everything pertaining to the common good, and, in everything social, separate like the fingers of the hand. And they believed it. They exulted in it. They stayed in their place, worked hard, and brought up my father to do the same. But my grandfather is the one. He was an odd old guy, my grandfather, and I am told I take after him. It was he who caused the trouble. On his deathbed he called my father to him and said, "Son, after I'm gone I want you to keep up the good fight. I never told you, but our life is a war and I have been a traitor all my born days, a spy in the enemy's country ever since I give up my gun back in the Reconstruction. Live with your head in the lion's mouth. I want you to overcome 'em with yeses, undermine 'em with grins, agree 'em to death and destruction, let 'em swoller you till they vomit or bust wide open." They thought the old man had gone out of his mind. He had been the meekest of men. The younger children were rushed from the room, the shades drawn and the flame of the lamp turned so low that it sputtered on the wick like the old man's breathing. "Learn it to the younguns," he whispered fiercely; then he died.

But my folks were more alarmed over his last words than over his dying. It was as though he had not died at all, his words caused so much anxiety. I was warned emphatically to forget what he had said and, indeed, this is the first time it has been mentioned outside the family circle. It had a tremendous effect upon me, however. I could never be sure of what he meant. Grandfather had been a quiet old man who never made any trouble, yet on his deathbed he had called himself a traitor and a spy, and he had spoken of his meekness as a dangerous activity. It became a constant puzzle which lay unanswered in the back of my mind. And whenever things went well for me I remembered my grandfather and felt guilty and uncomfortable. It was as though I was carrying out his advice in spite of myself. And to make it worse, everyone loved me for it. I was praised by the most lily-white men of the town. I was considered an example of desirable conduct — just as my grandfather had been. And what puzzled me was that the old man had defined it as *treachery*. When I was praised for my conduct I felt a guilt that in some way I was doing something that was really against the wishes of the white folks, that if they had understood they would have desired me to act just the opposite, that I should have been sulky and mean, and that that really would have been what they wanted, even though they were fooled and thought they wanted me to act as I did. It made me afraid that some day they would look upon me as a traitor and I would be lost. Still I was more afraid to act any other way because they didn't like that at all. The old man's words were like a curse. On my graduation day I delivered an oration in which I showed that humility was the secret, indeed, the very essence of progress. (Not that I believed this — how could I, remembering my grandfather? — I only believed that it worked.) It was a great success. Everyone praised me and I was invited to give the speech at a gathering of the town's leading white citizens. It was a triumph for our whole community.

It was the main ballroom of the leading hotel. When I got there I discovered that it was on the occasion of a smoker, and I was told that since I was to be there anyway I might as well take part in the battle royal to be fought by some of my schoolmates as part of the entertainment. The battle royal came first.

All of the town's big shots were there in their tuxedoes, wolfing down the buffet foods, drinking beer and whiskey and smoking black cigars. It was a large room with a high ceiling. Chairs were arranged in neat rows around three sides of a portable boxing ring. The fourth side was clear, revealing a gleaming space of polished floor. I had some misgivings over the battle royal, by the way. Not from a distaste for fighting, but because I didn't care too much for the other fellows who were to take part. They were tough guys who seemed to have no grandfather's curse worrying their minds. No one could mistake their toughness. And besides, I suspected that fighting a battle royal might detract from the dignity of my speech. In those pre-invisible days I visualized myself as a potential Booker T. Washington. But the other fellows didn't care too much for me either, and there were nine of them. I felt superior to them in my way, and I didn't like the manner in which we were all crowded together into the servants' elevator. Nor did they like my being there. In fact, as the warmly lighted floors flashed past the elevator we had words over the fact that I, by taking part in the fight, had knocked one of their friends out of a night's work.

We were led out of the elevator through a rococo hall into an anteroom and told to get into our fighting togs. Each of us was issued a pair of boxing gloves and ushered out into the big mirrored hall, which we entered looking cautiously about us and whispering, lest we might accidentally be heard above the noise of the room. It was foggy with cigar smoke. And already the whiskey was taking effect. I was shocked to see some of the most important men of the town quite tipsy. They were all there — bankers, lawyers, judges, doctors, fire chiefs, teachers, merchants. Even one of the more fashionable pastors. Something we could not see was going on up front. A clarinet was vibrating sensuously and the men were standing up and moving eagerly forward. We were a small tight group, clustered together, our bare upper bodies touching and shining with anticipatory sweat; while up front the big shots were becoming increasingly excited over something we still could not see. Suddenly I heard the school superintendent, who had told me to come, yell, "Bring up the shines, gentlemen! Bring up the little shines!"

We were rushed up to the front of the ballroom, where it smelled even more strongly of tobacco and whiskey. Then we were pushed into place. I almost wet my pants. A sea of faces, some hostile, some amused, ringed around us, and in the center, facing us, stood a magnificent blonde — stark naked. There was dead silence. I felt a blast of cold air chill me. I tried to back away, but they were behind me and around me. Some of the boys stood with lowered heads, trembling. I felt a wave of irrational guilt and fear. My teeth chattered, my skin turned to goose flesh, my knees knocked. Yet I was strongly attracted and looked in spite of myself. Had the price of looking been blindness, I would have looked. The hair was yellow like that of a circus kewpie doll, the face heavily powdered and rouged, as though to form an abstract mask, the eyes hollow and smeared a cool blue, the color of a baboon's butt. I felt a desire to spit upon her as my eyes brushed slowly over her body. Her breasts were firm and round as the domes of East Indian temples, and I stood so close as to see the fine skin texture and beads of pearly perspiration glistening like dew around the pink and erected buds of her nipples. I wanted at one and the same time to run from the room, to sink through the floor, or go to her and cover her from my eyes and the eyes of the others with my body; to feel the soft thigh, to caress her and destroy her, to love her and murder her, to hide from her, and yet to stroke where below the small American flag tattooed upon her belly her thighs formed a capital V. I had a notion that of all in the room she saw only me with her impersonal eyes.

And then she began to dance, a slow sensuous movement; the smoke of a hundred cigars clinging to her like the thinnest of veils. She seemed like a fair bird-girl girdled in veils calling to me from the angry surface of some gray and threatening sea. I was transported. Then I became aware of the clarinet playing and the big shots yelling at us. Some threatened us if we looked and others if we did not. On my right I saw one boy faint. And now a man grabbed a silver pitcher from a table and stepped close as he dashed ice water upon him and stood him up and forced two of us to support him as his head hung and moans issued from his thick bluish lips. Another boy began to plead to go home. He was the largest of the group, wearing dark red fighting trunks much too small to conceal the erection which projected from him as though in answer to the insinuating low-registered moaning of the clarinet. He tried to hide himself with his boxing gloves.

And all the while the blonde continued dancing, smiling faintly at the big shots who watched her with fascination, and faintly smiling at our fear. I noticed a certain merchant who followed her hungrily, his lips loose and drooling. He was a large man who wore diamond studs in a shirtfront which swelled with the ample paunch underneath, and each time the blonde swayed her undulating hips he ran his hand through the thin hair of his bald head and, with his arms upheld, his posture clumsy like that of an intoxicated panda, wound his belly in a slow and obscene grind. This creature was completely hypnotized. The music had quickened. As the dancer flung herself about with a detached expression on her face, the men began reaching out to touch her. I could see their beefy fingers sink into the soft flesh. Some of the others tried to stop them and she began to move around the floor in graceful circles, as they gave chase, slipping and sliding over the polished floor. It was mad. Chairs went crashing, drinks were spilt, as they ran laughing and howling after her. They caught her just as she reached the door, raised her from the floor, and tossed her as college boys are tossed at a hazing, and above her red, fixed-smiling lips I saw the terror and disgust in her eyes, almost like my own terror and that which I saw in some of the other boys. As I watched, they tossed her twice and her soft breasts seemed to flatten against the air and her legs flung wildly as she spun. Some of the more sober ones helped her to escape. And I started off the floor, heading for the anteroom with the rest of the boys.

Some were still crying and in hysteria. But as we tried to leave we were stopped and ordered to get into the ring. There was nothing to do but what we were told. All ten of us climbed under the ropes and allowed ourselves to be blindfolded with broad bands of white cloth. One of the men seemed to feel a bit sympathetic and tried to cheer us up as we stood with our backs against the ropes. Some of us tried to grin. "See that boy over there?" one of the men said. "I want you to run across at the bell and give it to him right in the belly. If you don't get him, I'm going to get you. I don't like his looks." Each of us was told the same. The blindfolds were put on. Yet even then I had been going over my speech. In my mind each word was as bright as flame. I felt the cloth pressed into place, and frowned so that it would be loosened when I relaxed.

But now I felt a sudden fit of blind terror. I was unused to darkness. It was as though I had suddenly found myself in a dark room filled with poisonous cottonmouths. I could hear the bleary voices yelling insistently for the battle royal to begin.

"Get going in there!"

"Let me at that big nigger!"

I strained to pick up the school superintendent's voice, as though to squeeze some security out of that slightly more familiar sound.

"Let me at those black sonsabitches!" someone yelled.

"No, Jackson, no!" another voice yelled. "Here, somebody, help me hold Jack."

"I want to get at that ginger-colored nigger. Tear him limb from limb," the first voice yelled.

I stood against the ropes trembling. For in those days I was what they called ginger-colored, and he sounded as though he might crunch me between his teeth like a crisp ginger cookie.

Quite a struggle was going on. Chairs were being kicked about and I could hear voices grunting as with a terrific effort. I wanted to see, to see more desperately than ever before. But the blindfold was as tight as a thick skin-puckering scab and when I raised my gloved hands to push the layers of white aside a voice yelled, "Oh, no you don't, black bastard! Leave that alone!"

"Ring the bell before Jackson kills him a coon!" someone boomed in the sudden silence. And I heard the bell clang and the sound of feet scuffling forward.

A glove smacked against my head. I pivoted, striking out stiffly as someone went past, and felt the jar ripple along the length of my arm to my shoulder. Then it seemed as though all nine of the boys had turned upon me at once. Blows pounded me from all sides while I struck out as best I could. So many blows landed upon me that I wondered if I were not the only blindfolded fighter in the ring, or if the man called Jackson hadn't succeeded in getting me after all.

Blindfolded, I could no longer control my emotions. I had no dignity. I stumbled about like a baby or a drunken man. The smoke had become thicker and with each new blow it seemed to sear and further restrict my lungs. My saliva became like hot bitter glue. A glove connected with my head, filling my mouth with warm blood. It was everywhere. I could not tell if the moisture I felt upon my body was sweat or blood. A blow landed hard against the nape of my neck. I felt myself going over, my head hitting the floor. Streaks of blue light filled the black world behind the blindfold. I lay prone, pretending that I was knocked out, but felt myself seized by hands and yanked to my feet. "Get going, black boy! Mix it up!" My arms were like lead, my head smarting from blows. I managed to feel my way to the ropes and held on, trying to catch my breath. A glove landed in my mid-section and I went over again, feeling as though the smoke had become a knife jabbed into my guts. Pushed this way and that by the legs milling around me I finally pulled erect and discovered that I could see the black, sweat-washed forms weaving in the smoky-blue atmosphere like drunken dancers weaving to the rapid drum-like thuds of blows.

Everyone fought hysterically. It was complete anarchy. Everybody fought everybody else. No group fought together for long. Two, three, four, fought one, then turned to fight each other, were themselves attacked. Blows landed below the belt and in the kidney, with the gloves open as well as closed, and with my eye partly opened now there was not so much terror. I moved carefully, avoiding blows, although not too many to attract attention, fighting from group to group. The boys groped about like blind, cautious crabs crouching to protect their mid-sections, their heads pulled in short against their shoulders, their arms stretched nervously before them, with their fists testing the smoke-filled air like the knobbed feelers of hypersensitive snails. In one corner I glimpsed a boy violently punching the air and heard him scream in pain as he smashed his hand against a ring post. For a second I saw him bent over holding his hand, then going down as a blow caught his unprotected head. I played one group against the other, slipping in and throwing a punch then stepping out of range while pushing the others into the melee to take the blows blindly aimed at me. The smoke was agonizing and there were no rounds, no bells at three minute intervals to relieve our exhaustion. The room spun round me, a swirl of lights, smoke, sweating bodies surrounded by tense white faces. I bled from both nose and mouth, the blood spattering upon my chest.

The men kept yelling, "Slug him, black boy! Knock his guts out!"

"Uppercut him! Kill him! Kill that big boy!"

Taking a fake fall, I saw a boy going down heavily beside me as though we were felled by a single blow, saw a sneaker-clad foot shoot into his groin as the two who had knocked him down stumbled upon him. I rolled out of range, feeling a twinge of nausea.

The harder we fought the more threatening the men became. And yet, I had begun to worry about my speech again. How would it go? Would they recognize my ability? What would they give me?

I was fighting automatically when suddenly I noticed that one after another of the boys was leaving the ring. I was surprised, filled with panic; as though I had been left alone with an unknown danger. Then I understood. The boys had arranged it among themselves. It was the custom for the two men left in the ring to slug it out for the winner's prize. I discovered this too late. When the bell sounded two men in tuxedoes leaped into the ring and removed the blindfold. I found myself facing Tatlock, the biggest of the gang. I felt sick at my stomach. Hardly had the bell stopped ringing in my ears than it clanged again and I saw him moving swiftly toward me. Thinking of nothing else to do I hit him smash on the nose. He kept coming, bringing the rank sharp violence of stale sweat. His face was a black blank of a face, only his eyes alive — with hate of me and aglow with a feverish terror from what had happened to us all. I became anxious. I wanted to deliver my speech and he came at me as though he meant to beat it out of me. I smashed him again and again, taking his blows as they came. Then on a sudden impulse I struck him lightly and as we clinched, I whispered, "Fake like I knocked you out, you can have the prize."

"I'll break your behind," he whispered hoarsely.

"For *them?*"

"For *me*, sonofabitch!"

They were yelling for us to break it up and Tatlock spun me half around with a blow, and as a joggled camera sweeps in a reeling scene, I saw the howling red faces crouching tense beneath the cloud of bluegray smoke. For a moment the world wavered, unraveled, flowed, then my head cleared and Tatlock bounced before me. That fluttering shadow before my eyes was his jabbing left hand. Then falling forward, my head against his damp shoulder, I whispered.

"I'll make it five dollars more."

"Go to hell!"

But his muscles relaxed a trifle beneath my pressure and I breathed, "Seven?"

"Give it to your ma," he said, ripping me beneath the heart.

And while I still held him I butted him and moved away. I felt myself bombarded with punches. I fought back with hopeless desperation. I wanted to deliver my speech more than anything else in the world, because I felt that only these men could judge truly my ability, and now this stupid clown was ruining my chances. I began fighting carefully now, moving in to punch him and out again with my greater speed. A lucky blow to his chin and I had him going too — until I heard a loud voice yell, "I got my money on the big boy."

Hearing this, I almost dropped my guard. I was confused: Should I try to win against the voice out there? Would not this go against my speech, and was not this a moment for humility, for nonresistance? A blow to my head as I danced about sent my right eye popping like a jack-in-the-box and settled my dilemma. The room went red as I fell. It was a dream fall, my body languid and fastidious as to where to land, until the floor became impatient and smashed up to meet me. A moment later I came to. An hypnotic voice said FIVE emphatically. And I lay there, hazily watching a dark red spot of my own blood shaping itself into a butterfly, glistening and soaking into the soiled gray world of the canvas.

When the voice drawled TEN I was lifted up and dragged to a chair. I sat dazed. My eye pained and swelled with each throb of my pounding heart and I wondered if now I would be allowed to speak. I was wringing wet, my mouth still bleeding. We were grouped along the wall now. The other boys ignored me as they congratulated Tatlock and speculated as to how much they would be paid. One boy whimpered over his smashed hand. Looking up front, I saw attendants in white jackets rolling the portable ring away and placing a small square rug in the vacant space surrounded by chairs. Perhaps, I thought, I will stand on the rug to deliver my speech.

Then the M.C. called to us, "Come on up here boys and get your money."

We ran forward to where the men laughed and talked in their chairs, waiting. Everyone seemed friendly now.

"There it is on the rug," the man said. I saw the rug covered with coins of all dimensions and a few crumpled bills. But what excited me, scattered here and there, were the gold pieces.

"Boys, it's all yours," the man said. "You get all you grab."

"That's right, Sambo," a blond man said, winking at me confidentially.

I trembled with excitement, forgetting my pain. I would get the gold and the bills, I thought. I would use both hands. I would throw my body against the boys nearest me to block them from the gold.

"Get down around the rug now," the man commanded, "and don't anyone touch it until I give the signal."

"This ought to be good," I heard.

As told, we got around the square rug on our knees. Slowly the man raised his freckled hand as we followed it upward with our eyes.

I heard, "These niggers look like they're about to pray!"

Then, "Ready," the man said. "Go!"

I lunged for a yellow coin lying on the blue design of the carpet, touching it and sending a surprised shriek to join those rising around me. I tried frantically to remove my hand but could not let go. A hot, violent force tore through my body, shaking me like a wet rat. The rug was electrified. The hair bristled up on my head as I shook myself free. My muscles jumped, my nerves jangled, writhed. But I saw that this was not stopping the other boys. Laughing in fear and embarrassment, some were holding back and scooping up the coins knocked off by the painful contortions of the others. The men roared above us as we struggled.

"Pick it up, goddammit, pick it up!" someone called like a bass-voiced parrot. "Go on, get it!"

I crawled rapidly around the floor, picking up the coins, trying to avoid the coppers and to get greenbacks and the gold. Ignoring the shock by laughing, as I brushed the coins off quickly, I discovered that I could contain the electricity — a contradiction, but it works. Then the men began to push us onto the rug. Laughing embarrassedly, we struggled out of their hands and kept after the coins. We were all wet and slippery and hard to hold. Suddenly I saw a boy lifted into the air, glistening with sweat like a circus seal, and dropped, his back landing flush upon the charged rug, heard him yell and saw him literally dance upon his back, his elbows beating a frenzied tattoo upon the floor, his muscles twitching like the flesh of a horse stung by many flies. When he finally rolled off, his face was gray and no one stopped him when he ran from the floor amid booming laughter.

"Get the money," the M.C. called. "That's good hard American cash!"

And we snatched and grabbed, snatched and grabbed. I was careful not to come too close to the rug now, and when I felt the hot whiskey breath descend upon me like a cloud of foul air I reached out and grabbed the leg of a chair. It was occupied and I held on desperately.

"Leggo, nigger! Leggo!"

The huge face wavered down to mine as he tried to push me free. But my body was slippery and he was too drunk. It was Mr. Colcord, who owned a chain of movie houses and "entertainment palaces." Each time he grabbed me I slipped out of his hands. It became a real struggle. I feared the rug more than I did the drunk, so I held on, surprising myself for a moment by trying to topple *him* upon the rug. It was such an enormous idea that I found myself actually carrying it out. I tried not to be obvious, yet when I grabbed his leg, trying to tumble him out of the chair, he raised up roaring with laughter, and, looking at me with soberness dead in the eye, kicked me viciously in the chest. The chair leg flew out of my hand and I felt myself going and rolled. It was as though I had rolled through a bed of hot coals. It seemed a whole century would pass before I would roll free, a century in which I was seared through the deepest levels of my body to the fearful breath within me and the breath seared and heated to the point of explosion. It'll all be over in a flash, I thought as I rolled clear. It'll all be over in a flash.

But not yet, the men on the other side were waiting, red faces swollen as though from apoplexy as they bent forward in their chairs. Seeing their fingers coming toward me I rolled away as a fumbled football rolls off the receiver's fingertips, back into the coals. That time I luckily sent the rug sliding out of place and heard the coins ringing against the floor and the boys scuffling to pick them up and the M.C. calling, "All right, boys, that's all. Go get dressed and get your money."

I was limp as a dish rag. My back felt as though it had been beaten with wires.

When we had dressed the M.C. came in and gave us each five dollars, except Tatlock, who got ten for being last in the ring. Then he told us to leave. I was not to get a chance to deliver my speech, I thought. I was going out into the dim alley in despair when I was stopped and told to go back. I returned to the ballroom, where the men were pushing back their chairs and gathering in groups to talk.

The M.C. knocked on a table for quiet. "Gentlemen," he said, "we almost forgot an important part of the program. A most serious part, gentlemen. This boy was brought here to deliver a speech which he made at his graduation yesterday . . ."

"Bravo!"

"I'm told that he is the smartest boy we've got out there in Greenwood. I'm told that he knows more big words than a pocket-sized dictionary."

Much applause and laughter.

"So now, gentlemen, I want you to give him your attention."

There was still laughter as I faced them, my mouth dry, my eye throbbing. I began slowly, but evidently my throat was tense, because they began shouting, "Louder! Louder!"

"We of the younger generation extol the wisdom of that great leader and educator," I shouted, "who first spoke these flaming words of wisdom: 'A ship lost at sea for many days suddenly sighted a friendly vessel. From the mast of the unfortunate vessel was seen a signal: "Water, water; we die of thirst!" The answer from the friendly vessel came back: "Cast down your bucket where you are." The captain of the distressed vessel, at last heeding the injunction, cast down his bucket, and it came up full of fresh sparkling water from the mouth of the Amazon River.' And like him I say, and in his words, 'To those of my race who depend upon bettering their condition in a foreign land, or who underestimate the importance of cultivating friendly relations with the Southern white man, who is his next-door neighbor, I would say: "Cast down your bucket where you are" — cast it down in making friends in every manly way of the people of all races by whom we are surrounded . . .' "

I spoke automatically and with such fervor that I did not realize that the men were still talking and laughing until my dry mouth, filling up with blood from the cut, almost strangled me. I coughed, wanting to stop and go to one of the tall brass, sand-filled spittoons to relieve myself, but a few of the men, especially the superintendent, were listening and I was afraid. So I gulped it down, blood, saliva and all, and continued. (What powers of endurance I had during those days! What enthusiasm! What a belief in the rightness of things!) I spoke even louder in spite of the pain. But still they talked and still they laughed, as though deaf with cotton in dirty ears. So I spoke with greater emotional emphasis. I closed my ears and swallowed blood until I was nauseated. The speech seemed a hundred times as long as before, but I could not leave out a single word. All had to be said, each memorized nuance considered, rendered. Nor was that all. Whenever I uttered a word of three or more syllables a group of voices would yell for me to repeat it. I used the phrase "social responsibility" and they yelled:

"What's that word you say, boy?"

"Social responsibility," I said.

"What?"

"Social . . ."

"Louder."

". . . responsibility."

"More!"

"Respon —"

"Repeat!"

"— sibility."

The room filled with the uproar of laughter until, no doubt, distracted by having to gulp down my blood, I made a mistake and yelled a phrase I had often seen denounced in newspaper editorials, heard debated in private.

"Social . . ."

"What?" they yelled.

". . . equality —"

The laughter hung smokelike in the sudden stillness. I opened my eyes, puzzled. Sounds of displeasure filled the room. The M.C. rushed forward. They shouted hostile phrases at me. But I did not understand.

A small dry mustached man in the front row blared out, "Say that slowly, son!"

"What sir?"

"What you just said!"

"Social responsibility, sir," I said.

"You weren't being smart, were you, boy?" he said, not unkindly.

"No, sir!"

"You sure that about 'equality' was a mistake?"

"Oh, yes, sir," I said. "I was swallowing blood."

"Well, you had better speak more slowly so we can understand. We mean to do right by you, but you've got to know your place at all times. All right, now, go on with your speech."

I was afraid. I wanted to leave but I wanted also to speak and I was afraid they'd snatch me down.

"Thank you, sir," I said, beginning where I had left off, and having them ignore me as before.

Yet when I finished there was a thunderous applause. I was surprised to see the superintendent come forth with a package wrapped in white tissue paper, and, gesturing for quiet, address the men.

"Gentlemen, you see that I did not overpraise this boy. He makes a good speech and some day he'll lead his people in the proper paths. And I don't have to tell you that that is important in these days and times. This is a good, smart boy, and so to encourage him in the right direction, in the name of the Board of Education I wish to present him a prize in the form of this . . ."

He paused, removing the tissue paper and revealing a gleaming calfskin brief case.

". . . in the form of this first-class article from Shad Whitmore's shop."

"Boy," he said, addressing me, "take this prize and keep it well. Consider it a badge of office. Prize it. Keep developing as you are and some day it will be filled with important papers that will help shape the destiny of your people."

I was so moved that I could hardly express my thanks. A rope of bloody saliva forming a shape like an undiscovered continent drooled upon the leather and I wiped it quickly away. I felt an importance that I had never dreamed.

"Open it and see what's inside," I was told.

My fingers a-tremble, I complied, smelling the fresh leather and finding an official-looking document inside. It was a scholarship to the state college for Negroes. My eyes filled with tears and I ran awkwardly off the floor.

I was overjoyed; I did not even mind when I discovered that the gold pieces I had scrambled for were brass pocket tokens advertising a certain make of automobile.

When I reached home everyone was excited. Next day the neighbors came to congratulate me. I even felt safe from grandfather, whose deathbed curse usually spoiled my triumphs. I stood beneath his photograph with my brief case in hand and smiled triumphantly into his stolid black peasant's face. It was a face that fascinated me. The eyes seemed to follow everywhere I went.

That night I dreamed I was at a circus with him and that he refused to laugh at the clowns no matter what they did. Then later he told me to open my brief case and read what was inside and I did, finding an official envelope stamped with the state seal; and inside the envelope I found another and another, endlessly, and I thought I would fall of weariness. "Them's years," he said. "Now open that one." And I did and in it I found an engraved document containing a short message in letters of gold. "Read it," my grandfather said. "Out loud."

"To Whom It May Concern," I intoned. "Keep This Nigger-Boy Running."

I awoke with the old man's laughter ringing in my ears.

(It was a dream I was to remember and dream again for many years after. But at that time I had no insight into its meaning. First I had to attend college.)

Suggestions for Discussion

1. Ellison begins the story by insisting, "It goes a long way back. . . ." Why? What is gained by this temporal distancing?

2. There are two time frames in the story: one for the events recalled, one for the telling. Yet when the narrator describes the smoker, he does so from the viewpoint of himself as a boy, without any adult comment on his memory. Why? How does this alter the distance? What limitations are implied in the boy's perceptions?

3. The narrator tells us that the grandfather's dying words "became a constant puzzle" and that he "had no insight" into the meaning of his dream about his grandfather. How do we as readers understand so clearly what the narrator claims not to have understood and does not explain?

4. Describe the distance, tangible or intangible, of the narrator from each of the following: himself as a boy, the grandfather, the town's leading white citizens, the dancer, and the other boys.

5. Show how the narrator's graduation speech is an extended irony.

6. What is our perspective on the boy's gratitude for the scholarship? How does Ellison manipulate tone to reveal the irony?

7. Like "Brownstone," the story "Battle Royal" was conceived, not as a short story, but as a chapter in a novel, *Invisible Man*. To what extent does it have the form of a short story, and in what ways is it unresolved?

The Loneliness of the Long-Distance Runner

ALAN SILLITOE

As soon as I got to Borstal they made me a long-distance cross-country runner. I suppose they thought I was just the build for it because I was long and skinny for my age (and still am) and in any case I didn't mind it much, to tell you the truth, because running had always been made much of in our family, especially running away from the police. I've always been a good runner, quick and with a big stride as well, the only trouble being that no matter how fast I run, and I did a very fair lick even though I do say so myself, it didn't stop me getting caught by the cops after that bakery job.

You might think it a bit rare, having long-distance cross-country runners in Borstal, thinking that the first thing a long-distance cross-country runner would do when they set him loose at them fields and woods would be to run as far away from the place as he could get on a bellyful of Borstal slumgullion — but you're wrong, and I'll tell you why. The first thing is that them bastards over us aren't as daft as they most of the time look, and for another thing I'm not so daft as I would look if I tried to make a break for it on my long-distance running, because to abscond and then get caught is nothing but a mug's game, and I'm not falling for it. Cunning is what counts in this life, and even that you've got to use in the slyest way you can; I'm telling you straight: they're cunning, and I'm cunning. If only them and us had the same ideas we'd get on like a house on fire, but they don't see eye to eye with us and we don't see eye to eye with them, so that's how it stands and how it will always stand. The one fact is that all of us are cunning, and because of this there's no love lost between us. So the thing is that they know I won't try to get away from them: they sit there like spiders in that crumbly manor house, perched like jumped-up jackdaws on the roof, watching out over the drives and fields like German generals from the tops of tanks. And even when I jog-trot on behind a wood and they can't see me anymore they know my sweeping-brush head will bob along that hedge-top in an hour's time and that I'll report to the bloke on the gate. Because when on a raw and frosty morning I get up at five o'clock and stand shivering my belly off on the stone floor and all the rest still have another hour to snooze before the bells go, I slink downstairs through all the corridors to the big outside door with a permit running-card in my fist, I feel like the first and last man on the world, both at once, if you can believe what I'm trying to say. I feel like the first man because I've hardly got a stitch on and am sent against the frozen fields in a shimmy and shorts — even the first poor bastard dropped on to the earth in midwinter knew how to make a suit of leaves, or how to skin a pterodactyl for a topcoat. But there I am, frozen stiff, with nothing to get me warm except a couple of hours' long-distance running before breakfast, not even a slice of bread-and-sheepdip. They're training me up fine for the big sports day when all the pig-faced snotty-nosed dukes and ladies — who can't add two and two together and would mess themselves like loonies if they didn't have slavies to beck-and-call — come and make speeches to us about sports being just the thing to get us leading an honest life and keep our itching finger-ends off them shop locks and safe handles and hairgrips to open gas meters. They give us a bit of blue ribbon and a cup for a prize after we've shagged ourselves out running or jumping, like race horses, only we don't get so well looked-after as race horses, that's the only thing.

So there I am, standing in the doorway in shimmy and shorts, not even a dry crust in my guts, looking out at frosty flowers on the ground. I suppose you think this is enough to make me cry? Not likely. Just because I feel like the first bloke in the world wouldn't make me bawl. It makes me feel fifty times better than when I'm cooped up in that dormitory with three hundred others. No, it's sometimes when I stand there feeling like the *last* man in the world that I don't feel so good. I feel like the last man in the world because I think that all those three hundred sleepers behind me are dead. They sleep so well I think that every scruffy head's kicked the bucket in the night and I'm the only one left, and when I look out into the bushes and frozen ponds I have the feeling that it's going to get colder and colder until everything I can see, meaning my red arms as well, is going to be covered with a thousand miles of ice, all the earth, right up to the sky and over every bit of land and sea. So I try to kick this feeling out and act like I'm the first man on earth. And that makes me feel good, so as soon as I'm steamed up enough to get this feeling in me, I take a flying leap out of the doorway, and off I trot.

I'm in Essex. It's supposed to be a good Borstal, at least that's what the governor said to me when I got here from Nottingham. "We want to trust you while you are in this establishment," he said, smoothing out his news-paper with lily-white workless hands, while I read the big words upside down: *Daily Telegraph*. "If you play ball with us, we'll play ball with you." (Honest to God, you'd have thought it was going to be one long tennis match.) "We want hard honest work and we want good athletics," he said as well. "And if you give us both these things you can be sure we'll do right by you and send you back into the world an honest man." Well, I could have died laughing, especially when straight after this I hear the barking sergeant-major's voice calling me and two others to attention and marching us off like we was Grenadier Guards. And when the governor kept saying how "we" wanted you to do this, and "we" wanted you to do that, I kept looking round for the other blokes, wondering how many of them there was. Of course, I knew there were thousands of them, but as far as I knew only one was in the room. And there *are* thousands of them, all over the poxeaten country, in shops, offices, railway stations, cars, houses, pubs — In-law blokes like you and them, all on the watch for Out-law blokes like me and us — and waiting to 'phone for the coppers as soon as we make a false move. And it'll always be there, I'll tell you that now, because I haven't finished making all my false moves yet, and I dare say I won't until I kick the bucket. If the In-laws are hoping to stop me making false moves they're wasting their time. They might as well stand me up against a wall and let fly with a dozen rifles. That's the only way they'll stop me, and a few million others. Because I've been doing a lot of thinking since coming here. They can spy on us all day to see if we're pulling our puddings and if we're working good or doing our "athletics" but they can't make an X-ray of our guts to find out what we're telling ourselves. I've been asking myself all sorts of questions, and thinking about my life up to now. And I like doing all this. It's a treat. It passes the time away and don't make Borstal seem half so bad as the boys in our street used to say it was. And this long-distance running lark is the best of all, because it makes me think so good that I learn things even better than when I'm on my bed at night. And apart from that, what with thinking so much while I'm running I'm getting to be one of the best runners in the Borstal. I can go my five miles round better than anybody else I know.

So as soon as I tell myself I'm the first man ever to be dropped into the world, and as soon as I take that first flying leap out into the frosty grass of an early morning when even birds haven't the heart to whistle, I get to thinking, and that's what I like. I go my rounds in a dream, turning at lane or footpath corners without knowing I'm turning, leaping brooks without knowing they're there, and shouting good morning to the early cow-milker without seeing him. It's a treat, being a long-distance runner, out in the world by yourself with not a soul to make you bad-tempered or tell you what to do or that there's a shop to break and enter a bit back from the next street. Sometimes I think that I've never been so free as during that couple of hours when I'm trotting up the path out of the gates and turning by that bare-faced, big-bellied oak tree at the lane end. Everything's dead, but good, because it's dead before coming alive, not dead after being alive. That's how I look at it. Mind you, I often feel frozen stiff at first. I can't feel my hands or feet or flesh at all, like I'm a ghost who wouldn't know the earth was under him if he didn't see it now and again through the mist. But even though some people would call this frost-pain suffering if they wrote about it to their mams in a letter, I don't, because I know that in half an hour I'm going to be warm, that by the time I get to the main road and am turning on to the wheatfield footpath by the bus stop I'm going to feel as hot as a potbellied stove and as happy as a dog with a tin tail.

It's a good life, I'm saying to myself, if you don't give in to coppers and Borstal-bosses and the rest of them bastard-faced In-laws. Trot-trot-trot.

Puff-puff-puff. Slap-slap-slap go my feet on the hard soil. Swish-swish-swish as my arms and side catch the bare branches of a bush. For I'm seventeen now, and when they let me out of this — if I don't make a break and see that things turn out otherwise — they'll try to get me in the army, and what's the difference between the army and this place I'm in now? They can't kid me, the bastards. I've seen the barracks near where I live, and if there weren't swaddies on guard outside with rifles you wouldn't know the difference between their high walls and the place I'm in now. Even though the swaddies come out at odd times a week for a pint of ale, so what? Don't I come out three mornings a week on my long-distance running, which is fifty times better than boozing. When they first said that I was to do my long-distance running without a guard pedalling beside me on a bike I couldn't believe it; but they called it a progressive and modern place, though they can't kid me because I know it's just like any other Borstal, going by the stories I've heard, except that they let me trot about like this. Borstal's Borstal no matter what they do; but anyway I moaned about it being a bit thick sending me out so early to run five miles on an empty stomach, until they talked me round to thinking it wasn't so bad — which I knew all the time — until they called me a good sport and patted me on the back when I said I'd do it and that I'd try to win them the Borstal Blue Ribbon Prize Cup for Long Distance Cross Country Running (All England). And now the governor talks to me when he comes on his rounds, almost as he'd talk to his prize race horse, if he had one.

"All right, Smith?" he asks.

"Yes, sir," I answer.

He flicks his grey moustache: "How's the running coming along?"

"I've set myself to trot round the grounds after dinner just to keep my hand in, sir," I tell him.

The pot-bellied pop-eyed bastard gets pleased at this: "Good show. I know you'll get us that cup," he says.

And I swear under my breath: "Like boggery, I will." No, I won't get them that cup, even though the stupid tash-twitching bastard has all his hopes in me. Because what does his barmy hope mean? I ask myself. Trot-trot-trot, slap-slap-slap, over the stream and into the wood where it's almost dark and frosty-dew twigs sting my legs. It won't mean a bloody thing to me, only to him, and it means as much to him as it would mean to me if I picked up the racing paper and put my bet on a hoss I didn't know, had never seen, and didn't care a sod if I ever did see. That's what it means to him. And I'll lose that race, because I'm not a race horse at all, and I'll let him know it when I'm about to get out — if I don't sling my hook even before the race. By Christ I will. I'm a human being and I've got thoughts and secrets and bloody life inside me that he doesn't know is there, and he'll never know what's there because he's stupid. I suppose you'll laugh at this, me saying the governor's a stupid bastard when I know hardly how to write and he can read and write and add-up like a professor. But what I say is true right enough. He's stupid, and I'm not, because I can see further into the likes of him than he can see into the likes of me. Admitted, we're both cunning, but I'm more cunning and I'll win in the end even if I die in gaol at eighty-two, because I'll have more fun and fire out of my life than he'll ever get out of his. He's read a thousand books I suppose, and for all I know he might even have written a few, but I know for a dead cert, as sure as I'm sitting here, that what I'm scribbling down is worth a million to what he could ever scribble down. I don't care what anybody says, but that's the truth and can't be denied. I know when he talks to me and I look into his army mug that I'm alive and he's dead. He's as dead as a doornail. If he ran ten yards he'd drop dead. If he got ten yards into what goes on in my guts he'd drop dead as well — with surprise. At the moment it's dead blokes like him as have the whip-hand over blokes like me, and I'm almost dead sure it'll always be like that, but even so, by Christ, I'd rather be like I am — always on the run and breaking into shops for a packet of fags and a jar of jam — than have the whip-hand over somebody else and be dead from the toe nails up. Maybe as soon as you get the whip-hand over somebody you do go dead. By God, to say that last sentence has needed a few hundred miles of long-distance running. I could no more have said that at first than I could have took a million-pound note from my back pocket. But it's true, you know, now I think of it again, and has always been true, and always will be true, and I'm surer of it every time I see the governor open that door and say Goodmorning lads.

As I run and see my smoky breath going out into the air as if I had ten cigars stuck in different parts of my body I think more on the little speech the governor made when I first came. Honesty. Be honest. I laughed so much one morning I went ten minutes down in my timing because I had to stop and get rid of the stitch in my side. The governor was so worried when I got back late that he sent me to the doctor's for an X-ray and heart check. Be honest. It's like saying: Be dead, like me, and then you'll have no more pain of leaving your nice slummy house for Borstal or prison. Be honest and settle down in a cosy six pounds a week job. Well, even with all this long-distance running I haven't yet been able to decide what he means by this, although I'm just about beginning to — and I don't like what it means. Because after all my thinking I found that it adds up to something that can't be true about me, being born and brought up as I was. Because another thing people like the governor will never understand is that I *am* honest, that I've never been anything else but honest, and that I'll always be honest. Sounds funny. But it's true because I know what honest means according to me and he only knows what it means according to him. I think my honesty is the only sort in the world, and he thinks his is the only sort in the world as well. That's why this dirty great walled-up and fenced-up manor house in the middle of nowhere has been used to coop-up blokes like me. And if I had the whip-hand I wouldn't even bother to build a place like this to put all the cops, governors, posh whores, penpushers, army officers, Members of Parliament in; no, I'd stick them up against a wall and let them have it, like they'd have done with blokes like us years ago, that is, if they'd ever known what it means to be honest, which they don't and never will so help me God Almighty.

I was nearly eighteen months in Borstal before I thought about getting out. I can't tell you much about what it was like there because I haven't got the hang of describing buildings or saying how many crumby chairs and slatted windows make a room. Neither can I do much complaining, because to tell you the truth I didn't suffer in Borstal at all. I gave the same answer a pal of mine gave when someone asked him how much he hated it in the army. "I didn't hate it," he said. "They fed me, gave me a suit, and pocket-money, which was a bloody sight more than I ever got before, unless I worked myself to death for it, and most of the time they wouldn't let me work but sent me to the dole office twice a week." Well, that's more or less what I say. Borstal didn't hurt me in that respect, so since I've no complaints I don't have to describe what they gave us to eat, what the dorms were like, or how they treated us. But in another way Borstal does something to me. No, it doesn't get my back up, because it's always been up, right from when I was born. What it does do is show me what they've been trying to frighten me with. They've got other things as well, like prison and, in the end, the rope. It's like me rushing up to thump a man and snatch the coat off his back when, suddenly, I pull up because he whips out a knife and lifts it to stick me like a pig if I come too close. That knife is Borstal, clink, the rope. But once you've seen the knife you learn a bit of unarmed combat. You have to, because you'll never get that sort of knife in your own hands, and this unarmed combat doesn't amount to much. Still, there it is, and you keep on rushing up to this man, knife or not, hoping to get one of your hands on his wrist and the other on his elbow both at the same time, and press back until he drops the knife.

You see, by sending me to Borstal they've shown me the knife, and from now on I know something I didn't know before: that it's war between me and them. I always knew this, naturally, because I was in Remand Homes as well and the boys there told me a lot about their brothers in Borstal, but it was only touch and go then, like kittens, like boxing-gloves, like dobbie. But now that they've shown me the knife, whether I ever pinch another thing in my life again or not, I know who my enemies are and what war is. They can drop all the atom bombs they like for all I care: I'll never call it war and wear a soldier's uniform, because I'm in a different sort of war, that they think is child's play. The war they think is war is suicide, and those that go and get killed in war should be put in clink for attempted suicide because that's the feeling in blokes' minds when they rush to join up or let themselves be called up. I know, because I've thought how good it would be sometimes to do myself in and the easiest way to do it, it occurred to me, was to hope for a big war so's I could join up and get killed. But I got past that when I knew I already was in a war of my own, that I was born into one, that I grew up hearing the sound of "old soldiers" who'd been over the top at Dartmoor, half-killed at Lincoln, trapped in no-man's-land at Borstal, that sounded louder than any Jerry bombs. Government wars aren't my wars; they've got nowt to do with me, because my own war's all that I'll ever be bothered about. I remember when I was fourteen and I went out into the country with three of my cousins, all about the same age, who later went to different Borstals, and then to different regiments, from which they soon deserted, and then to different gaols where they still are as far as I know. But anyway, we were all kids then, and wanted to go out to the woods for a change, to get away from the roads of stinking hot tar one summer. We climbed over fences and went through fields, scrumping a few sour apples on our way, until we saw the wood about a mile off. Up Colliers' Pad we heard another lot of kids talking in high-school voices behind a hedge. We crept up on them and peeped through the brambles, and saw they were eating a picnic, a real posh spread out of baskets and flasks and towels. There must have been about seven of them, lads and girls sent out by their mams and dads for the afternoon. So we went on our bellies through the hedge like crocodiles and surrounded them, and then dashed into the middle, scattering the fire and batting their tabs and snatching up all there was to eat, then running off over Cherry Orchard fields into the wood, with a man chasing us who'd come up while we were ransacking their picnic. We got away all right, and had a good feed into the bargain, because we'd been clambed to death and couldn't wait long enough to get our chops ripping into them thin lettuce and ham sandwiches and creamy cakes.

Well, I'll always feel during every bit of my life like those daft kids should have felt before we broke them up. But they never dreamed that what happened was going to happen, just like the governor of this Borstal who spouts to us about honesty and all that wappy stuff don't know a bloody thing, while I know every minute of my life that a big boot is always likely to smash any nice picnic I might be barmy and dishonest enough to make for myself. I admit that there've been times when I've thought of telling the governor all this so as to put him on his guard, but when I've got as close as seeing him I've changed my mind, thinking to let him either find out for himself or go through the same mill as I've gone through. I'm not hard-hearted (in fact I've helped a few blokes in my time with the odd quid, lie, fag, or shelter from the rain when they've been on the run) but I'm boggered if I'm going to risk being put in the cells just for trying to give the governor a bit of advice he don't deserve. If my heart's soft I know the sort of people I'm going to save it for. And any advice I'd give the governor wouldn't do him the least bit of good; it'd only trip him up sooner than if he wasn't told at all, which I suppose is what I want to happen. But for the time being I'll let things go on as they are, which is something else I've learned in the last year or two. (It's a good job I can only think of these things as fast as I can write with this stub of pencil that's clutched in my paw, otherwise I'd have dropped the whole thing weeks ago.)

By the time I'm half-way through my morning course, when after a frost-bitten dawn I can see a phlegmy bit of sunlight hanging from the bare twigs of beech and sycamore, and when I've measured my half-way mark by the short-cut scrimmage down the steep bush-covered bank and into the sunken lane, when still there's not a soul in sight and not a sound except the neighing of a piebald foal in a cottage stable that I can't see, I get to thinking the deepest and daftest of all. The governor would have a fit if he could see me sliding down the bank because I could break my neck or ankle, but I can't not do it because it's the only risk I take and the only excitement I ever get, flying flat-out like one of them pterodactyls from the "Lost World" I once heard on the wireless, crazy like a cut-balled cockerel, scratching myself to bits and almost letting myself go but not quite. It's the most wonderful minute because there's not one thought or word or picture of anything in my head while I'm going down. I'm empty, as empty as I was before I was born, and I don't let myself go, I suppose, because whatever it is that's farthest down inside me don't want me to die or hurt myself bad. And it's daft to think deep, you know, because it gets you nowhere, though deep is what I am when I've passed this half-way mark because the long-distance run of an early morning makes me think that every run like this is a life — a little life, I know — but a life as full of misery and happiness and things happening as you can ever get really around yourself — and I remember that after a lot of these runs I thought that it didn't need much know-how to tell how a life was going to end once it had got well started. But as usual I was wrong, caught first by the cops and then by my own bad brain, I could never trust myself to fly scot-free over these traps, was always tripped up sooner or later no matter how many I got over to the good without even knowing it. Looking back I suppose them big trees put their branches to their snouts and gave each other the wink, and there I was whizzing down the bank and not seeing a bloody thing.

II

I don't say to myself: "You shouldn't have done the job and then you'd have stayed away from Borstal"; no, what I ram into my runner-brain is that my luck had no right to scram just when I was on my way to making the coppers think I hadn't done the job after all. The time was autumn and the night foggy enough to set me and my mate Mike roaming the streets when we should have been rooted in front of the telly or stuck into a plush posh seat at the pictures, but I was restless after six weeks away from any sort of work, and well you might ask me why I'd been bone-idle for so long because normally I sweated my thin guts out on a milling-machine with the rest of them, but you see, my dad died from cancer of the throat, and mam collected a cool five hundred in insurance and benefits from the factory where he'd worked, "for your bereavement," they said, or words like that.

Now I believe, and my mam must have thought the same, that a wad of crisp blue-back fivers ain't a sight of good to a living soul unless they're flying out of your hand into some shopkeeper's till, and the shopkeeper is passing you tip-top things in exchange over the counter, so as soon as she got the money, mam took me and my five brothers and sisters out to town and got us dolled-up in new clothes. Then she ordered a twenty-one-inch telly, a new carpet because the old one was covered with blood from dad's dying and wouldn't wash out, and took a taxi home with bags of grub and a new fur coat. And do you know — you wain't believe me when I tell you — she'd still near three hundred left in her bulging handbag the next day, so how could any of us go to work after that? Poor old dad, he didn't get a look in, and he was the one who'd done the suffering and dying for such a lot of lolly.

Night after night we sat in front of the telly with a ham sandwich in one hand, a bar of chocolate in the other, and a bottle of lemonade between our boots, while mam was with some fancy-man upstairs on the new bed she'd ordered, and I'd never known a family as happy as ours was in that couple of months when we'd got all the money we needed. And when the dough ran out I didn't think about anything much, but just roamed the streets — looking for another job. I told mam — hoping I suppose to get my hands on another five hundred nicker so's the nice life we'd got used to could go on and on for ever. Because it's surprising how quick you can get used to a different life. To begin with, the adverts on the telly had shown us how much more there was in the world to buy than we'd ever dreamed of when we'd looked into shop windows but hadn't seen all there was to see because we didn't have the money to buy it with anyway. And the telly made all these things seem twenty times better than we'd ever thought they were. Even adverts at the cinema were cool and tame, because now we were seeing them in private at home. We used to cock our noses up at things in shops that didn't move, but suddenly we saw their real value because they jumped and glittered around the screen and had some pasty-faced tart going head over heels to get her nail-polished grabbers on to them or her lipstick lips over them, not like the crumby adverts you saw on posters or in newspapers as dead as doornails; these were flickering around loose, half-open packets and tins, making you think that all you had to do was finish opening them before they were yours, like seeing an unlocked safe through a shop window with the man gone away for a cup of tea without thinking to guard his lolly. The films they showed were good as well, in that way, because we couldn't get our eyes unglued from the cops chasing the robbers who had satchel-bags crammed with cash and looked like getting away to spend it — until the last moment. I always hoped they would end up free to blow the lot, and could never stop wanting to put my hand out, smash into the screen (it only looked a bit of rag-screen like at the pictures) and get the copper in a half-nelson so's he'd stop following the bloke with the money-bags. Even when he'd knocked off a couple of bank clerks I hoped he wouldn't get nabbed. In fact then I wished more than ever he wouldn't because it meant the hot-chair if he did and I wouldn't wish that on anybody no matter what they'd done, because I'd read in a book where the hot-chair worn't a quick death at all, but that you just sat there scorching to death until you were dead. And it was when these cops were chasing the crooks that we played some good tricks with the telly, because when one of them opened his big gob to spout about getting their man I'd turn the sound down and see his mouth move like a goldfish or mackerel or a minnow mimicking what they were supposed to be acting — it was so funny the whole family nearly went into fits on the brand-new carpet that hadn't yet found its way to the bedroom. It was the best of all though when we did it to some Tory telling us about how good his government was going to be if we kept on voting for them — their slack chops rolling, opening and bumbling, hands lifting to twitch moustaches and touching their button-holes to make sure the flower hadn't wilted, so that you could see they didn't mean a word they said, especially with not a murmur coming out because we'd cut off the sound. When the governor of the Borstal first talked to me I was reminded of those times so much that I nearly killed myself trying not to laugh. Yes, we played so many good stunts on the box of tricks that mam used to call us the Telly Boys, we got so clever at it.

My pal Mike got let off with probation because it was his first job — anyway the first they ever knew about — and because they said he would never have done it if it hadn't been for me talking him into it. They said I was a menace to honest lads like Mike — hands in his pockets so that they looked stone-empty, head bent forward as if looking for half-crowns to fill 'em with, a ripped jersey on and his hair falling into his eyes so that he could go up to women and ask them for a shilling because he was hungry — and that I was the brains behind the job, the guiding light when it came to making up anybody's mind, but I swear to God I worn't owt like that because really I ain't got no more brains than a gnat after hiding the money in the place I did. And I — being cranky like I am — got sent to Borstal because to tell you the honest truth I'd been to Remand Homes before — though that's another story and I suppose if ever I tell it it'll be just as boring as this one is. I was glad though that Mike got away with it, and I only hope he always will, not like silly bastard me.

So on this foggy night we tore ourselves away from the telly and slammed the front door behind us, setting off up our wide street like slow tugs on a river that'd broken their hooters, for we didn't know where the housefronts began what with the perishing cold mist all around. I was snatched to death without an overcoat: mam had forgotten to buy me one in the scrummage of shopping, and by the time I thought to remind her of it the dough was all gone. So we whistled "The Teddy Boys Picnic" to keep us warm, and I told myself that I'd get a coat soon if it was the last thing I did. Mike said he thought the same about himself, adding that he'd also get some brand-new glasses with gold rims, to wear instead of the wire frames they'd given him at the school clinic years ago. He didn't twig it was foggy at first and cleaned his glasses every time I pulled him back from a lamp-post or car, but when he saw the lights on Alfreton Road looking like octopus eyes he put them in his pocket and didn't wear them again until we did the job. We hadn't got two ha-pennies between us, and though we weren't hungry we wished we'd got a bob or two when we passed the fish and chip shops because the delicious sniffs of salt and vinegar and frying fat made our mouths water. I don't mind telling you we walked the town from one end to the other and if our eyes worn't glued to the ground looking for lost wallets and watches they was swivelling around house windows and shop doors in case we saw something easy and worth nipping into.

Neither of us said as much as this to each other, but I know for a fact that that was what we was thinking. What I don't know — and as sure as I sit here I know I'll never know — is which of us was the first bastard to latch his peepers on to that baker's backyard. Oh yes, it's all right me telling myself it was me, but the truth is that I've never known whether it was Mike or not, because I do know that I didn't see the open window until he stabbed me in the ribs and pointed it out. "See it?" he said.

"Yes," I told him, "so let's get cracking."

"But what about the wall though?" he whispered, looking a bit closer.

"On your shoulders," I chipped in.

His eyes were already up there: "Will you be able to reach?" It was the only time he ever showed any life.

"Leave it to me," I said, ever-ready. "I can reach anywhere from your ham-hock shoulders."

Mike was a nipper compared to me, but underneath the scruffy draught-board jersey he wore were muscles as hard as iron, and you wouldn't think to see him walking down the street with glasses on and hands in pockets that he'd harm a fly, but I never liked to get on the wrong side of him in a fight because he's the sort that don't say a word for weeks on end — sits plugged in front of the telly, or reads a cowboy book, or just sleeps — when suddenly BIFF — half kills somebody for almost nothing at all, such as beating him in a race for the last Football Post on a Saturday night, pushing in before him at a bus stop, or bumping into him when he was day-dreaming about Dolly-on-the-Tub next door. I saw him set on a bloke once for no more than fixing him in a funny way with his eyes, and it turned out that the bloke was cockeyed but nobody knew it because he'd just that day come to live in our street. At other times none of these things would matter a bit, and I suppose the only reason why I was pals with him was because I didn't say much from one month's end to another either.

He puts his hands up in the air like he was being covered with a Gatling-Gun, and moved to the wall like he was going to be mowed down, and I climbed up him like he was a stile or step-ladder, and there he stood, the palms of his upshot maulers flat and turned out so's I could step on 'em like they was the adjustable jack-spanner under a car, not a sound of a breath nor the shiver of a flinch coming from him. I lost no time in any case, took my coat from between my teeth, chucked it up to the glass-topped wall (where the glass worn't too sharp because the jags had been worn down by years of accidental stones) and was sitting astraddle before I knew where I was. Then down the other side, with my legs rammed up into my throat when I hit the ground, the crack coming about as hard as when you fall after a high parachute drop, that one of my mates told me was like jumping off a twelve-foot wall, which this must have been. Then I picked up my bits and pieces and opened the gate for Mike, who was still grinning and full of life because the hardest part of the job was already done. "I came, I broke, I entered," like that clever-dick Borstal song.

I didn't think about anything at all, as usual, because I never do when I'm busy, when I'm draining pipes, looting sacks, yaling locks, lifting latches, forcing my bony hands and lanky legs into making something move, hardly feeling my lungs going in-whiff and out-whaff, not realizing whether my mouth is clamped tight or gaping, whether I'm hungry, itching from scabies, or whether my flies are open and flashing dirty words like muck and spit into the late-night final fog. And when I don't know anything about all this then how can I honest-to-God say I think of anything at such times? When I'm wondering what's the best way to get a window open or how to force a door, how can I be thinking or have anything on my mind? That's what the four-eyed white-smocked bloke with the note-book couldn't understand when he asked me questions for days and days after I got to Borstal; and I couldn't explain it to him then like I'm writing it down now; and even if I'd been able to maybe he still wouldn't have caught on because I don't know whether I can understand it myself even at this moment, though I'm doing my best you can bet.

So before I knew where I was I was inside the baker's office watching Mike picking up that cash box after he'd struck a match to see where it was, wearing a tailor-made fifty-shilling grin on his square crew-cut nut as his paws closed over the box like he'd squash it to nothing. "Out," he suddenly said, shaking it so's it rattled. "Let's scram."

"Maybe there's some more," I said, pulling half a dozen drawers out of a rollertop desk.

"No," he said, like he'd already been twenty years in the game, "this is the lot," patting his tin box, "this is it."

I pulled out another few drawers, full of bills, books and letters. "How do you know, you loony sod?"

He barged past me like a bull at a gate. "Because I do."

Right or wrong, we'd both got to stick together and do the same thing. I looked at an ever-loving babe of a brand-new typewriter, but I knew it was too traceable, so blew it a kiss, and went out after him. "Hang on," I said, pulling the door to, "we're in no hurry."

"Not much we aren't," he says over his shoulder.

"We've got months to splash the lolly," I whispered as we crossed the yard, "only don't let that gate creak too much or you'll have the narks tuning-in."

"You think I'm barmy?" he said, creaking the gate so that the whole street heard.

I don't know about Mike, but now I started to think, of how we'd get back safe through the streets with that money-box up my jumper. Because he'd clapped it into my hand as soon as we'd got to the main road, which might have meant that he'd started thinking as well, which only goes to show how you don't know what's in anybody else's mind unless you think about things yourself. But as far as my thinking went at that moment it wasn't up to much, only a bit of fright that wouldn't budge not even with a hot blow-lamp, about what we'd say if a copper asked us where we were off to with that hump in my guts.

"What is it?" he'd ask, and I'd say: "A growth." "What do you mean, a growth, my lad?" he'd say back, narky like. I'd cough and clutch myself like I was in the most tripe-twisting pain in the world, and screw my eyes up like I was on my way to the hospital, and Mike would take my arm like he was the best pal I'd got. "Cancer," I'd manage to say to Narker, which would make his slow punch-drunk brain suspect a thing or two. "A lad of your age?" So I'd groan again, and hope to make him feel a real bully of a bastard, which would be impossible, but anyway: "It's in the family. Dad died of it last month, and I'll die of it next month by the feel of it." "What, did he have it in the guts?" "No, in the throat. But it's got me in the stomach." Groan and cough. "Well, you shouldn't be out like this if you've got cancer, you should be in the hospital." I'd get ratty now: "That's where I'm trying to go if only you'd let me and stop asking so many questions. Aren't I, Mike?" Grunt from Mike as he unslung his cosh. Then just in time the copper would tell us to get on our way, kind and considerate all of a sudden, saying that the outpatient department of the hospital closes at twelve, so hadn't he better call us a taxi? He would if we liked, he says, and he'd pay for it as well. But we tell him not to bother, that he's a good bloke even if he is a copper, that we know a short cut anyway. Then just as we're turning a corner he gets it into his big batchy head that we're going the opposite way to the hospital, and calls us back. So we'd start to run . . . if you can call all that thinking.

Up in my room Mike rips open that money-box with a hammer and chisel, and before we know where we are we've got seventy-eight pounds fifteen and fourpence ha'penny *each* lying all over my bed like tea spread out on Christmas Day: cake and trifle, salad and sandwiches, jam tarts and bars of chocolate: all shared and shared alike between Mike and me because we believed in equal work and equal pay, just like the comrades my dad was in until he couldn't do a stroke anymore and had no breath left to argue with. I thought how good it was that blokes like that poor baker didn't stash all his cash in one of the big marble-fronted banks that take up every corner of the town, how lucky for us that he didn't trust them no matter how many millions of tons of concrete or how many iron bars and boxes they were made of, or how many coppers kept their blue pop-eyed peepers glued on to them, how smashing it was that he believed in money-boxes when so many shopkeepers thought it old-fashioned and tried to be modern by using a bank, which wouldn't give a couple of sincere, honest, hard-working, conscientious blokes like Mike and me a chance.

Now you'd think, and I'd think, and anybody with a bit of imagination would think, that we'd done as clean a job as could ever be done, that, with the baker's shop being at least a mile from where we lived, and with not a soul having seen us, and what with the fog and the fact that we weren't more than five minutes in the place, that the coppers should never have been able to trace us. But then, you'd be wrong, I'd be wrong, and everybody else would be wrong, no matter how much imagination was diced out between us.

Even so, Mike and I didn't splash the money about, because that would have made people think straightaway that we'd latched on to something that didn't belong to us. Which wouldn't do at all, because even in a street like ours there are people who love to do a good turn for the coppers, though I never know why they do. Some people are so mean-gutted that even if they've only got tuppence more than you and they think you're the sort that would take it if you have half the chance, they'd get you put inside if they saw you ripping lead out of a lavatory, even if it weren't their lavatory — just to keep their tuppence out of your reach. And so we didn't do anything to let on about how rich we were, nothing like going down town and coming back dressed in brand-new Teddy boy suits and carrying a set of skiffle-drums like another pal of ours who'd done a factory office about six months before. No, we took the odd bobs and pennies out and folded the notes into bundles and stuffed them up the drainpipe outside the door in the backyard. "Nobody'll ever think of looking for it there," I said to Mike. "We'll keep it doggo for a week or two, then take a few quid a week out till it's all gone. We might be thieving bastards, but we're not green."

Some days later a plain-clothes dick knocked at the door. And asked for me. I was still in bed, at eleven o'clock, and had to unroll myself from the comfortable black sheets when I heard mam calling me. "A man to see you," she said. "Hurry up, or he'll be gone."

I could hear her keeping him at the back door, nattering about how fine it had been but how it looked like rain since early this morning — and he didn't answer her except to snap out a snotty yes or no. I scrambled into my trousers and wondered why he'd come — knowing it was a copper because "a man to see you" always meant just that in our house — and if I'd had any idea that one had gone to Mike's house as well at the same time I'd have twigged it to be because of that hundred and fifty quid's worth of paper stuffed up the drainpipe outside the back door about ten inches away from that plain-clothed copper's boot, where mam still talked to him thinking she was doing me a favour, and I wishing to God she'd ask him in, though on second thoughts realizing that that would seem more suspicious than keeping him outside, because they know we hate their guts and smell a rat if they think we're trying to be nice to them. Mam wasn't born yesterday, I thought, thumping my way down the creaking stairs.

I'd seen him before: Borstal Bernard in nicky-hat, Remand Home Ronald in rowing-boat boots, Probation Pete in a pit-prop mackintosh, three-months clink in collar and tie (all this out of a Borstal skiffle-ballad that my new mate made up, and I'd tell you it in full but it doesn't belong in this story), a 'tec who'd never had as much in his pockets as that drainpipe had up its jackses. He was like Hitler in the face, right down to the paint-brush tash, except that being six-foot tall made him seem worse. But I straightened my shoulders to look into his illiterate blue eyes — like I always do with any copper.

Then he started asking me questions, and my mother from behind said: "He's never left that television set for the last three months, so you've got nowt on him, mate. You might as well look for somebody else, because you're wasting the rates you get out of my rent and the income-tax that comes out of my pay-packet standing there like that" — which was a laugh because she'd never paid either to my knowledge, and never would, I hoped.

"Well, you know where Papplewick Street is, don't you?" the copper asked me, taking no notice of mam.

"Ain't it off Alfreton Road?" I asked him back, helpful and bright.

"You know there's a baker's half-way down on the left-hand side, don't you?"

"Ain't it next door to a pub, then?" I wanted to know.

He answered me sharp: "No, it bloody well ain't." Coppers always lose their tempers as quick as this, and more often than not they gain nothing by it. "Then I don't know it," I told him, saved by the bell.

He slid his big boot round and round on the doorstep. "Where were you last Friday night?" Back in the ring, but this was worse than a boxing match.

I didn't like him trying to accuse me of something he wasn't sure I'd done. "Was I at that baker's you mentioned? Or in the pub next door?"

"You'll get five years in Borstal if you don't give me a straight answer," he said, unbuttoning his mac even though it was cold where he was standing.

"I was glued to the telly, like mam says," I swore blind. But he went on and on with his looney questions: "Have you got a television?"

The things he asked wouldn't have taken in a kid of two, and what else could I say to the last one except: "Has the aerial fell down? Or would you like to come in and see it?"

He was liking me even less for saying that. "We know you weren't listening to the television set last Friday, and so do you, don't you?"

"P'raps not, but I was *looking* at it, because sometimes we turn the sound down for a bit of fun." I could hear mam laughing from the kitchen, and I hoped Mike's mam was doing the same if the cops had gone to him as well.

"We know you weren't in the house," he said, starting up again, cranking himself with the handle. They always say "We" "We," never "I" "I" — as if they feel braver and righter knowing there's a lot of them against only one.

"I've got witnesses," I said to him. "Mam for one. Her fancy-man, for two. Ain't that enough? I can get you a dozen more, or thirteen altogether, if it was a baker's that got robbed."

"I don't want no lies," he said, not catching on about the baker's dozen. Where do they scrape cops up from anyway? "All I want is to get from you where you put that money."

Don't get mad, I kept saying to myself, don't get mad — hearing mam setting out cups and saucers and putting the pan on the stove for bacon. I stood back and waved him inside like I was a butler. "Come and search the house. If you've got a warrant."

"Listen, my lad," he said, like the dirty bullying jumped-up bastard he was, "I don't want too much of your lip, because if we get you down to the Guildhall you'll get a few bruises and black-eyes for your trouble." And I knew he wasn't kidding either, because I'd heard about all them sort of tricks. I hoped one day though that him and all his pals would be the ones to get the black-eyes and kicks; you never knew. It might come sooner than anybody thinks, like in Hungary. "Tell me where the money is, and I'll get you off with probation."

"What money?" I asked him, because I'd heard that one before as well.

"You know what money."

"Do I look as though I'd know owt about money?" I said, pushing my fist through a hole in my shirt.

"The money that was pinched, that you know all about," he said. "You can't trick me, so it's no use trying."

"Was it three-and-eightpence ha'penny?" I asked.

"You thieving young bastard. We'll teach you to steal money that doesn't belong to you."

I turned my head around: "Mam," I called out, "get my lawyer on the blower, will you?"

"Clever, aren't you?" he said in a very unfriendly way, "but we won't rest until we clear all this up."

"Look," I pleaded, as if about to sob my socks off because he'd got me wrong, "it's all very well us talking like this, it's like a game almost, but I wish you'd tell me what it's all about, because honest-to-God I've just got out of bed and here you are at the door talking about me having pinched a lot of money, money that I don't know anything about."

He swung around now as if he'd trapped me, though I couldn't see why he might think so. "Who said anything about money? I didn't. What made you bring money into this little talk we're having?"

"It's you," I answered, thinking he was going barmy, and about to start foaming at the chops, "you've got money on the brain, like all policemen. Baker's shops as well."

He screwed his face up. "I want an answer from you: where's that money?"

But I was getting fed-up with all this. "I'll do a deal."

Judging by his flash-bulb face he thought he was suddenly on to a good thing. "What sort of a deal?"

So I told him: "I'll give you all the money I've got, one and fourpence ha'penny, if you stop this third-degree and let me go in and get my breakfast. Honest, I'm clambed to death. I ain't had a bite since yesterday. Can't you hear my guts rollin'?"

His jaw dropped, but on he went, pumping me for another half hour. A routine check-up, as they say on the pictures. But I knew I was winning on points.

Then he left, but came back in the afternoon to search the house. He didn't find a thing, not a French farthing. He asked me questions again and I didn't tell him anything except lies, lies, lies, because I can go on doing that forever without batting an eyelid. He'd got nothing on me and we both of us knew it, otherwise I'd have been down at the Guildhall in no time, but he kept on keeping on because I'd been in a Remand Home for a high-wall job before; and Mike was put through the same mill because all the local cops knew he was my best pal.

When it got dark me and Mike were in our parlour with a low light on and the telly off, Mike taking it easy in the rocking chair and me slouched out on the settee, both of us puffing a packet of Woods. With the door bolted and curtains drawn we talked about the dough we'd crammed up the drainpipe. Mike thought we should take it out and both of us do a bunk to Skegness or Cleethorpes for a good time in the arcades, living like lords in a boarding house near the pier, then at least we'd both have had a big beano before getting sent down.

"Listen, you daft bleeder," I said, "we aren't going to get caught at all *and* we'll have a good time, later." We were so clever we didn't even go out to the pictures, though we wanted to.

In the morning old Hitler-face questioned me again, with one of his pals this time, and the next day they came, trying as hard as they could to get something out of me, but I didn't budge an inch. I know I'm showing off when I say this, but in me he'd met his match, and I'd never give in to questions no matter how long it was kept up. They searched the house a couple of times as well, which made me think they thought they really had something to go by, but I know now that they hadn't, and that it was all buckshee speculation. They turned the house upside down and inside out like an old sock, went from top to bottom and front to back but naturally didn't find a thing. The copper even poked his face up the front-room chimney (that hadn't been used or swept for years) and came down looking like Al Jolson so that he had to swill himself clean at the scullery sink. They kept tapping and pottering around the big aspidistra plant that grandma had left to mam, lifting it up from the table to look under the cloth, putting it aside so's they could move the table and get at the boards under the rug — but the big headed stupid ignorant bastards never once thought of emptying the soil out of the plant pot, where they'd have found the crumpled-up money-box that we'd buried the night we did the job. I suppose it's still there, now I think about it, and I suppose mam wonders now and again why the plant don't prosper like it used to — as if it could with a fistful of thick black tin lapped around its guts.

The last time he knocked at our door was one wet morning at five minutes to nine and I was sleep-logged in my crumby bed as usual. Mam had gone to work that day so I shouted for him to hold on a bit, and then went down to see who it was. There he stood, six-feet tall and sopping wet, and for the first time in my life I did a spiteful thing I'll never forgive myself for: I didn't ask him to come in out of the rain, because I wanted him to get double pneumonia and die. I suppose he could have pushed by me and come in if he'd wanted, but maybe he'd got used to asking questions on the doorstep and didn't want to be put off by changing his ground even though it was raining. Not that I don't like being spiteful because of any barmy principle I've got, but this bit of spite, as it turned out, did me no good at all. I should have treated him as a brother I hadn't seen for twenty years and dragged him in for a cup of tea and a fag, told him about the picture I hadn't seen the night before, asked him how his wife was after her operation and whether they'd shaved her moustache off to make it, and then sent him happy and satisfied out by the front door. But no, I thought, let's see what he's got to say for himself now.

He stood a little to the side of the door, either because it was less wet there, or because he wanted to see me from a different angle, perhaps having found it monotonous to watch a bloke's face always tell lies from the same side. "You've been identified," he said, twitching raindrops from his tash. "A woman saw you and your mate yesterday and she swears blind you are the same chaps she saw going into that bakery."

I was dead sure he was still bluffing, because Mike and I hadn't even seen each other the day before, but I looked worried. "She's a menace then to innocent people, whoever she is, because the only bakery I've been in lately is the one up our street to get some cut-bread on tick for mam."

He didn't bite on this. "So now I want to know where the money is" — as if I hadn't answered him at all.

"I think mam took it to work this morning to get herself some tea in the canteen." Rain was splashing down so hard I thought he'd get washed away if he didn't come inside. But I wasn't much bothered, and went on: "I remember I put it in the telly-vase last night — it was my only one-and-three and I was saving it for a packet of tips this morning — and I nearly had a jibbering black fit just now when I saw it had gone. I was reckoning on it for getting me through today because I don't think life's worth living without a fag, do you?"

I was getting into my stride and began to feel good, twigging that this would be my last pack of lies, and that if I kept it up for long enough this time I'd have the bastards beat: Mike and me would be off to the coast in a few weeks time having the fun of our lives, playing at penny football and latching on to a couple of tarts that would give us all they were good for. "And this weather's no good for picking-up fag-ends in the street," I said, "because they'd be sopping wet. Course, I know you could dry 'em out near the fire, but it don't taste the same you know, all said and done. Rainwater does summat to 'em that don't bear thinkin' about: it turns 'em back into hoss-tods without the taste though."

I began to wonder, at the back of my brainless eyes, why old copper-lugs didn't pull me up sharp and say he hadn't got time to listen to all this, but he wasn't looking at me anymore, and all my thoughts about Skegness went bursting to smithereens in my sludgy loaf. I could have dropped into the earth when I saw what he'd fixed his eyes on.

He was looking at it, an ever-loving fiver, and I could only jabber: "The one thing is to have some real fags because new hoss-tods is always better than stuff that's been rained on and dried, and I know how you feel about not being able to find money because one-and-three's one-and-three in anybody's pocket, and naturally if I see it knocking around I'll get you on the blower tomorrow straightaway and tell you where you can find it."

I thought I'd go down in a fit: three green-backs as well had been washed down by the water, and more were following, lying flat at first after their fall, then getting tilted at the corners by wind and rainspots as if they were alive and wanted to get back into the dry snug drainpipe out of the terrible weather, and you can't imagine how I wished they'd be able to. Old Hitler-face didn't know what to make of it but just kept staring down and down, and I thought I'd better keep on talking, though I knew it wasn't much good now.

"It's a fact, I know, that money's hard to come by and half-crowns don't get found on bus seats or in dustbins, and I didn't see any in bed last night because I'd 'ave known about it, wouldn't I? You can't sleep with things like that in the bed because they're too hard, and anyway at first they're. . . ." It took Hitler-boy a long time to catch on; they were beginning to spread over the yard a bit, reinforced by the third colour of a ten-bob note, before his hand clamped itself on to my shoulder.

III

The pop-eyed potbellied governor said to a pop-eyed potbellied Member of Parliament who sat next to his pop-eyed potbellied whore of a wife that I was his only hope for getting the Borstal Blue Ribbon Prize Cup For Long Distance Cross Country Running (All England), which I was, and it set me laughing to myself inside, and I didn't say a word to any potbellied pop-eyed bastard that might give them real hope, though I knew the governor anyway took my quietness to mean he'd got that cup already stuck on the bookshelf in his office among the few other mildewed trophies.

"He might take up running in a sort of professional way when he gets out," and it wasn't until he'd said this and I'd heard it with my own flap-tabs that I realized it might be possible to do such a thing, run for money, trot for wages on piece work at a bob a puff rising bit by bit to a guinea a gasp and retiring through old age at thirty-two because of lace-curtain lungs, a football heart, and legs like varicose beanstalks. But I'd have a wife and car and get my grinning long-distance clock in the papers and have a smashing secretary to answer piles of letters sent by tarts who'd mob me when they saw who I was as I pushed my way into Woolworth's for a packet of razor blades and a cup of tea. It was something to think about all right, and sure enough the governor knew he'd got me when he said, turning to me as if I would at any rate have to be consulted about it all: "How does this matter strike you, then, Smith, my lad?"

A line of potbellied pop-eyes gleamed at me and a row of goldfish mouths opened and wiggled gold teeth at me, so I gave them the answer they wanted because I'd hold my trump card until later. "It'd suit me fine, sir," I said.

"Good lad. Good show. Right spirit. Splendid."

"Well," the governor said, "get that cup for us today and I'll do all I can for you. I'll get you trained so that you whack every man in the Free World." And I had a picture in my brain of me running and beating everybody in the world, leaving them all behind until only I was trot-trotting across a big wide moor alone, doing a marvellous speed as I ripped between boulders and reed-clumps, when suddenly: CRACK! CRACK! — bullets that can go faster than any man running, coming from a copper's rifle planted in a tree, winged me and split my gizzard in spite of my perfect running, and down I fell.

The potbellies expected me to say something else. "Thank you, sir," I said.

Told to go, I trotted down the pavilion steps, out onto the field because the big cross-country was about to begin and the two entries from Gunthorpe had fixed themselves early at the starting line and were ready to move off like white kangaroos. The sports ground looked a treat: with big tea-tents all round and flags flying and seats for families — empty because no mam or dad had known what opening day meant — and boys still running heats for the hundred yards, and lords and ladies walking from stall to stall, and the Borstal Boys Brass Band in blue uniforms; and up on the stands the brown jackets of Hucknall as well as our own grey blazers, and then the Gunthorpe lot with shirt sleeves rolled. The blue sky was full of sunshine and it couldn't have been a better day, and all of the big show was like something out of Ivanhoe that we'd seen on the pictures a few days before.

"Come on, Smith," Roach the sports master called to me, "we don't want you to be late for the big race, eh? Although I dare say you'd catch them up if you were." The others cat-called and grunted at this, but I took no notice and placed myself between Gunthorpe and one of the Aylesham trusties, dropped on my knees and plucked a few grass blades to suck on the way round. So the big race it was, for them, watching from the grand-stand under a fluttering Union Jack, a race for the governor, that he had been waiting for, and I hoped he and all the rest of his pop-eyed gang were busy placing big bets on me, hundred to one to win, all the money they had in their pockets, all the wages they were going to get for the next five years, and the more they placed the happier I'd be. Because here was a dead cert going to die on the big name they'd built for him, going to go down dying with laughter whether it choked him or not. My knees felt the cool soil pressing into them, and out of my eye's corner I saw Roach lift his hand. The Gunthorpe boy twitched before the signal was given; some-body cheered too soon; Medway bent forward; then the gun went; and I was away.

We went once around the field and then along a half-mile drive of elms, being cheered all the way, and I seemed to feel I was in the lead as we went out by the gate and into the lane, though I wasn't interested enough to find out. The five-mile course was marked by splashes of whitewash gleaming on gateposts and trunks and stiles and stones, and a boy with a waterbottle and bandage-box stood every half-mile waiting for those that dropped out or fainted. Over the first stile, without trying, I was still nearly in the lead but one; and if any of you want tips about running, never be in a hurry, and never let any of the other runners know you are in a hurry even if you are. You can always overtake on long-distance running without letting the others smell the hurry in you; and when you've used your craft like this to reach the two or three up front then you can do a big dash later that puts everybody else's hurry in the shade because you've not had to make haste up till then. I ran to a steady jog-trot rhythm, and soon it was so smooth that I forgot I was running, and I was hardly able to know that my legs were lifting and falling and my arms going in and out, and my lungs didn't seem to be working at all, and my heart stopped that wicked thumping I always get at the beginning of a run. Because you see I never race at all; I just run, and somehow I know that if I forget I'm racing and only jog-trot along until I don't know I'm running I always win the race. For when my eyes recognize that I'm getting near the end of the course — by seeing a stile or cottage corner — I put on a spurt, and such a fast big spurt it is because I feel that up till then I haven't been running and that I've used up no energy at all. And I've been able to do this because I've been thinking; and I wonder if I'm the only one in the running business with this system of forgetting that I'm running because I'm too busy thinking; and I wonder if any of the other lads are on to the same lark, though I know for a fact that they aren't. Off like the wind along the cobbled footpath and rutted lane, smoother than the flat grass track on the field and better for thinking because it's not too smooth, and I was in my element that afternoon knowing that nobody could beat me at running but intending to beat myself before the day was over. For when the governor talked to me of being honest when I first came in he didn't know what the word meant or he wouldn't have had me here in this race, trotting along in shimmy and shorts and sunshine. He'd have had me where I'd have had him if I'd been in his place: in a quarry breaking rocks until he broke his back. At least old Hitler-face the plain-clothes dick was honester than the governor, because he at any rate had had it in for me and I for him, and when my case was coming up in court a copper knocked at our front door at four o'clock in the morning and got my mother out of bed when she was paralytic tired, reminding her she had to be in court at dead on half past nine. It was the finest bit of spite I've ever heard of, but I would call it honest, the same as my mam's words were honest when she really told that copper what she thought of him and called him all the dirty names she'd ever heard of, which took her half an hour and woke the terrace up.

I trotted on along the edge of a field bordered by the sunken lane, smelling green grass and honeysuckle, and I felt as though I came from a long line of whippets trained to run on two legs, only I couldn't see a toy rabbit in front and there wasn't a collier's cosh behind to make me keep up the pace. I passed the Gunthorpe runner whose shimmy was already black with sweat and I could just see the corner of the fenced-up copse in front where the only man I had to pass to win the race was going all out to gain the half-way mark. Then he turned into a tongue of trees and bushes where I couldn't see him anymore, and I couldn't see anybody, and I knew what the loneliness of the long-distance runner running across country felt like, realizing that as far as I was concerned this feeling was the only honesty and realness there was in the world and knowing it would be no different ever, no matter what I felt at odd times, and no matter what anybody else tried to tell me. The runner behind me must have been a long way off because it was so quiet, and there was even less noise and movement than there had been at five o'clock of a frosty winter morning. It was hard to understand, and all I knew was that you had to run, run, run, without knowing why you were running, but on you went through fields you didn't understand and into woods that made you afraid, over hills without knowing you'd been up and down, and shooting across streams that would have cut the heart out of you had you fallen into them. And the winning post was no end to it, even though crowds might be cheering you in, because on you had to go before you got your breath back, and the only time you stopped really was when you tripped over a tree trunk and broke your neck or fell into a disused well and stayed dead in the darkness forever. So I thought: they aren't going to get me on this racing lark, this running and trying to win, this jog-trotting for a bit of blue ribbon, because it's not the way to go on at all, though they swear blind that it is. You should think about nobody and go your own way, not on a course marked out for you by people holding mugs of water and bottles of iodine in case you fall and cut yourself so that they can pick you up — even if you want to stay where you are — and get you moving again.

On I went, out of the wood, passing the man leading without knowing I was going to do so. Flip-flap, flip-flap, jog-trot, jog-trot, crunchslap-crunchslap, across the middle of a broad field again, rhythmically running in my greyhound effortless fashion, knowing I had won the race though it wasn't half over, won it if I wanted it, could go on for ten or fiften or twenty miles if I had to and drop dead at the finish of it, which would be the same, in the end, as living an honest life like the governor wanted me to. It amounted to: win the race and be honest, and on trot-trotting I went, having the time of my life, loving my progress because it did me good and set me thinking which by now I liked to do, but not caring at all when I remembered that I had to win this race as well as run it. One of the two, I had to win the race or run it, and I knew I could do both because my legs had carried me well in front — now coming to the short cut down the bramble bank and over the sunken road — and carry me further because they seemed made of electric cable and easily alive to keep on slapping at those ruts and roots, but I'm not going to win because the only way I'd see I came in first would be if winning meant that I was going to escape the coppers after doing the biggest bank job of my life, but winning means the exact opposite, no matter how they try to kill or kid me, means running right into their white-gloved wall-barred hands and grinning mugs and staying there for the rest of my natural long life of stone-breaking anyway, but stone-breaking in the way I want to do it and not in the way they tell me.

Another honest thought that comes is that I could swing left at the next hedge of the field, and under its cover beat my slow retreat away from the sports ground winning post. I could do three or six or a dozen miles across the turf like this and cut a few main roads behind me so's they'd never know which one I'd taken; and maybe on the last one when it got dark I could thumb a lorry-lift and get a free ride north with somebody who might not give me away. But no, I said I wasn't daft didn't I? I won't pull out with only six months left, and besides there's nothing I want to dodge and run away from; I only want a bit of my own back on the In-laws and Potbellies by letting them sit up there on their big posh seats and watch me lose this race, though as sure as God made me I know that when I do lose I'll get the dirtiest crap and kitchen jobs in the months to go before my time is up. I won't be worth a threpp'ny-bit to anybody here, which will be all the thanks I get for being honest in the only way I know. For when the governor told me to be honest it was meant to be in his way not mine, and if I kept on being honest in the way he wanted and won my race for him he'd see I got the cushiest six months still left to run; but in my own way, well, it's not allowed, and if I find a way of doing it such as I've got now then I'll get what-for in every mean trick he can set his mind to. And if you look at it in my way, who can blame him? For this is war — and ain't I said so? — and when I hit him in the only place he knows he'll be sure to get his own back on me for not collaring that cup when his heart's been set for ages on seeing himself standing up at the end of the afternoon to clap me on the back as I take the cup from Lord Earwig or some such chinless wonder with a name like that. And so I'll hit him where it hurts a lot, and he'll do all he can to get his own back, tit for tat, though I'll enjoy it most because I'm hitting first, and because I planned it longer. I don't know why I think these thoughts are better than any I've ever had, but I do, and I don't care why. I suppose it took me a long time to get going on all this because I've had no time and peace in all my bandit life, and now my thoughts are coming pat and the only trouble is I often can't stop, even when my brain feels as if it's got cramp, frostbite and creeping paralysis all rolled into one and I have to give it a rest by slap-dashing down through the brambles of the sunken lane. And all this is another uppercut I'm getting in first at people like the governor, to show him — if I can — his races are never won even though some bloke always comes unknowingly in first, how in the end the governor is going to be doomed while blokes like me will take the pickings of his roasted bones and dance like maniacs around his Borstal's ruins. And so this story's like the race and once again I won't bring off a winner to suit the governor: no, I'm being honest, like he told me to, without him knowing what he means, though I don't suppose he'll ever come in with a story of his own, even if he reads this one of mine and knows who I'm talking about.

I've just come up out of the sunken lane, kneed and elbowed, thumped and bramble-scratched, and the race is two-thirds over, and a voice is going like a wireless in my mind saying that when you've had enough of feeling good like the first man on earth of a frosty morning, and you've known how it is to be taken bad like the last man on earth on a summer's afternoon, then you get at last to being like the only man on earth and don't give a bogger about either good or bad, but just trot on with your slippers slapping the good dry soil that at least would never do you a bad turn. Now the words are like coming from a crystal-set that's broken down, and something's happening inside the shell-case of my guts that bothers me and I don't know why or what to blame it on, a grinding near my ticker as though a bag of rusty screws is loose inside me and I shake them up every time I trot forward. Now and again I break my rhythm to feel my left shoulderblade by swinging a right hand across my chest as if to rub the knife away that has somehow got stuck there. But I know it's nothing to bother about, that more likely it's caused by too much thinking that now and again I take for worry. For sometimes I'm the greatest worrier in the world I think (as you twigged I'll bet from me having got this story out) which is funny anyway because my mam don't know the meaning of the word so I don't take after her, though dad had a hard time of worry all his life up to when he filled his bedroom with hot blood and kicked the bucket that morning when nobody was in the house. I'll never forget it, straight I won't, because I was the one that found him and I often wished I hadn't. Back from a session on the fruit-machines at the fish-and-chip shop, jingling my three-lemon loot to a nail-dead house, as soon as I got in I knew something was wrong, stood leaning my head against the cold mirror above the mantelpiece trying not to open my eyes and see my stone-cold clock — because I knew I'd gone as white as a piece of chalk since coming in as if I'd been got at by a Dracula-vampire and even my penny-pocket winnings kept quiet on purpose.

Gunthorpe nearly caught me up. Birds were singing from the briar hedge, and a couple of thrushes flew like lightning into some thorny bushes. Corn had grown high in the next field and would be cut down soon with scythes and mowers; but I never wanted to notice much while running in case it put me off my stroke, so by the haystack I decided to leave it all behind and put on such a spurt, in spite of nails in my guts, that before long I'd left both Gunthorpe and the birds a good way off; I wasn't far now from going into that last mile and a half like a knife through margarine, but the quietness I suddenly trotted into between two pickets was like opening my eyes underwater and looking at the pebbles on a stream bottom, reminding me again of going back that morning to the house in which my old man had croaked, which is funny because I hadn't thought about it at all since it happened and even then I didn't brood much on it. I wonder why? I suppose that since I started to think on these long-distance runs I'm liable to have anything crop up and pester at my tripes and innards, and now that I see my bloody dad behind each grass-blade in my barmy runner-brain I'm not so sure I like to think and that it's such a good thing after all. I choke my phlegm and keep on running anyway and curse the Borstal-builders and their athletics — flappity-flap, slop-slop, crunchslap-crunchslap-crunchslap — who've maybe got their own back on me from the bright beginning by sliding magic-lantern slides into my head that never stood a chance before. Only if I take whatever comes like this in my runner's stride can I keep on keeping on like my old self and beat them back; and now I've thought on this far I know I'll win, in the crunchslap end. So anyway after a bit I went upstairs one step at a time not thinking anything about how I should find dad and what I'd do when I did. But now I'm making up for it by going over the rotten life mam led him ever since I can remember, knocking-on with different men even when he was alive and fit and she not caring whether he knew it or not, and most of the time he wasn't so blind as she thought and cursed and roared and threatened to punch her tab, and I had to stand up to stop him even though I knew she deserved it. What a life for all of us. Well, I'm not grumbling, because if I did I might just as well win this bleeding race, which I'm not going to do, though if I don't lose speed I'll win it before I know where I am, and then where would I be?

Now I can hear the sports ground noise and music as I head back for the flags and the lead-in drive, the fresh new feel of underfoot gravel going against the iron muscles of my legs. I'm nowhere near puffed despite that bag of nails that rattles as much as ever, and I can still give a big last leap like gale-force wind if I want to, but everything is under control and I know now that there ain't another long-distance cross-country running runner in England to touch my speed and style. Our doddering bastard of a governor, our half-dead gangrened gaffer is hollow like an empty petrol drum, and he wants me and my running life to give him glory, to put in him blood and throbbing veins he never had, wants his potbellied pals to be his witnesses as I gasp and stagger up to his winning post so's he can say: "My Borstal gets that cup, you see. I win my bet, because it pays to be honest and try to gain the prizes I offer to my lads, and they know it, have known it all along. They'll always be honest now, because I made them so." And his pals will think: "He trains his lads to live right, after all; he deserves a medal but we'll get him made a Sir" — and at this very moment as the birds come back to whistling I can tell myself I'll never care a sod what any of the chinless spineless In-laws think or say. They've seen me and they're cheering now and loudspeakers set around the field like elephant's ears are spreading out the big news that I'm well in the lead, and can't do anything else but stay there. But I'm still thinking of the Out-law death my dad died, telling the doctors to scat from the house when they wanted him to finish up in hospital (like a bleeding guinea-pig, he raved at them). He got up in bed to throw them out and even followed them down the stairs in his shirt though he was no more than skin and stick. They tried to tell him he'd want some drugs but he didn't fall from it, and only took the pain-killer that mam and I got from a herb-seller in the next street. It's not till now that I know what guts he had, and when I went into the room that morning he was lying on his stomach with the clothes thrown back, looking like a skinned rabbit, his grey head resting just on the edge of the bed, and on the floor must have been all the blood he'd had in his body, right from his toe-nails up, for nearly all of the lino and carpet was covered in it, thin and pink.

And down the drive I went, carrying a heart blocked up like Boulder Dam across my arteries, the nail-bag clamped down tighter and tighter as though in a woodwork vice, yet with my feet like birdwings and arms like talons ready to fly across the field except that I didn't want to give anybody that much of a show, or win the race by accident. I smell the hot dry day now as I run towards the end, passing a mountain-heap of grass emptied from cans hooked on to the fronts of lawnmowers pushed by my pals; I rip a piece of tree-bark with my fingers and stuff it in my mouth, chewing wood and dust and maybe maggots as I run until I'm nearly sick, yet swallowing what I can of it just the same because a little birdie whistled to me that I've got to go on living for at least a bloody sight longer yet but that for six months I'm not going to smell that grass or taste that dusty bark or trot this lovely path. I hate to have to say this but something bloody-well made me cry, and crying is a thing I haven't bloody-well done since I was a kid of two or three. Because I'm slowing down now for Gunthorpe to catch me up, and I'm doing it in a place just where the drive turns in to the sports field — where they can see what I'm doing, especially the governor and his gang from the grandstand, and I'm going so slow I'm almost marking time. Those on the nearest seats haven't caught on yet to what's happening and are still cheering like mad ready for when I make that mark, and I keep on wondering when the bleeding hell Gunthorpe behind me is going to nip by on to the field because I can't hold this up all day, and I think Oh Christ it's just my rotten luck that Gunthorpe's dropped out and that I'll be here for half an hour before the next bloke comes up, but even so, I say, I won't budge, I won't go for that last hundred yards if I have to sit down cross-legged on the grass and have the governor and his chinless wonders pick me up and carry me there, which is against their rules so you can bet they'd never do it because they're not clever enough to break the rules — like I would be in their place — even though they are their own. No, I'll show him what honesty means if it's the last thing I do, though I'm sure he'll never understand because if he and all them like him did it'd mean they'd be on my side which is impossible. By God I'll stick this out like my dad stuck out his pain and kicked them doctors down the stairs: if he had guts for that then I've got guts for this and here I stay waiting for Gunthorpe or Aylesham to bash that turf and go right slap-up against that bit of clothes-line stretched across the winning post. As for me, the only time I'll hit that clothes-line will be when I'm dead and a comfortable coffin's been got ready on the other side. Until then I'm a long-distance runner, crossing country all on my own no matter how bad it feels.

The Essex boys were shouting themselves blue in the face telling me to get a move on, waving their arms, standing up and making as if to run at that rope themselves because they were only a few yards to the side of it. You cranky lot, I thought, stuck at that winning post, and yet I knew they didn't mean what they were shouting, were really on my side and always would be, not able to keep their maulers to themselves, in and out of cop-shops and clink. And there they were now having the time of their lives letting themselves go in cheering me which made the governor think they were heart and soul on his side when he wouldn't have thought any such thing if he'd had a grain of sense. And I could hear the lords and ladies now from the grandstand, and could see them standing up to wave me in: "Run!" they were shouting in their posh voices. "Run!" But I was deaf, daft and blind, and stood where I was, still tasting the bark in my mouth and still blubbing like a baby, blubbing now out of gladness that I'd got them beat at last.

Because I heard a roar and saw the Gunthorpe gang throwing their coats up in the air and I felt the pat-pat of feet on the drive behind me getting closer and closer and suddenly a smell of sweat and a pair of lungs on their last gasp passed me by and went swinging on towards that rope, all shagged out and rocking from side to side, grunting like a Zulu that didn't know any better, like the ghost of me at ninety when I'm heading for that fat upholstered coffin. I could have cheered him myself: "Go on, go on, get cracking. Knot yourself up on that piece of tape." But he was already there, and so I went on, trot-trotting after him until I got to the rope, and collapsed, with a murderous sounding roar going up through my ears while I was still on the wrong side of it.

It's about time to stop; though don't think I'm not still running, because I am, one way or another. The governor at Borstal proved me right; he didn't respect my honesty at all; not that I expected him to, or tried to explain it to him, but if he's supposed to be educated then he should have more or less twigged it. He got his own back right enough, or thought he did, because he had me carting dustbins about every morning from the big full-working kitchens to the garden-bottoms where I had to empty them; and in the afternoon I spread out slops over spuds and carrots growing in the allotments. In the evenings I scrubbed floors, miles and miles of them.

But it wasn't a bad life for six months, which was another thing he could never understand and would have made it grimmer if he could, and it was worth it when I look back on it, considering all the thinking I did, and the fact that the boys caught on to me losing the race on purpose and never had enough good words to say about me, or curses to throw out (to themselves) at the governor.

The work didn't break me; if anything it made me stronger in many ways, and the governor knew, when I left, that his spite had got him nowhere. For since leaving Borstal they tried to get me in the army, but I didn't pass the medical and I'll tell you why. No sooner was I out, after that final run and six-months hard, that I went down with pleurisy, which means as far as I'm concerned that I lost the governor's race all right, and won my own twice over, because I know for certain that if I hadn't raced my race I wouldn't have got this pleurisy, which keeps me out of khaki but doesn't stop me doing the sort of work my itchy fingers want to do.

I'm out now and the heat's switched on again, but the rats haven't got me for the last big thing I pulled. I counted six hundred and twenty-eight pounds and am still living off it because I did the job all on my own, and after it I had the peace to write all this, and it'll be money enough to keep me going until I finish my plans for doing an even bigger snatch, something up my sleeve I wouldn't tell to a living soul. I worked out my systems and hiding-places while pushing scrubbing-brushes around them Borstal floors, planned my outward life of innocence and honest work, yet at the same time grew perfect in the razor-edges of my craft for what I knew I had to do once free; and what I'll do again if netted by the poaching coppers.

In the meantime (as they say in one or two books I've read since, useless though because all of them ended on a winning post and didn't teach me a thing) I'm going to give this story to a pal of mine and tell him that if I do get captured again by the coppers he can try and get it put into a book or something, because I'd like to see the governor's face when he reads it, if he does, which I don't suppose he will; even if he did read it though I don't think he'd know what it was all about. And if I don't get caught the bloke I give this story to will never give me away; he's lived in our terrace for as long as I can remember, and he's my pal. That I do know.

Suggestions for Discussion

1. Who speaks? What aspects of type are significant to the narrator's character? In what way does his individuality transcend these typical traits? By what details of character is his individuality achieved?

2. To whom? Who is the "you" of the narrative? To what extent do you accept and/or reject the characterization of "you"?

3. In what form? How does it affect the point of view of the story that the narrator is "scribbling down" (page 243) his thoughts with a "stub of a pencil" (page 246)?

4. At what distance? How much time has elapsed from the events recalled? How significant is it that the narrator writes of being "inside" from the "outside"? How keen a perspective does he show on the events through tone?

5. With what limitations? Identify passages where you emotionally, morally, or intellectually reject what the narrator says; others where you identify completely with his judgment.

6. On page 243 the narrator discusses honesty in the paragraph beginning, "As I run and see my smoky breath. . . ." What distance do we take on his concept of honesty? Has it changed by the end of the story? See also the paragraph beginning, "We went once around the field . . ." (page 259).

7. Analyze the irony of this sentence: "I can't tell you much about what it was like there because I haven't got the hang of describing buildings or saying how many crumby chairs and slatted windows make a room" (page 244).

8. How reliable are the narrator's values as depicted in two paragraphs, the first of which begins, "Now I believe, and my mam must have thought the same . . ." (page 247)? How much of the responsibility for these values lies with the narrator? How much with society? How does Sillitoe indicate such responsibility?

9. With the paragraph beginning, "I didn't think about anything at all . . ." (page 250), the narrator clearly outlines what he means by "thinking." What is your intellectual distance from his ideas? How do these ideas alter in two paragraphs, the first of which begins, "I've just come up out of the sunken lane . . ." (page 263)? Why is there a knife stuck in his chest from "too much thinking"?

10. Are you convinced that the narrator "wins" the race?

RETROSPECT

1. How many time periods are involved in "The Masked Marvel's Last Toehold"? To what extent does the narrator retain an adult perspective on the child's experience? To what extent does he enter that experience and see it from the child's viewpoint?

2. How would you describe the authorial distance of "The Bella Lingua"? How do time, place, and tone affect and inform that distance?

3. How reliable is the narrator of "Brownstone"? Is the author's perspective identical with that of the narrator, or is some distance implied? Moral? Intellectual? Emotional?

4. In "Jamal the Constable," where is Jamal's judgment accurate and where is he an unreliable narrator? With which of his values do you identify, to which are you in opposition? Why?

WRITING ASSIGNMENTS

1. Choose a crucial incident from a child's life (your own or invented) and write about it from the temporally distanced perspective of an adult narrator.

2. Rewrite the same incident in the child's language from the point of view of the child as narrator.

3. Write a passage from the point of view of a central narrator who is spatially distanced from the events she or he describes. Make the contrast significant — write of a sea voyage from prison, of home from an alien country, of a closet from a mountaintop, or the like.

4. Write a short scene from the point of view of anything nonhuman (a plant, object, animal, Martian, angel). We may sympathize or not with the perceptions of the narrator, but try to imagine yourself into the terms, logic, and frame of reference this character would use.

5. Write a scene from the point of view of a narrator who passes moral judgments that we totally reject.

6. Let your narrator begin with a totally unacceptable premise — illogical, ignorant, bigoted, insane. In the passage, let us gradually come to sympathize with his or her view.

7. Take any assignment you have previously done and recast it from another point of view. This may (but will not simply) involve changing the person in which it is written. Alter the means of perception or point-of-view character so that we have an entirely different perspective on the events. But let your attitude as author remain the same.

8. From the stance of the editorial omniscient, write an ironic scene in which we are to disbelieve your explicit judgments about at least four characters. Side with the villains and condemn the virtuous, but let us know that you mean the opposite of what you say.

9. Write the first paragraph of the story outlined on page 225 five times, from five different points of view.

IS AND IS NOT
Comparison

Types of Metaphor and Simile
Metaphoric Faults to Avoid
Allegory
Symbol
The Objective Correlative

As the concept of distance implies, every reader reading is a self-deceiver. We simultaneously "believe" a story and know that it is a fiction, a fabrication. Our belief in the reality of the story may be so strong that it produces real physical reactions — tears, trembling, sighs, gasps, a headache. At the same time, as long as the fiction is working for us, we know that our submission is voluntary; that we have, as Samuel Taylor Coleridge pointed out, suspended disbelief. "It's just a *movie*," says the exasperated father as he takes his shrieking six-year-old out to the lobby. For the father the fiction is working; for the child it is not.

The necessity of disbelief was demonstrated for me some years ago with the performance of a play that ended with too "good" a hanging. The harness was too well hidden, the actor too adept at purpling and bloating his face when the trap fell. Consternation rippled through the audience: my God, they've hanged the *actor*. Because the illusion was too like reality the illusion was destroyed, and the audience was jolted from its belief in the story back into the real world of the performance.

Simultaneous belief and awareness of illusion are present in both the content and the craft of literature, and what is properly called artistic pleasure derives from the tension of this *is and is not*.

The content of a plot tells us that something happens that does not happen, that people who do not exist behave in such a way, and that the events of life — which we know to be random, unrelated, and unfinished — are necessary, patterned, and come to closure. When someone declares interest or pleasure in a story "because it really happened," he or she is expressing an unartistic and antiartistic preference, subscribing to the lie that events can be accurately translated into the medium of words. Pleasure in artistry comes precisely when the illusion rings true without, however, destroying the knowledge that it is an illusion.

In the same way, the techniques of every art offer us the tension of things that are and are not *alike*. This is true of poetry, in which rhyme is interesting because *tend* sounds like *mend* but not exactly like; it is true of music, whose interest lies in variations on a theme; of composition, where shapes and colors are balanced in asymmetry. And it is the fundamental nature of metaphor, from which literature derives.

Just as the content of a work must not be too like life to destroy the knowledge that it is an illusion, so the likenesses in the formal elements of art must not be too much alike. Rich rhyme, in which *tend* rhymes with *contend* and *pretend*, is boring and restrictive, and virtually no poet chooses to write a whole poem in it. Repetitive tunes jingle; symmetrical compositions tend toward decor.

Metaphor is the literary device by which we are told that something is, or is like, something that it clearly is not, or is not exactly like. What a good metaphor does is surprise us with the unlikeness of the two things compared, while at the same time convincing us of the aptness or truth of the likeness. A bad metaphor fails to surprise, or to convince, or both.

Types of Metaphor and Simile

The simplest distinction between types of comparison, and usually the first one grasped by beginning students of literature, is between *metaphor* and *simile*. A simile makes a comparison with the use of *like* or *as*, a metaphor without. Though this distinction is technical, it is not entirely trivial, for a metaphor demands a more literal acceptance. If you say, "a woman is a rose," you ask for an extreme suspension of disbelief, whereas "a woman is like a rose" is a more sophisticated form, acknowledging the artifice in the statement.

Historically, metaphor preceded simile, originating in a purely sensuous comparison. When we speak of "the eyes of a potato," or "the eye of a needle," we mean simply that the leafbud and the thread hole *look like* eyes. We don't mean to suggest that the potato or the needle can *see*. The comparisons do not suggest any essential or abstract quality to do with sight.

Both metaphor and simile have developed, however, so that the resonance of comparison is precisely in the essential or abstract quality that the two objects share. When a writer speaks of "the eyes of the houses" or "the windows of the soul," the comparison of eyes to windows does contain the idea of transmitting vision between the inner and the outer. When we speak of "the king of beasts," we don't mean that a lion wears a crown or sits on a throne (though it is relevant that in children's stories the lion often does precisely that, in order to suggest a primitive physical likeness); we mean that king and lion share abstract qualities of power, position, pride, and bearing.

In both metaphor and simile a physical similarity can yield up a characterizing abstraction. So "a woman" may be either "a rose" or "like a rose." The significance of either lies not in the physical similarity but in the essential qualities that such similarity implies: slenderness, suppleness, fragrance, beauty, color — and perhaps the hidden threat of thorns.

Every metaphor and simile I have used so far is either a cliché or a dead metaphor (both of which will be discussed later): each of them may at one time have surprised by their aptness, but by now each has been used so often that the surprise is gone. I wished to use familiar examples in order to clarify that *the resonance of comparison depends on the abstractions conveyed in the likeness of the things compared.* A good metaphor reverberates with the essential; this is the writer's principle of choice.

So Flannery O'Connor, in "A Good Man Is Hard to Find," describes the mother as having "a face as round and innocent as a cabbage." A soccer ball is also round and innocent; so is a schoolroom globe; so is a streetlamp. But if the mother's face had been as round and innocent as any of these things, she would be a different woman altogether. A cabbage is also rural, heavy, dense, and cheap, and so it conveys a whole complex of abstractions about the woman's class and mentality. There is, on the other hand, no innocence in the face of Shrike, in Nathanael West's *Miss Lonelyhearts,* who "buried his triangular face like a hatchet in her neck."

Sometimes the aptness of a comparison is achieved by taking it from an area of reference relevant to the thing compared. In *Dombey and Son,* Charles Dickens describes the ships' instrument maker Solomon Gills as having "eyes as red as if they had been small suns looking at you through a fog." The simile suggests a seascape, whereas in *One Flew Over the Cuckoo's Nest,* Ken Kesey's Ruckly, rendered inert by shock therapy, has eyes "all smoked up and gray and deserted inside like blown fuses." But the metaphor may range further from its original, in which case the abstraction conveyed must strike us as strongly and essentially appropriate. William Faulkner's Emily Grierson in "A Rose for Emily" has "haughty black eyes in a face the flesh of which was strained across the temple and about the eyesockets as you imagine a lighthouse-keeper's face ought to look." Miss Emily has no connection with the sea, but the metaphor reminds us, not only of her sternness and self-sufficiency, but also that she has isolated herself in a locked house. The same character as an old woman has eyes that "looked like two pieces of coal pressed into a lump of dough," and the image domesticates her, robs her of her light.

Both metaphors and similes can be *extended*, meaning that the writer continues to present aspects of likeness in the things compared.

> There was a white fog . . . standing all around you like something solid. At eight or nine, perhaps, it lifted as a shutter lifts. We had a glimpse of the towering multitude of trees, of the immense matted jungle, with the blazing little ball of the sun hanging over it — all perfectly still — and then the shutter came down again, smoothly, as if sliding in greased grooves.
>
> JOSEPH CONRAD, *Heart of Darkness*

Notice that Conrad moves from a generalized image of "something solid" to the specific simile, "as a shutter lifts"; reasserts the simile as a metaphor, "then the shutter came down again"; and becomes still more specific in the extension, "as if sliding in greased grooves." Also note that Conrad emphasizes the dumb solidity of the fog by comparing the larger natural image with the smaller domestic one. Metaphor may equally work when the smaller or more ordinary image is compared with one larger or more intense, as in this example from Katherine Anne Porter's "Flowering Judas."

> Sometimes she wishes to run away, but she stays. Now she longs to fly out of this room, down the narrow stairs, and into the street where the houses lean together like conspirators under a single mottled lamp.

A *conceit*, which can be either metaphor or simile, is a comparison of two things radically and startlingly unlike — in Samuel Johnson's words, "yoked by violence together." A conceit is as far removed as possible from the purely sensuous comparison of "the eyes of the potato." It compares two things that have very little or no immediately apprehensible similarity; and so it is the nature of the conceit to be long. The author must explain to us, sometimes at great length, why these things can be said to be alike. When John Donne compares a flea to the Holy Trinity, the two images have no areas of reference in common, and we don't understand. He must explain to us that the flea, having bitten both the poet and his lover, now has the blood of three souls in its body.

The conceit is more common to poetry than to prose because of the density of its imagery, but it can be used to good effect in fiction. In *The Day of the Locust*, Nathanael West uses a conceit in an insistent devaluation of love. The screenwriter Claude Estee says:

> Love is like a vending machine, eh? Not bad. You insert a coin and press home the lever. There's some mechanical activity inside the bowels of the device. You receive a small sweet, frown at yourself in the dirty mirror, adjust your hat, take a firm grip on your umbrella and walk away, trying to look as though nothing had happened.

"Love is like a vending machine" is a conceit; if the writer didn't explain to us in what way love is like a vending machine, we'd founder trying to figure it out. So he goes on to develop the vending machine in images that suggest, not "love," but seamy sex. The last image — "trying to look as though nothing had happened" — has nothing to do with the vending machine; we accept it because by this time we've fused the two ideas in our minds.

Tom Robbins employs conceit in *Even Cowgirls Get the Blues,* in a playfully self-conscious, mock-scientific comparison of Sissy Hankshaw's thumbs to a pearl.

> As for the oyster, its rectal temperature has never been estimated, although we must suspect that the tissue heat of the sedentary bivalve is as far below good old 98.6 as that of the busy bee is above. Nonetheless, the oyster, could it fancy, should fancy its excremental equipment a hot item, for what other among Creation's crapping creatures can convert its bodily wastes to treasure?
>
> There is a metaphor here, however strained. The author is attempting to draw a shaky parallel between the manner in which the oyster, when beset by impurities or disease, coats the offending matter with its secretions — and the manner in which Sissy Hankshaw, adorned with thumbs that many might consider morbid, coated the offending digits with glory.

The vignette of the oyster is a frivolous digression, relevant only in the making of the pearl. The comparison of pearl and thumbs is a conceit because sensuous similarity is not the point: Sissy's thumbs are not necessarily pale or shiny. The similarity is in the abstract idea of converting "impurities" to "glory."

A *dead metaphor* is one so familiar that it has in effect ceased to be a metaphor; has lost the force of the original comparison and acquired a new definition. Fowler's *Modern English Usage* uses the word *sift* to demonstrate the dead metaphor, one that has "been used so often that speaker and hearer have ceased to be aware that the words used are not literal."

> Thus, in *The men were sifting the meal* we have a literal use of *sift;* in *Satan hath desired to have you, that he may sift you as wheat, sift* is a live metaphor; in *the sifting of evidence,* the metaphor is so familiar that it is about equal chances whether *sifting* or *examination* will be used, and that a sieve is not present to the thought.

English abounds in dead metaphors. *Abounds* is one, where the over-flowing of liquid is not present to the thought. When a man *runs* for office, his legs are not present to the thought, nor is an arrow when we speak of his *aim*, hot stones when we go through an *ordeal*, headgear when someone *caps* a joke. Unlike clichés, dead metaphors enrich the language. There is a residual resonance from the original metaphor but no pointless effort on the part of the mind to resolve the tension of like and unlike. English is fertile with metaphors (including those eyes of the potato and the needle) that have died and been resurrected as *idiom*, a "manner of speaking."

Metaphoric Faults to Avoid

Comparison is not a frivolity. It is, on the contrary, the primary business of the brain. Some eighteenth-century philosophers spoke of the human mind as a *tabula rasa*, a blank sheet on which sense impressions were recorded, compared, and grouped. Now we're more likely to speak of the mind as a "computer" (notice that both images are metaphors), "storing" and "sorting" "data." What both acknowledge is that comparison is the basis of all learning and all reasoning. When a child burns his hand on the stove and his mother says, "It's hot," and then goes toward the radiator and the mother says, "It's hot," the child learns not to burn his fingers. But the goal of reasoning is fact, toward a mode of behavior. When we speak of "the flames of torment," our impulse is comprehension and com-passion. The goal of literary comparison is not fact but perception, toward scope of understanding.

Nevertheless, *metaphor* is a dirty word in some critical circles, because of the strain of the pursuit. Clichés, mixed metaphors, similes that are inept, unapt, obscure, or done to death mar good prose and tax the patience of the most willing reader. After eyes have been red suns, burnt-out fuses, lighthouse keepers, and lumps of coal, what else can they be?

The answer is: always something. But because by definition metaphor introduces an alien image into the flow of the story, metaphor is to some degree always self-conscious. Badly handled, it calls attention to the writer rather than the meaning, and produces a sort of hiccup in the reader's involvement. A good metaphor fits so neatly that it fuses to and illuminates the meaning; or, like the Robbins passage quoted above, it acknowledges its self-consciousness so as to take the reader into the game. Generally speaking, where metaphors are concerned, less is more and, if in doubt, don't.

(Now I want to analyze the preceding paragraph. It contains at least seven dead metaphors: *alien, flow, handled, calls, fits, fuses,* and *illuminates.*

A metaphor is not a foreigner; a story is not water; we do not take comparisons in our fingers; they have no vocal cords; they are not puzzle pieces; they do not congeal; and they give off no light rays. But each of these words has acquired a new definition and so settles into its context without strain. At the same time, the metaphoric echoes of these words make them more interesting than their abstract synonyms: *introduces an image from a different context into the meaning of the story . . . badly written, it makes us aware of the writer . . . a good metaphor is so directly relevant that it makes the meaning more understandable* — these abstract synonyms contain no imagery, and so they make for flatter writing. I have probably used what Fowler speaks of as a "moribund or dormant, but not stone-dead" metaphor when I speak of Robbins "taking the reader into the game." If I were Robbins, I'd probably have said, "inviting the reader to sit down at the literary pinochle table," which is a way of acknowledging that "taking the reader into the game" is a familiar metaphor; that is, it's a way of taking us into the game. I have used one live metaphor — "produces a sort of hiccup in the reader's involvement" — and I think I will leave it there to defend itself.)

There are more *dont's* than *do's* to record for the writing of metaphor and simile, because every good comparison is its own justification by virtue of being apt and original.

To study good metaphor: read. In the meantime, avoid the following:

Cliché metaphors are metaphors on their way to being dead. They are inevitably apt comparisons; if they were not, they wouldn't have been repeated often enough to become clichés. But they have not acquired new definitions, and so the reader's mind must make the imaginative leap to an image. The image fails to surprise, and we blame the writer for this expenditure of energy without a payoff. The metaphor is not original. Or, to put it a worse way:

> Clichés are *the last word* in bad writing, and it's *a crying shame* to see all you *bright young things* spoiling your *deathless prose* with phrases *as old as the hills.* You must *keep your nose to the grindstone,* because *the sweet smell of success* only comes to those who *march to the tune of a different drummer.*

It's a sad fact that because you have been born into the twentieth century you may not say that eyes are like pools or stars, and you should be very wary of saying that they flood with tears. These have been so often repeated that they've become shorthand for emotions (attraction in the first and second instances, grief in the third) without the felt force of those emotions. Anytime you as writer record an emotion without convincing us to feel that emotion, you introduce a fatal distance between author and reader. Therefore, neither may your characters be hawk-eyed nor eagle-eyed; nor may they have ruby lips or pearly teeth or peaches-and-cream complexions or necks like swans or breasts like melons or thighs like hams. I once gave a character spatulate fingers — and have been worrying about it ever since. If you sense — and you may — that the moment calls for the special intensity of metaphor, you may have to sift through a whole stock of clichés that come readily to mind before you find the fresh comparison that is both apt and startling.

Nevertheless, *pools* and *stars* have become clichés for *eyes* because they capture and manifest something essential about the nature of eyes. As long as eyes continue to contain liquid and light, there will be a new way of saying so. And a metaphor freshly pursued can even take advantage of the shared writer-reader consciousness of familiar images. Here William Golding, in *The Inheritors*, describes his Neanderthal protagonist's first tears, which mark his evolution into a human being:

> There was a light now in each cavern, lights faint as the starlight reflected in the crystals of a granite cliff. The lights increased, acquired definition, brightened, lay each sparkling at the lower edge of a cavern. Suddenly, noiselessly, the lights became thin crescents, went out, and streaks glistened on each cheek. The lights appeared again, caught among the silvered curls of the beard. They hung, elongated, dropped from curl to curl and gathered at the lowest tip. The streaks on the cheeks pulsed as the drops swam down them, a great drop swelled at the end of a hair of the beard, shivering and bright. It detached itself and fell in a silver flash.

In this sharply focused and fully extended metaphor of eyes as caverns, Golding asks us to draw on a range of familiar light imagery: starlight, crystal, the crescent moon, silver. The light imagery usually associated with eyes attaches to the water imagery of tears, though neither eyes nor tears are named. There is a submerged acknowledgment of cliché, but there is no cliché; Golding has reinvested the familiar images with their comparative and emotional force.

In both serious and comic writing, the consciousness of the familiar can be a peripheral advantage if you find a new way of exploiting it. It is a cliché to say, "You'll break my heart," but when Linda Ronstadt sings, "Break my mind, break my mind . . . ," the heart is still there, and the old image takes on new force. Although you may not say *her eyes are like pools*, you may probably say *her eyes are like the scummy duck pond out back*, and we'll find it comic partly because we know the cliché is lurking under the scum.

Cliché can also be useful as a device for establishing authorial distance toward a character or narrator. If the author tells us that Rome wasn't built in a day, we're likely to think the author has little to contribute to human insight; but if a character says so, in speech or thought, the judgment attaches to the character rather than to the author.

The door closed and he turned to find the dumpy figure, surmounted by the atrocious hat, coming toward him. "Well," she said, *"you only live once* and paying a little more for it, I at least won't *meet myself coming and going."*

"Some day I'll start making money . . ."

"I think you're doing fine," she said, drawing on her gloves. "You've only been out of school a year. *Rome wasn't built in a day."*

(italics mine)

FLANNERY O'CONNOR, "Everything That Rises Must Converge"

Though you can exploit the familiar by acknowledging it in a new way, it is never sufficient to put a cliché in quotation marks: *They hadn't seen each other for "eons."* Writers are sometimes tempted to do this in order to indicate that they know a cliché when they see one. Unfortunately, quotation marks have no power to renew emotion. All they say is, "I'm being lazy and I know it."

Farfetched metaphors are the opposite of clichés; they surprise but are not apt. As the dead metaphor *farfetched* suggests, the mind must travel too far to carry back the likeness, and too much is lost on the way. When such a comparison does work, we speak laudatorily of a "leap of the imagination." But when it does not, what we face is in effect a failed conceit: the explanation of what is alike about these two things does not convince. Very good writers in the search for originality sometimes fetch too far. Ernest Hemingway's talent was not for metaphor, and on the rare occasions that he used a metaphor, he was likely to strain. In this passage from *A Farewell to Arms,* the protagonist has escaped a firing squad and is fleeing the war:

You had lost your cars and your men as a floorwalker loses the stock of his department in a fire. There was, however, no insurance. You were out of it now. You had no more obligation. If they shot floorwalkers after a fire in the department store because they spoke with an accent they had always had, then certainly the floorwalkers would not be expected to return when the store opened again for business. They might seek other employment; if there was any other employment and the police did not get them.

Well, this doesn't work. We may be willing to see the likeness between stock lost in a department store fire and men and cars lost in a military skirmish; but "they" *don't* shoot floorwalkers as they shoot prisoners of war; and although a foreign accent might be a disadvantage behind enemy lines, it is hard to see how a floorwalker could be killed because of one, although it might make it hard for him to get hired in the first place, if. . . . The mind twists trying to find any illuminating or essential logic in the comparison of a soldier to a floorwalker, and fails, so that the protagonist's situation is trivialized in the attempt.

Mixed metaphors are so called because they ask us to compare the original image with things from two or more different areas of reference: *as you walk the path of life, don't founder on the reefs of ignorance.* Life can be a path or a sea, but it cannot be both at the same time. The point of metaphor is to fuse two images in a single tension. The mind is adamantly unwilling to fuse three.

Separate metaphors or similes too close together, especially if they come from areas of reference very different in value or tone, disturb in the same way the mixed metaphor does. The mind doesn't leap; it staggers. The cliché paragraph on page 276 gives an example of metaphors packed too closely. Here is another example, less cliché.

> They fought like rats in a Brooklyn sewer. Nevertheless her presence was the axiom of his heart's geometry, and when she was away you would see him walking up and down the street dragging his cane along the picket fence like an idle boy's stick.

Any of these metaphors or similes might be acceptable by itself, but rats, axioms, and boy's sticks connote three different areas and tones, and two sentences cannot contain them all.

Mixed metaphors and metaphors too close together may be used for comic or characterizing effect, and *The New Yorker* has been amusing its readers for decades with a filler item called "Block That Metaphor." But the laugh is always on the writer/speaker, and put-down humor, like a bad pun, is more likely to produce a snicker than an insight. Just as writers are sometimes tempted to put a cliché in quotation marks, they are sometimes tempted to mix metaphors and then apologize for it, in some such phrase as "to mix the metaphor," or, "If I may be permitted a mixed metaphor." It doesn't work. Don't apologize and don't mix.

Obscure and *overdone metaphors* falter because the author has misjudged the difficulty of the comparison. The result is either confusion or an insult to the reader's intelligence. In the case of obscurity, a similarity in the author's mind isn't getting onto the page. One student described the spines on a prickly pear cactus as being "slender as a fat man's fingers." I was completely confused by this. Was it ironic, that the spines weren't slender at all? Ah no, he said, hadn't I noticed how startling it was when someone with a fleshy body had bony fingers and toes? The trouble here was that the author knew what he meant but had left out the essential abstraction in the comparison, the startling quality of the contrast: "the spines of the fleshy prickly pear, like slender fingers on a fat man."

In this case, the simile was underexplained. It's probably a more common impulse — we're so anxious to make sure the reader gets it — to explain the obvious. In the novel *Raw Silk*, I had the narrator describe quarrels with her husband, "which I used to face with my dukes up in high confidence that we'd soon clear the air. The air can't be cleared now. We live in marital Los Angeles. This is the air — polluted, poisoned." A critic friend pointed out to me that anybody who didn't know about LA smog wouldn't get it anyway, and that all the last two words did was ram the comparison down his throat. He was right. "The air can't be cleared now. We live in marital Los Angeles. This is the air." The rewrite is much stronger because it neither explains nor exaggerates; and the reader enjoys supplying the metaphoric link.

Allegory

Allegory is a narrative form in which comparison is structural rather than stylistic. An allegory is a continuous fictional comparison of events, in which the action of the story represents a different action or a philosophical idea. The simplest illustration of an allegory is a fable, in which, for example, the race between the tortoise and the hare is used to illustrate the philosophical notion that "the race is not always to the swift." Such a story can be seen as an extended simile, with the original figure of the comparison suppressed: the tortoise and the hare represent types of human beings, but people are never mentioned and the comparison takes place in the reader's mind. George Orwell's *Animal Farm* is a less naive animal allegory, exploring ideas about corruption in a democratic society. Muriel Spark's *The Abbey* is a historical allegory, representing, without any direct reference to Richard Nixon, the events of Nixon's presidential term, through allegorical machinations in a nunnery. The plots of such stories are self-contained, but their significance lies in the reference to outside events or ideas.

Allegory is a tricky form. In the hands of Dante, John Bunyan, Edmund Spenser, John Keats, Franz Kafka, Henrik Ibsen, and Samuel Beckett, it has yielded works of the highest philosophical insight. But most allegories seem to smirk. A naive philosophical fable leads to a simpleminded idea that can be stated in a single phrase; a historical allegory relies on our familiarity with the Watergate scandal or the tribulations of the local football team, and so appeals to a limited and insular readership.

Symbol

A *symbol* differs from metaphor and simile in that it need not contain a comparison. A symbol is an object or event that, by virtue of association, represents something more or something other than itself. Sometimes an object is invested arbitrarily with such meaning, as a flag represents a nation and patriotism. Sometimes a single event stands for a whole complex of events, as the crucifixion of Christ stands as well for resurrection and redemption. Sometimes an object is invested with a complex of qualities through its association with the event, like the cross itself. These symbols are not metaphors; the cross represents redemption, but is not similar to redemption, which cannot be said to be wooden or T-shaped. The mother's hat in "Everything That Rises Must Converge" is such a symbol; it cannot be said to "resemble" desegregation, but in the course of the story it comes to represent the tenacious nostalgia of gentility and the aspirations of the new black middle class, and therefore the unacknowledged "converging" of equality.

Nevertheless, most literary symbols, including this one, do in the course of the action derive their extra meaning from some sort of likeness on the level of emotional or ideological abstraction. The hat is not "like" desegregation, but the action of the story reveals that both women are able to buy such a hat and choose it; this is a concrete example of equality, and so represents the larger concept of equality.

Margaret Drabble's novel *The Garrick Year* recounts the disillusionment of a young wife and mother who finds no escape from her situation. The book ends with a family picnic in an English meadow, and the return home.

> On the way back to the car, Flora dashed at a sheep that was lying in the path, but unlike all the others it did not get up and move: it stared at us instead with a sick and stricken indignation. Flora passed quickly on, pretending for pride's sake that she had not noticed its recalcitrance; but as I passed, walking slowly, supported by David, I looked more closely and I saw curled up and clutching at the sheep's belly a real snake. I did not say anything to David: I did not want to admit that I had seen it, but I did see it, I can see it still. It is the only wild snake that I have ever seen. In my book on Herefordshire it says that that part of the country is notorious for its snakes. But "Oh, well, so what," is all that one can say, the Garden of Eden was crawling with them too, and David and I managed to lie amongst them for one whole pleasant afternoon. One just has to keep on and to pretend, for the sake of the children, not to notice. Otherwise one might just as well stay at home.

The sheep is a symbol of the young woman's emotional situation. It does resemble her, but only on the level of the abstractions: sickness, indignation, and yet resignation at the fatal dangers of the human condition. There is here a metaphor that could be expressed as such (*she was sick and resigned as the sheep*), but the strength of the symbol is that such literal expression does not take place: we let the sheep stand in the place of the young woman while it reaches out to the larger significance.

A symbol may also begin as and grow from a metaphor, so that it finally contains more qualities than the original comparison. In John Irving's novel *The World According to Garp*, the young Garp mishears the word *undertow* as *under toad* and compares the danger of the sea to the lurking fantasies of his childish imagination. Throughout the novel the "under toad" persists, and it comes symbolically to represent all the submerged dangers of ordinary life, ready to drag Garp under just when he thinks he is swimming under his own power. Likewise the African continent in *Heart of Darkness* is dark like the barbaric reaches of the soul; but in the course of the novella we come to understand that darkness is shot with light and light with darkness, that barbarity and civilization are inextricably intermixed, and that the heart of darkness is the darkness of the heart.

One important distinction in the use of literary symbols is between those symbols of which the character is aware, and therefore "belong" to him or her; and those symbols of which only writer and reader are aware, and that therefore belong to the work. This distinction is often important to characterization, theme, and distance. In the passage quoted from *The Garrick Year*, the narrator is clearly aware of the import of the sheep, and her awareness suggests her intelligence and the final acceptance of her situation, so that we identify with her in recognizing the symbol. But the protagonist's tumbling hair in "Not Your Singing, Dancing Spade," expensively pomaded and swinging irritatingly into his eyes, is a symbol introduced by the author and not recognized as such by the character, and so distances us from his perception of himself. To the star, his hair is an expression of wealth and professionalism, but the author and the reader see it from the first as a rejection of his black heritage and so as a symbol of the cause of his misery.

Sometimes the interplay between these types of symbol — those recognized by the characters and those seen only by writer and reader — can enrich the story in scope or irony. In *The Inheritors*, from which I've quoted several times, the Neanderthal tribe has its own religious symbols — a root, a grave, shapes in the ice cap — that represent its life-cycle worship. But in the course of the action, flood, fire, and a waterfall recall biblical symbols that allow the reader to supply an additional religious interpretation, which the characters would be incapable of doing. Again, in "Everything That Rises Must Converge," the mother sees her hat as representing, first, her taste and pride, and later the outrageousness of black presumption. For the reader it has the opposite and ironic significance, as a symbol of equality.

Symbols are subject to all the same faults as metaphor: cliché, strain, obscurity, obviousness, and overwriting. For these reasons, and because the word *Symbolism* also describes a particular late-nineteenth-century movement in French poetry, with connotations of obscurity, dream, and magical incantation, *symbolism* as a method has sometimes been treated with scorn in the hard-nosed twentieth century.

Yet it seems to me incontrovertible that the writing process is inherently and by definition symbolic. In the structuring of events; the creation of character and atmosphere; the choice of object, detail, and language, you are selecting and arranging toward the goal that these elements should signify more than their mute material existence. If this were not so, then you would have no principle of choice, and might just as well write about any other set of events, characters, and objects. If you so much as say, "as innocent as a cabbage," the image is minutely symbolic, not a statement of fact but selected to mean "something more and something other" than itself.

There is another and more mundane reason that symbol cannot be avoided in literature, and should not, which is that people also, constantly, function symbolically. We must do so because we rarely know exactly what we mean, and if we do we are not willing to express it, and if we are willing we are not able, and if we are able we are not heard, and if we are heard we are not understood. Words are unwieldy and unyielding, and we leap them with intuition, body language, tone, and symbol. "Is the oven supposed to be on?" he asks. He is only peripherally curious about whether the oven is supposed to be on. He is really complaining: *You're scatterbrained and extravagant with the money I go out and earn.* "If I don't preheat it, the muffins won't crest," she says, meaning: *You didn't catch me this time! You're always complaining about the food, and God knows I wear myself out trying to please you.* "We used to have *salade niçoise* in the summertime," he recalls, meaning: *Don't be so damn triumphant. You're still extravagant, and you haven't got the class you used to have when we were young.* "We used to keep a garden," she says, meaning: *You're always away on weekends and never have time to do anything with me because you don't love me anymore; I think you have a mistress.* "What do you expect of me!" he explodes, and neither of them is surprised that ovens, muffins, salads, and gardens have erupted. When people say "we quarreled over nothing," this is what they mean. They quarreled over symbols.

The Objective Correlative

But the conflict in a fiction cannot be "over nothing," and as a writer you must search for the concrete external manifestations that are adequate to the inexpressible feeling. T. S. Eliot used the term "objective correlative" to describe this process and this necessity.

> The only way of expressing emotion in the form of art is by finding an "objective correlative"; in other words, a set of objects, a situation, a chain of events which shall be the formula of that particular emotion; such that when the external facts, which must terminate in sensory experience, are given, the emotion is immediately invoked.
>
> *The Sacred Wood*

Some critics have argued that Eliot's *objective correlative* is really no more than a synonym for *symbol,* but the term and its definition make several important distinctions. An artistic symbol, unlike a scientific or notational symbol, contains and invokes an *emotion*. Unlike a political or religious symbol, the emotion it evokes is particular to the work, and that specific emotion is evoked by no other objective correlative. The wine in a religious ceremony, the raised fist at a Black Power rally, the peace sign at a love-in, may evoke a generalized communal emotion; but using any of these symbols in a literary work will not evoke that emotion, and not only may an author not choose for them to do otherwise, but the author *may not* rely on them to do so. The objects, situations, and events of a particular work contain its particular emotional effect; conversely, if they do not contain the desired emotional effect, that effect cannot be produced in that work, either by its statement in abstractions or by appeal to outside symbols. The "objective" sensory experience must be "co-relative" to the emotion, each corresponding to the other, for that is *the only way* of expressing emotion in the form of art.

When literary symbols fail, it is most often in this difficult and essential mutuality. In a typical example, we begin the story in a room of a dying woman alone with her collection of perfume bottles. The story ranges back over her rich and sensuous life, and at the end we focus on an empty perfume bottle. It is meant to move us at her death, but it does not. Yet the fault is not in the perfume bottle. Presumably a perfume bottle may express mortality as well as a hat may express racial equality. The fault is in the use of the symbol, which has not been integrated into the texture of the story. We would need to be convinced, perhaps, of the importance this woman placed on perfume as essence, need to know how the collection has played a part in the conflicts of her life, perhaps to see her fumbling now toward her favorite, so that we could emotionally equate the spilling or evaporation of the scent with her own spirit.

Writers of the first rank have had this difficulty dealing with the two holocausts of World War II, the extermination camps and the bombing of Hiroshima and Nagasaki, not because fact is stranger than fiction, but because the two horrors are of such magnitude that it is almost impossible to find a particular series of objects, situations, and events adequate to invoke the emotion of the historical facts. Arthur Miller's play *Incident at Vichy*, Lina Wertmuller's film *Seven Beauties*, and William Styron's novel *Sophie's Choice* — all these seem to some extent to borrow from the emotion invoked by the extermination camps, rather than to co-relate the facts and the emotions.

A symbolic object, situation, or event may err because it is insufficiently integrated into the story, and so seems to exist for its own sake rather than to emanate naturally from the characters' lives. It may err because the objective correlative is inadequate to the emotion it is supposed to evoke. Or it may err because it is too heavy or heavy-handed; that is, the author keeps pushing the symbol at us, nudging us in the ribs to say: Get it? In any of these cases we will say that the symbol is *artificial* — a curious word in the critical vocabulary, analogous to the charge of a *formula* plot, since *art*, like *form*, is a word of praise. All writing is "artificial," and when we charge it with being so, we mean that it isn't artificial enough, that the artifice has not concealed itself so as to give the illusion of the natural, and that the artificer must go back to work.

Signs and Symbols

VLADIMIR NABOKOV

I

For the fourth time in as many years they were confronted with the problem of what birthday present to bring a young man who was incurably deranged in his mind. He had no desires. Man-made objects were to him either hives of evil, vibrant with a malignant activity that he alone could perceive, or gross comforts for which no use could be found in his abstract world. After eliminating a number of articles that might offend him or frighten him (anything in the gadget line for instance was taboo), his parents chose a dainty and innocent trifle: a basket with ten different fruit jellies in ten little jars.

At the time of his birth they had been married already for a long time; a score of years had elapsed, and now they were quite old. Her drab gray hair was done anyhow. She wore cheap black dresses. Unlike other women of her age (such as Mrs. Sol, their next-door neighbor, whose face was all pink and mauve with paint and whose hat was a cluster of brookside flowers), she presented a naked white countenance to the fault-finding light of spring days. Her husband, who in the old country had been a fairly successful businessman, was now wholly dependent on his brother Isaac, a real American of almost forty years' standing. They seldom saw him and had nicknamed him "the Prince."

That Friday everything went wrong. The underground train lost its life current between two stations, and for a quarter of an hour one could hear nothing but the dutiful beating of one's heart and the rustling of newspapers. The bus they had to take next kept them waiting for ages; and when it did come, it was crammed with garrulous high-school children. It was raining hard as they walked up the brown path leading to the sanitarium. There they waited again; and instead of their boy shuffling into the room as he usually did (his poor face blotched with acne, ill-shaven, sullen, and confused), a nurse they knew, and did not care for, appeared at last and brightly explained that he had again attempted to take his life. He was all right, she said, but a visit might disturb him. The place was so miserably understaffed, and things got mislaid or mixed up so easily, that they decided not to leave their present in the office but to bring it to him next time they came.

She waited for her husband to open his umbrella and then took his arm. He kept clearing his throat in a special resonant way he had when he was upset. They reached the bus-stop shelter on the other side of the street and he closed his umbrella. A few feet away, under a swaying and dripping tree, a tiny half-dead unfledged bird was helplessly twitching in a puddle.

During the long ride to the subway station, she and her husband did not exchange a word; and every time she glanced at his old hands (swollen veins, brown-spotted skin), clasped and twitching upon the handle of his umbrella, she felt the mounting pressure of tears. As she looked around trying to hook her mind onto something, it gave her a kind of soft shock, a mixture of compassion and wonder, to notice that one of the passengers, a girl with dark hair and grubby red toenails, was weeping on the shoulder of an older woman. Whom did that woman resemble? She resembled Rebecca Borisovna, whose daughter had married one of the Soloveichiks — in Minsk, years ago.

The last time he had tried to do it, his method had been, in the doctor's words, a masterpiece of inventiveness; he would have succeeded, had not an envious fellow patient thought he was learning to fly — and stopped him. What he really wanted to do was to tear a hole in his world and escape.

The system of his delusions had been the subject of an elaborate paper in a scientific monthly, but long before that she and her husband had puzzled it out for themselves. "Referential mania," Herman Brink had called it. In these very rare cases the patient imagines that everything happening around him is a veiled reference to his personality and existence. He excludes real people from the conspiracy — because he considers himself to be so much more intelligent than other men. Phenomenal nature shadows him wherever he goes. Clouds in the staring sky transmit to one another, by means of slow signs, incredibly detailed information regarding him. His inmost thoughts are discussed at nightfall, in manual alphabet, by darkly gesticulating trees. Pebbles or stains or sun flecks form patterns representing in some awful way messages which he must intercept. Everything is a cipher and of everything he is the theme. Some of the spies are detached observers, such are glass surfaces and still pools; others, such as coats in store windows, are prejudiced witnesses, lynchers at heart; others again (running water, storms) are hysterical to the point of insanity, have a distorted opinion of him and grotesquely misinterpret his actions. He must be always on his guard and devote every minute and module of life to the decoding of the undulation of things. The very air he exhales is indexed and filed away. If only the interest he provokes were limited to his immediate surroundings — but alas it is not! With distance the torrents of wild scandal increase in volume and volubility. The silhouettes of his blood corpuscles, magnified a million times, flit over vast plains; and still farther, great mountains of unbearable solidity and height sum up in terms of granite and groaning firs the ultimate truth of his being.

II

When they emerged from the thunder and foul air of the subway, the last dregs of the day were mixed with the street lights. She wanted to buy some fish for supper, so she handed him the basket of jelly jars, telling him to go home. He walked up to the third landing and then remembered he had given her his keys earlier in the day.

In silence he sat down on the steps and in silence rose when some ten minutes later she came, heavily trudging upstairs, wanly smiling, shaking her head in deprecation of her silliness. They entered their two-room flat and he at once went to the mirror. Straining the corners of his mouth apart by means of his thumbs, with a horrible masklike grimace he removed his new hopelessly uncomfortable dental plate and severed the long tusks of saliva connecting him to it. He read his Russian-language newspaper while she laid the table. Still reading, he ate the pale victuals that needed no teeth. She knew his moods and was also silent.

When he had gone to bed, she remained in the living room with her pack of soiled cards and her old albums. Across the narrow yard where the rain tinkled in the dark against some battered ash cans, windows were blandly alight and in one of them a black-trousered man with his bare elbows raised could be seen lying supine on an untidy bed. She pulled the blind down and examined the photographs. As a baby he looked more surprised than most babies. From a fold in the album, a German maid they had had in Leipzig and her fat-faced fiancé fell out. Minsk, the Revolution, Leipzig, Berlin, Leipzig, a slanting house front badly out of focus. Four years old, in a park: moodily, shyly, with puckered forehead, looking away from an eager squirrel as he would from any other stranger. Aunt Rosa, a fussy, angular, wild-eyed old lady, who had lived in a tremulous world of bad news, bankruptcies, train accidents, cancerous growths — until the Germans put her to death, together with all the people she had worried about. Age six — that was when he drew wonderful birds with human hands and feet, and suffered from insomnia like a grown-up man. His cousin, now a famous chess player. He again, aged about eight, already difficult to understand, afraid of the wallpaper in the passage, afraid of a certain picture in a book which merely showed an idyllic landscape with rocks on a hillside and an old cart wheel hanging from the branch of a leafless tree. Aged ten: the year they left Europe. The shame, the pity, the humiliating difficulties, the ugly, vicious, backward children he was with in that special school. And then came a time in his life, coinciding with a long convalescence after pneumonia, when those little phobias of his which his parents had stubbornly regarded as the eccentricities of a prodigiously gifted child hardened as it were into a dense tangle of logically interacting illusions, making him totally inaccessible to normal minds.

This, and much more, she accepted — for after all living did mean accepting the loss of one joy after another, not even joys in her case — mere possibilities of improvement. She thought of the endless waves of pain that for some reason or other she and her husband had to endure; of the invisible giants hurting her boy in some unimaginable fashion; of the incalculable amount of tenderness contained in the world; of the fate of this tenderness, which is either crushed, or wasted, or transformed into madness; of neglected children humming to themselves in unswept corners; of beautiful weeds that cannot hide from the farmer and helplessly have to watch the shadow of his simian stoop leave mangled flowers in its wake, as the monstrous darkness approaches.

III

It was past midnight when from the living room she heard her husband moan; and presently he staggered in, wearing over his nightgown the old overcoat with astrakhan collar which he much preferred to the nice blue bathrobe he had.

"I can't sleep," he cried.

"Why," she asked, "why can't you sleep? You were so tired."

"I can't sleep because I am dying," he said and lay down on the couch.

"Is it your stomach? Do you want me to call Dr. Solov?"

"No doctors, no doctors," he moaned. "To the devil with doctors! We must get him out of there quick. Otherwise we'll be responsible. Responsible!" he repeated and hurled himself into a sitting position, both feet on the floor, thumping his forehead with his clenched fist.

"All right," she said quietly, "we shall bring him home tomorrow morning."

"I would like some tea," said her husband and retired to the bathroom.

Bending with difficulty, she retrieved some playing cards and a photograph or two that had slipped from the couch to the floor: knave of hearts, nine of spades, ace of spades, Elsa and her bestial beau.

He returned in high spirits, saying in a loud voice:

"I have it all figured out. We will give him the bedroom. Each of us will spend part of the night near him and the other part on this couch. By turns. We will have the doctor see him at least twice a week. It does not matter what the Prince says. He won't have to say much anyway because it will come out cheaper."

The telephone rang. It was an unusual hour for their telephone to ring. His left slipper had come off and he groped for it with his heel and toe as he stood in the middle of the room, and childishly, toothlessly, gaped at his wife. Having more English than he did, it was she who attended to calls.

"Can I speak to Charlie," said a girl's dull little voice.

"What number you want? No. That is not the right number."

The receiver was gently cradled. Her hand went to her old tired heart.

"It frightened me," she said.

He smiled a quick smile and immediately resumed his excited monologue. They would fetch him as soon as it was day. Knives would have to be kept in a locked drawer. Even at his worst he presented no danger to other people.

The telephone rang a second time. The same toneless anxious young voice asked for Charlie.

"You have the incorrect number. I will tell you what you are doing: you are turning the letter O instead of the zero."

They sat down to their unexpected festive midnight tea. The birthday present stood on the table. He sipped noisily; his face was flushed; every now and then he imparted a circular motion to his raised glass so as to make the sugar dissolve more thoroughly. The vein on the side of his bald head where there was a large birthmark stood out conspicuously and, although he had shaved that morning, a silvery bristle showed on his chin. While she poured him another glass of tea, he put on his spectacles and re-examined with pleasure the luminous yellow, green, red little jars. His clumsy moist lips spelled out their eloquent labels: apricot, grape, beach plum, quince. He had got to crab apple, when the telephone rang again.

Suggestions for Discussion

1. In the third paragraph of the story we read, "The underground train lost its life current between two stations . . ."; and at the beginning of section II, "they emerged from the thunder and foul air of the subway." How do these metaphors relate to the situation of the story and to its symbolic pattern?

2. Is the "tiny half-dead unfledged bird . . . helplessly twitching in a puddle" at the end of the fourth paragraph of the first section a symbol? Of what?

3. The "referential mania" described on pages 286–287 is the symbolic system of a madman, in which every natural phenomenon means something other and some-

thing more than itself. What distance do we take on this system when we first encounter it? How has that distance altered by the end of the story?

4. What place do the following have in the symbolic meaning of the story: The description of Aunt Rosa on page 287? The shadow of the farmer's "simian stoop" at the end of section II on page 288? The old woman's explanation, "you are turning the letter O instead of the zero," on page 289?

5. This is a "Lady or the Tiger" tale, ending with an unanswered and unanswerable question. Why has Nabokov chosen this form for this particular story? Who do *you* think is on the other end of the telephone at the third call? What significance does it have for the symbolic meaning of the story if it should be the wrong-number caller again? The hospital?

Lost in the Funhouse

JOHN BARTH

For whom is the funhouse fun? Perhaps for lovers. For Ambrose it is *a place of fear and confusion.* He has come to the seashore with his family for the holiday, *the occasion of their visit is Independence Day, the most important secular holiday of the United States of America.* A single straight underline is the manuscript mark for italic type, *which in turn* is the printed equivalent to oral emphasis of words and phrases as well as the customary type for titles of complete works, not to mention. Italics are also employed, in fiction stories especially, for "outside," intrusive, or artificial voices, such as radio announcements, the texts of telegrams and newspaper articles, et cetera. They should be used *sparingly.* If passages originally in roman type are italicized by someone repeating them, it's customary to acknowledge the fact. *Italics mine.*

Ambrose was "at that awkward age." His voice came out high-pitched as a child's if he let himself get carried away; to be on the safe side, therefore, he moved and spoke with *deliberate calm* and *adult gravity.* Talking soberly of unimportant or irrelevant matters and listening consciously to the sound of your own voice are useful habits for maintaining control in this difficult interval. *En route* to Ocean City he sat in the back seat of the family car with his brother Peter, age fifteen, and Magda G——, age fourteen, a pretty girl an exquisite young lady, who lived not far from them on B—— Street in the town of D——, Maryland. Initials, blanks, or both were often substituted for proper names in nineteenth-century fiction to enhance the illusion of reality. It is as if the author felt it necessary to delete the names for reasons of tact or legal liability. Interestingly, as with other aspects of realism, it is an *illusion* that is being enhanced, by purely artificial means. Is it likely, does it violate the principle of verisimilitude, that a thirteen-year-old boy could make such a sophisticated observation? A girl of fourteen is *the psychological coeval* of a boy of fifteen or sixteen; a thirteen-year-old boy, therefore, even one precocious in some other respects, might be three years *her emotional junior.*

Thrice a year — on Memorial, Independence, and Labor Days — the family visits Ocean City for the afternoon and evening. When Ambrose and Peter's father was their age, the excursion was made by train, as mentioned in the novel *The 42nd Parallel* by John Dos Passos. Many families from the same neighborhood used to travel together, with dependent relatives and often with Negro servants; schoolfuls of children swarmed through the railway cars; everyone shared everyone else's Maryland fried chicken, Virginia ham, deviled eggs, potato salad, beaten biscuits, iced tea. Nowadays (that is, in 19 — , the year of our story) the journey is made by automobile — more comfortably and quickly though without the extra fun though without the *camaraderie* of a general excursion. It's all part of the deterioration of American life, their father declares; Uncle Karl supposes that when the boys take *their* families to Ocean City for the holidays they'll fly in Autogiros. Their mother, sitting in the middle of the front seat like Magda in the second, only with her arms on the seat-back behind the men's shoulders, wouldn't want the good old days back again, the steaming trains and stuffy long dresses; on the other hand she can do without Autogiros, too, if she has to become a grandmother to fly in them.

Description of physical appearance and mannerisms is one of several standard methods of characterization used by writers of fiction. It is also important to "keep the senses operating"; when a detail from one of the five senses, say visual, is "crossed" with a detail from another, say auditory, the reader's imagination is oriented to the scene, perhaps unconsciously. This procedure may be compared to the way surveyors and navigators determine their positions by two or more compass bearings, a process known as triangulation. The brown hair on Ambrose's mother's forearms gleamed in the sun like. Though right-handed, she took her left arm from the seat-back to press the dashboard cigar lighter for Uncle Karl. When the glass bead in its handle glowed red, the lighter was ready for use. The smell of Uncle Karl's cigar smoke reminded one of. The fragrance of the ocean came strong to the picnic ground where they always stopped for lunch, two miles inland from Ocean City. Having to pause for a full hour almost within sound of the breakers was difficult for Peter and Ambrose when they were younger; even at their present age it was not easy to keep their anticipation, *stimulated by the briny spume,* from turning into short temper. The Irish author James Joyce, in his unusual novel entitled *Ulysses,* now available in this country, uses the adjectives *snot-green* and *scrotum-tightening* to describe the sea. Visual, auditory, tactile, olfactory, gustatory. Peter and Ambrose's father, while steering their black 1936 LaSalle sedan with one hand, could with the other remove the first cigarette from a white pack of Lucky Strikes and, more remarkably, light it with a match forefingered from its book and thumbed against the flint paper without being detached. The matchbook cover merely advertised U.S. War Bonds and Stamps. A fine metaphor, simile, or other figure of speech, in addition to its obvious "first-order" relevance to the thing it describes, will be seen upon reflection to have a second order of significance: it may be drawn from the *milieu* of the action, for example, or be particularly appropriate to the sensibility of the narrator, even hinting to the reader things of which the narrator is unaware; or it may cast further and subtler lights upon the thing it describes, sometimes ironically qualifying the more evident sense of the comparison.

To say that Ambrose's and Peter's mother was *pretty* is to accomplish nothing; the reader may acknowledge the proposition, but his imagination is not engaged. Besides, Magda was also pretty, yet in an altogether different way. Although she lived on B ——— Street she had very good manners and did better than average in school. Her figure was very well developed for her age. Her right hand lay casually on the plush upholstery of the seat, very near Ambrose's left leg, on which his own hand rested. The space between their legs, between her right and his left leg, was out of the line of sight of anyone sitting on the other side of Magda, as well as anyone glancing into the rearview mirror. Uncle Karl's face resembled Peter's — rather, vice versa. Both had dark hair and eyes, short husky statures, deep voices. Magda's left hand was probably in a similar position on her left side. The boy's father is difficult to describe; no particular feature of his appearance or manner stood out. He wore glasses and was principal of a T ——— County grade school. Uncle Karl was a masonry contractor.

Although Peter must have known as well as Ambrose that the latter, because of his position in the car, would be the first to see the electrical towers of the power plant at V ——— , the half-way point of their trip, he leaned forward and slightly toward the center of the car and pretended to be looking for them through the flat pinewoods and tuckahoe creeks along the highway. For as long as the boys could remember, "looking for the Towers" had been a feature of the first half of their excursions to Ocean City, "looking for the standpipe" of the second. Though the game was childish, their mother preserved the tradition of rewarding the first to see the Towers with a candybar or piece of fruit. She insisted now that Magda play the game; the prize, she said, was "something hard to get nowadays." Ambrose decided not to join in; he sat far back in his seat. Magda, like Peter, leaned forward. Two sets of straps were discernible through the shoulders of her sun dress; the inside right one, a brassiere-strap, was fastened or shortened with a small safety pin. The right armpit of her dress, presumably the left as well, was damp with perspiration. The simple strategy for being first to espy the Towers, which Ambrose had understood by the age of four, was to sit on the right-hand side of the car. Whoever sat there, however, had also to put up with the worst of the sun, and so Ambrose without mentioning the matter, chose sometimes the one and sometimes the other. Not impossibly Peter had never caught on to the trick, or thought that his brother hadn't simply because Ambrose on occasion preferred shade to a Baby Ruth or tangerine.

The shade-sun situation didn't apply to the front seat, owing to the windshield; if anything the driver got more sun, since the person on the passenger side not only was shaded below by the door and dashboard but might swing down his sunvisor all the way too.

"Is that them?" Magda asked. Ambrose's mother teased the boys for letting Magda win, insinuating that "somebody [had] a girlfriend." Peter and Ambrose's father reached a long thin arm across their mother to butt his cigarette in the dashboard ashtray, under the lighter. The prize this time for seeing the Towers first was a banana. Their mother bestowed it after chiding their father for wasting a half-smoked cigarette when everything was so scarce. Magda, to take the prize, moved her hand from so near Ambrose's that he could have touched it as though accidentally. She offered to share the prize, things like that were so hard to find; but everyone insisted it was hers alone. Ambrose's mother sang an iambic trimeter couplet from a popular song, femininely rhymed:

> *"What's good is in the Army;*
> *What's left will never harm me."*

Uncle Karl tapped his cigar ash out the ventilator window; some particles were sucked by the slipstream back into the car through the rear window on the passenger side. Magda demonstrated her ability to hold a banana in one hand and peel it with her teeth. She still sat forward; Ambrose pushed his glasses back onto the bridge of his nose with his left hand, which he then negligently let fall to the seat cushion immediately behind her. He even permitted the single hair, gold, on the second joint of his thumb to brush the fabric of her skirt. Should she have sat back at that instant, his hand would have been caught under her.

Plush upholstery prickles uncomfortably through gabardine slacks in the July sun. The function of the *beginning* of a story is to introduce the principal characters, establish their initial relationships, set the scene for the main action, expose the background of the situation if necessary, plant motifs and foreshadowings where appropriate, and initiate the first complication or whatever of the "rising action." Actually, if one imagines a story called

"The Funhouse," or "Lost in the Funhouse," the details of the drive to Ocean City don't seem especially relevant. The *beginning* should recount the events between Ambrose's first sight of the funhouse early in the afternoon and his entering it with Magda and Peter in the evening. The *middle* would narrate all relevant events from the time he goes in to the time he loses his way; middles have the double and contradictory function of delaying the climax while at the same time preparing the reader for it and fetching him to it. Then the *ending* would tell what Ambrose does while he's lost, how he finally finds his way out, and what everybody makes of the experience. So far there's been no real dialogue, very little sensory detail, and nothing in the way of a *theme*. And a long time has gone by already without anything happening; it makes a person wonder. We haven't even reached Ocean City yet: we will never get out of the funhouse.

The more closely an author identifies with the narrator, literally or metaphorically, the less advisable it is, as a rule, to use the first-person narrative viewpoint. Once three years previously the young people *aforementioned* played Niggers and Masters in the backyard; when it was Ambrose's turn to be Master and theirs to be Niggers Peter had to go serve his evening papers; Ambrose was afraid to punish Magda alone, but she led him to the whitewashed Torture Chamber between the woodshed and the privy in the Slaves Quarters; there she knelt sweating among bamboo rakes and dusty Mason jars, pleadingly embraced his knees, and while bees droned in the lattice as if on an ordinary summer afternoon, purchased clemency at a surprising price set by herself. Doubtless she remembered nothing of this event; Ambrose on the other hand seemed unable to forget the least detail of his life. He even recalled how, standing beside himself with awed impersonality in the reeky heat, he'd stared the while at an empty cigar box in which Uncle Karl kept stone-cutting chisels: beneath the words *El Producto*, a laureled, loose-toga'd lady regarded the sea from a marble bench; beside her, forgotten or not yet turned to, was a five-stringed lyre. Her chin reposed on the back of her right hand; her left depended negligently from the bench-arm. The lower half of scene and lady was peeled away; the words EXAMINED BY — were inked there into the wood. Nowadays cigar boxes are made of pasteboard. Ambrose wondered what Magda would have done, Ambrose wondered what Magda would do when she sat back on his hand as he resolved she should. Be angry. Make a teasing joke of it. Give no sign at all. For a long time she leaned forward, playing cow-poker with Peter against Uncle Karl and Mother and watching for the first sign of Ocean City. At nearly the same instant, picnic ground and Ocean City standpipe hove into view; an Amoco filling station on their side of the road cost Mother and Uncle Karl fifty cows and the game; Magda bounced back, clapping her right hand on Mother's right arm; Ambrose moved clear "in the nick of time."

At this rate our hero, at this rate our protagonist will remain in the funhouse forever. Narrative ordinarily consists of alternating dramatization and summarization. One symptom of nervous tension, paradoxically, is repeated and violent yawning; neither Peter nor Magda nor Uncle Karl nor Mother reacted in this manner. Although they were no longer small children, Peter and Ambrose were each given a dollar to spend on boardwalk amusements in addition to what money of their own they'd brought along. Magda too, though she protested she had ample spending money. The boys' mother made a little scene out of distributing the bills; she pretended that her sons and Magda were small children and cautioned them not to spend the sum too quickly or in one place. Magda promised with a merry laugh and, having both hands free, took the bill with her left. Peter laughed also and pledged in a falsetto to be a good boy. His imitation of a child was not clever. The boys' father was tall and thin, balding, fair-complexioned. Assertions of that sort are not effective; the reader may acknowledge the proposition, but. We should be much farther along than we are; something has gone wrong; not much of this preliminary rambling seems relevant. Yet everyone begins in the same place; how is it that most go along without difficulty but a few lose their way?

"Stay out from under the boardwalk," Uncle Karl growled from the side of his mouth. The boys' mother pushed his shoulder *in mock annoyance.* They were all standing before Fat May the Laughing Lady who advertised the funhouse. Larger than life, Fat May mechanically shook, rocked on her heels, slapped her thighs while recorded laughter — uproarious, female — came amplified from a hidden loudspeaker. It chuckled, wheezed, wept; tried in vain to catch its breath; tittered, groaned, exploded raucous and anew. You couldn't hear it without laughing yourself, no matter how you felt. Father came back from talking to a Coast-Guardsman on duty and reported the surf was spoiled with crude oil from tankers recently torpedoed offshore. Lumps of it, difficult to remove, made tarry tidelines on the beach and stuck on swimmers. Many bathed in the surf nevertheless and came out speckled; others paid to use a municipal pool and only sunbathed on the beach. We would do the latter. We would do the latter. We would do the latter.

Under the boardwalk, matchbook covers, grainy other things. What is the story's theme? Ambrose is ill. He perspires in the dark passages; candied apples-on-a-stick, delicious-looking, disappointing to eat. Funhouses need men's and ladies' rooms at intervals. Others perhaps have also vomited in corners and corridors; may even have had bowel movements liable to be stepped in in the dark. The word *fuck* suggests suction and / or and / or flatulence. Mother and Father; grandmothers and grandfathers on both sides; great-grandmothers and great-grandfathers on four sides, et cetera. Count a generation as thirty years: in approximately the year when Lord Baltimore was granted charter to the province of Maryland by Charles I, five hundred twelve women — English, Welsh, Bavarian, Swiss — of every class and character, received into themselves the penises the intromittent organs of five hundred twelve men, ditto, in every circumstance and posture, to conceive the five hundred twelve ancestors of the two hundred fifty-six ancestors of the et cetera et cetera et cetera et cetera et cetera et cetera et cetera et cetera of the author, of the narrator, of this story, *Lost in the Funhouse.* In alleyways, ditches, canopy beds, pinewoods, bridal suites, ship's cabins, coach-and-fours, coaches-and-four, sultry toolsheds; on the cold sand under boardwalks, littered with *El Producto* cigar butts, treasured with Lucky Strike cigarette stubs, Coca-Cola caps, gritty turds, cardboard lollipop sticks, matchbook covers warning that A Slip of the Lip Can Sink a Ship. The shluppish whisper, continuous as seawash round the globe, tidelike falls and rises with the circuit of dawn and dusk.

Magda's teeth. She *was* left-handed. Perspiration. They've gone all the way, through, Magda and Peter, they've been waiting for hours with Mother and Uncle Karl while Father searches for his lost son; they draw french-fried potatoes from a paper cup and shake their heads. They've named the children they'll one day have and bring to Ocean City on holidays. Can spermatozoa properly be thought of as male animalcules when there are no female spermatozoa? They grope through hot, dark windings, past Love's Tunnel's fearsome obstacles. Some perhaps lose their way.

Peter suggested then and there that they do the funhouse; he had been through it before, so had Magda, Ambrose hadn't and suggested, his voice cracking on account of Fat May's laughter, that they swim first. All were chuckling, couldn't help it; Ambrose's father, Ambrose's and Peter's father came up grinning like a lunatic with two boxes of syrup-coated popcorn, one for Mother, one for Magda; the men were to help themselves. Ambrose walked on Magda's right; being by nature left-handed, she carried the box in her left hand. Up front the situation was reversed.

"What are you limping for?" Magda inquired of Ambrose. He supposed in a husky tone that his foot had gone to sleep in the car. Her teeth flashed. "Pins and needles?" It was the honeysuckle on the lattice of the former privy that drew the bees. Imagine being stung there. How long is this going to take?

The adults decided to forgo the pool; but Uncle Karl insisted they change into swimsuits and do the beach. "He wants to watch the pretty girls," Peter teased, and ducked behind Magda from Uncle Karl's pretended wrath. "You've got all the pretty girls you need right here," Magda declared, and Mother said: "Now that's the gospel truth." Magda scolded Peter, who reached over her shoulder to sneak some popcorn. "Your brother and father aren't getting any." Uncle Karl wondered if they were going to have fireworks that night, what with the shortages. It wasn't the shortages, Mr. M ——— replied; Ocean City had fireworks from pre-war. But it was too risky on account of the enemy submarines, some people thought.

"Don't seem like Fourth of July without fireworks," said Uncle Karl. The inverted tag in dialogue writing is still considered permissible with proper names or epithets, but sounds old-fashioned with personal pronouns. "We'll have 'em again soon enough," predicted the boys' father. Their mother declared she could do without fireworks: they reminded her too much of the real thing. Their father said all the more reason to shoot off a few now and again. Uncle Karl asked *rhetorically* who needed reminding, just look at people's hair and skin.

"The oil, yes," said Mrs. M ——— .

Ambrose had a pain in his stomach and so didn't swim but enjoyed watching the others. He and his father burned red easily. Magda's figure was exceedingly well developed for her age. She too declined to swim, and got mad, and became angry when Peter attempted to drag her into the pool. She always swam, he insisted; what did she mean not swim? Why did a person come to Ocean City?

"Maybe I want to lay here with Ambrose," Magda teased.

Nobody likes a pedant.

"Aha," said Mother. Peter grabbed Magda by one ankle and ordered Ambrose to grab the other. She squealed and rolled over on the beach blanket. Ambrose pretended to help hold her back. Her tan was darker than even Mother's and Peter's. "Help out, Uncle Karl!" Peter cried. Uncle Karl went to seize the other ankle. Inside the top of her swimsuit, however, you could see the line where the sunburn ended and, when she hunched her shoulders and squealed again, one nipple's auburn edge. Mother made them behave themselves. "*You* should certainly know," she said to Uncle Karl. Archly. "That when a lady says she doesn't feel like swimming, a gentleman doesn't ask questions." Uncle Karl said excuse *him*; Mother winked at Magda; Ambrose blushed; stupid Peter kept saying "Phooey on *feel like!*" and tugging at Magda's ankle; then even he got the point, and cannonballed with a holler into the pool.

"I swear," Magda said, in mock *in feigned* exasperation.

The diving would make a suitable literary symbol. To go off the high board you had to wait in a line along the poolside and up the ladder. Fellows tickled girls and goosed one another and shouted to the ones at the top to hurry up, or razzed them for bellyfloppers. Once on the springboard some took a great while posing or clowning or deciding on a dive or getting up their nerve; others ran right off. Especially among the younger fellows the idea was to strike the funniest pose or do the craziest stunt as you fell, a thing that got harder to do as you kept on and kept on. But whether you hollered *Geronimo!* or *Sieg heil!*, held your nose or "rode a bicycle," pretended to be shot or did a perfect jacknife or changed your mind halfway down and ended up with nothing, it was over in two seconds, after all that wait. Spring, pose, splash. Spring, neat-o, splash. Spring, aw fooey, splash.

The grown-ups had gone on; Ambrose wanted to converse with Magda; she was remarkably well developed for her age; it was said that that came from rubbing with a turkish towel, and there were other theories. Ambrose could think of nothing to say except how good a diver Peter was, who was showing off for her benefit. You could pretty well tell by looking at their bathing suits and arm muscles how far along the different fellows were. Ambrose was glad he hadn't gone in swimming, the cold water shrank you up so. Magda pretended to be uninterested in the diving; she probably weighed as much as he did. If you knew your way around in the funhouse like your own bedroom, you could wait until a girl came along and then slip away without ever getting caught, even if her boyfriend was right with her. She'd think *he* did it! It would be better to be the boyfriend, and act outraged, and tear the funhouse apart.

Not act; *be.*

"He's a master diver," Ambrose said. In feigned admiration. "You really have to slave away at it to get that good." What would it matter anyhow if he asked her right out whether she remembered, even teased her with it as Peter would have?

There's no point in going farther; this isn't getting anybody anywhere; they haven't even come to the funhouse yet. Ambrose is off the track, in some new or old part of the place that's not supposed to be used; he strayed into it by some one-in-a-million chance, like the time the roller-coaster car left the tracks in the nineteen-teens against all the laws of physics and sailed over the boardwalk in the dark. And they can't locate him because they don't know where to look. Even the designer and operator have forgotten this other part, that winds around on itself like a whelk shell. That winds around the right part like the snakes on Mercury's caduceus. Some people, perhaps, don't "hit their stride" until their twenties, when the growing-up business is over and women appreciate other things besides wisecracks and teasing and strutting. Peter didn't have one-tenth the imagination *he* had, not one-tenth. Peter did this naming-their-children thing as a joke, making up names like Aloysius and Murgatroyd, but Ambrose knew *exactly* how it would feel to be married and have children of your own, and be a loving husband and father, and go comfortably to work in the mornings and to bed with your wife at night, and wake up with her there. With a breeze coming through the sash and birds and mockingbirds singing in the Chinese-cigar trees. His eyes watered, there aren't enough ways to say that. He would be quite famous in his line of work. Whether Magda was his wife or not, one evening when he was wise-lined and gray at the temples he'd smile gravely, at a fashionable dinner party, and remind her of his youthful passion. The time they went with his family to Ocean City; the *erotic fantasies* he used to have about her. How long ago it seemed, and childish! Yet tender, too, *n'est-ce pas?* Would she have imagined that the world-famous whatever remembered how many strings were on the lyre on the bench beside the girl on the label of the cigar box he'd stared at in the toolshed at age ten while she, age eleven. Even then he had felt *wise beyond his years;* he'd stroked her hair and said in his deepest voice and correctest English, as to a dear child: "I shall never forget this moment."

But though he had breathed heavily, groaned as if ecstatic, what he'd really felt throughout was an odd detachment, as though someone else were Master. Strive as he might to be transported, he heard his mind take notes upon the scene: *This is what they call* passion. *I am experiencing it.* Many of the digger machines were out of order in the penny arcades and could not be repaired or replaced for the duration. Moreover the prizes, made now in USA, were less interesting than formerly, pasteboard items for the most part, and some of the machines wouldn't work on white pennies. The gypsy fortune-teller machine might have provided a foreshadowing of the climax of this story if Ambrose had operated it. It was even dilapidateder than most: the silver coating was worn off the brown metal handles, the glass windows around the dummy were cracked and taped, her kerchiefs and silks long-faded. If a man lived by himself, he could take a department-store mannequin with flexible joints and modify her in certain ways. *However:* by the time he was that old he'd have a real woman. There was a machine that stamped your name around a white-metal coin with a star in the middle: A ———— . His son would be the second, and when the lad reached thirteen or so he would put a strong arm around his shoulder and tell him calmly: "It is perfectly normal. We have all been through it. It will not last forever." Nobody knew how to be what they were right. He'd smoke a pipe, teach his son how to fish and softcrab, assure him he needn't worry about himself. Magda would certainly give, Magda would certainly yield a great deal of milk, although guilty of occasional solecisms. It don't taste so bad. Suppose the lights came on now!

The day wore on. You think you're yourself, but there are other persons in you. Ambrose gets hard when Ambrose doesn't want to, *and obversely.* Ambrose watches them disagree; Ambrose watches him watch. In the funhouse mirror-room you can't see yourself go on forever, because no matter how you stand, your head gets in the way. Even if you had a glass periscope, the image of your eye would cover up the thing you really wanted to see. The police will come; there'll be a story in the papers. That must be where it happened. Unless he can find a surprise exit, an unofficial backdoor or escape hatch opening on an alley, say, and then stroll up to the family in front of the funhouse and ask where everybody's been; *he's* been out of the place for ages. That's just where it happened, in that last lighted room: Peter and Magda found the right exit; he found one that you weren't supposed to find and strayed off into the works somewhere. In a perfect funhouse you'd be able to go only one way, like the divers off the high-board; getting lost would be impossible; the doors and halls would work like minnow traps or the valves in veins.

On account of German U-boats, Ocean City was "browned out": street-lights were shaded on the seaward side; shop-windows and boardwalk amusement places were kept dim, not to silhouette tankers and Liberty-ships for torpedoing. In a short story about Ocean City, Maryland, during World War II, the author could make use of the image of sailors on leave in the penny arcades and shooting galleries, sighting through the crosshairs of toy machine guns at swastika'd subs, while out in the black Atlantic a U-boat skipper squints through his periscope at real ships outlined by the glow of penny arcades. After dinner the family strolled back to the amusement end of the boardwalk. The boys' father had burnt red as always and was masked with Noxzema, a minstrel in reverse. The grown-ups stood at the end of the boardwalk where the Hurricane of '33 had cut an inlet from the ocean to Assawoman Bay.

"Pronounced with a long o," Uncle Karl reminded Magda with a wink. His shirt sleeves were rolled up; Mother punched his brown biceps with the arrowed heart on it and said his mind was naughty. Fat May's laugh came suddenly from the funhouse, as if she'd just got the joke; the family laughed too at the coincidence. Ambrose went under the boardwalk to search for out-of-town matchbook covers with the aid of his pocket flashlight; he looked out from the edge of the North American continent and wondered how far their laughter carried over the water. Spies in rubber rafts; survivors in lifeboats. If the joke had been beyond his understanding, he could have said: *"The laughter was over his head."* And let the reader see the serious wordplay on second reading.

He turned the flashlight on and then off at once even before the woman whooped. He sprang away, heart athud, dropping the light. What had the man grunted? Perspiration drenched and chilled him by the time he scrambled up to the family. "See anything?" his father asked. His voice wouldn't come; he shrugged and violently brushed sand from his pants legs.

"Let's ride the old flying horses!" Magda cried. I'll never be an author. It's been forever already, everybody's gone home, Ocean City's deserted, the ghost-crabs are tickling across the beach and down the littered cold streets. And the empty halls of clapboard hotels and abandoned funhouses. A tidal wave; an enemy air raid; a monster-crab swelling like an island from the sea. *The inhabitants fled in terror.* Magda clung to his trouser leg; he alone knew the maze's secret. "He gave his life that we might live," said Uncle Karl with a scowl of pain, as he. The fellow's hands had been tattooed; the woman's legs, the woman's fat white legs had. *An astonishing coincidence.* He yearned to tell Peter. He wanted to throw up for excitement. They hadn't even chased him. He wished he were dead.

One possible ending would be to have Ambrose come across another lost person in the dark. They'd match their wits together against the funhouse, struggle like Ulysses past obstacle after obstacle, help and encourage each other. Or a girl. By the time they found the exit they'd be close friends, sweethearts if it were a girl; they'd know each other's inmost souls, be bound together *by the cement of shared adventure*; then they'd emerge into the light and it would turn out that his friend was a Negro. A blind girl. President Roosevelt's son. Ambrose's former archenemy.

Shortly after the mirror room he'd groped along a musty corridor, his heart already misgiving him at the absence of phosphorescent arrows and other signs. He'd found a crack of light — not a door, it turned out, but a seam between the plyboard wall panels — and squinting up to it, espied a small old man, *in appearance not unlike* the photographs at home of Ambrose's late grandfather, nodding upon a stool beneath a bare, speckled bulb. A crude panel of toggle- and knife-switches hung beside the open fuse box near his head; elsewhere in the little room were wooden levers and ropes belayed to boat cleats. At the time, Ambrose wasn't lost enough to rap or call; later he couldn't find the crack. Now it seemed to him that he'd possibly dozed off for a few minutes somewhere along the way; certainly he was exhausted from the afternoon's sunshine and the evening's problems; he couldn't be sure he hadn't dreamed part or all of the sight. Had an old black wall fan droned like bees and shimmied two flypaper streamers? Had the funhouse operator — gentle, somewhat sad and tired-appearing, in expression not unlike the photographs at home of Ambrose's late Uncle Konrad — murmured in his sleep? Is there really such a person as Ambrose, or is he a figment of the author's imagination? Was it Assawoman Bay or Sinepuxent? Are there other errors of fact in this fiction? Was there another sound besides the little slap slap of thigh on ham, like water suckling at the chine-boards of a skiff?

When you're lost, the smartest thing to do is stay put till you're found, hollering if necessary. But to holler guarantees humiliation as well as rescue; keeping silent permits some saving of face — you can act surprised at the fuss when your rescuers find you and swear you weren't lost, if they do. What's more you might find your own way yet, *however belatedly*.

"Don't tell me your foot's still asleep!" Magda exclaimed as the three young people walked from the inlet to the area set aside for ferris wheels, carrousels, and other carnival rides, they having decided in favor of the vast and ancient merry-go-round instead of the funhouse. What a sentence, everything was wrong from the outset. People don't know what to make of him, he doesn't know what to make of himself, he's only thirteen, *athletically and socially inept*, not astonishingly bright, but there are antennae; he has . . . some sort of receivers in his head; things speak to him, he understands more than he should, the world winks at him through its objects, grabs grinning at his coat. Everybody else is in on some secret he doesn't know; they've forgotten to tell him. Through simple *procrastination* his mother put off his baptism until this year. Everyone else had it done as a baby; he'd assumed the same of himself, as had his mother, so she claimed, until it was time for him to join Grace Methodist-Protestant and the oversight came out. He was mortified, but pitched sleepless through his private catechizing, intimidated by the ancient mysteries, a thirteen year old would never say that, resolved to experience conversion like St. Augustine. When the water touched his brow and Adam's sin left him, he contrived by a strain like defecation to bring tears into his eyes — but felt nothing. There was some simple, radical difference about him; he hoped it was genius, feared it was madness, devoted himself to amiability and inconspicuousness. Alone on the seawall near his house he was seized by the terrifying transports he'd thought to find in toolshed, in Communion-cup. The grass was alive! The town, the river, himself, were not imaginary; time roared in his ears like wind; the world was *going on!* This part ought to be dramatized. The Irish author James Joyce once wrote, Ambrose M ——— is going to scream.

There is no *texture of rendered sensory detail,* for one thing. The faded distorting mirrors beside Fat May; the impossibility of choosing a mount when one had but a single ride on the great carrousel; the *vertigo attendant on his recognition* that Ocean City was worn out, the place of fathers and grandfathers, straw-boatered men and parasoled ladies survived by their amusements. Money spent, the three paused at Peter's insistence beside Fat May to watch the girls get their skirts blown up. The object was to tease Magda, who said: "I swear, Peter M ———, you've got a one-track mind! Amby and me aren't *interested* in such things." In the tumbling-barrel, too, just inside the Devil's-mouth entrance to the funhouse, the girls were up-ended and their boyfriends and others could see up their dresses if they cared to. Which was the whole point, Ambrose realized. Of the entire funhouse! If you looked around, you noticed that almost all the people on the boardwalk were paired off into couples except the small children; in a way, that was the whole point of Ocean City! If you had X-ray eyes and could see everything going on at that instant under the boardwalk and in all the hotel rooms and cars and alleyways, you'd realize that all that normally *showed,* like restaurants and dance halls and clothing and test-your-strength machines, was merely preparation and intermission. Fat May screamed.

Because he watched the goings-on from the corner of his eye, it was Ambrose who spied the half-dollar on the boardwalk near the tumbling-barrel. Losers weepers. The first time he'd heard some people moving through a corridor not far away, just after he'd lost sight of the crack of light, he'd decided not to call to them, for fear they'd guess he was scared and poke fun; it sounded like roughnecks; he'd hoped they'd come by and he could follow in the dark without their knowing. Another time he'd heard just one person, unless he imagined it, bumping along as if on the other side of the plywood; perhaps Peter coming back for him, or Father, or Magda lost too. Or the owner and operator of the funhouse. He'd called out once, as though merrily: "Anybody know where the heck we are?" But the query was too stiff, his voice cracked, when the sounds stopped he was terrified: maybe it was a queer who waited for fellows to get lost, or a longhaired filthy monster that lived in some cranny of the funhouse. He stood rigid for hours it seemed like, scarcely respiring. His future was shockingly clear, in outline. He tried holding his breath to the point of unconsciousness. There ought to be a button you could push to end your life absolutely without pain; disappear in a flick, like turning out a light. He would push it instantly! He despised Uncle Karl. But he despised his father too, for not being what he was supposed to be. Perhaps his father hated *his* father, and so on, and his son would hate him, and so on. Instantly!

Naturally he didn't have nerve enough to ask Magda to go through the funhouse with him. With incredible nerve and to everyone's surprise he invited Magda, quietly and politely, to go through the funhouse with him. "I warn you, I've never been through it before," he added, *laughing easily;* "but I reckon we can manage somehow. The important thing to remember, after all, is that it's meant to be a *fun*house; that is, a place of amusement. If people really got lost or injured or too badly frightened in it, the owner'd go out of business. There'd even be lawsuits. No character in a work of fiction can make a speech this long without interruption or acknowledgment from the other characters."

Mother teased Uncle Karl: "Three's a crowd, I always heard." But actually Ambrose was relieved that Peter now had a quarter too. Nothing was what it looked like. Every instant, under the surface of the Atlantic Ocean, millions of living animals devoured one another. Pilots were falling in flames over Europe; women were being forcibly raped in the South Pacific. His father should have taken him aside and said: "There is a simple secret to getting through the funhouse, as simple as being first to see the Towers. Here it is. Peter does not know it; neither does your Uncle Karl. You and I are different. Not surprisingly, you've often wished you weren't. Don't think I haven't noticed how unhappy your childhood has been! But you'll understand, when I tell you, why it had to be kept secret until now. And you won't regret not being like your brother and your uncle. *On the contrary!*" If you knew all the stories behind all the people on the boardwalk, you'd see that *nothing* was what it looked like. Husbands and wives often hated each other; parents didn't necessarily love their children; et cetera. A child took things for granted because he had nothing to compare his life to and everybody acted as if things were as they should be. Therefore each saw himself as the hero of the story, when the truth might turn out to be that he's the villain, or the coward. And there wasn't one thing you could do about it!

Hunchbacks, fat ladies, fools — that no one chose what he was was unbearable. In the movies he'd meet a beautiful young girl in the funhouse; they'd have hairs-breadth escapes from real dangers; he'd do and say the right things; she also; in the end they'd be lovers; their dialogue lines would match up; he'd be perfectly at ease; she'd not only like him well enough, she'd think he was *marvelous*; she'd lie awake thinking about *him*, instead of vice versa — the way *his* face looked in different lights and how he stood and exactly what he'd said — and yet that would be only one small episode in his wonderful life, among many many others. Not a *turning point* at all. What had happened in the toolshed was nothing. He hated, he loathed his parents! One reason for not writing a lost-in-the-funhouse story is that either everybody's felt what Ambrose feels, in which case it goes without saying, or else no normal person feels such things, in which case Ambrose is a freak. "Is anything more tiresome, in fiction, than the problems of sensitive adolescents?" And it's all too long and rambling, as if the author. For all a person knows the first time through, the end could be just around any corner; perhaps, *not impossibly* it's been within reach any number of times. On the other hand he may be scarcely past the start, with everything yet to get through, an intolerable idea.

Fill in: His father's raised eyebrows when he announced his decision to do the funhouse with Magda. Ambrose understands now, but didn't then, that his father was wondering whether he knew what the funhouse was *for* — especially since he didn't object, as he should have, when Peter decided to come along too. The ticket-woman, witchlike, mortifying him when inadvertently he gave her his name-coin instead of the half-dollar, then unkindly calling Magda's attention to the birthmark on his temple: "Watch out for him, girlie, he's a marked man!" She wasn't even cruel, he understood, only vulgar and insensitive. Somewhere in the world there was a young woman with such splendid understanding that she'd see him entire, like a poem or story, and find his words so valuable after all that when he confessed his apprehensions she would explain why they were in fact the very things that made him precious to her . . . and to Western Civilization! There was no such girl, the simple truth being. Violent yawns as they approached the mouth. Whispered advice from an old-timer on a bench near the barrel: "Go crabwise and ye'll get an eyeful without upsetting!" Composure vanished at the first pitch: Peter hollered joyously, Magda tumbled, shrieked, clutched her skirt; Ambrose scrambled crabwise, tight-lipped with terror, was soon out, watched his dropped name-coin slide among the couples. Shame-faced he saw that to get through expeditiously was not the point; Peter feigned assistance in order to trip Magda up, shouted "I see Christmas!" when her legs went flying. The old man, his latest betrayer, cackled approval. A dim hall then of black-thread cobwebs and recorded gibber: he took Magda's elbow to steady her against revolving discs set in the slanted floor to throw your feet out from under, and explained to her in a calm, deep voice his theory that each phase of the funhouse was triggered either automatically, by a series of photoelectric devices, or else manually by operators stationed at peepholes. But he lost his voice thrice as the discs unbalanced him; Magda was anyhow squealing; but at one point she clutched him about the waist to keep from falling, and her right cheek pressed for a moment against his belt-buckle. Heroically he drew her up, it was his chance to clutch her close as if for support and say: "I love you." He even put an arm lightly about the small of her back before a sailor-and-girl pitched into them from behind, sorely treading his left big toe and knocking Magda asprawl with them. The sailor's girl was a string-haired hussy with a loud laugh and light blue drawers; Ambrose realized that he wouldn't have said "I love you" anyhow, and was smitten with self-contempt. How much better it would be to be that common sailor! A wiry little Seaman 3rd, the fellow squeezed a girl to each side and stumbled hilarious into the mirror room, closer to Magda in thirty seconds than Ambrose had got in thirteen years. She giggled at something the fellow said to Peter; she drew her hair from her eyes with a movement so womanly it struck Ambrose's heart; Peter's smacking her backside then seemed particularly coarse. But Magda made a pleased indignant face and cried, "All right for *you*, mister!" and pursued Peter into the maze without a backward glance. The sailor followed after, leisurely, drawing his girl against his hip; Ambrose understood not only that they were also relieved to be rid of his burdensome company that they didn't even notice his absence, but that he himself shared their relief. Stepping from the treacherous passage at last into the mirror-maze, he saw once again, more clearly than ever, how readily he deceived himself into supposing he was a person. He even foresaw, wincing at his dreadful self-knowledge, that he would repeat the deception, at ever-rarer intervals, all his wretched life, so fearful were the alternatives. Fame, madness, suicide; perhaps all three. It's not believable that so young a boy could articulate that reflection, and in fiction the merely true must always yield to the plausible. Moreover, the symbolism is in places heavy-footed. Yet Ambrose M ——— understood, as few adults do, that the famous loneliness of the great was no popular myth but a general truth — furthermore, that it was as much cause as effect.

All the preceding except the last few sentences is exposition that should've been done earlier or interspersed with the present action instead of lumped together. No reader would put up with so much with such *prolixity*. It's interesting that Ambrose's father, though presumably an intelligent man (as indicated by his role as grade-school principal), neither encouraged nor discouraged his sons at all in any way — as if he either didn't care about them or cared all right but didn't know how to act. If this fact should contribute to one of them's becoming a celebrated but wretchedly unhappy scientist, was it a good thing or not? He too might someday face the question; it would be useful to know whether it had tortured his father for years, for example, or never once crossed his mind.

In the maze two important things happened. First, our hero found a name-coin someone else had lost or discarded: AMBROSE, suggestive of the famous lightship and of his late grandfather's favorite dessert, which his mother used to prepare on special occasions out of coconut, oranges, grapes, and what else. Second, as he wondered at the endless replication of his image in the mirrors, second, as he *lost himself in the reflection* that the necessity for an observer makes perfect observation impossible, better make him eighteen at least, yet that would render other things unlikely, he heard Peter and Magda chuckling somewhere together in the maze. "Here!" "No, here!" they shouted to each other; Peter said, "Where's Amby?" Magda murmured. "Amb?" Peter called. In a pleased, friendly voice. He didn't reply. The truth was, his brother was a *happy-go-lucky youngster* who'd've been better off with a regular brother of his own, but who seldom complained of his lot and was generally cordial. Ambrose's throat ached; there aren't enough different ways to say that. He stood quietly while the two young people giggled and thumped through the glittering maze, hurrah'd their discovery of its exit, cried out in joyful alarm at what next beset them. Then he set his mouth and followed after, as he supposed, took a wrong turn, strayed into the pass *wherein he lingers yet.*

The action of conventional dramatic narrative may be represented by a diagram called Freitag's Triangle:

or more accurately by a variant of that diagram:

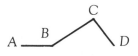

in which *AB* represents the exposition, *B* the introduction of conflict, *BC* the "rising action," complication, or development of the conflict, *C* the climax, or turn of the action, *CD* the dénouement, or resolution of the conflict. While there is no reason to regard this pattern as an absolute necessity, like many other conventions it became conventional because great numbers of people over many years learned by trial and error that it was effective; one ought not to forsake it, therefore, unless one wishes to forsake as well the effect of drama or has clear cause to feel that deliberate violation of the "normal" pattern can better can better effect that effect.

This can't go on much longer; it can go on forever. He died telling stories to himself in the dark; years later, when that vast unsuspected area of the funhouse came to light, the first expedition found his skeleton in one of its labyrinthine corridors and mistook it for part of the entertainment. He died of starvation telling himself stories in the dark; but unbeknownst unbeknownst to him, an assistant operator of the funhouse, happening to overhear him, crouched just behind the plyboard partition and wrote down his every word. The operator's daughter, an exquisite young woman with a figure unusually well developed for her age, crouched just behind the partition and transcribed his every word. Though she had never laid eyes on him, she recognized that here was one of Western Culture's truly great imaginations, the eloquence of whose suffering would be an inspiration to unnumbered. And her heart was torn between her love for the misfortunate young man (yes, she loved him, though she had never laid though she knew him only — but how well! — through his words, and the deep, calm voice in which he spoke them) between her love et cetera and her womanly intuition that only in suffering and isolation could he give voice et cetera. Lone dark dying. Quietly she kissed the rough plyboard, and a tear fell upon the page. Where she had written in shorthand *Where she had written in shorthand* Where she had written in shorthand *Where she* et cetera. A long time ago we should have passed the apex of Freitag's Triangle and made brief work of the *dénouement*; the plot doesn't rise by meaningful steps but winds upon itself, digresses, retreats, hesitates, sighs, collapses, expires. The climax of the story must be its protagonist's discovery of a way to get through the funhouse. But he has found none, may have ceased to search.

What relevance does the war have to the story? Should there be fireworks outside or not?

Ambrose wandered, languished, dozed. Now and then he fell into his habit of rehearsing to himself the unadventurous story of his life, narrated from the third-person point of view, from his earliest memory parenthesis of maple leaves stirring in the summer breath of tidewater Maryland end of parenthesis to the present moment. Its principal events, on this telling, would appear to have been A, B, C, and D.

He imagined himself years hence, successful, married, at ease in the world, the trials of his adolescence far behind him. He has come to the seashore with his family for the holiday: how Ocean City has changed! But at one seldom at one ill-frequented end of the boardwalk a few derelict amusements survive from times gone by: the great carrousel from the turn of the century, with its monstrous griffins and mechanical concert band; the roller coaster rumored since 1916 to have been condemned; the mechanical shooting gallery in which only the image of our enemies changed. His own son laughs with Fat May and wants to know what a funhouse is; Ambrose hugs the sturdy lad close and smiles around his pipestem at his wife.

The family's going home. Mother sits between Father and Uncle Karl, who teases him good-naturedly who chuckles over the fact that the comrade with whom he'd fought his way shoulder to shoulder through the funhouse had turned out to be a blind Negro girl — to their mutual discomfort, as they'd opened their souls. But such are the walls of custom, which even. Whose arm is where? How must it feel. He dreams of a funhouse vaster by far than any yet constructed; but by then they may be out of fashion, like steamboats and excursion trains. Already quaint and seedy: the draperied ladies on the frieze of the carrousel are his father's father's mooncheeked dreams; if he thinks of it more he will vomit his apple-on-a-stick.

He wonders: will he become a regular person? Something has gone wrong; his vaccination didn't take; at the Boy-Scout initiation campfire he only pretended to be deeply moved, as he pretends to this hour that it is not so bad after all in the funhouse, and that he has a little limp. How long will it last? He envisions a truly astonishing funhouse, incredibly complex yet utterly controlled from a great central switchboard like the console of a pipe organ. Nobody had enough imagination. He could design such a place himself, wiring and all, and he's only thirteen years old. He would be its operator: panel lights would show what was up in every cranny of its cunning of its multifarious vastness; a switch-flick would ease this fellow's way, complicate that's, to balance things out; if anyone seemed lost or frightened, all the operator had to do was.

He wishes he had never entered the funhouse. But he has. Then he wishes he were dead. But he's not. Therefore he will construct funhouses for others and be their secret operator — though he would rather be among the lovers for whom funhouses are designed.

Suggestions for Discussion

1. Experimental fiction in which narrative forms and techniques become part of the content has been given the name *metafiction*. How do forms and techniques described in *Writing Fiction* operate as an extended metaphor in "Lost in the Funhouse"? Here are some specific points to consider.

2. Barth sets up the situation of the story and immediately launches into a digression on the use of italics. What sort of "contract" does this set up between author and reader? For what sorts of effect does he use italics throughout the story?

3. The paragraph beginning "Description of physical appearance . . ." on page 291 contains a parody of advice given in several chapters of this book, including those on significant detail and character presentation. Why does Barth include this parody? Why does he fail to supply the simile in the sentence, "The brown hair on Ambrose's mother's forearms gleamed in the sun like"?

4. At the end of the paragraph mentioned in item 3, Barth describes the way a good metaphor operates. This description is itself a metaphor. How does it operate?

How is it "particularly appropriate to the sensibility of the narrator"? This story is told in the third person: What does he mean by "the narrator"? (Clues are to be found on page 294 in the paragraph beginning "The more closely . . ." and on page 307 in the paragraph beginning, "Ambrose wandered . . .")

5. On page 293, the paragraph beginning "Plush upholstery . . ." makes several complaints about the story's structure, dialogue, detail, and theme. How reliable are these complaints? The paragraph ends: "we will never get out of the funhouse." Explain the irony of this judgment.

6. On page 294 Barth puts a cliché in quotation marks: "Ambrose moved clear 'in the nick of time.'" Obviously, he knows better. What is his purpose?

7. The story contains two metaphors extended so far as to become symbols: fictional techniques and the funhouse. What is their relation to each other?

8. How is the point of view, or the level of reality, of the piece altered by the position of the quotation marks on page 303, in the paragraph beginning, "Naturally he didn't have nerve enough . . ."?

9. Ambrose steps into the mirror-maze (page 305); not long after, he loses himself in reflection. What is the significance of the mirror metaphor?

10. On page 306, Barth parodies "Freitag's Triangle." Does "Lost in the Funhouse" in fact follow the "variant diagram" of story form?

11. Nabokov's "Signs and Symbols" denies us a resolution. Barth's "Lost in the Funhouse" offers a number of mutually exclusive possible endings. Do we know which of these is the "real" resolution of the story? If so, what is the purpose of the others?

RETROSPECT

Explain how each of the following metaphors or symbols operates in its context:

1. "Cutting Edge," page 18: " 'It fills out his face,' Mr. Zeller said, looking at the wallpaper and surprised he had never noticed what a pattern it had before; it showed the sacrifice of some sort of animal by a youth."

2. "Everything That Rises Must Converge," page 43: "while he, his hands behind him, appeared pinned to the door frame, waiting like Saint Sebastian for the arrows to begin piercing him."

3. "In the Absence of Angels," pages 94–95: "We know this on the instant, recognition clamoring between us, two animals who touch each other's scent in the prowling dark."

4. "Brownstone," page 149: "The camel, I had noticed, was passing, with great difficulty, through the eye of the needle."

5. "The Masked Marvel's Last Toehold," page 208: "And . . . *I am masked.*"

6. "Battle Royal," page 229: "the eyes hollow and smeared a cool blue, the color of a baboon's butt."

WRITING ASSIGNMENTS

1. Write a passage using at least three cliché metaphors, wringing a change on each cliché so that it becomes new.

2. Take any dead metaphor and write a comic or serious scene that reinvests the metaphor with its original comparative force. Here are a few sample suggestions (your own will be better):

Sifting the evidence. (The lawyer uses a colander, a tea strainer, two coffee filters, and a garlic press to decide the case.)

Speakeasy. (Chicago, 1916. A young libertine tricks a beautiful but repressed young woman into an illegal basement bar. He thinks drink will loosen her up. What it loosens is not her sensuality but her tongue, and what she says he doesn't want to hear.)

Peck on the cheek.
(Alfred Hitchcock has done this one already, perhaps?)
Bus terminal.   *Don't spoil your lunch.*
Advertising jingle.   *Broken home.*
Soft shoulders.   *Good-bye.*

3. Write two one-page scenes, each containing an extended metaphor or simile. In one, compare an ordinary object to something of great size or significance. In the other, compare a major thing or phenomenon to something smaller and more mundane or less intense.

4. Write a short scene involving a conflict between two people over an object. Let the object take on symbolic significance. It may have the same significance to the two people, or a different significance to each.

5. Let an object smaller than a breadbox symbolize hope, redemption, or love to the central character. Let it symbolize something else entirely to the reader.

9

I GOTTA USE WORDS
WHEN I TALK TO YOU
Theme

Theme as a Fusion of Emotion, Idea, and Judgment
Theme as a Speculation
Theme as the Total Pattern of the Work

In an essay, your goal is to say as clearly and directly as possible what you mean. In fiction, your goal is to make people and make them do things and, ideally, never to say what you mean at all. What you mean emerges in the reading experience and takes shape in the reader's mind. It is a reverberation and a resonance, "not," as the narrator says of Marlowe's tales in *Heart of Darkness*, "inside like a kernel but outside, enveloping the tale which brought it out."

Theoretically, an outline can never harm an essay: this is what I have to say, and I'll say it through points A, B, and C. But if a fiction writer sets out to write a story in order to illustrate an idea, the fiction will almost inevitably be thin. Even if you begin with an outline, as many writers do, it will be an outline of the action and not of your "points." You may not know what the meaning of the story is until the characters begin to tell you; you'll begin with an image of a person or a situation that seems vaguely to embody something important, and you'll learn as you go what that something is. Vladimir Nabokov's advice to readers might equally apply to the author of fiction.

. . . fondle details. There is nothing wrong about the moonshine of generalization *after* the sunny trifles of the book have been lovingly collected. If one begins with a ready-made generalization, one begins at the wrong end and travels away from the book before one has started to understand it.

As a writer you are in control of your theme but it must not be in control of you; and you must also start at the right end and travel toward what your story has to say before you indulge in the moonshine of generalization.

Theme as a Fusion of Emotion, Idea, and Judgment

Yet it is very likely that at some point in the writing process, early or late, you will find yourself impelled by, under pressure of, interested primarily in, your theme more than your plot. It will seem that the reason you must set yourself this lonely, austere, and torturous task is that you do have something to say. Every author has the experience of being asked: *What is your new story/novel about?* I have seen writers go pigeon-toed, stammer, stumble, and fumble for an answer — and have felt myself do the same. I have learned to answer: *It's about a costume designer in a crummy little town in southern Georgia, whose ex-husband comes to work in the same town.* In other words, I answer with character and plot, which is what my interlocutor wants to know about. But in doing so I feel dishonest and detached. I could answer more truthfully and with more enthusiasm: *It's about digging up graves* (but that would give the false impression that I'm writing a horror novel), or: *It's about dreams coming true* (which would give the equally false impression that I'm writing a romance), or: *It's about professionalism, trash and treasure, getting rid of the past, opening and openings, permission, the occult as a metaphor for the horrors of ordinary life* (none of which, I think, would give much impression at all.) Jane Austen once wrote her sister that the theme of her novel *Mansfield Park* was "ordination." In the two hundred years since that letter, critics have written many times the number of words in the novel trying to explain what she meant. And yet the novel is well understood, forcefully experienced, and intelligently appreciated. The difficulty is not in understanding the book but in applying the "kernel" definition to its multiplicity of ideas and richness of theme.

Literature is stuck with ideas in a way the other arts are not. Music, paradoxically the most abstract of the arts, creates a logical structure that need make no reference to the world outside itself. It may express a mood, but it needs to draw no conclusions and offer no morality. Shapes in painting and sculpture may suggest forms in the physical world, but they need not represent the world, and they need contain no message. But words mean.

The grammatical structure of the simplest sentence contains a concept, whatever else it may contain, so that an author who wishes to treat words solely as sound or shape may be said to make strange music or pictures but not literature. And yet, "I take it as my principle," said Antonin Artaud, "that words do not mean everything." Artaud was a theatrical writer and director, concerned with the impact of the visual and aural in live performance, but his principle is also relevant to theme in literature. If it were not, it would be possible to extract in words a moral or a message from every great story and novel; which is to say, an essay would have done as well.

In the human experience, emotion, judgment, and logic are inextricably mixed, and we make continual cross-reference between and among them. *You've just got the sulks today.* (I pass judgment on your emotion.) *What do you think of this idea?* (How do you judge this logic?) *Why do I feel this way?* (What is the logic of this emotion?) *It makes no sense to be angry about it.* (I pass judgment on the logic of your emotion.) Literature attempts to fuse three areas of experience organically, denying the force of none of them, positing that no one is more real than the others. This is why I have insisted throughout this book on detail and scene (immediate felt experience), the essential abstractions conveyed therein (ideas), and the attitude implied thereby (judgment).

"Literature," says John Ciardi, "is never only about ideas, but about the experience of ideas." The writer's primary task is in the creation of the experience, but in that process she or he inevitably also conveys an idea, and also an attitude toward that idea. I would go further and define theme, in literature, as *the emotional experience of a moral idea.* Rust Hills says:

> . . . coherence in the world [an author] creates is constituted of two concepts he holds, which may be in conflict: one is his world view, his sense of the way the world is; and the other is his sense of morality, the way the world ought to be.
>
> *Writing in General and the Short Story in Particular*

Wayne C. Booth calls his analysis of point of view *The Rhetoric of Fiction,* deliberately implying that the purpose of fiction is persuasion. Joan Didion suggests that the phrase "Why I Write" contains its own answer in the repetition of the sound, *I, I, I;* and she goes on to say of the act of writing that it is:

> a way of imposing oneself upon other people, of saying *listen to me, see it my way, change your mind.* It's an aggressive, even a hostile act.

Imamu Amiri Baraka (LeRoi Jones) agrees when he asks for "poems that kill / Assassin poems, Poems that shoot guns"; yet neither is fundamentally at odds with F. R. Leavis when he insists that literature must be "life-affirming." I know no writer in the 1980s who would be willing to say with Thomas Bulfinch that "literature is one of the best allies of virtue and prompters of happiness," but I suspect every writer hopes that is the case. The morality each of these writers espouses is different from that of the others, but each confirms the tautology of literary judgment, that fiction is "good" if it's "good." No writer who fails to convince us of the validity of his vision of the world can convince us of his greatness. Literature is willy-nilly, ineluctably moral, whatever the morality.

The Victorians used literature to teach piety, and the Aesthetes asserted that Victorian piety was a deadening lie. Albert Camus believed that no serious writer in the twentieth century could avoid political commitment, whereas for Joyce the true artist could be a God but *must not* be a preacher. Each of these stances is a moral one. Those who defend escape literature do so on the grounds that people *need* to escape. Those who defend hard-core pornography argue that we can't prove an uncensored press makes for moral degeneracy, whereas it can be historically demonstrated that a censored press makes for political oppression. Anarchistic, nihilistic, and antisocial literature is always touted as offering a neglected truth. I have yet to hear anyone assert that literature leads to laziness, madness, and brutality and then say that it doesn't matter.

But to say that literature is a persuasive art, and that it is moral, is a very different thing than to say that a work of literature "has a moral." Any literary text of significant worth will begin a discussion of theme by warning that theme is not *the moral*, not *the message*, and that *the meaning* of the piece cannot be paraphrased.

Why not? Joan Didion suggests the beginning of an answer as she continues to discuss, "Why I Write":

> I am not a scholar. I am not in the least an intellectual, which is not to say that when I hear the word "intellectual" I reach for my gun, but only to say that I do not think in abstracts. During the years when I was an undergraduate at Berkeley I tried, with a kind of hopeless late-adolescent energy, to buy some temporary visa into the world of ideas, to forge for myself a mind that could deal with the abstract.
>
> In short I tried to think. I failed. My attention veered inexorably back to the specific, to the tangible, to what was generally considered, by everyone I knew then and for that matter have known since, the peripheral. I would try to contemplate the Hegelian dialectic and would find myself concentrating instead on the flowering pear tree outside my window and the particular way the petals fell on the floor.

Didion takes a Socratic stance here, ironically pretending to naïveté and modesty as she equates "thinking" with "thinking in the abstract." Certainly her self-deprecation is ironic in light of the fact that she is not only a novelist but one of the finest intellects among our contemporary essayists. But she acknowledges an assumption very general and very seriously taken, that *thought* means *dealing with the abstract,* and that abstract thought is more real, central, and valid than specific concrete thought.

Vladimir Nabokov confronts this attitude head-on, defending the writer's "irrational belief in the goodness of man":

> What exactly do these irrational standards mean? They mean the supremacy of the detail over the general, of the part that is more alive than the whole, of the little thing which a man observes and greets with a friendly nod of the spirit while the crowd around him is being driven by some common impulse to some common goal. . . . This capacity to wonder at trifles — no matter the imminent peril — these asides of the spirit, these footnotes in the volume of life are the highest forms of consciousness.

T. S. Eliot faces the issue less lyrically but no less directly in his *Elizabethan Essays,* when he considers Shakespeare's "philosophy":

> We talk as if thought was precise and emotion was vague. In reality there is precise emotion and there is vague emotion. To express precise emotion requires as great intellectual power as to express precise thought.

This is not to say that Eliot makes no distinction between those who express in art the ideas of their time and situation and those who break and remold philosophical concepts in the abstract. But the intellectual power of the writer of fiction is to capture the precise emotional force of the ideas that fiction contains.

> When Dante says *la sua voluntade e nostre pace* it is great poetry, and there is a great philosophy behind it. When Shakespeare says
>
> > As flies to wanton boys are we to the gods;
> > They kill us for their sport,
>
> it is *equally* great poetry, though the philosophy behind it is not great. But the essential is that each expresses in perfect language, some permanent human impulse. Emotionally, the latter is just as strong, just as true, and just as informative — just as useful and beneficial in the sense in which poetry is useful and beneficial, as the former.

In other words, literature is "useful and beneficial" when it brings home to us with emotional force an idea together with an attitude toward that idea. Every story in this volume does that; each invites, asks, or forces us to experience its moral idea. In "The Loneliness of the Long-Distance

Runner" we experience the idea that it is possible to win one's honor by losing a race. In the story "In the Absence of Angels" we experience the idea that the final value of civilization may lie in the ability to forgive one's executioner. In "The Masked Marvel's Last Toehold" we experience the idea that mortality is an unfair fight. It is the pervasive presence of these ideas that gives each story its coherence; it is the moral value of each that makes the story significant. Yet ultimately the purpose of the story is not the idea itself but the reader's experience of that idea.

Not all experience reveals, but all revelation comes through experience. All books aspire to become a part of that revelatory experience, and the books that are made in the form of fiction attempt to do so by re-creating the experience of revelation.

There is a curious prejudice built into our language that makes us speak of *telling the truth* but *telling a lie*. No one supposes that all conceivable falsehood can be wrapped up in a single statement called "the lie"; lies are manifold, varied, and specific. But truth is supposed to be absolute: the truth, the whole truth, and nothing but the truth. This is, of course, impossible nonsense, and *telling a lie* is a truer phrase than *telling the truth*. Fiction does not have to tell the truth, but a truth.

The implied contrast with the law here is relevant. Abstract reasoning works toward generalization and results in definitions, laws, and absolute judgments. Imaginative reasoning and concrete thought work toward instances and result in emotional experience, revelation, and the ability to contain life's paradoxes in tension — which may explain the notorious opposition of writers to the laws and institutions of their time. Lawmakers struggle to define a moral position in abstract terms such that it will justly account for every instance to which it is applied. (This is why the language of law is so tedious and convoluted.) Poets and novelists continually goad them by producing instances for which the law does not account and referring by resonance and implication to the principle behind and beyond the law. (This is why the language of literature is so dense and compact.) So the author may create a situation in which the spirit is violated by the letter and say: this mental hospital is run by psychotics; this university is run by dolts; this marriage is run on hate; this church is run on sin; this government is run on corruption; this court is run on injustice. And/or the fictional instance may have as its moral exploration: here insanity is sanity, stupidity wisdom, anger love, sin purity, and injustice justice. To cite Nabokov again:

It is instructive to think that there is not a single person in this room, or for that matter in any room in the world, who, at some nicely chosen point in historical time-space, would not be put to death there and then, here and now, by a commonsensical majority in a righteous rage. The color of one's creed, necktie, eyes, thoughts, manners, speech, is sure to meet somewhere in time or space with a fatal objection from a mob that hates that particular tone. And the more brilliant, the more unusual the man, the nearer he is to the stake. "Stranger" always rhymes with "danger."

Theme as a Speculation

Theme is not a moral but the emotional experience of a moral idea. Equally, it is not a law but a speculation, a supposition, a possibility, an exploration. The value of such speculation is not that a better law may be built out of it but that it may not; that literature asks us to acknowledge and to hold in a single tension in our minds-feelings-beliefs the manifold beauties and uncertainties of the human condition. Anton Chekhov wrote that "the writer of fiction should not try to solve such questions as those of God, pessimism and so forth." What is "obligatory for the artist," he said, is not "solving a problem," but "stating a problem correctly." Every story reaches in its climax and resolution an interim solution to a specifically realized dilemma. But it offers no final solutions and no Final Solution.

Further, this refusal to solve is not the writer's intellectual weakness, but his intellectual strength. "A great enough writer," Ernest Hemingway said, "seems to be born with an intelligence to accept or reject what is already presented as knowledge." John Keats went even further in pursuing a definition of the artist's "disinterestedness," his receptivity, and the "impersonality of genius": "The only means of strengthening one's intellect is to make up one's mind about nothing — to let the mind be a thoroughfare for all thoughts." And he defined genius as negative capability: "that is when a man is capable of being in uncertainties, Mysteries, doubts, without any irritable reaching after fact & reason."

The critic F. R. Leavis has described the process of literary criticism as a "yes-but dialogue": This is true, isn't it? Yes, but this is also true. Yes, except for this.

Literature applies to life the process that criticism applies to literature. An eye for an eye and a tooth for a tooth (says the Old Testament). Yes (says the New Testament), but the meek shall inherit the earth. Yes, but you must submit to a higher truth, not temporal authority (Sophocles' Antigone). Yes, but the powers of darkness can disguise themselves as higher truth (Shakespeare's Macbeth). Yes, but submitting to established authority can be a way of serving higher truth (Jane Austen's Persuasion). Yes, but even so you may lose your soul (Henry James's Portrait of a Lady). Yes, but sometimes your soul is precisely what you must lose to achieve greatness (Thomas Mann's Dr. Faustus). Yes, but sometimes you fail to recognize that you have a choice (Kafka's The Trial). Yes, but . . .

Some time ago I had a conversation, extending over several days, with a friend who is a family counselor, about the differences between our professions. We agreed that our concerns and our methods had much in common, but that her work remained a process, intangible and invisible except through fleeting signs, whereas my work at least yielded a product that could be held in the hand and pointed to as a "result." I was dissatisfied with this, since a book as an object seems to me of no value unless it also represents an invisible process in the reader's mind. But eventually we identified a much more significant distinction: as a social worker my friend is unequivocally committed to health. She may urge her clients to consider only those possibilities that may lead to their greater strength, happiness, and active functioning. As a practical daily person I share this commitment, but as a writer I am committed, not to life, but to the life cycle; in the speculations that are my themes I do, and must, equally celebrate disease, decay, despair, and death. I spoke of this with Richard Selzer, the surgeon whose story "The Masked Marvel's Last Toehold" appears in this volume. He agreed that an alternative or dual vision was one of the purposes of writing for him — that in the operating room he must always see disease and deformity as the enemy, whereas as an author he can step back from this struggle and acknowledge, in the words of one of his narrators, the "black joy" of our ephemerality.

The writer, of course, may be powerfully impelled to impose a limited vision of the world as it ought to be, and even to tie that vision to a social institution, wishing not only to persuade and convince but to propagandize. But because the emotional force of literary persuasion is in the realization of the particular, he or she is doomed to fail. The greater the work, the more it refers us to "some permanent human impulse" rather than a given institutional embodiment of that impulse. Fine writing expands our scope by continually presenting a new way of seeing, a further possibility of emotional identification; it flatly refuses to become a law. I am not a Roman Catholic like Gerard Manley Hopkins, and cannot be persuaded by his poetry to become one; but in a moment near despair I can drive along an Illinois street in a Chevrolet station wagon and take strength from the lines of a Jesuit in the Welsh wasteland. I am not a communist as Bertolt Brecht was and cannot be convinced by his plays to become one; but I can see the hauteur of wealth displayed on the Gulf of Mexico and recognize, from a parable of the German Marxist, the difference between a possession and a belonging.

The theme that is proposed, supposed, or speculated upon in a fiction may be very simple and untrue, like the notion in "Cinderella" that the good and beautiful will triumph. Or it may be profound and unprovable, like the theme in *Oedipus Rex* that man cannot escape his destiny but may be ennobled in the attempt. It may be deliberately paradoxical and offer no guidelines that can be made use of in life, as in Jane Austen's *Persuasion*, where the heroine, in order to adhere to her principles, must follow advice given on principles less sound than her own. The fiction may speculate that life is meaningless and communication impossible, like the novels and plays of Samuel Beckett — which communicate the meaning of these philosophies. It can propound that the events of life are random and offer no pattern whatsoever, like the novels of William Burroughs, in which case randomness and lack of pattern amount to a concept and a form.

Theme as the Total Pattern of the Work

Whatever the supposition is, it will bring that theme into the realm of experience through its particular and unique pattern. It is the nature of art that disparate elements are fused into a single unity. So theme involves emotion, logic, and judgment — all three — but the pattern that forms the particular experience of that theme involves every element of fiction this book has discussed: the arrangement, shape, and flow of the characters realized in their details, seen in their atmosphere and their actions from a unique point of view through the imagery and rhythm of the language.

This fusion of elements into a unified pattern is the nature of creativity, a word devalued in latter years to the extent that it has come to mean a random gush of self-expression. God, perhaps, created out of the void; but in the world as we know it, all creativity, from the sprouting of an onion to the painting of *Guernica*, is a matter of selection and arrangement. A child learns to draw one circle on top of another, to add two triangles at the top and a line at the bottom, and in this particular pattern of circles, triangles, and lines has made a creature of an altogether different nature: a cat! The child draws one square on top of another and connects the corners and has made three dimensions where there are only two. And although these are tricks that can be taught and learned, they partake of the essential nature of creativity, in which several elements are joined to produce, not merely a whole that is greater than the sum of its parts, but a whole that is something altogether other. At the conception of a fetus or a short story, there occurs a conjunction of two unlike things, whether cells or ideas, that have never been joined before. Around this conjunction other cells, other ideas, accumulate in a deliberate pattern. That pattern is the unique personality of the creature, and if the pattern does not cohere it miscarries or is stillborn.

The organic unity of a work of literature cannot be taught — or, if it can, I have not discovered a way to teach it. I can suggest from time to time that concrete image is not separate from character, which is revealed in dialogue and point of view, which may be illuminated by simile, which may reveal theme, which is contained in plot as water is contained in an apple. But I cannot tell you how to achieve this; nor, if you achieve it, will you be able to explain very clearly how you have done so. Analysis separates in order to focus; it assumes that an understanding of the parts contributes to an understanding of the whole; but it does not produce the whole. Scientists can determine with minute accuracy the elements, in their proportions, contained in a piece of human skin. They can gather these elements, stir and warm them, but they will not be skin. A good critic can show you where a metaphor does or does not illuminate character, where the character does or does not ring true in an action. But the critic cannot tell you how to make a character breathe; the breath is talent, and can neither be explained nor produced.

Both Joseph Conrad in *Heart of Darkness* and Ralph Ellison in *Invisible Man* deal with issues of race, isolation, money, moral contamination, and human cruelty. Both do so partly through the use of symbolic black-and-white imagery, which in both books derives from common assumptions about black people and white people. In both, the recurrent coupling and fusing of light and dark imagery suggest the complexity of moral attitude and the difficulty of choice. The ultimate moral stances of the authors are quite compatible, and both suggest that their protagonists must return to the world with their visions expanded, keeping a difficult balance between the horrors they have seen and the principles they hold. If you were to insist on extracting a moral from both works, you would come up with some such banality as: cruelty is part of human nature and we must try to maintain individual integrity as we see it without repudiating the rest of mankind.

The experience of these books is by no means so banal as any moral stated in abstract terms. The themes of the two books are different because the experiences they recount are different, their forms are different, and the experience of the reader is therefore different. The protagonist of one is white and the other black. One takes place in Africa, the other in America; one in the nineteenth century, the other in the twentieth. The black-white imagery of one is fused out of iron, gold, ivory, rags, mourning, fog, clouds, and gunfire; of the other out of light bulbs, electrified carpet, teeth, paint, two-tone shoes, basements, and blindness. The one borrows a rhetorical rhythm from the sea and the other from a church. As we read each of these books an experience unfolds that makes reference, perhaps, to many of the same moral ideas and permanent human impulses, but it is the pattern that is the force of each and the precision of its emotional expression.

As you write, the experience of your story also unfolds itself to you, and you begin to see connections occur, images recur, a pattern emerge.

Students irritated by the analysis of literature often ask, "How do you know she did that on purpose? How do you know it didn't just happen to come out that way?" The answer is: you don't. But what is on the page is on the page. An author no less than a reader or critic can see an emerging pattern, and the author has both the possibility and the obligation of manipulating it. When you have put something on the page, you have two possibilities, and only two: you may cut it or you are committed to it. Gail Godwin asks:

> But what about the other truths you lost by telling it that way? . . .
> Ah, my friend, that is my question too. The choice is always a killing one. One option must die so that another may live. I do little murders in my workroom every day.

Often the choice to commit yourself to a phrase, an image, a line of dialogue will reveal, in a minor convulsion of understanding, what you mean. I have written no story or novel in which this did not occur once or several times in trivial or dramatic ways. I once sat bolt upright at 4:00 A.M. in a strange town, with the realization that my sixty-year-old male narrator had been lying to me for two hundred pages. I once had a female narrator say of her sister, "She needs to be important, especially if it's dangerous." I did not know why I used the phrase, "especially if it's dangerous." I supposed I wanted it for the rhythm, or used it simply because I knew that the sister was to be murdered in the last chapter of the book. I cut it, but it would not be cut. So I faced it and quarreled with it, and I discovered that the narrator knew her sister better than I did and also that the phrase contained the clue to her character, her relationship with her politician father, to the plot, and to my central theme: this girl was courting the *publicity* of her own assassination.

It has become a popular — a cliché — stance for modern writers to claim that they haven't the faintest idea what they meant in their writing. *Don't ask me; read the book. If I knew what it meant, I wouldn't have written it. It means what it says.* When an author makes such a response, it is well to remember that an author is a professional liar. What he or she means is not that there are no themes, ideas, or meanings in the work but that these are not separable from the pattern of fictional experience in which they are embodied.

No one can tell you what to mean, and no one can tell you how. I am conscious of having avoided the phrase *creative writing* in these pages, largely because all of us who teach creative writing find the words sticking in our throats. I myself would like to see courses taught in creative algebra, creative business administration, creative nursing, and creative history. I also fully and seriously intend one day to teach an advanced seminar in destructive writing (polemic, invective, libel, actionable obscenity, and character defamation). The mystique and the false glamour of the writing profession grow partly out of a mistaken belief that people who can express profound ideas and emotions have ideas and emotions more profound than the rest of us. It isn't so. The ability to express is a special gift with a special craft to support it and is spread fairly equally among the profound, the shallow, and the mediocre.

All the same, I am abashedly conscious that the creative exists — in algebra and nursing as in words — and that it mysteriously surfaces in the trivia of human existence: numbers, bandages, words. In the unified pattern of a fiction there is even something to which the name of magic may be given, where one empty word is placed upon another and tapped with a third, and a flaming scarf or a long-eared hope is pulled out of the tall black heart. The most magical thing about this magic is that once the trick is explained, it is not explained, and the better you understand how it works, the better it will work again.

Birth, death, work, and love continue to occur. Their meaning changes from time to time and place to place, and new meanings engender new forms, which capture and create new meanings until they tire, while birth, death, work, and love continue to recur. Something to which we give the name of "honor" seems to persist, though in one place and time it is embodied in choosing to die for your country, in another, choosing not to. A notion of "progress" survives, though it is expressed, now in technology, now in ecology, now in the survival of the fittest, now in the protection of the weak. There seems to be something corresponding to the human invention of "love," though it takes its form, now in tenacious loyalty, now in letting go.

Ideas are not new, but the form in which they are expressed is constantly renewed, and new forms give life to what used to be called (in the old form) the eternal verities. An innovative writer tries to forge, and those who follow try to perfect, forms that so fuse with meaning that form itself expresses.

Mobius the Stripper

A TOPOLOGICAL EXERCISE

GABRIEL JOSIPOVICI

No one ever knew the origins and background of Mobius the stripper. "I'm not English," he would say, "that's for certain." His language was an uneasy mixture of idioms and accents, jostling each other as the words fell from his thick lips. He was always ready to talk. To anyone who would listen. He had to explain. It was a need.

"You see. What I do. My motive. Is not seshual. Is metaphysical. A metaphysical motive, see? I red Jennett. Prust. Nitch. Those boys. All say the same. Is a metaphysical need. To strip. To take off what society has put on me. What my father and my mother have put on me. What my friends have put on me. What I have put on me. And I say to me: What are you Mobius? a man? A wooman? A vedge table? Are you a stone, Mobius? This fat. You feel here. Here. Like it's folds of fat, see. And it's

---

I first heard of Mobius the stripper from a girl with big feet called Jenny. She was one of those girls who make a point of always knowing what's going on, and in those days she was constantly coming up with bright and bizarre little items of information in which she tried to interest me. Once she dragged me to Ealing where, in the small and smoke-filled back room of a dingy terrace, a fakir of sorts first turned a snake into a rope, then climbed the rope and sat fanning himself with a mauve silk handkerchief with his greasy hair just touching the flaking ceiling, then redescended and turned the rope back into a snake before finally returning the snake to the little leather bag from which he had taken it. A cheap trick. Another time she took me to Greenwich, where a friend of hers knew a man who kept six seals in his bathtub, but the man was gone or dead or simply unwilling to answer her friend's urgent ring at the doorbell. Most of all, though, Jenny's interest centred on deviant sexuality, and she was forever urging me to go with her to some dreary nightclub or "ned of wice" as she liked to call it, where men, women, children and monsters of every description did their best to plug the gaps in creation which a thoughtful Nature had benevolently provided for just such a purpose. Usually I didn't respond to these invitations of Jenny's, partly because her big feet embarrassed me (though she was a likeable girl with some distinction as a lacrosse player I believe), and partly because this kind of thing did not greatly interest me anyway.

"But it *must* interest you," Jenny would say. "They're all part of our world, aren't they?"

me. Mobius. This the mystery. I want to get right down behind this fat to the centre of me. And you can help me. Yes you. Everybody. Everybody can help Mobius. That the mystery. You and you and you and you. You think you just helping yourself but you helping me. And for why? Because in ultimate is not seshual. Is metaphysical. Maybe religious."

When Mobius spoke other people listened. He had presence. Not just size or melancholy but presence. There was something about the man that demanded attention and got it. No one knew where he lived, not even the manager of the club in Notting Hill, behind the tube station, where he stripped in public seven nights a week.

"You want to take Sundays off?" Tony the manager asked when he engaged him.

"Off?" Mobius said.

"We allow you one night a week," the manager said. "We treat our artists proper."

"I doan understand," Mobius said. "You employ me or you doan employ me. There an end."

"You have rights," the manager said. "We treat our artists proper here.

I agreed, but explained that not all parts of the world held out an equal interest for me.

"I don't understand you," she said. "You say you want to be a writer and then you *shut* your mind to experience. You simply *shut* your mind to it. You live in an ivory bower."

I accepted what she said. My mistake was ever to have told her I wanted to be a writer. The rest I deserved.

"Did Shakespeare have your attitude?" Jenny said. "Did Leonardo?"

No, I had to admit. Shakespeare had not had my attitude. Neither had Leonardo.

"Well then," Jenny said.

Sometimes, at this point, I'd be sorry for Jenny, for her big feet and her fresh English face. Mobius. Mobius the stripper. I could just imagine him. His real name was Ted Binks. He had broad shoulders and a waist narrow as a girl's. When he walked he pranced and when he laughed he.

"Well then," Jenny repeated, as if my admission made further discussion unnecessary. I sighed and said:

"All right. I'll come if you want me to. But if we're going to go all the way across London again only to find the door closed in our faces and the —"

"That only happened once," Jenny said. "I don't see why you have to bring it up like this every time. Anyway, it was you who wanted to see those seals. As soon as I told you about them you wanted to see them."

We're not in the business to exploit them."

"You not exploitin," Mobius said. "You doin me a favour. You payin me and givin me pleasure both."

"All right," the manager said. "I'm easy."

"You easy with me, I easy with you," Mobius said. "Okydoke?"

"You're on at six this evening then," the manager said, getting up and opening the door of his little office.

Mobius wanted to kiss him but the manager, a young man with a diamond tiepin, hastily stepped back behind his desk. When the door shut behind Mobius he slumped back in his chair, buried his face in his hands, and burst into tears. Nor was he ever afterwards able to account for this uncharacteristic gesture or forget it, hard as he tried.

Mobius arrived at five that afternoon and every subsequent afternoon as well. "You need concentration," he would say. "A good stripper needs to get in the right mood. Is like Yoga. All matter of concentration."

"Yes," the manager would say. "Yes. Of course. Of course."

"With me," Mobius explained to him, "is not seshual, is metaphysical. A metaphysical motive. Not like the rest of this garbage."

"All right," I said, resigned. "All right."

"It's yourself you're doing a favour to, not me," Jenny would add at this point. "You can't write without experience, and how the hell are you going to gain experience if you stay shut up in here all day long?"

Indeed, the girl had a point. She wasn't strictly accurate, since my mornings were spent delivering laundry for NU-nap, the new nappy service ("We clean dirt" they modestly informed the world in violet letters on their cream van — I used to wake up whispering that phrase to myself, at times it seemed to be the most beautiful combination of the most beautiful words in the language), and my evenings kicking the leaves in the park as I watched the world go by. But not quite inaccurate either, since I recognized within myself a strong urge towards seclusion, a shutting out of the world and its too urgent claims, Jenny included. And not just the world. The past too I would have liked to banish from my consciousness at times, and with it all the books I had ever read. As I bent over my desk in the afternoons, staring at the virgin paper, I would wish fervently, pray desperately to whatever deity would answer my prayers, that all the print which had ever been conveyed by my eyes to my brain and thence buried deep inside me where it remained to fester could be removed by a sharp painless and efficient knife. Not that I felt history to be a nightmare from which I wanted to awake etcetera etcetera, but simply that I felt the little self I once possessed to be dangerously threatened by the size and the *assurance* of all the great men who had come before me. There they were, solid,

But they didn't mind him saying that. Everybody liked Mobius except Tony the manager. The girls liked him best. "Hi Moby," they shouted. "How's your dick?"

"Is keeping up," he would reply. "How's yours?"

They wanted to know about his private life but he gave nothing away. "We're always telling you about our problems," they complained. "Why don't you ever tell us about yours?"

"I doan have problems," Mobius said.

"Come off it," they said, laughing. "Everyone's got problems."

"You have problems?" he asked them, surprised.

"Would we be in this lousy joint if we didn't?"

"Problems, problems," Mobius said. "Is human invention, problems."

But they felt melancholy in the late afternoons, far from their families, and in the early hours of the morning, when the public had all departed. "Where do you live?" they asked him. "Do you have a man or a woman? Do you have any children, Moby?"

To all these questions he replied with the same kindly smile, but once, when he caught one of them tailing him after a show he came back and

---

smiling, melancholy or grim as the case might be, Virgil and Dante and Descartes and Wordsworth and Joyce, lodged inside me, each telling me the truth — and who could doubt it was the truth, their very lives bore witness to the fact — but was it *my* truth, that was the question. And behind that, of course, another question and another: Was I entitled to a truth of my own at all, and if so, was it not precisely by following Jenny out into the cold streets of Richmond or Bermondsey or Highgate that I should find it?

At other times I'd catch myself before I spoke and, furious at the degree of condescension involved in feeling sorry for Jenny — who was I to feel sorry for anyone? — would say to her instead: "Fuck off. I want to work."

"Work later."

"No. I've got to work now."

"It's good for your work. You can't create out of your own entrails."

"There are always excuses. It's always either too early or too late."

"You want to be another of those people who churn out tepid trivia because it's the thing to be a writer? Why not forget that bit and live a little for a change?"

Dear Jenny. Despite her big feet — no, no, because of them — she never let go. She knew I'd give way in the end and if she'd come to me with the news in the first place it was only because she hadn't found anyone else to take her anyway. Jenny had a nose for the peculiar, but she was an old-fashioned girl at heart and felt the need of an escort wherever she went.

hit her across the face with his glove so that none of them ever tried anything like that again.

"I doan ask you you doan ask me," he said to them after the incident. "I have no secrets but my life is my own business." And when Tony came to have a talk with him about the girl's disfigured cheek he just closed his eyes and didn't answer.

"If it happens again you're out," Tony said, but although he would, in his heart of hearts, have been relieved had this in fact occurred, they both of them knew it was just talk. For Mobius was a gold mine. He really drew them in.

Alone in his little room, not many streets away from the club, he sat on the edge of the bed and stuffed himself sick on bananas. "Meat is meat," he would say. "I'm no cannibal." Bananas he ate by the hundredweight, sitting with bowed shoulders and sagging folds of fat on the narrow unmade bed, staring at the blank wall.

Those were good hours, the hours spent staring at the wall, waiting for four o'clock. Not as good as the hours after four, but good hours all the same. For what harm was he doing? If you don't pick a banana when it's ripe it rots, so again, what harm was he doing? Who was he hurting?

"Look," I said to her. "I don't want to live. I want to be left in peace to work."

"But this guy," she said. "The rolls of fat on him. It's fantastic. And the serenity. My God. You should see the serenity in his eyes when he strips."

"Serenity?" I said. "What are you talking about?"

"It's like a Buddha or something," Jenny said.

"What are you trying to do to me?" I said.

"Am I one of those people who fall for Zen and Yoga and all the rest of that Eastern crap?" Jenny said.

I had to admit she wasn't.

"I'm telling you," she said. "It's a great experience."

"Another time," I said.

Cheltenham hadn't prepared her for this. Her eyes popped.

"Another time," I said again.

"You mean — you're not going to come?"

"Another time," I said.

"Wow!" Jenny said. "Something must be happening to you. Are you in love or something?"

"I just want to work," I said.

"You always say that," Jenny said, suddenly deflated.

"I'm sorry," I said, and I was. Desperately. What sort of luck is it to be born with big feet? "Another time," I said. "O.K.?"

Sometimes the voices started and he sat back and listened to them with pride. "Who's talking of Mobius?" he would say. "I tell you, everybody's talking of Mobius. When I walk I hear them. When I sleep I hear them. When I sit in my room I hear them. Mobius the stripper. The best in the business. I've seen many strippers in my time but there's none to beat Mobius. I first met Mobius. I first saw Mobius. I first heard of Mobius. A friend of mine. A cousin. A duchess, the Duchess of Folkestone. We had been childhood friends. I remember her remarking that Mobius the stripper was the most amazing man she ever knew. I hear them all. But what do I care? That too must be stripped off." Give him the choice and he preferred the beautiful silence. The peace of stripping. But if they came he accepted them. They did him no harm.

He flicked another skin into the metal waste-paper basket and bit into another banana. When it was gone he would feel in the corners, between the molars, with his tongue, and sigh with contentment. How many doctors, wise men, had told him to pack it in, to have a change of diet and start a new life? But then how many doctors had told him he was too fat, needed to take more exercise, had bad teeth, incipient arthritis, a weak heart, bad

---

"You don't know what you're missing," Jenny said.

True enough, but I could guess. Mobius the stripper, six foot eight and round as a barrel: "That time Primo Carnera was chewing my big toe off. I couldn't get a proper grip on the slimy bastard so I grope around and he's chewing my toe like it'll come off any minute and then I find I've got my finger up his nostril and." Yes. Very good. He was another one I could do without.

After Jenny had gone I stared at the virgin sheet of paper on the table in front of me. When I did that I always wanted to scream. And when I left it there and got out, anywhere, just out, away from it all, then all I ever wanted to do was get back and start writing. Crazy. In those days I had a recurrent nightmare. I was in my shorts, playing rugger in the mud against the giants. Proust, languid and bemonocled, kept guard behind the pack; Joyce, small and fiery, his moustache in perfect trim, darted through their legs, whisking out the ball and sending it flying to the wings; Dostoyevsky, manic and bearded, Swift, ferocious and unstoppable; Chaucer, going like a terrier. And the pack, the pack itself, Tolstoy and Hugo and Homer and Goethe, Lawrence and Pascal and Milton and Descartes. Bearing down on me. Huge. Powerful. Totally confident. The ball kept coming out at me on the wing. It was a parcel of nappies neatly wrapped in plastic, "We clean dirt" in violet lettering across it. I always seemed to be out there by myself, there was never anyone else on my side, but the ball would keep coming out of the loose at me. It always began like that, with the ball flying

circulation, bronchitis, pneumonia, traces of malarial fever, smallpox? He was a man, a mound of flesh, heir to all that flesh is heir to. Mobius sighed and rubbed the folds of his stomach happily. It was a miracle he had survived this long when you thought of all the things that could have happened to him. And if so long then why not longer? "Time," he would say, "she mean nothing to me. You see this? This fat? My body she my clock. When I die she stop." And after all he had no need of clocks, there was a church the other side of the street and it sounded for him, especially for him, a particular peal, at four o'clock. Then he would get up and make the bed ("You got to have order. Disorder in the little thing and that's the beginning of the end"), wash his teeth and get his things together. No one had ever known him to get to the club after five ("You need time to meditate if you do a show like mine. Is like Yoga, all meditation").

When Tony the manager took his annual holiday in the Bermudas he locked up the place and carried the keys away with him. Mobius, a stickler for routine and with a metaphysical need to satisfy, still got up at four, made his bed, emptied the banana skins into the communal dustbin in the back yard, cleaned his teeth, packed his things, and went on down to the

---

through the grey air towards my outstretched arms and then the pack bearing down, boots pounding the turf as in desperation I swung further and further out, knowing all the time that I would never be able to make it into touch or have the nerve to steady and kick ahead. There was just me and this ball that was a parcel of nappies and all of them coming at me. Descartes in particular obsessed me. I would wake up sweating and wondering how it was possible to be so sure and yet so wrong. And why did they all have to keep coming for me like that, with Proust always drifting nonchalantly behind them, hair gleaming, boots polished, never in any hurry but always blocking my path? What harm had I done any of them except read them? And now I wanted to forget them. Couldn't I be allowed to do that in peace? You don't think of it when you look at a tempting spine in a libary or bookshop, but once you touch it you've had it. You're involved. It's worse than a woman. It's there in your body till the day you die and the harder you try and forget it the clearer it gets.

I tried aphorisms:

"If a typewriter could read what it had written it would sue God."

"He is another."

"The trouble with the biological clock is it has no alarm."

No good. They weren't even good enough to fit end to end and send in as a poem to the *T. L. S.* In the streets Rilke walked beside me and whispered in my ear. He said beautiful things but I preferred whatever nonsense I might have thought up for myself if he hadn't been there. In the mornings

club. He rattled on the door and even tried to push it open with his shoulder, but it wouldn't give and he wasn't one to be put off by a thing like that. "I got my rights, same as you," he said to the policeman who took him in. "Nobody going to shut a door in my face and get away with it."

"That's no reason to break it down," the policeman said, staring in wonder at Mobius.

"I got my rights," Mobius said.

"You mean they don't pay you?" the policeman asked.

"Sure they pay me," Mobius said.

"I mean in the holidays."

"Sure," Mobius said.

"Well then," the policeman said.

"I got my rights," Mobius said. "He employ me, no?"

"If it's a holiday why not go away somewhere?" the policeman said. "Give yourself a break."

"I doan want a break," Mobius said. "I want my rights."

"I don't know about that," the policeman said. "You've committed an offence against the law. I'm afraid I'll have to book you for it."

I drove my cream van through the suburbs of west London and that kept me sane. I screamed to a halt, leapt out with my neat parcel of clean nappies, swapped it for the dirty ones waiting on the doorstep in the identical plastic wrapper, "We clean dirt" in violet lettering. "Like hell you do," said a note pinned to the wrapper once. "Take it back and try again."

I took it back. They weren't my babies or my nappies and I didn't give a damn but my life was sliding off the rails and I didn't know what in God's good name to do about it.

"Why don't you come and see Mobius the stripper?" Jenny said. "It'll change your ideas. Give it a break and you'll all of a sudden see the light."

"That's fine," I said, "except I've been saying just that for the last fifteen years and I'm still in the dark."

"That's because you don't trust," Jenny said. "You've got no faith."

I had to admit she might be right. Unto those who have etcetera etcetera. But how does one contrive to have in the first place? There was a flaw somewhere but who was I to spot it?

"All right," Jenny said. "Make an effort. Anybody can write *something*. Just put something down and then you'll feel better and you can come out with me."

Something. Mobius the stripper was a genial man when in the bosom of his family. Etcetera. Etcetera etcetera. "Oh, fuck off," I said. "I told you I didn't want to be disturbed."

"You doan understand," Mobius said to the policeman. "This is my life. Just because he want to go to the fucking Bermudas doan mean I got to have my life ruined, eh?"

"Are you American or something?" the policeman asked, intrigued.

"You want to see my British passport?" Mobius said.

"Stay at home," the policeman advised him. "Take it easy for a few days. We'll look into the matter when the manager returns."

The next time Tony took his holiday he gave Mobius the key of the club, but without the audience it wasn't the same, and after a day or two he just stayed in his room the whole time except for the occasional stroll down to the park and back, heavily protected by his big coat and Russian fur hat. But he wasn't used to the streets, especially in the early evening when the tubes disgorged their contents, and it did him no good, no good at all. Inside the room he felt happier, but the break in the routine stopped him going to sleep and he spent the night with the light switched on. The bulb swung in the breeze and the voices dissolved him into a hundred parts. I first saw Mobius at a club in Buda. In Rio. In Albuquerque. A fine guy, Mobius. Is he? Oh yes, a fine guy. I remember going to see him and. I first heard of Mobius the stripper from a kid down on the front in Marseilles.

"It'll do you good," she said, standing her ground. The worse the language I used the more she responded. She had a lot of background to make up for. "Besides," she said, "it's all good experience."

"I don't need experience," I said. "I need peace and quiet. And, if I'm lucky, a bit of inspiration."

"He'd give you that," Jenny said. "Just to look at him is to feel inspired."

"What do you mean just to look at him?" I said. "What else are we expected to do?"

"Go to hell," Jenny said.

"Tomorrow," I said.

"You said that yesterday."

"Nevertheless," I said. "Tomorrow."

Jenny began to sob. It was impressive. I was impressed. "Just because I have big feet," she said, "you think you can push me around like that."

"Jenny," I said. "Please. I like big feet."

"You don't," she sobbed. "You find them ridiculous." When she sobbed she really sobbed. Nothing could stem the tide.

"In men," I said. "I find them ridiculous in men. In women I find them a sign of solidity. Stability."

"You're just laughing at me," she said. "You despise me because of my big feet."

M.E. the foot fetishist. He was a quiet man, scholarly and abstemious.

From a girl in Vienna. She was over there on a scholarship to study the cello and she. I met her in a restaurant. In a bar. She was blond. Dark. A sort of dark skin. Long fingers. A cellist's fingers. There's nobody like Mobius, she said.

Mobius smiled and listened to the voices. They came and went inside his head and if that's where they liked to be he had no objection. There was room and more. But he missed his sleep and he knew bronzed Tony had a point when he said: "Mobius, you look a sight."

That was the day the club re-opened. "Why don't you take a holiday same as everyone?" Tony said. "You must have a tidy bit stacked away by now."

"A holiday from what?" Mobius asked him.

"I don't know," Tony said. Mobius upset him, he didn't know which way to take him. Maybe one of these days he'd cease to pull them in and then he could get rid of him. "Just a holiday," he said. "From work."

"Look," Mobius said to him. "That the difference between us, Tony. You work and you spit on your work. But for me my work is my life."

"O.K.," Tony said. "I'm not complaining."

Everyone who ever met him said he was almost a saint. Not quite but almost. Yet deep inside there throbbed etcetera etcetera.

"But I don't," I said. "You've no idea what I feel about feet. I can't have enough of them. That's just what I like about you, Jenny. Your big feet."

She stopped crying. Just like that. "You're despicable," she said. "You're obscene."

"Look Jenny," I said. "I'll come with you. I'd love to see this chap. But tomorrow, O.K.?"

An incredible girl, Jenny. A great tactician. "You promise?" she said before I had time to draw breath.

"You know I'd love to go," I said. "I just don't want to be a drag on you. And if I'm sitting there thinking of my work all the time instead of being convivial and all I —"

"You'll see," Jenny said. "You'll love him. He's a lovely man."

Lovely or not I didn't think I could face them, either Jenny or her stripper, so I locked the door and went out into the park. Walking around there and kicking my feet in the leaves and seeing all those nannies and things kept the rest of it at bay. Had Rilke seen this nanny? Or Proust that child? Had Hopkins seen this tree, this leaf? So what did they have to teach me? They were talking about something else altogether. They were just about as much use to me as I was to them. And if it's eternity they wanted, why pick on me? There are plenty of other fools around for them to try their vampire tricks on. I can do without them, thank you very much. And

"Is there a holiday from life?" Mobius asked him. "Answer me that, Tony."

"For God's sake!" Tony said. "Can't you talk straight ever? You're not on stage now you know."

"You just answer me first," Mobius said. "Is there a holiday from life, Tony?"

"I don't know what you're talking about," Tony said, and when Mobius began to laugh, his great belly heaving, he added under his breath: "You shit."

At home he said to his wife: "That guy Mobius. He's a nut."

"Is he still drawing them in?" his wife asked as she passed him the toast.

"I don't know what they see in him," Tony said. "A fat bloody foreigner stripping in public. Downright obscene it is. And they roll in to see him. It makes you despair of the British public."

"Try the blackcurrant jam," his wife said. And then: "You hired him. You couldn't go on enough about him at first."

"It makes you sick," Tony said. He pulled the jam towards him. "Bloody perverted they are," he said. "Bloody twisted."

---

if it's this tree I want to see they only get in the way. And if it isn't what use am I to myself? Their trees they've already seen.

After a while, though, I felt the urge to get back in there and sit down in front of that blasted sheet of white paper. What use is this tree even if I do see it? No use to me or to the world. And even if it is, who says I *can* see it? When I sit down in front of that sheet of paper I have this feeling I want to tear right in and get everything down. Everything. And then what happens? He was a small man with a. I remember once asking Charles and. Gerald looked round. Christopher turned. When Jill saw. When Robert saw. Elizabeth Nutely was. Geraldine Bluett was. Hilary McPherson wasn't exactly the. Everything is the enemy of something, and when my pen touches the paper I go blank. Stories. Stories and stories. Mobius the stripper sat in his penthouse flat and filed his nails. Sat in his bare room and picked his nose. Stories and stories. Anyone can write them. All you need is a hide thick enough to save you from boring yourself sick. Jack turned suddenly and said. Count Frederick Prokovsky, a veteran of the Crimea. Horst Voss, the rowing coach. Peter Bender, overseer of a rubber plantation in. Etcetera etcetera. This one and this one and this one. When all the time it's crying out in me (Henry James was much obsessed by this but there the similarity between us ends, Good-bye, Henry James, good-bye, Virginia Woolf, good-bye, good-bye) crying out in me to say *everything, everything.*

They keep peacocks in the park. I don't know why. But they do. One

But when Mobius said it wasn't sexual it was metaphysical he had a point. Take off the layers and get down to the basics. One day the flesh would go and then the really basic would come to light. Mobius waited patiently for that day.

"You read Prust," he would say. "Nitch. Jennett. Those boys. See what they say. All the same. They know the truth. Is all a matter of stripping."

"You talk too much Moby," the girls said to him. "You're driving us crazy with all your talk."

"You gotta talk when you strip," Mobius explained to them. "You gotta get the audience involved."

"You can have music," the girls said. "Music's nice. Whoever heard of a stripper talking?"

"O.K.," Mobius admitted. "Perhaps I do like to talk. Like that I talk I feel my essential self emerging. Filling the room."

Outside the club, though, Mobius rarely opened his mouth. Certainly he never spoke to himself, and as for the voices, if they wanted to settle for a while inside his head, who was he to order them away? He sat on the bed and stared at the wall, eating bananas and dozing. I first saw. I first

---

of them was strutting about in the path in front of me. With big feet like Jenny. Who was I to say if big feet are attractive or not? And why ask me anyway? Think of the stripper Mobius with his nightly ritual, slowly getting down to the primal scene and after that what? Why do men do things like that and do they even know themselves etcetera etcetera? All the stories in the world but you've only got one body and who would ever exchange the former for the latter except every single second-rate writer who's ever lived? And they still live. Proliferate. And believe in themselves, what's more. Why then the daily anguish and the certainty that if I could only start the pen moving over that sheet of paper my life would alter, alter, as they say, beyond the bounds of recognition? Because I've read them all? The Van Gogh letters and the life of Rimbaud and the Hopkins Notebooks and the N. of M.L.B. Have they conned me even into this? It was possible. Everything is possible. "Tell me the truth," I said to the peacock with the big feet. "Go on, you bastard. Tell me the truth or just fuck off."

A woman with an unpleasant little runt of a white poodle backed away down an alley. "Don't you want the truth?" I asked her. She turned and beetled off towards the gates. "Lady!" I shouted after her. "Don't you want the truth?"

It's always the same. That's what gets me down. If I can say *anything* then why say anything? And yet everything's there to be said. Round and round. Mobius sat on his bed and ate one banana after another. But did he? Did he?

heard. I remember His Excellency telling me about Mobius the stripper. In Prague it was, that wonderful city. I was acting as private secretary to the Duke and had time on my hands. I was down and out in Paris and London. A girl called Bertha Pappenheim first mentioned Mobius to me. Not the famous Bertha Pappenheim, another.

Once or twice he would pull a chair up to the mirror on the dressing-table which stood inevitably in the bay window, and stare and stare into his own grey eyes. Then he would push the chair violently back and go over to the bed again.

"For what is life?" he would say. "Chance. And what is my life? The result of a million and one chances. But behind chance is truth. The whole problem is to get behind chance to the TRUTH!" That was when the jock strap came off and it brought the house down. But Mobius hadn't finished with them. Sitting cross-legged on the little wooden stage, staring down at more than his navel, he let them have the facts of life, straight from the chest:

"Beyond a man's chance is his necessity. But how many find? I ask you. You think this is seshual thing, but for why you come to see me? Because I give you the truth. Is a metaphysical something, is the truth. Is the

---

The bird had gone and I sat down on a bench and looked up at the sky through the trees. Jenny would have been and gone by now. Or perhaps not been at all. I sometimes wondered if Jenny knew quite as many people as she said she did. Wondered if perhaps there was only me she knew in the whole of London. Otherwise how to explain her persistence? Unless those feet of hers kept perpetually carrying her back over the ground they had once trodden. Myth. Ritual. An idea. More than an idea. A metaphor for life. "It is!" I shouted, suddenly understanding. "It is! It is! A metaphor for life!"

A little group of people were standing under the trees a little way along the path. One or two park wardens. A fat man with one of those Russian fur hats. My friend the poodle woman. I waved to them politely. They seemed to expect it. One of the wardens stepped forward and asked politely why I was chasing the peacocks and using bad language. The man was preposterous. Couldn't he see me sitting silent on the bench? I'd chased Pascal down a back alley once, but peacocks? What am I to peacocks or they to me? I said to the man.

"I saw you," the poodle woman said. "Chasin and abusin."

"Don't be more absurd than you can help," I said to her.

"Don't you dare talk to me like that, young man," she said.

What would Descartes have done in my place?

"Chasin peacocks and usin abusin language," she said.

necessity behind the chance. For each man is only one truth and so many in the world as each man is truths."

Mobius, staring into his own grey eyes in the little room in Notting Hill, occasionally sighed, and his gaze would wander over the expanse of flesh exposed and exposable. Sometimes his right hand would hover over the drawer of his dressing-table, where certain private possessions were kept, but would as quickly move away again. That was too easy. Yet if you talk of necessity how many versions are there? His hand hovered but the drawer remained unopened.

"These girls," he would say, "they excite you seshually. But once you seen me your whole life is change." He had a way of riding the laughter, silencing it. "For why? For you learn from me the difference between on one hand clockwork and on other hand necessity. Clockwork is clockwork. One. Two. In. Out. But Necessity she a goddess. She turn your muscles to water and your bones to oil. One day you meet her and you will see that Mobius is right."

He went home after that session more slowly than usual. If he was giving them the truth where was his truth? His heart heavy with the weight of

---

"Are you going to stand there and listen to this woman's grotesque accusations?" I asked them.

"It is an offence under the regulations," the warden said, "to chase the peacocks."

"But I love those birds," I said. "I love their big feet." For some reason I was still sitting there on that bench and they were standing grouped together under the trees staring in my direction. "What would I want to go chasing them for?" I said.

How could they be expected to understand? Or, understanding, to believe? Had I a beard like Tolstoy's? A moustache like Rilke's? "Gentlemen," I said. "I apologize. Good evening."

"He's goin away," the woman said. "You can't let him go away like that. He insulted and abused me."

"In that case, madam," the warden said, "I suggest you consult a lawyer." Bless his silver tongue. The first thing I'm going to do when success comes my way is give a donation to the wardens of the London parks.

I was shaken, though. And who wouldn't be? Examples of prejudice are always upsetting. Upsetting but exhilarating, too. They make you want to fight back. Something had happened down there inside me in those few minutes and now I couldn't wait to get back. This was it. After all those years.

There was no message from Jenny on the door. Not even a single word

years he opened the drawer and took out his little friend. Cupping it in his hand he felt its weight. There was no hesitation in his movements now and why should there be? If his life had a logic then this was it. The weight on his heart pressed him to this point. When you have stripped away everything the answer will be there, but if so, why wait? Easy to say it's too easy but why easier than waiting? As always, he did everything methodically. When he had found the right spot on his temple he straightened a little and waited for the steel to gather a little warmth from his flesh. "So I come to myself at last," Mobius said. "To the centre of myself." And he said: "Is my necessity and my truth. And is example to all." He stared into his own grey eyes and felt the coldness of the metal. His finger tightened on the trigger and the voices were there again. Cocking his head on one side and smiling, Mobius listened to what they had to say. He had time on his hands and to spare. Resting the barrel against his brow and smiling to himself in the mirror as the bulb swung in the breeze over his head, Mobius waited for them to finish.

---

like "Bastard!" or "Fuck you!" or any of the other affectionate little words we use when we are sufficiently intimate with a person. Well fuck her. I could do without her. Without them all. I was sitting at my desk with this white sheet of paper in front of me and suddenly it was easy. I bent over it, pen poised, wrist relaxed, the classic posture. It was all suddenly so easy I couldn't understand what had kept me back for so long.

I looked at the white page. At the pen. At my wrist. I began to laugh. You have to laugh at moments like that. It's the only thing to do. When I had finished laughing I got up and went to the window. What I couldn't work out was if I had actually believed it or really known all along that today was going to be no different from any other day. That between everything and something would once again fall the shadow. Leaving me with nothing. Nothing.

I turned round and sat down at the desk again. At least if Jenny had been there it wouldn't have been so bad. We could have talked. I looked at my watch. There was still time. She might still come.

I picked up the pen and wrote my name across the top of the sheet, for no reason that I could fathom. And then, suddenly, out of the blue it started to come. Perhaps it was only one story, arbitrary, incomplete, but suddenly I knew that it would make its own necessity and in the process give me back my lost self. Dear Jenny. Dear Mobius. Dear Peacock. "Gone out. Do not disturb." I scrawled on a sheet of paper, pinned it to the door and locked it. Then I sat down and began to write.

1. If you don't know what a Möbius strip is, demonstrate the form to yourself like this: cut an inch-wide strip of newspaper and form it into a single loop. Turn over one end of the strip so that there is a single twist in the loop. Tape or staple the ends together. Now begin drawing a line down the middle of the strip; keep going until you meet the beginning of your line. You will have proved that the strip of paper, which self-evidently has two sides, has only one; and that a line drawn in a single direction makes, in fact, a circle.

How does this concept of the Möbius strip relate to, illuminate, or reflect emotion and judgment in "Mobius the Stripper"? How, in particular, does it illuminate the final clause of Mobius' story, "Mobius waited for them to finish"?

2. Suppose you were told that the theme of this story is commitment to a profession; is the metaphysical need to strip; is the need for others; is self-regard; is self-expression; is truth; is fiction itself. How would you respond? Is it none, one, two, all of these?

3. Mobius can't stop talking. The writer can't start writing. How does this contrast (is it really a contrast?) contribute to the theme?

4. Mobius won't take a holiday; the writer won't leave his desk to go see Mobius. How does this parallel contribute to the theme?

5. On page 325 the writer says that NU-nap's motto, "We clean dirt," seemed to be the most beautiful combination of the most beautiful words in the language." Is this mere whimsy, or a clue to the story's meaning? Is it significant that Mobius insists, "You got to have order" (page 329)? How?

6. How do the writer's various mental images of Mobius relate to the story of Mobius as it is written?

7. The writer says that each of the authors in his head is "telling me the truth . . . but was it *my* truth . . ." (page 326). Mobius says, "The whole problem is to get behind chance to the TRUTH!" (page 335). If theme in fiction can be described as a speculation on a truth, is the theme of this story a speculation on speculation?

8. The writer wants to cut out the other authors he has read but that are "in your body till the day you die" (page 329). Mobius hears voices but says, "That too must be stripped off," (page 328). How do these feelings relate to each other and to the theme?

9. Nabokov's "Signs and Symbols" frustrates us at the resolution, but "Mobius the Stripper" frustrates us from the beginning. Did you read it page by page, or across the tops of the pages till you had finished Mobius' story, then across the lower portions until you had read the writer's? Which way should it be read? Would it be more satisfying if it were printed on a Möbius strip? How symbolic, revealing, and essential is the relation between the top and bottom of each page as the story is printed?

10. How is it significant to the total pattern of the story that Mobius' half is written in the third person, the writer's in the first? How much of "Mobius the Stripper" does the writer write?

The Babysitter

ROBERT COOVER

She arrives at 7:40, ten minutes late, but the children, Jimmy and Bitsy, are still eating supper, and their parents are not ready to go yet. From other rooms come the sounds of a baby screaming, water running, a television musical (no words: probably a dance number — patterns of gliding figures come to mind). Mrs. Tucker sweeps into the kitchen, fussing with her hair, and snatches a baby bottle full of milk out of a pan of warm water, rushes out again. "Harry!" she calls. "The babysitter's here already!"

That's My Desire? I'll Be Around? He smiles toothily, beckons faintly with his head, rubs his fast balding pate. Bewitched, maybe? Or, What's the Reason? He pulls on his shorts, gives his hips a slap. The baby goes silent in mid-scream. Isn't this the one who used their tub last time? Who's Sorry Now, that's it.

Jack is wandering around town, not knowing what to do. His girlfriend is babysitting at the Tuckers', and later, when she's got the kids in bed, maybe he'll drop over there. Sometimes he watches TV with her when she's babysitting, it's about the only chance he gets to make out a little since he doesn't own wheels, but they have to be careful because most people don't like their sitters to have boyfriends over. Just kissing her makes her nervous. She won't close her eyes because she has to be watching the door all the time. Married people really have it good, he thinks.

"Hi," the babysitter says to the children, and puts her books on top of the refrigerator. "What's for supper?" The little girl, Bitsy, only stares at her obliquely. She joins them at the end of the kitchen table. "I don't have to go to bed until nine," the boy announces flatly, and stuffs his mouth full of potato chips. The babysitter catches a glimpse of Mr. Tucker hurrying out of the bathroom in his underwear.

Her tummy. Under her arms. And her feet. Those are the best places. She'll spank him, she says sometimes. Let her.

That sweet odor that girls have. The softness of her blouse. He catches a glimpse of the gentle shadows amid her thighs, as she curls her legs up under her. He stares hard at her. He has a lot of meaning packed into that stare, but she's not even looking. She's popping her gum and watching television. She's sitting right there, inches away, soft, fragrant, and ready: but what's his next move? He notices his buddy Mark in the drugstore, playing the pinball machine, and joins him. "Hey, this mama's cold, Jack baby! She needs your touch!"

Mrs. Tucker appears at the kitchen doorway, holding a rolled-up diaper. "Now, don't just eat potato chips, Jimmy! See that he eats his hamburger, dear." She hurries away to the bathroom. The boy glares sullenly at the babysitter, silently daring her to carry out the order. "How about a little of that good hamburger now, Jimmy?" she says perfunctorily. He lets half of it drop to the floor. The baby is silent and a man is singing a love song on the TV. The children crunch chips.

He loves her. She loves him. They whirl airily, stirring a light breeze, through a magical landscape of rose and emerald and deep blue. Her light brown hair coils and wisps softly in the breeze, and the soft folds of her white gown tug at her body and then float away. He smiles in a pulsing crescendo of sincerity and song.

"You mean she's alone?" Mark asks. "Well, there's two or three kids," Jack says. He slides the coin in. There's a rumble of steel balls tumbling, lining up. He pushes a plunger with his thumb, and one ball pops up in place, hard and glittering with promise. His stare? to say he loves her. That he cares for her and would protect her, would shield her, if need be, with his own body. Grinning, he bends over the ball to take careful aim: he and Mark have studied this machine and have it figured out, but still it's not that easy to beat.

On the drive to the party, his mind is partly on the girl, partly on his own high-school days, long past. Sitting at the end of the kitchen table there with his children, she had seemed to be self-consciously arching her back, jutting her pert breasts, twitching her thighs: and for whom if not for him? So she'd seen him coming out of there, after all. He smiles. Yet what could he ever do about it? Those good times are gone, old man. He glances over at his wife, who, readjusting a garter, asks: "What do you think of our babysitter?"

He loves her. She loves him. And then the babies come. And dirty diapers and one goddamn meal after another. Dishes. Noise. Clutter. And fat. Not just tight, her girdle actually hurts. Somewhere recently she's read about women getting heart attacks or cancer or something from too-tight girdles. Dolly pulls the car door shut with a grunt, strangely irritated, not knowing why. Party mood. Why is her husband humming, "Who's Sorry Now?" Pulling out of the drive, she glances back at the lighted kitchen window. "What do you think of our babysitter?" she asks. While her husband stumbles all over himself trying to answer, she pulls a stocking tight, biting deeper with the garters.

"Stop it!" she laughs. Bitsy is pulling on her skirt and he is tickling her in the ribs. "Jimmy! Don't!" But she is laughing too much to stop him. He leaps on her, wrapping his legs around her waist, and they all fall to the carpet in front of the TV, where just now a man in a tuxedo and a little girl in a flouncy white dress are doing a tapdance together. The babysitter's blouse is pulling out of her skirt, showing a patch of bare tummy: the target. "I'll spank!"

Jack pushes the plunger, thrusting up a steel ball, and bends studiously over the machine. "You getting any off her?" Mark asks, and clears his throat, flicks ash from his cigarette. "Well, not exactly, not yet," Jack says, grinning awkwardly, but trying to suggest more than he admits to, and fires. He heaves his weight gently against the machine as the ball bounds off a rubber bumper. He can feel her warming up under his hands, the flippers suddenly coming alive, delicate rapid-fire patterns emerging in the flashing of the lights. 1000 WHEN LIT: now! "Got my hand on it, that's about all." Mark glances up from the machine, cigarette dangling from his lip. "Maybe you need some help," he suggests with a wry one-sided grin. "Like maybe together, man, we could do it."

She likes the big tub. She uses the Tuckers' bath salts, and loves to sink into the hot fragrant suds. She can stretch out, submerged, up to her chin. It gives her a good sleepy tingly feeling.

"What do you think of our babysitter?" Dolly asks, adjusting a garter. "Oh, I hardly noticed," he says. "Cute girl. She seems to get along fine with the kids. Why?" "I don't know." His wife tugs her skirt down, glances at a lighted window they are passing, adding: "I'm not sure I trust her completely, that's all. With the baby, I mean. She seems a little careless. And the other time, I'm almost sure she had a boyfriend over." He grins, claps one hand on his wife's broad gartered thigh. "What's wrong with that?" he asks. Still in anklets, too. Bare thighs, no girdles, nothing up there but a flimsy pair of panties and soft adolescent flesh. He's flooded with vague remembrances of football rallies and movie balconies.

How tiny and rubbery it is! she thinks, soaping between the boy's legs, giving him his bath. Just a funny jiggly little thing that looks like it shouldn't even be there at all. Is that what all the songs are about?

Jack watches Mark lunge and twist against the machine. Got her running now, racked them up. He's not too excited about the idea of Mark fooling around with his girlfriend, but Mark's a cooler operator than he is, and maybe, doing it together this once, he'd get over his own timidity. And if she didn't like it, there were other girls around. If Mark went too far, he could cut him off too. He feels his shoulders tense: enough's enough, man . . . but sees the flesh, too. "Maybe I'll call her later," he says.

"Hey, Harry! Dolly! Glad you could make it!" "I hope we're not late." "No, no, you're one of the first, come on in! By golly, Dolly, you're looking younger every day! How do you do it? Give my wife your secret, will you?" He pats her on her girdled bottom behind Mr. Tucker's back, leads them in for drinks.

8:00. The babysitter runs water in the tub, combs her hair in front of the bathroom mirror. There's a western on television, so she lets Jimmy watch it while she gives Bitsy her bath. But Bitsy doesn't want a bath. She's angry and crying because she has to be first. The babysitter tells her if she'll take her bath quickly, she'll let her watch television while Jimmy takes his bath, but it does no good. The little girl fights to get out of the bathroom, and the babysitter has to squat with her back against the door and forcibly undress the child. There are better places to babysit. Both children mind badly, and then, sooner or later, the baby is sure to wake up for a diaper change and more bottle. The Tuckers do have a good color TV, though, and she hopes things will be settled down enough to catch the 8:30 program. She thrusts the child into the tub, but she's still screaming and thrashing around. "Stop it now, Bitsy, or you'll wake the baby!" "I have to go potty!" the child wails, switching tactics. The babysitter sighs, lifts the girl out of the tub and onto the toilet, getting her skirt and blouse all wet in the process. She glances at herself in the mirror. Before she knows it, the girl is off the seat and out of the bathroom. "Bitsy! Come back here!"

"Okay, that's enough!" Her skirt is ripped and she's flushed and crying. "Who says?" "I do, man!" The bastard goes for her, but she tackles him. They roll and tumble. Tables tip, lights topple, the TV crashes to the floor. He slams a hard right to the guy's gut, clips his chin with a rolling left.

"We hope it's a girl." That's hardly surprising, since they already have four boys. Dolly congratulates the woman like everybody else, but she doesn't envy her, not a bit. That's all she needs about now. She stares across the room at Harry, who is slapping backs and getting loud, as usual. He's spreading out through the middle, so why the hell does he have to complain about her all the time? "Dolly, you're looking younger every day!" was the nice greeting she got tonight. "What's your secret?" And Harry: "It's all those calories. She's getting back her baby fat." "Haw haw! Harry, have a heart!"

"Get her feet" he hollers at Bitsy, his fingers in her ribs, running over her naked tummy, tangling in the underbrush of straps and strange clothing. "Get her shoes off!" He holds her pinned by pressing his head against her soft chest. "No! No, Jimmy! Bitsy, stop!" But though she kicks and twists and rolls around, she doesn't get up, she can't get up, she's laughing too hard, and the shoes come off, and he grabs a stockinged foot and scratches the sole ruthlessly, and she raises up her legs, trying to pitch him off, she's wild, boy, but he hangs on, and she's laughing, and on the screen there's a rattle of hooves, and he and Bitsy are rolling around and around on the floor in a crazy rodeo of long bucking legs.

He slips the coin in. There's a metallic fall and a sharp click as the dial tone begins. "I hope the Tuckers have gone," he says. "Don't worry, they're at our place," Mark says. "They're always the first ones to come and the last to go home. My old man's always bitching about them." Jack laughs nervously and dials the number. "Tell her we're coming over to protect her from getting raped," Mark suggests, and lights a cigarette. Jack grins, leaning casually against the door jamb of the phonebooth, chewing gum, one hand in his pocket. He's really pretty uneasy, though. He has the feeling he's somehow messing up a good thing.

Bitsy runs naked into the livingroom, keeping a hassock between herself and the babysitter. "Bitsy . . . !" the babysitter threatens. Artifical reds and greens and purples flicker over the child's wet body, as hooves clatter, guns crackle, and stagecoach wheels thunder over rutted terrain. "Get outa the way, Bitsy!" the boy complains. "I can't see!" Bitsy streaks past and the babysitter chases, cornering the girl in the back bedroom. Bitsy throws something that hits her softly in the face: a pair of men's undershorts. She grabs the girl scampering by, carries her struggling to the bathroom, and with a smart crack on her glistening bottom, pops her back into the tub. In spite, Bitsy peepees in the bathwater.

Mr. Tucker stirs a little water into his bourbon and kids with his host and another man, just arrived, about their golf games. They set up a match for the weekend, a threesome looking for a fourth. Holding his drink in his right hand, Mr. Tucker swings his left through the motion of a tee-shot. "You'll have to give me a stroke a hole," he says. "I'll give you a stroke!" says his host: "Bend over!" Laughing, the other man asks: "Where's your boy Mark tonight?" "I don't know," replies the host, gathering up a trayful of drinks. Then he adds in a low growl: "Out chasing tail probably." They chuckle loosely at that, then shrug in commiseration and return to the livingroom to join their women.

Shades pulled. Door locked. Watching the TV. Under a blanket maybe. Yes, that's right, under a blanket. Her eyes close when he kisses her. Her breasts, under both their hands, are soft and yielding.

A hard blow to the belly. The face. The dark beardy one staggers, the lean-jawed sheriff moves in, but gets a spurred boot in his face. The dark one hurls himself forward, drives his shoulder into the sheriff's hard midriff, her own tummy tightens, withstands, as the sheriff smashes the dark man's nose, slams him up against a wall, slugs him again! and again! The dark man grunts rhythmically, backs off, then plunges suicidally forward — her own knees draw up protectively — the sheriff staggers! caught low! but instead of following through, the other man steps back — a pistol! the dark one has a pistol! the sheriff draws! shoots from the hip! explosions! she clutches her hands between her thighs — no! the sheriff spins! wounded! the dark man hesitates, aims, her legs stiffen toward the set, the sheriff rolls desperately in the straw, fires: dead! the dark man is dead! groans, crumples, his pistol drooping in his collapsing hand, dropping, he drops. The sheriff, spent, nicked, watches weakly from the floor where he lies. Oh, to be whole! to be good and strong and right! to embrace and be embraced by harmony and wholeness! The sheriff, drawing himself painfully up on one elbow, rubs his bruised mouth with the back of his other hand.

"Well, we just sorta thought we'd drop over," he says, and winks broadly at Mark. "Who's we?" "Oh, me and Mark here." "Tell her, good thing like her, gotta pass it around," whispers Mark, dragging on his smoke, then flicking the butt over under the pinball machine. "What's that?" she asks. "Oh, Mark and I were just saying, like two's company, three's an orgy," Jack says, and winks again. She giggles. "Oh Jack!" Behind her, he can hear shouts and gunfire. "Well, okay, for just a little while, if you'll both be good." Way to go, man.

Probably some damn kid over there right now. Wrestling around on the couch in front of his TV. Maybe he should drop back to the house. Just to check. None of that stuff, she was there to do a job! Park the car a couple doors down, slip in the front door before she knows it. He sees the disarray of clothing, the young thighs exposed to the flickering television light, hears his baby crying. "Hey, what's going on here! Get outa here, son, before I call the police!" Of course, they haven't really been doing anything. They probably don't even know how. He stares benignly down upon the girl, her skirt rumpled loosely around her thighs. Flushed, frightened, yet excited, she stares back at him. He smiles. His finger touches a knee, approaches the hem. Another couple arrives. Filling up here with people. He wouldn't be missed. Just slip out, stop back casually to pick up something or other he forgot, never mind what. He remembers that the other time they had this babysitter, she took a bath in their house. She had a date afterwards, and she'd come from cheerleading practice or something. Aspirin maybe. Just drop quietly and casually into the bathroom to pick up some aspirin. "Oh, excuse me, dear! I only . . . !" She gazes back at him, astonished, yet strangely moved. Her soft wet breasts rise and fall in the water, and her tummy looks pale and ripply. He recalls that her pubic hairs, left in the tub, were brown. Light brown.

She's no more than stepped into the tub for a quick bath, when Jimmy announces from outside the door that he has to go to the bathroom. She sighs: just an excuse, she knows. "You'll have to wait." The little nuisance. "I can't wait." "Okay, then come ahead, but I'm taking a bath." She supposes that will stop him, but it doesn't. In he comes. She slides down into the suds until she's eyelevel with the edge of the tub. He hesitates. "Go ahead, if you have to," she says, a little awkwardly, "but I'm not getting out." "Don't look," he says. She: "I will if I want to."

She's crying. Mark is rubbing his jaw where he's just slugged him. A lamp lies shattered. "Enough's enough, Mark! Now get outa here!" Her skirt is ripped to the waist, her bare hip bruised. Her panties lie on the floor like a broken balloon. Later, he'll wash her wounds, help her dress, he'll take care of her. Pity washes through him, giving him a sudden hard-on. Mark laughs at it, pointing. Jack crouches, waiting, ready for anything.

Laughing, they roll and tumble. Their little hands are all over her, digging and pinching. She struggles to her hands and knees, but Bitsy leaps astride her neck, bowing her head to the carpet. "Spank her, Jimmy!" His swats sting: is her skirt up? The phone rings. "The cavalry to the rescue!" she laughs, and throws them off to go answer.

Kissing Mark, her eyes closed, her hips nudge toward Jack. He stares at the TV screen, unsure of himself, one hand slipping cautiously under her skirt. Her hand touches his arm as though to resist, then brushes on by to rub his leg. This blanket they're under was a good idea. "Hi! This is Jack!"

Bitsy's out and the water's running. "Come on, Jimmy, your turn!" Last time, he told her he took his own baths, but she came in anyway. "I'm not gonna take a bath," he announces, eyes glued on the set. He readies for the struggle. "But I've already run your water. Come on, Jimmy, please!" He shakes his head. She can't make him, he's sure he's as strong as she is. She sighs. "Well, it's up to you. I'll use the water myself then," she says. He waits until he's pretty sure she's not going to change her mind, then sneaks in and peeks through the keyhole in the bathroom door: just in time to see her big bottom as she bends over to stir in the bubblebath. Then she disappears. Trying to see as far down as the keyhole will allow, he bumps his head on the knob. "Jimmy, is that you?" "I — I have to go to the bathroom!" he stammers.

Not actually in the tub, just getting in. One foot on the mat, the other in the water. Bent over slightly, buttocks flexed, teats swaying, holding on to the edge of the tub. "Oh, excuse me! I only wanted. . . . !" He passes over her astonishment, the awkward excuses, moves quickly to the part where he reaches out to — "What on earth are you doing, Harry?" his wife asks, staring at his hand. His host, passing, laughs. "He's practicing his swing for Sunday, Dolly, but it's not going to do him a damn bit of good!" Mr. Tucker laughs, sweeps his right hand on through the air as though lifting a seven-iron shot onto the green. He makes a *dok!* sound with his tongue. "In there!"

"No, Jack, I don't think you'd better." "Well, we just called, we just, uh, thought we'd, you know, stop by for a minute, watch television for thirty minutes, or, or something." "Who's we?" "Well, Mark's here, I'm with him, and he said he'd like to, you know, like if it's all right, just — " "Well, it's *not* all right. The Tuckers said no." "Yeah, but if we only — " "And they seemed awfully suspicious about last time." "Why? We didn't — I mean, I just thought — " "No, Jack, and that's period." She hangs up. She returns to the TV, but the commercial is on. Anyway, she's missed most of the show. She decides maybe she'll take a quick bath. Jack might come by anyway, it'd make her mad, that'd be the end as far as he was concerned, but if he should, she doesn't want to be all sweaty. And besides, she likes the big tub the Tuckers have.

He is self-conscious and stands with his back to her, his little neck flushed. It takes him forever to get started, and when it finally does come, it's just a tiny trickle. "See, it was just an excuse," she scolds, but she's giggling inwardly at the boy's embarrassment. "You're just a nuisance, Jimmy." At the door, his hand on the knob, he hesitates, staring timidly down on his shoes. "Jimmy?" She peeks at him over the edge of the tub, trying to keep a straight face, as he sneaks a nervous glance back over his shoulder. "As long as you bothered me," she says, "you might as well soap my back."

"The aspirin . . ." They embrace. She huddles in his arms like a child. Lovingly, paternally, knowledgeably, he wraps her nakedness. How compact, how tight and small her body is! Kissing her ear, he stares down past her rump at the still clear water. "I'll join you," he whispers hoarsely.

She picks up the shorts Bitsy threw at her. Men's underwear. She holds them in front of her, looks at herself in the bedroom mirror. About twenty sizes too big for her, of course. She runs her hand inside the opening in front, pulls out her thumb. How funny it must feel!

"Well, man, I say we just go rape her," Mark says flatly, and swings his weight against the pinball machine. "Uff! Ahh! Get in there, you mother! Look at that! Hah! Man, I'm gonna turn this baby over!" Jack is embarrassed about the phone conversation. Mark just snorted in disgust when he hung up. He cracks down hard on his gum, angry that he's such a chicken. "Well, I'm game if you are," he says coldly.

8:30 "Okay, come on, Jimmy, it's time." He ignores her. The western gives way to a spy show. Bitsy, in pajamas, pads into the livingroom. "No, Bitsy, it's time to go to bed." "You said I could watch!" the girl whines, and starts to throw another tantrum. "But you were too slow and it's late. Jimmy, you get in that bathroom, and right now!" Jimmy stares sullenly at the set, unmoving. The babysitter tries to catch the opening scene of the television program so she can follow it later, since Jimmy gives himself his own baths. When the commercial interrupts, she turns off the sound, stands in front of the screen. "Okay, into the tub, Jimmy Tucker, or I'll take you in there and give you your bath myself!" "Just try it," he says, "and see what happens."

They stand outside, in the dark, crouched in the bushes, peeking in. She's on the floor, playing with the kids. Too early. They seem to be tickling her. She gets to her hands and knees, but the little girl leaps on her head, pressing her face to the floor. There's an obvious target, and the little boy proceeds to beat on it. "Hey, look at that kid go!" whispers Mark, laughing and snapping his fingers softly. Jack feels uneasy out here. Too many neighbors, too many cars going by, too many people in the world. That little boy in there is one up on him, though: he's never thought about tickling her as a starter.

His little hand, clutching the bar of soap, lathers shyly a narrow space between her shoulderblades. She is doubled forward against her knees, buried in rich suds, peeking at him over the edge of her shoulder. The soap slithers out of his grip and plunks into the water. "I . . . I dropped the soap," he whispers. She: "Find it."

"I dream of Jeannie with the light brown pubic hair!" "Harry! Stop that! You're drunk!" But they're laughing, they're all laughing, damn! he's feeling pretty goddamn good at that, and now he just knows he needs that aspirin. Watching her there, her thighs spread for him, on the couch, in the tub, hell, on the kitchen table for that matter, he tees off on Number Nine, and — whap! — swats his host's wife on the bottom. "Hole in one!" he shouts. "Harry!" Why can't his goddamn wife Dolly ever get happy-drunk instead of sour-drunk all the time? "Gonna be tough Sunday, old buddy!" "You're pretty tough right now, Harry," says his host.

The babysitter lunges forward, grabs the boy by the arms and hauls him off the couch, pulling two cushions with him, and drags him toward the bathroom. He lashes out, knocking over an endtable full of magazines and ashtrays. "You leave my brother alone!" Bitsy cries and grabs the sitter around the waist. Jimmy jumps on her and down they all go. On the silent screen, there's a fade-in to a dark passageway in an old apartment building in some foreign country. She kicks out and somebody falls between her legs. Somebody else is sitting on her face. "Jimmy! Stop that!" the babysitter laughs, her voice muffled.

She's watching television. All alone. It seems like a good time to go in. Just remember: really, no matter what she says, she wants it. They're standing in the bushes, trying to get up the nerve. "We'll tell her to be good," Mark whispers, "and if she's not good, we'll spank her." Jack giggles softly, but his knees are weak. She stands. They freeze. She looks right at them. "She can't see us." Mark whispers tensely. "Is she coming out?" "No," says Mark, "She's going into — that must be the bathroom!" Jack takes a deep breath, his heart pounding. "Hey, is there a window back there?" Mark asks.

The phone rings. She leaves the tub, wrapped in a towel. Bitsy gives a tug on the towel. "Hey, Jimmy, get the towel!" she squeals. "Now stop that, Bitsy!" the babysitter hisses, but too late: with one hand on the phone, the other isn't enough to hang on to the towel. Her sudden nakedness awes them and it takes them a moment to remember about tickling her. By then, she's in the towel again. "I hope you got a good look," she says angrily. She feels chilled and oddly a little frightened. "Hello?" No answer. She glances at the window — is somebody out there? Something, she saw something, and a rustling — footsteps?

"Okay, I don't care, Jimmy, don't take a bath," she says irritably. Her blouse is pulled out and wrinkled, her hair is all mussed, and she feels sweaty. There's about a million things she'd rather be doing than babysitting with these two. Three: at least the baby's sleeping. She knocks on the overturned endtable for luck, rights it, replaces the magazines and ashtrays. The one thing that really makes her sick is a dirty diaper. "Just go on to bed." "I don't have to go to bed until nine," he reminds her. Really, she couldn't care less. She turns up the volume on the TV, settles down on the couch, poking her blouse back into her skirt, pushing her hair out of her eyes. Jimmy and Bitsy watch from the floor. Maybe, once they're in bed, she'll take a quick bath. She wishes Jack would come by. The man, no doubt the spy, is following a woman, but she doesn't know why. The woman passes another man. Something seems to happen, but it's not clear what. She's probably already missed too much. The phone rings.

Mark is kissing her. Jack is under the blanket, easing her panties down over her squirming hips. Her hand is in his pants, pulling it out, pulling it toward her, pulling it hard. She knew just where it was! Mark is stripping, too. God, it's really happening! he thinks with a kind of pious joy, and notices the open door. "Hey! What's going on here?"

He soaps her back, smooth and slippery under his hand. She is doubled over, against her knees, between his legs. Her light brown hair, reaching to her gleaming shoulders, is wet at the edges. The soap slips, falls between her legs. He fishes for it, finds it, slips it behind him. "Help me find it," he whispers in her ear. "Sure Harry," says his host, going around behind him. "What'd you lose?"

Soon be nine, time to pack the kids off to bed. She clears the table, dumps paper plates and leftover hamburgers into the garbage, puts glasses and silverware into the sink, and the mayonnaise, mustard, and ketchup in the refrigerator. Neither child has eaten much supper finally, mostly potato chips and ice cream, but it's really not her problem. She glances at the books on the refrigerator. Not much chance she'll get to them, she's already pretty worn out. Maybe she'd feel better if she had a quick bath. She runs water into the tub, tosses in bubblebath salts, undresses. Before pushing down her panties, she stares for a moment at the smooth silken panel across her tummy, fingers the place where the opening would be if there were one. Then she steps quickly out of them, feeling somehow ashamed, unhooks her brassiere. She weighs her breasts in the palms of her hands, watching herself in the bathroom mirror, where, in the open window behind her, she sees a face. She screams.

She screams: "Jimmy! Give me that!" "What's the matter?" asks Jack on the other end. "Jimmy! Give me my towel! Right now!" "Hello? Hey, are you still there?" "I'm sorry, Jack," she says, panting. "You caught me in the tub. I'm just wrapped in a towel and these silly kids grabbed it away!" "Gee, I wish I'd been there!" "Jack — !" "To protect you, I mean." "Oh, sure," she says, giggling. "Well, what do you think, can I come over and watch TV with you?" "Well, not right this minute," she says. He laughs lightly. He feels very cool. "Jack?" "Yeah?" "Jack, I . . . I think there's somebody outside the window!"

She carries him, fighting all the way, to the tub, Bitsy pummeling her in the back and kicking her ankles. She can't hang on to him and undress him at the same time. "I'll throw you in, clothes and all, Jimmy Tucker!" she gasps. "You better not!" he cries. She sits on the toilet seat, locks her legs around him, whips his shirt up over his head before he knows what's happening. The pants are easier. Like all little boys his age, he has almost no hips at all. He hangs on desperately to his underpants, but when she succeeds in snapping these down out of his grip, too, he gives up, starts to bawl, and beats her wildly in the face with his fists. She ducks her head, laughing hysterically, oddly entranced by the spectacle of that pale little thing down there, bobbing and bouncing rubberlike about the boy's helpless fury and anguish.

"Aspirin? Whaddaya want aspirin for, Harry! I'm sure they got aspirin here, if you — " "Did I say aspirin? I meant uh, my glasses. And, you know, I thought, well, I'd sorta check to see if everything was okay at home." Why the hell is it his mouth feels like it's got about six sets of teeth packed in there, and a tongue the size of that liverwurst his host's wife is passing around? "Whaddaya want your glasses for, Harry? I don't understand you at all!" "Aw, well, honey, I was feeling kind of dizzy or something, and I thought — " "Dizzy is right. If you want to check on the kids, why don't you just call on the phone?"

They can tell she's naked and about to get into the tub, but the bathroom window is frosted glass, and they can't see anything clearly. "I got an idea," Mark whispers. "One of us goes and calls her on the phone, and the other watches when she comes out." "Okay, but who calls?" "Both of us, we'll do it twice. Or more."

Down forbidden alleys. Into secret passageways. Unlocking the world's terrible secrets. Sudden shocks: a trapdoor! a fall! or the stunning report of a rifle shot, the *whaaii-ii-ing!* of the bullet biting concrete by your ear! Careful! Then edge forward once more, avoiding the light, inch at a time, now a quick dash for an open doorway — *look out!* there's a knife! a struggle!

no! the long blade glistens! jerks! thrusts! *stabbed!* No, no, it missed! The assailant's down, yes! the spy's on top, pinning him, a terrific thrashing about, the spy rips off the assailant's mask: *a woman!*

Fumbling behind her, she finds it, wraps her hand around it, tugs. "Oh!" she gasps, pulling her hand back quickly, her ears turning crimson. "I . . . I thought it was the soap!" He squeezes her close between his thighs, pulls her back toward him, one hand sliding down her tummy between her legs. I Dream of Jeannie — "I have to go to the bathroom!" says someone outside the door.

She's combing her hair in the bathroom when the phone rings. She hurries to answer it before it wakes the baby. "Hello, Tuckers." There's no answer. "Hello?" A soft click. Strange. She feels suddenly alone in the big house, and goes in to watch TV with the children.

"Stop it!" she screams, "Please stop!" She's on her hands and knees, trying to get up, but they're too strong for her. Mark holds her head down. "Now, baby, we're gonna teach you how to be a nice girl," he says coldly, and nods at Jack. When she's doubled over like that, her skirt rides up her thighs to the leg bands of her panties. "C'mon, man, go! This baby's cold! She needs your touch!"

Parks the car a couple blocks away. Slips up to the house, glances in his window. Just like he's expected. Her blouse is off and the kid's shirt is unbuttoned. He watches, while slowly, clumsily, childishly, they fumble with each other's clothes. My God, it takes them forever. "Some party!" "You said it!" When they're more or less naked, he walks in. "Hey! What's going on here?" They go white as blue cheese. Haw haw! "What's the little thing you got sticking out there, boy?" "Harry, behave yourself!" No, he doesn't let the kid get dressed, he sends him home bareassed. "Bareassed!" He drinks to that. "Promises, promises," says his host's wife. "I'll mail you your clothes, son!" He gazes down on the naked little girl on his couch. "Looks like you and me, we got a little secret to keep, honey," he says coolly. "Less you wanna go home the same way your boyfriend did!" He chuckles at his easy wit, leans down over her, and unbuckles his belt. "Might as well make it two secrets, right?" "What in God's name are you talking about, Harry?" He staggers out of there, drink in hand, and goes to look for his car.

"Hey! What's going on here?" They huddle half-naked under the blanket, caught utterly unawares. On television: the clickety-click of frightened running feet on foreign pavements. Jack is fumbling for his shorts, tangled somehow around his ankles. The blanket is snatched away. "On your feet there!" Mr. Tucker, Mrs. Tucker, and Mark's mom and dad, the police, the neighbors, everybody comes crowding in. Hopelessly, he has a terrific erection. So hard it hurts. Everybody stares down at it.

Bitsy's sleeping on the floor. The babysitter is taking a bath. For more than an hour now, he'd had to use the bathroom. He doesn't know how much longer he can wait. Finally, he goes to knock on the bathroom door. "I have to use the bathroom." "Well, come ahead, if you have to." "Not while you're in there." She sighs loudly. "Okay, okay, just a minute," she says, "but you're a real nuisance, Jimmy!" He's holding on, pinching it as tight as he can. *"Hurry!"* He holds his breath, squeezing shut his eyes. No. Too late. At last, she opens the door. "Jimmy!" "I *told* you to hurry!" he sobs. She drags him into the bathroom and pulls his pants down.

He arrives just in time to see her emerge from the bathroom, wrapped in a towel, to answer the phone. His two kids sneak up behind her and pull the towel away. She's trying to hang on to the phone and get the towel back at the same time. It's quite a picture. She's got a sweet ass. Standing there in the bushes, pawing himself with one hand, he lifts his glass with the other and toasts her sweet ass, which his son now swats. Haw haw, maybe that boy's gonna shape up, after all.

They're in the bushes, arguing about their next move, when she comes out of the bathroom, wrapped in a towel. They can hear the baby crying. Then it stops. They see her running, naked, back to the bathroom like she's scared or something. "I'm going in after her, man, whether you're with me or not!" Mark whispers, and he starts out of the bushes. But just then, a light comes sweeping up through the yard, as a car swings in the drive. They hit the dirt, hearts pounding. "Is it the cops?" "I don't know!" "Do you think they saw us?" "Sshh!" A man comes staggering up the walk from the drive, a drink in his hand, stumbles on in the kitchen door and then straight into the bathroom. "It's Mr. Tucker!" Mark whispers. A scream. "Let's get outa here, man!"

9:00. Having missed most of the spy show anyway and having little else to do, the babysitter has washed the dishes and cleaned the kitchen up a little. The books on the refrigerator remind her of her better intentions, but she decides that first she'll see what's next on TV. In the livingroom, she finds little Bitsy sound asleep on the floor. She lifts her gently, carries her into her bed, and tucks her in. "Okay, Jimmy, it's nine o'clock, I've let you stay up, now be a good boy." Sullenly, his sleepy eyes glued still to the set, the boy backs out of the room toward his bedroom. A drama comes on. She switches channels. A ballgame and a murder mystery. She switches back to the drama. It's a love story of some kind. A man married to an aging invalid wife, but in love with a younger girl. "Use the bathroom and brush your teeth before going to bed, Jimmy!" she calls, but as quickly regrets it, for she hears the baby stir in its crib.

Two of them are talking about mothers they've salted away in rest homes. Oh boy, that's just wonderful, this is one helluva party. She leaves them to use the john, takes advantage of the retreat to ease her girdle down awhile, get a few good deep breaths. She has this picture of her three kids carting her off to a rest home. In a wheelbarrow. That sure is something to look forward to, all right. When she pulls her girdle back up, she can't seem to squeeze into it. The host looks in. "Hey, Dolly, are you all right?" "Yeah, I just can't get into my damn girdle, that's all." "Here, let me help."

She pulls them on, over her own, standing in front of the bedroom mirror, holding her skirt bundled up around the waist. About twenty sizes too big for her, of course. She pulls them tight from behind, runs her hand inside the opening in front, pulls out her thumb. "And what a good boy am I!" She giggles: how funny it must feel! Then, in the mirror, she sees him: in the doorway behind her, sullenly watching. "Jimmy! You're supposed to be in bed!" "Those are my daddy's!" the boy says. "I'm gonna tell!"

"Jimmy!" She drags him into the bathroom and pulls his pants down. "Even your shoes are wet! Get them off!" She soaps up a warm washcloth she's had with her in the bathtub, scrubs him from the waist down with it. Bitsy stands in the doorway, staring. "Get out! Get out!" the boy screams at his sister. "Go back to bed, Bitsy. It's just an accident." "Get out!" The baby wakes and starts to howl.

The young lover feels sorry for her rival, the invalid wife; she believes the man has a duty toward the poor woman and insists she is willing to wait. But the man argues that he also has a duty toward himself: his life, too, is short, and he could not love his wife now even were she well. He embraces the young girl feverishly; she twists away in anguish. The door opens. They stand there grinning, looking devilish, but pretty silly at the same time. "Jack! I thought I told you not to come!" She's angry, but she's also glad in a way: she was beginning to feel a little too alone in the big house, with the children all sleeping. She should have taken that bath, after all. "We just came by to see if you were being a good girl," Jack says and blushes. The boys glance at each other nervously.

She's just sunk down into the tubful of warm fragrant suds, ready for a nice long soaking, when the phone rings. Wrapping a towel around her, she goes to answer: no one there. But now the baby's awake and bawling. She wonders if that's Jack bothering her all the time. If it is, brother, that's the end. Maybe it's the end anyway. She tries to calm the baby with the half-empty bottle, not wanting to change it until she's finished her bath. The bathroom's where the diapers go dirty, and they make it stink to high heaven. "Shush, shush!" she whispers, rocking the crib. The towel slips away, leaving an airy empty tingle up and down her backside. Even before she stoops for the towel, even before she turns around, she knows there's somebody behind her.

"We just came by to see if you were being a good girl," Jack says, grinning down at her. She's flushed and silent, her mouth half open. "Lean over," says Mark amiably. "We'll soap your back, as long as we're here." But she just huddles there, down in the suds, staring up at them with big eyes.

"Hey! What's going on here?" It's Mr. Tucker, stumbling through the door with a drink in his hand. She looks up from the TV. "What's the matter, Mr. Tucker?" "Oh, uh, I'm sorry, I got lost — no, I mean, I had to get some aspirin. Excuse me!" And he rushes past her into the bathroom, caroming off the livingroom door jamb on the way. The baby awakes.

"Okay, get off her, Mr. Tucker!" "Jack!" she cries, "what are *you* doing here?" He stares hard at them a moment: so that's where it goes. Then, as Mr. Tucker swings heavily off, he leans into the bastard with a hard right to the belly. Next thing he knows, though, he's got a face full of an old man's fist. He's not sure, as the lights go out, if that's his girlfriend screaming or the baby . . .

Her host pushes down on her fat fanny and tugs with all his might on her girdle, while she bawls on his shoulder: "I don't *wanna* go to a rest home!" "Now, now, take it easy, Dolly, nobody's gonna make you — " "Ouch! Hey, you're hurting!" "You should buy a bigger girdle, Dolly." "You're telling me?" Some other guy pokes his head in. "Whatsa-matter? Dolly fall in?" "No, she fell out. Give me a hand."

By the time she's chased Jack and Mark out of there, she's lost track of the program she's been watching on television. There's another woman in the story now for some reason. That guy lives a very complicated life. Impatiently, she switches channels. She hates ballgames, so she settles for the murder mystery. She switches just in time, too: there's a dead man sprawled out on the floor of what looks like an office or a study or something. A heavyset detective gazes up from his crouch over the body: "He's been strangled." Maybe she'll take that bath, after all.

She drags him into the bathroom and pulls his pants down. She soaps up a warm washcloth she's had in the tub with her, but just as she reaches between his legs, it starts to spurt, spraying her arms and hands. "Oh, Jimmy! I thought you were done!" she cries, pulling him toward the toilet and aiming it into the bowl. How moist and rubbery it is! And you can turn it every which way. How funny it must feel!

"Stop it!" she screams. "Please stop!" She's on her hands and knees and Jack is holding her head down. "Now we're gonna teach you how to be a nice girl," Mark says and lifts her skirt. "Well, I'll be damned!" "What's the matter?" says Jack, his heart pounding. "Look at this big pair of men's underpants she's got on!" "Those are my daddy's!" says Jimmy, watching them from the doorway. "I'm gonna tell!"

People are shooting at each other in the murder mystery, but she's so mixed up, she doesn't know which ones are the good guys. She switches back to the love story. Something seems to have happened, because now the man is kissing his invalid wife tenderly. Maybe she's finally dying. The baby wakes, begins to scream. Let it. She turns up the volume on the TV.

Leaning down over her, unbuckling his belt. It's all happening just like he's known it would. Beautiful! The kid is gone, though his pants, poor lad, remain. "Looks like you and me, we got a secret to keep, child!" But he's cramped on the couch and everything is too slippery and small. "Lift your legs up, honey. Put them around my back." But instead, she screams. He rolls off, crashing to the floor. There they all come, through the front door. On television, somebody is saying: "Am I a burden to you, darling?" "Dolly! My God! Dolly, I can explain . . . !"

The game of the night is Get Dolly Tucker Back in Her Girdle Again. They've got her down on her belly in the livingroom and the whole damn crowd is working on her. Several of them are stretching the girdle, while others try to jam the fat inside. "I think we made a couple inches on this side! Roll her over!" Harry?

She's just stepped into the tub, when the phone rings, waking the baby. She sinks down in the suds, trying not to hear. But that baby doesn't cry, it screams. Angrily, she wraps a towel around herself, stamps peevishly into the baby's room, just letting the phone jangle. She tosses the baby down on its back, unpins its diapers hastily, and gets yellowish baby stool all over her hands. Her towel drops away. She turns to find Jimmy staring at her like a little idiot. She slaps him in the face with her dirty hand, while the baby screams, the phone rings, and nagging voices argue on the TV. There are better things she might be doing.

What's happening? Now there's a young guy in it. Is he after the young girl or the old invalid? To tell the truth, it looks like he's after the same man the women are. In disgust, she switches channels. "The strangler again," growls the fat detective, hands on hips, staring down at the body of a half-naked girl. She's considering either switching back to the love story or taking a quick bath, when a hand suddenly clutches her mouth.

"You're both chicken," she says, staring up at them. "But what if Mr. Tucker comes home?" Mark asks nervously.

How did he get here? He's standing pissing in his own goddamn bathroom, his wife is still back at the party, the three of them are, like good kids, sitting in there in the livingroom watching TV. One of them is his host's boy Mark. "It's a good murder mystery, Mr. Tucker," Mark said, when he came staggering in on them a minute ago. "Sit still!" he shouted, "I am just home for a moment!" Then whump thump on into the bathroom. Long hike for a wee-wee, Mister. But something keeps bothering him. Then it hits him: the girl's panties hanging like a broken balloon fron the rabbit-ear antennae on the TV! He barges back in there, giving his shoulder a helluva crack on the livingroom door jamb on the way — but they're not hanging there any more. Maybe he's only imagined it. "Hey, Mr. Tucker," Mark says flatly. "Your fly's open."

The baby's dirty. Stinks to high heaven. She hurries back to the livingroom, hearing sirens and gunshots. The detective is crouched outside a house, peering in. Already, she's completely lost. The baby screams at the top of its lungs. She turns up the volume. But it's all confused. She hurries back in there, claps an angry hand to the baby's mouth. "Shut up!" she cries. She throws the baby down on its back, starts to unpin the diaper, as the baby tunes up again. The phone rings. She answers it, one eye on the TV. "*What!*" The baby cries so hard it starts to choke. Let it. "I said, hi, this is Jack!" Then it hits her: oh no! the diaper pin!

"The aspirin . . ." But she's already in the tub. Way down in the tub. Staring at him through the water. Her tummy looks pale and ripply. He hears sirens, people on the porch.

Jimmy gets up to go to the bathroom and gets his face slapped and smeared with baby poop. Then she hauls him off to the bathroom, yanks off his pajamas, and throws him into the tub. That's okay, but next she gets naked and acts like she's gonna get in the tub, too. The baby's screaming and the phone's ringing like crazy and in walks his dad. Saved! he thinks, but, no, his dad grabs him right back out of the tub and whales the dickens out of him, no questions asked, while she watches, then sends him — *whack!* — back to bed. So he's lying there, wet and dirty and naked and sore, and he still has to go to the bathroom, and outside his window he hears two older guys talking. "Listen, you know where to do it if we get her pinned?" "No! Don't you?"

"Yo ho heave ho! *Ugh!*" Dolly's on her back and they're working on the belly side. Somebody got the great idea of buttering her down first. Not to lose the ground they've gained, they've shot it inside with a basting syringe. But now suddenly there's this big tug-of-war under way between those who want to stuff her in and those who want to let her out. Something rips, but she feels better. The odor of hot butter makes her think of movie theaters and popcorn. "Hey, has anybody seen Harry?" she asks. "Where's Harry?"

Somebody's getting chased. She switches back to the love story, and now the man's back kissing the young lover again. What's going on? She gives it up, decides to take a quick bath. She's just stepping into the tub, one foot in, one foot out, when Mr. Tucker walks in. "Oh, excuse me! I only wanted some aspirin . . ." She grabs for a towel, but he yanks it away. "Now, that's not how it's supposed to happen, child," he scolds. "Please! Mr. Tucker . . . !" He embraces her savagely, his calloused old hands clutching roughly at her backside. "Mr. Tucker!" she cries, squirming. "Your wife called — !" He's pushing something between her legs, hurting her. She slips, they both slip — something cold and hard slams her in the back, cracks her skull, she seems to be sinking into a sea . . .

They've got her over the hassock, skirt up and pants down. "Give her a little lesson there, Jack baby!" The television lights flicker and flash over her glossy flesh, 1000 WHEN LIT. Whack! Slap! Bumper to bumper! He leans into her, feeling her come alive.

The phone rings, waking the baby. "Jack, is that you? Now, you listen to me — " "No, dear, this is Mrs. Tucker. Isn't the TV awfully loud?" "Oh, I'm sorry, Mrs. Tucker! I've been getting — " "I tried to call you before, but I couldn't hang on. To the phone, I mean. I'm sorry, dear." "Just a minute, Mrs. Tucker, the baby's — " "Honey, listen! Is Harry there? Is Mr. Tucker there, dear?"

"Stop it!" she screams and claps a hand over the baby's mouth. "Stop it! Stop it! *Stop it!*" Her other hand is full of baby stool and she's afraid she's going to be sick. The phone rings. "No!" she cries. She's hanging on to the baby, leaning woozily away, listening to the phone ring. "Okay, okay," she sighs, getting ahold of herself. But when she lets go of the baby, it isn't screaming any more. She shakes it. Oh no . . .

"Hello?" No answer. Strange. She hangs up and, wrapped only in a towel, stares out the window at the cold face staring in — she screams!

She screams, scaring the hell out of him. He leaps out of the tub, glances up at the window she's gaping at just in time to see two faces duck away, then slips on the bathroom tiles, and crashes to his ass, whacking his head on the sink on the way down. She stares down at him, trembling, a towel over her narrow shoulders. "Mr. Tucker! Mr. Tucker, are you all right . . . ?" Who's Sorry Now? Yessir, who's back is breaking with each . . . He stares up at the little tufted locus of all his woes, and passes out, dreaming of Jeannie . . .

The phone rings. "Dolly! It's for you!" "Hello?" "Hello, Mrs. Tucker?" "Yes, speaking." "Mrs. Tucker, this is the police calling . . ."

It's cramped and awkward and slippery, but he's pretty sure he got it in her, once anyway. When he gets the suds out of his eyes, he sees her staring up at them. Through the water. "Hey, Mark! Let her up!"

Down in the suds. Feeling sleepy. The phone rings, startling her. Wrapped in a towel, she goes to answer. "No, he's not here, Mrs. Tucker." Strange. Married people act pretty funny sometimes. The baby is awake and scream-ing. Dirty, a real mess. Oh boy, there's a lot of things she'd rather be doing than babysitting in this madhouse. She decides to wash the baby off in her own bathwater. She removes her towel, unplugs the tub, lowers the water level so the baby can sit. Glancing back over her shoulder, she sees Jimmy staring at her. "Go back to bed, Jimmy." "I have to go to the bathroom." "Good grief, Jimmy! It looks like you already have!" The phone rings. She doesn't bother with the towel — what can Jimmy see he hasn't already seen? — and goes to answer. "No, Jack, and that's final." Sirens, on the TV, as the police move in. But wasn't that the channel with the love story? Ambulance maybe. Get this over with so she can at least catch the news. "Get those wet pajamas off, Jimmy, and I'll find clean ones. Maybe you better get in the tub, too." "I think something's wrong with the baby," he says. "It's down in the water and it's not swimming or anything."

She's staring up at them from the rug. They slap her. Nothing happens. "You just tilted her, man!" Mark says softly. "We gotta get outa here!" Two little kids are standing wide-eyed in the doorway. Mark looks hard at Jack. "No, Mark, they're just little kids . . . !" "We gotta, man, or we're dead."

"Dolly! My God! Dolly, I can explain!" She glowers down at them, her ripped girdle around her ankles. "What the four of you are doing in the bathtub with *my* babysitter?" she says sourly. "I can hardly wait!"

Police sirens wail, lights flash. "I heard the scream!" somebody shouts. "There were two boys!" "I saw a man!" "She was running with the baby!" "My God!" somebody screams "they're *all* dead!" Crowds come running. Spotlights probe the bushes.

"Harry, where the hell you been?" his wife whines, glaring blearily up at him from the carpet. "I can explain," he says. "Hey, whatsa-matter, Harry?" his host asks, smeared with butter for some goddamn reason. "You look like you just seen a ghost!" Where did he leave his drink? Everybody's laughing, everybody except Dolly, whose cheeks are streaked with tears. "Hey, Harry, you won't let them take me to a rest home, will you, Harry?"

10:00. The dishes done, children to bed, her books read, she watches the news on television. Sleepy. The man's voice is gentle, soothing. She dozes — awakes with a start: a babysitter? Did the announcer say something about a babysitter?

"Just want to catch the weather," the host says, switching on the TV. Most of the guests are leaving, but the Tuckers stay to watch the news. As it comes on, the announcer is saying something about a babysitter. The host switches channels. "They got a better weatherman on four," he explains. "Wait!" says Mrs. Tucker. "There was something about a babysitter . . . !" The host switches back. "Details have not yet been released by the police," the announcer says. "Harry, maybe we'd better go . . ."

They stroll casually out of the drugstore, run into a buddy of theirs. "Hey! Did you hear about the babysitter?" the guy asks. Mark grunts, glances at Jack. "Got a smoke?" he asks the guy.

"I think I hear the baby screaming!" Mrs. Tucker cries, running across the lawn from the drive.

She wakes, startled, to find Mr. Tucker hovering over her. "I must have dozed off!" she exclaims. "Did you hear the news about the babysitter?" Mr. Tucker asks. "Part of it," she says, rising. "Too bad, wasn't it?" Mr. Tucker is watching the report of the ball scores and golf tournaments. "I'll drive you home in just a minute, dear," he says. "Why, how nice!" Mrs. Tucker exclaims from the kitchen. "The dishes are all done!"

"What can I say, Dolly?" the host says with a sigh, twisting the buttered strands of her ripped girdle between his fingers. "Your children are murdered, your husband gone, a corpse in your bathtub, and your house is wrecked. I'm sorry. But what can I say?" On the TV, the news is over, and they're selling aspirin. "Hell, *I* don't know," she says. "Let's see what's on the late late movie."

Suggestions for Discussion

1. What *really* happens in "The Babysitter"? Is it possible to know? How many kinds of reality does the story suggest? To what extent are speculations on the nature of reality its theme?

2. How often are you uncertain, at the beginning of a section, not only about whether the events are real or imagined, but about who is the point-of-view character of that section? Confusion usually leads to alienation of the reader from the author. What purpose does it serve that Coover runs this risk? Are you willing to be so alienated? Why or why not?

3. Confusion also inevitably results from leaps backward and forward in time. What would be lost, in terms of the story's theme, if the events were given chronologically?

4. On page 341 Dolly wonders, "Why is her husband humming, 'Who's Sorry Now?'" Why, in terms of the story's theme, is he?

5. How does the pinball machine operate as an objective correlative for the relation between sex and violence?

6. How do the various television shows reflect the action and fantasies of the characters? What function do they serve in the story's structure? In the illumination of the theme?

7. Consider authorial distance in "The Babysitter" by trying to pinpoint your attitude toward each of the characters. Do you identify with some more than others, find yourself in moral, emotional, or intellectual opposition to some or all? To what extent do these judgments contribute to the theme?

8. Consider how the total pattern of the story is formed by the fusion of these elements: action and fantasies of action; characterization; the five points of view; recurring details of object and action; leaps backward and forward in time; settings; metaphors and symbols. How does the interrelation of these elements reveal the theme? How might that theme alter if any of them were significantly altered?

RETROSPECT

1. Both "Brownstone" and "The Only Way to Make It in New York" offer speculations on sanity and survival in New York City. How do differences in structure, tone, detail, and characterization differentiate their themes?

2. Consider the themes of home, homesickness, foreignness, and patriotism in "The Bella Lingua." What speculative conclusions does the story suggest?

3. Which of the stories in this volume offer an inversion of a "truth" that you ordinarily accept — about, for instance, the nature of reality, sanity, time, goodness? How successfully does each offer its alternative truth?

4. In which of the stories in this volume can a central character be said to "find" himself or herself in the crisis and resolution? How do emotion, judgment, and logic fuse in these epiphanies to suggest theme?

WRITING ASSIGNMENTS

These final four exercises are arranged in order of ascending difficulty. The first is the easiest, and it is likely to produce a bad story. If it produces a bad story, it will be invaluably instructive to you, and you will be relieved of the onus of ever doing it again. If it produces a good story, then you have done something else, something more, and something more original than the assignment asks for. If you prefer to do exercises 3 or 4, then you may already have doomed yourself to the writing craft, and should prepare to be very poor for a few years while you discover what place writing will have in your life.

1. Take a simple but specific political, religious, scientific, or moral idea. It may be one already available to us in a formula of words, or it may be one of your own, but it should be possible to state it in less than ten words. Write a short story that illustrates the idea. Do not state the idea at all. Your goals are two: that the idea should be perfectly clear to us, so that it could be extracted as a moral or message, and that we should feel we have experienced it.

2. Take as your title a common proverb or maxim, such as: *power corrupts; honesty is the best policy; walk softly and carry a big stick; haste makes waste.* Let the story make the title ironic. That is, explore a situation in which the advice or statement does not apply.

3. Identify the belief you hold most passionately and profoundly. Write a short story that explores an instance in which this belief is untrue.

4. Write the short story that you have wanted to write all term and have not written because you knew it was too big for you and you would fail. You may fail. Write it anyway.

APPENDIX A

NARRATIVE TECHNIQUES
Workshop Symbol Code

Format

Manuscripts should be typed, double-spaced, with generous margins, on one side of 8½ × 11-inch white paper. Use a new black ribbon and well-cleaned keys. Title and author's name and address (or class identification) should appear on a cover page. Some editors (and teachers) will not accept Corrasable bond or Xerox copies. Always keep a copy of your work.

The symbols listed here are a suggested shorthand for identifying common errors in usage and style. A few of the marks are standard copy-editing and proofreading symbols.

Usage

sp.   Misspelling.

gram.   Grammar at fault. Consult Strunk's *Elements of Style,* Fowler's *Modern English Usage,* or any good grammar text.

¢	Paragraph. Begin a new one here.
⸂	No new paragraph needed.
⌃	Comma needed. Insert one here.
⌿	No comma needed.
p/c	You have used a possessive for a contraction or vice versa. *Its*, *their*, and *your* are possessives. *It's*, *they're*, and *you're* are contractions of *it is*, *they are*, and *you are*. They're going to take their toll if you're not sure of your usage.
p/p	Participial phrase at the beginning of a sentence must refer to the grammatical subject. "Failing to understand this, your prose will read awkwardly," means that your prose fails to understand.
s/i	Split infinitives tend to always read awkwardly. Try to immediately correct it and to never do it again.
T	A pointless change of tense. It leaves the reader not knowing *when* he is.
n/s	Not a sentence. Technique okay if effective, otherwise not. Here, not.
tr.	Transpose. This can refer to letters, words, phrases, sentences, whole paragraphs.
#	Insert a space here (between words, paragraphs, etc.).

Style

V   This is definitely vague. Or, you have used a generalization or an abstraction where you need a concrete detail. Specify.

A/   Use the active voice. If "she was happy" or "she felt happy," she was not nearly as happy as if she laughed, grinned, jumped, or threw her arms around a tree.

ůn.   Unnecessary. Delete.

↓↑   Compress this passage to half the words for twice the strength. You're writing *long*.

?   Either you are confusing or the reader is confused or both. What do you *really* mean?

awk.   Awkward. This sentence is related to the auk, a thick-bodied, short-necked bird without grace. Restyle it.

R   Repetition to unintended or undesirable effect.

∝   Cliché.

m/m   Mixed metaphor.

o/w ⎫
o/s ⎬   Overwritten, overstated, overinsistent. You're straining. Lower the key to raise the effect.
o/i ⎭

conv.   In the exceedingly likely and, one might say, almost inevitable event, in view of your enrollment in this class, that you are not Henry James, the use of convoluted language is considerably less than certain to contribute to the augmenting of your intended effect. Simplify.

Coy, pompous, precious, pretentious — all meaning that you are enjoying yourself more than the reader is. No reader will forgive you.

chron.

Chronology unnecessarily violated. "She sat down after having crossed to the couch." Except for very special effects, let the reader's mind follow events in their order.

d/t

Unnecessary dialogue tag. " 'Shut your stupid mouth!' he said angrily." We do not need to be told that he said this angrily. If he said it sweetly, then we would probably need to be told.

dial.

Dialect is overwritten. You are probably misspelling too much, so that your character sounds stupid rather than regional. Let the syntax do the work; keep misspellings and grammatical mistakes to a minimum.

int.

Author intrusion. You are explaining, judging, or interpreting too much. Show us, and let us understand and judge.

SUGGESTIONS
FOR FURTHER READING

This is a short list of books of various sorts that can be useful to the practicing writer

Books on Technique

Authors of the books in this first group address themselves more or less directly to techniques of writing and the problems writers face; all contain useful insights and advice.

Aristotle, *The Poetics*. The first extant work of literary criticism, and the essay from which all later criticism derives. There are numerous good translations, of which one of the best (particularly for its full and helpful comments by O. B. Hardison, Jr.), is that by Leon Golden, *Aristotle's Poetics*, Prentice-Hall, 1968.

Booth, Wayne C., *The Rhetoric of Fiction*. University of Chicago Press, 1961. This is a thorough, brilliant, and difficult discussion of point of view, which well repays the effort of its reading.

Braine, John, *Writing a Novel*. McGraw-Hill, 1974. Braine gives writerly advice very much from the perspective of his own experience, which will not be useful to everyone. But *Writing a Novel* is anecdotal, interesting, and readable.

Forster, E. M., *Aspects of the Novel*. Harcourt, Brace, 1927, 1947. Forster delivered these Clark Lectures at Trinity College, Cambridge, England, in 1927. They are talkative, informal, and informative; still the best analysis by a writer of literature from a writer's point of view. A must.

Gibson, Walker, *Seeing and Writing*. David McKay, 1974. This is a book of exercises in perception, aimed primarily at the writer of essays rather than fiction, but nonetheless provocative, fresh, even startling, in its ideas for observing and capturing sense detail — and therefore useful to the fiction writer as well.

Hills, Rust, *Writing in General and the Short Story in Particular*. Bantam, 1979. A former literary editor of *Esquire Magazine*, Hills has written a breezy, enjoyable guide to fictional technique with good advice on every page.

Knott, William C., *The Craft of Fiction*. Reston (Prentice-Hall), 1973. An excellent practical text with useful exercises.

Lubbock, Percy, *The Craft of Fiction*. Viking, 1957. A classic of practical criticism, now however of more historical than practical interest.

Minot, Stephen, *Three Genres*, 3rd ed. Prentice-Hall, 1982. This text covers the writing of poetry, fiction, and drama, so that each is necessarily treated briefly. Nevertheless Minot is direct and insightful, well worth reading.

Strunk, William C., and White, E. B. *The Elements of Style*, 3rd ed. Macmillan, 1979. Strunk barks the rules for correct usage and vigorous writing in this briefest and most useful of handbooks.

Sloane, William, *The Craft of Writing*, edited by Julia Sloane. W. W. Norton, 1979. This book was culled posthumously from the notes of one of the great teachers of fiction writing. The advice he gives is solid and memorable, and the reader's only regret is that there isn't more of it.

Surmelian, Leon, *Techniques of Fiction Writing: Measure and Madness*. Anchor Books (Doubleday), 1969. Surmelian occasionally falls into some strange observations ("The exclamation point has all but vanished from rugged masculine prose like Hemingway's, but women still use it"), but his discussion of narrative elements, especially characterization, is insightful.

Anthologies

Short-story anthologies abound, and you will find your own favorites. Here are a few I've particularly liked, for their selection or their comments or both:

Cassill, R. V., *The Norton Anthology of Short Fiction*. Norton, 1978.

Hogins, James Burl, *Literature: Fiction*. Science Research Associates, 1973, 1974.

Howard, Daniel F., *The Modern Tradition*. Little, Brown, 1979.

Gasarch, Pearl, and Paul Gasarch, *Fiction: The Universal Elements*. Van Nostrand Reinhold, 1972.

Mizener, Arthur, *Modern Short Stories*. Norton, 1979.

Pickering, James H., *Fiction 100*. Macmillan, 1974.

Scott, Virgil, and David Madden, *Studies in the Short Story*. Holt Rinehart & Winston, 4th ed., 1976.

Personal Statements

These diaries, interviews, and essays are of particular interest because they give a candid view of the personal problems, predilections, and writing methods of practicing authors.

Plimpton, George, ed., *Writers at Work. The Paris Review Interviews*. There are now four volumes of this valuable collection of interviews, all originally published in *The Paris Review*. The collections are published by Viking Press and Penguin.

Porter, Katherine Anne, *The Days Before*. Harcourt, Brace, 1952.

Sternburg, Janet, ed., *The Writer on Her Work*. Norton, 1980.

Woolf, Virginia, *A Writer's Diary*. Harcourt, Brace, 1954.

Critical Works

These are works of literary criticism, aimed at the reader rather than the writer of fiction. But each is a classic in its way, and each provides a valuable perspective for the writer.

Daiches, David, *The Novel and the Modern World*. University of Chicago Press, 1960.

Fiedler, Leslie, *Love and Death in the American Novel*. Stein & Day, 1966.

James, Henry, *The Art of Fiction and Other Essays*, ed. Morris Roberts. Oxford University Press, 1948.

Josipovici, Gabriel, *The World and the Book: A Study of Modern Fiction*. Paladin (London), 1973.

Leavis, F. R., *The Great Tradition*. Chatto & Windus, 1948.

Robbe-Grillet, Alain, *For a New Novel: Essays on Fiction*, trans. Richard Howard. Grove Press, 1965.

Sarraute, Nathalie, *The Age of Suspicion: Essays on the Novel*, trans. Maria Jolas. Grove Press, 1963.

Marketing

Of the guides and services offered to writers, two of the most helpful are these:

Writer's Market, edited by Jane Koester and Paula Arnett Sandhage, Writer's Digest (Cincinnati). A new edition comes out each year with practical advice on how to sell your manuscripts as well as lists of book and magazine publishers, agents, foreign markets, and other services for writers.

Poets & Writers, Inc. (201 W. 54th St., New York, N.Y. 10019). Poets & Writers issues a bimonthly newsletter, *Coda*, which has articles of high quality and interest, and keeps you up to date on contests and magazines and publishers soliciting manuscripts. The organization also has a number of useful publications that are periodically revised; a *Directory of American Poets and Fiction Writers*, a *Sponsors List*, an *Awards List*, guides to agents and bookstores, and a trade publishing survey. Poets & Writers maintains an information center for the literary world, with a toll-free number. It's well worth subscribing to *Coda*, thereby gaining access to the other services and publications.

APPENDIX C

STUDENT FICTION

There follow three stories written by students in fiction workshops at the University of Iowa and Florida State University. The stories vary widely in subject matter and treatment, but each writer makes successful use of techniques described in this book, and each gives an indication of the high quality that can be achieved in student writing. Examine the stories for plot, detail, characterization, atmosphere, point of view, imagery, and theme. What are the particular successes of each, and why? What might you have done differently in each, and why?

JUDAS

Joe Taylor

On weekdays, released from school to play alone behind the barn, she would imagine that the row of black plank fencing stared at her with knot-hole eyes. She would drop to the grass and imagine that peacocks just like her own Judas gracefully mounted the posts of the fencing to spread their plumage. Then she would see that their feathery eyes were staring too. She would see their beaks open in a scream like they do, though no sound came. The eyes and the posts and the beaks stretched as far as she could see. A peafowl would lift its foot like a rooster lifts its spur: it would lift its foot and teeter on the post, ready to jump. When she saw this, she would cross her eyes until her nose intruded upon the scene. She knew it was her nose because it was ugly.

With Saturday came pie-day. It was the day when she got to scrape at a bowl of sugared, half-cooked fruit and chew strips of dough. (God sakes, stop! Don't eat any more of that, Leslie — it'll swell your belly./ She knows when to stop. It's instinctive with children./ Instinctive? How can you look at her and say instinctive? Tell me that one thing, will you, George? Someone has to watch her every minute. Don't lecture me about instinct!/ Stop it, Alice. Look./ Come here, Leslie, honey. Momma loves you. And daddy too. We didn't mean to yell. Come here and let Momma wipe your pie-face.)

This Saturday was different. Aunt Lena was visiting and had brought one of her boys over. Not the tall one, the one who wasn't afraid of the fence out back, the one who used to let her ride piggy-back along the row. (The fence won't hurt you when I'm around. Touch it now. See?) That one never came any more. Aunt Lena said he was married now. (Bill's wife thinks she's p-r-e-g-n-a-n-t. They've been fixing up their second room./ That's wonderful, Lena. We'll give them Leslie's old crib./ No! — Bill's father is making them one already. You know how he likes to do things like that.)

It wasn't that one. It was the short and skinny one. Leslie could see him through the car's rear window. Aunt Lena was twirling his curly blonde hair with one hand while she pointed to Leslie with the other. The boy turned to stare, then rubbed his head against his mother's hand.

Leslie had been talking to Judas, but the car scared the peacock away. She watched as the two finally got out of the car. Aunt Lena took the boy's hand.

"Joe, I want you and Leslie to play together while your Aunt Alice and I talk. Leslie, why don't you show Joe your peacock?"

As soon as Aunt Lena walked away, Leslie drooled at the boy with her tongue hanging to one side. He didn't pay any attention, though: he kept staring at the brace on her leg. She started to go talk with Judas. Between steps she listened to see if the boy was following: she didn't think he was, so she stopped and turned. He pretended to be looking at something in his hand, though she knew well enough what he had been staring at. She moved her hands to her hips, like she had seen her mother do.

"Do you want to see Judas?" Her voice sounded like a foghorn. It reminded her of the fire department's whistle which was supposed to sound at noon, which always howled at ten after instead. She hated the whistle and would sometimes sit in the barn in a stall and scream when its time came.

The boy only stared at her, squeezing his hand closed. Leslie slung her leg forward.

He didn't move until she tried to grab his hand, then he spun away quickly and looked to the back door where his mother had disappeared.

"Do you want to see Judas? Let me see what's in your hand first." Leslie held her open palm in front of his face. He looked from it to her, then stuck out his own open palm in the same way. It held a buckeye with a big white splotch running down one side.

"I found it in the street yesterday," the boy said.

Leslie had seen plenty of buckeyes behind the barn, but never one with a white spot like this. It looked like an airplane. She watched his fingers rubbing it. Then, she watched him put it to his nose. She thought at first he was going to eat it and decided she would let him, but changed her mind.

"Don't eat it!"

He laughed and held it out to her again. Leslie took it and fingered it as he had, and shifted her weight.

"It's pretty." She started to giggle and rub it against her nose when she saw the boy staring at her brace. Leslie flung the buckeye toward the barn.

His face puckered and Leslie could see he was going to cry. She remembered the family dog shaking her teddy bear, tossing its insides all over the rug in the bedroom. The dog bit into the bear when she tried to take it away, leaving it to stare at her with two button eyes and a blue-gray tuft of lint protruding from its nose. She hit the dog over its head with a book, sending it howling like a fire whistle, like herself. She hated the dog. Her mother walked in as she was trying to re-stuff the bear. (God help me! Sometimes I swear I wish I could just slap the living daylights out of you. If you were only — go to your room, just go to your room. Go!)

The boy put his fist to his eyes.

"Come on, I was just teasing. It's right near the barn. I can find it."

He followed, steps behind her.

The grass was tall. Leslie cocked her body at the spot she thought she had thrown the buckeye, and the boy peered downward too. They walked in a circle around one another.

The peacock screamed shrilly and the boy slid behind Leslie.

"He won't hurt you." Leslie took some corn from her pocket and threw it at Judas, who began pecking it from the ground.

"See? That's just Judas. He doesn't do anything but eat and show his tail feathers off. It's because he's so pretty."

The boy remained behind Leslie.

"When he's finished, I'll show you something."

The bird found the last kernel, then hunted some more before dipping his neck toward Leslie.

"Do it, Judas, show Joe."

The bird blinked and wobbled its head. Leslie reached into her pocket and waited. Judas shifted his weight and looked to the boy. Leslie rattled the kernels in her pocket. The peacock spread his tail.

"See! See! I taught Judas that." Leslie started to throw the corn but stopped, handing it to the boy instead. Joe took it and held it with his palm open for the peacock.

"No! Don't do that! He'll peck your hand. You can't trust him. That's how he got his name in the first place." Leslie made a motion for the boy to throw the corn instead. They stood watching after he did.

"Do you know who Judas was?"

"A bird."

Leslie rolled her eyes at the peacock.

"Do you want to see where buckeyes come from?"

The boy stared blankly.

"The thing you had in your hand. Do you want to see more?"

He nodded. They began walking to the other side of the barn.

"My mother said it was a chestnut."

"It's a buckeye. We have a whole tree of them in the back. They fall over the fence this time of year. I get as many as I want. You can't eat them like chestnuts."

"Cre-ew!" Judas cried.

The boy jumped and Leslie reassured him: "That's only Judas. He's following us for more corn. I sound loud like him, but I don't eat corn." She watched the boy, but he only stared at the ground.

The heat of October's Indian summer reflected off the black barn onto Leslie's face, reminding her of the fire her parents would sometimes start late at night when they were watching t.v. If she was real quiet she could sneak from her room and watch Baretta talk to a white bird and shoot at people. She always tried not to laugh.

But she hadn't done that in a while. (I don't want her in a home. She belongs here with us. I have to watch her./ With us? She's not with us and never will be. Something else is wrong with her besides her leg and that voice. She's my flesh and blood too, but you know what I say is true as well as I do. What did her teacher tell you?/ Not tonight, I don't want to talk about it any more tonight./ We'll have to talk about it some night — I warn you, Alice, I'll not raise a normal infant alongside her.) Leslie touched her hand to the dried, black wood of the barn. Joe did the same. They both looked to the sun, then to Judas, three steps behind.

"Can I give him some more corn?"

"Wait 'til we get to the tree."

They turned the corner. Leslie banged on the barn's black drainpipe, heard Joe bang on it behind her, heard Judas peck at it once. She stopped short as she saw the shadow of the barn falling on the fence row and its spiny planks and posts. Joe tumbled into her.

When Leslie first learned to walk with her brace, her mother warned her about the fence. It was "bad," "no." When Leslie began to play in the yard, her mother told her the fence's planks were devil lips which gobbled up any little girls who came near them. When Leslie came to supper, late and out of breath from playing behind the barn, her mother told her the fence circled the farm at dark, looking for anything stray to eat. After this, Leslie would memorize certain planks before she went inside for the evening, then check each morning to see if they were out of place. Most of the time, the fence came right back to where it started. Sometimes not. Those were the nights, she decided, that the fence had found something to eat. She told her father. (What God-awful horror stories have you been telling this child?/ I had to keep her away somehow. What if she crossed it and got lost? Or fell somewhere so she couldn't get back up?/ How do you expect her to climb a fence with that damned brace? She's lucky to walk.)

The planks today looked like they always did, except they were in the barn's shadow. She hadn't really seen them move for nearly a year now. She hardly even checked anymore. (See the tree way over there, Leslie? That's a persimmon. Come this fall and we'll go get some. Right over the fence. Go ahead, you can touch it while I'm here.)

She started looking around for buckeyes. Joe pulled her arm and pointed to Judas pecking at something beneath the drainpipe.

"Okay. But throw them. Remember what I said."

Joe took the kernels from Leslie and sifted them from hand to hand. Leslie rattled the remainder in her pocket and Judas spread his tail.

"Toss them now."

Joe threw the kernels and stared at the pecking bird. Leslie began searching the yard's collection of prickly shells, the same ones she had busted open for the last week and a half. At last, she spotted one containing a buckeye.

"Cre-ew!"

"Go, Judas! We want to play now. Come here, Joe." Leslie stepped on the full shell she had found and picked up a halved one she had emptied days before. "These have buckeyes in them when they're full. All we have to do is look."

"Will it have an airplane on it?"

"If we look hard enough."

Joe circled Leslie, kicking through the opened shells. Leslie pretended to look, then moved when Joe came back.

"Here's one!" Joe shouted, pointing to the buckeye she had stood on.

Leslie showed him how to crack the outer shell with a rock.

"It doesn't have a plane. It doesn't even have any white anywhere."

They kept looking, but Leslie had picked over the shells too carefully in the past days. Joe finally wandered over to the fence.

"I bet we could find a plane and all kinds of things on the ones over there." He leaned against the fence, then lifted his foot to the first plank.

Leslie stared at the boy poised like a frog ready to hop. She stared at the fence, its planks reassuringly the same as they had been for the past year, a knothole still spying from the middle board, the upper and lower boards still curving upward like a troll's fat belly. Joe bounced on the first rung. The fence made no movement at all: it didn't even seem to notice.

"Wait for me!" Leslie slung her leg forward as the boy climbed to the top to straddle the post and look down at her. She reached to touch the middle plank, carefully avoiding its knothole.

"It's just like walking up stairs. But you use your arms to pull too. See?" Joe backed down one step and demonstrated.

"I know how!"

She did as he suggested on the first rung, which was easy. She did the same on the next, then looked down to where her foot was. It stood right over the knothole. Joe climbed down the other side.

Leslie lifted her brace over the top and looked upward to the sky. Her insides stretched with cool, sky air.

She heard a tiny noise from the barn and turned to see Judas still pecking beneath the drainpipe near the corner timbering. She flapped her elbows at him and turned away, crossing her eyes until she could see the tip of her nose. She aimed it down the fence row, lifting her face as the posts stretched into the distance. Her skin tingled, even tightened, in the sun's warmth. But she was cool and light and in the air. As she looked down the row, she realized it wasn't straight at all like she had thought, but that it wavered in and out with each post until it disappeared over the small hill before the road. Leslie imagined herself hopping from one post to another until she too reached the road. Then she saw herself skipping to the neighbor's fence and continuing her trip until she reached the highway.

"Come on! They're all over the place!"

Leslie stepped down the planks. She and Joe scoured the grass for the prickly buckeye shells, slapping the gray-green husks against the fencepost with a fieldstone. They stacked a pile of empty shells there, and the buckeyes left their pockets bulging.

There weren't any airplanes, though they found a white spot that resembled South America, one that looked like a three-pointed star, and one that Joe said looked like his teacher.

"A big, round face with no ears. She's mean too. She made me stand in the corner for making a noise." Joe squeezed his palm underneath his armpit.

"Well, she should have made you stay after school. My teacher made me stay after school."

"She said she would the next time I did it." Joe fingered a buckeye and looked to Leslie. "Why'd your teacher do that?"

"Because I beat up three boys and two girls," she said.

"By yourself? Why'd you do that?"

"Come on. Let's look at the shells."

"Tell me."

"I'll tell you the next time you come. We'll be friends then."

"Promise?"

"Promise."

They kicked their way nearly to the tree when Judas started crying out, his screams echoing off the barn.

"Won't he stop? It hurts my ears."

Leslie walked to the fence and Judas headed for her. She shook her pants pocket, but it was too full of buckeyes and wouldn't rattle.

"Hush, Judas. Hush, or they'll wonder what's going on."

"My mom would spank me if she knew I was over here."

"Well, what makes you think mine wouldn't?" Leslie picked up a buckeye shell and threw it at the peacock, who stepped backward and was quiet for a moment. Then he began crying again. She and Joe both threw shells this time, bouncing one off the bird's neck and sending him loping.

They returned to the tree and first began breaking up the shells for the buckeyes, then just leaving them in their husks, stacking cannonballs for the fort to use against Apache, then heaving them as chinkers against blackbirds in a nearby black cherry tree, finally counting the full husks as gold pirate's ingots.

"What if they're really dragon's teeth?"

"Leslie! Joe!"

Leslie imagined that her mother was in the hayloft spying on her. She wanted to run into the woods with Joe and hide there forever, eating persimmons and wild cherries, sowing dragon's teeth.

"Aren't you going to answer?" Joe whispered.

"We're here!"

"You and Joe come on. It's time for pie."

The two scrambled for the fence.

"Race!"

"Race!"

Joe was well across while Leslie was still trying to swing her brace over the top rung. Suddenly the back of her leg was scraping against a splintering plank. She grabbed the top board and its black mashed her nose. She hung there, smelling pitch. Her eyes began to hurt, then she cried. Joe pushed her leg, boosting her upward.

Leslie straddled the topmost plank, shaking, feeling the back of her leg burning, a drop of blood trickling. She looked to where her hands rested on the fencepost, expecting to see hungry black lips gaping upward. But beneath was only Joe looking up. She wiped her eyes.

"Are you okay."

"Yes."

They walked to the house together.

"You tore your pantsleg. And there's blood."

Leslie looked around for Judas, but couldn't find him.

"What are you going to tell your mother?"

"Just that I fell behind the barn. That's all."

Aunt Lena met them at the back door.

"Child, what have you done to your leg?"

Leslie could hear a pan clatter in the kitchen.

"I fell behind the barn and cut it a little bit. That's all." She looked to the kitchen doorway. Her mother ran through it, furiously wiping her hands on her apron.

"My God! What have you done? What have you done to your leg?"

Leslie watched Joe back away, still holding a buckeye in his hand.

"I just fell behind the barn and cut myself a little. That's all."

"That's all? What were you doing there? What? Here, let me see that." Her mother began pulling at her shoes and trying to unzip her pants.

"Momma!" Leslie fell backward against the wall to avoid her mother's grip and the wide, staring eyes of Joe.

"Hold still!"

"Momma! I'm okay!"

"You're not okay! You've got one good leg and you've torn it to shreds!"

"What were you two doing, young man?" Aunt Lena asked.

"For God's sake, Leslie, let me pull down your pants and see that leg!"

"Momma-uh! Momma-uh!"

"She told me it was all right to climb the fence. She told me she did it all the time. She said if I didn't go with her, she'd hit me until I screamed like her!"

Leslie thought of the twelve o'clock horn, how it echoed out across the country all the way from town. She thought of Judas screaming, of the children at school yelling. She slapped her mother's hand away and reached into her pocket to hurl the buckeyes, then the remaining corn, at everything moving in front of her.

From her room she heard the car starting. She stared at the window and saw her nose. She closed her eyes. (I'm sorry, Lena, I don't know what to do with her: she's as sweet as can be, then she's a fury. Joe, she didn't hurt you, did she?/ No, ma'am./ Lena, I can't say how sorry I am./ That's all right. It's a burden the whole family has to bear with you. I just thank God for Bill and Joe. I just thank God.) Leslie wandered ahead to the space that wasn't allowed her. She saw rows of black fences, just like the ones in her back yard, staring with their knothole eyes. And teetering on the posts were peacocks just like Judas. They sat with their plumage spread, their feathery eyes staring at her. Their mouths opened in a scream like they do.

"A-aaaa-uh!" She opened her eyes and saw her nose. She knew it was her nose.

PULLING PROOFS

Bruce Brooks

One evening eight months ago, Buzzy and I were giggling over glasses of yellow champagne to celebrate her first day as my "cohabitor" (her word), when she brought an especially snappy laugh to an upbeat stop, rubbed her bubble-invaded nose to compose herself, and solemnly pulled a package out of a nearby suitcase I had thought was emptied. To my expectant eye, the package had all the markings of a large tin of smoked oysters that I had openly admired that afternoon during our first official joint grocery binge. I had already presented to Buzzy a bottle of Spanish olives stuffed with almonds and a set of Scandinavian measuring spoons, which I had slyly snatched from shelves and hidden beneath bulbous packages of paper products in our burgeoning cart. Certainly she could have bought me a similar gift. I smiled, salivated, and reached for the packet with a gracious nod.

As soon as I touched it I knew it was not a tin of oysters. Nevertheless, I enjoyed the tender excitement a mysterious gift brings, and I placed the thing on the table to open it. Now, I like to unwrap gifts with patience, peeling away my illusions about them as they peek out from layers of paper. But this package would not be toyed with. The instant I touched it, the tape let go, and the stiff white paper sprang open like a box lid on a spring. There it was: a black paperback book with gaudy gold letters all over it. I nodded my thanks, and rotated it so that I could read the title. While I did this, Buzzy delivered a serious little speech.

"Toby. If you are going to live with me, live with a woman, then, really, you simply must know this book. You have to *read* it, Toby. If we were twenty, or even twenty-five, it wouldn't matter. But we are both thirty, and we can't afford to fool around many more years, and, well, this book sort of provokes *adult* considerations of the way people contend. It's all in there, Toby; it *matters*."

I nodded soberly, and did a fine job of hiding my disappointment. Not only had I set my hopes on the smoked oysters; I had also hoped that the package would *not* contain a book. Buzzy had never given me a book, in the months that we had known each other, and I had been quite happy about her restraint. Books make bad gifts. What the giver extends as an intimate code, the recipient might regard as an impenetrable artifice. Too often, a person depends on a book to communicate to a friend something that could be simply said without the unnecessary intrusion of a third voice using words unnatural to either person. Books are especially dangerous when they are presented to mark an auspicious occasion — they do not transmit multiple significance very precisely. It has always been difficult enough for me to read a book and figure out what was going on *inside* it; when I was also required to apply this hard-won interior sense to the mercurial movements of life outside the print, I had no luck. Many masterpieces have earned my disdain because they served as important gifts — in my life I have hated *The Little Prince*, which my grandmother gave me when I discovered at age six that I enjoyed cultivating potted flowers, *Great Expectations*, which my fifth-grade teacher gave me shortly after I was orphaned at ten, and *The Autobiography of Benjamin Franklin*, which the same eager grandmother presented to me on the occasion of my formal apprenticeship to a letterpress printer, at seventeen.

Now there was another. I thanked Buzzy, and promised to read it right away. But I was not optimistic about the project. I disliked the book from my first glance at its cover, which had been designed by a typographical fool who flaunted his incompetence in the hope of being flashy, by breaking half a dozen timeless laws of graphic design and good taste. Gold cartoon letters with fake ligatures and bogus serifs had been crammed into a flush-right alignment so grossly unfit for the book's title that the last of the three words in the title had to be *hyphenated*, of all things:

T H E
G O L D E N
N O T E
B O O K

I pitied Doris Lessing, the author, for being made to bear the bad impression her novel's icky cover implanted. I was certain that no one could begin to read the book with a perfectly open mind. However, I promised Buzzy that I would do just that, and did not bother her with my misgivings.

I kept my word: the next day I started reading *The Golden Notebook*. I made myself a pot of Swiss cocoa, put on my red mukluks with the navy-blue manatees embroidered on the toes, took the telephone off the hook, and curled myself into an armchair. These preparations were necessary — if I were to read intelligently, my concentration had to be coddled by comforts and silence. Perhaps this is because I rarely read books. Buzzy reads constantly, and her attention has an uncanny durability. I always admired the way she used reading to make full use of the moments that slip away in the course of days — she reads while waiting for her coffee to cool, while listening to records of chamber music (the complexity of ensembles containing more than six instruments demands her full attention, however), even while flossing her teeth, if she happens to have a heavy limp book that can be propped open while her hands are occupied. I once measured her progress through an old gift edition of *Seven Pillars of Wisdom* in terms of yards of unwaxed string instead of weeks; it took her 150 yards to get through 598 pages. All this amazes me. If I am to skim one of the four printing journals to which I subscribe, I have to retreat to the printery I have built out in back of my apartment, where the distractions surrounding me at least bear a relevance to the material I peruse. As for novels — the only one I have finished in the past ten years is *Tristram Shandy*, which to me is notable only because it is so innovatively printed in the antique edition I own.

So I set myself up for *The Golden Notebook*, and cracked it open. Right away, I had trouble getting started; I had to read the first page four or five times, to get my mental wheels spinning. But then I felt myself settle, and relax. A certain ease came over me. The process felt very smooth. Lessing's story caught me: these two women were talking, and then a man came in, and the three of them shifted into a new discussion, and talked, and then the man suggested that they all go skiing. So they all put on bright clothing, dressing right there in the same room, and then they went out into the snow and set out across the countryside. It was lovely country. They kept talking all the while, about abstract aspects of relationships, and then they came upon a pond and saw a manatee in it. While they watched the manatee two people appeared and skied over to say hello and, lo and behold, the two newcomers were Buzzy and me! Well, hello! I thought, look at us right here in this book, but then some part of my awareness performed the realization that our presence did not fit with the act of reading this novel, and my mind made a little twist, pulling me awake. I blinked. The pond was gone, and I stared at the black and gold cover of the book, which had closed in my lap as soon as I slipped into sleep. I thumbed through the first few pages and found that I had made it up to page three. I yawned, vowed to do better the next day, and went out to the printery to finish up a stationery order that was to be picked up that afternoon.

The next day I tried again. This time I spread the book out on the cold white enamel of the kitchen table, next to a steaming cup of black coffee. I leaned over it with my head in my hands. The cold enamel stung my elbows, keeping me alert. I cut into the novel with determination. This time I made it up to page five, where everyone starts saying "*Well?*" in italics. "*Well?*" says one, and then "*Well?*" says another, and so on — it really put me off, as I thought that "well" was hardly the sort of word that demanded italic emphasis. Lessing and her publisher were constructing a cheap reliance on typography for articulations that ought to have come from textual substance, I thought; such dependences not only indicated a shortcoming of the story, but worst of all tended to devalue the impact of italic typefaces. This sort of abuse typified the foolish liberties that writers and publishers took with print, without a thought to the fact that they were ruining the equipoise of type and idea upon which their business depended. I slammed the book shut and stormed out to my printery. On the linotype I dashed out a sardonic letter to the editor of *Printing Impressions* on the general escalation of italic abuse. When I had finished, I read it over, and decided that perhaps it might make a fair article, if I revised it coolly. I spent the next hour rewriting it, then I set it in 12-point Bodoni Modern, slipped it into a manila envelope, and walked to the post office to send it off to the magazine. (Three weeks later I received a notice of acceptance and a check for $300.) I never quite returned to my reading on that day.

In the next few weeks I gave *The Golden Notebook* numerous chances to fascinate me. I tried to read it in every possible situation conducive to concentration. I read it stretched out in a hot bath laced with sandalwood oil, and I read it sitting upright in a ladderback chair. I read it by the pink light of sun at dawn, and the yellow light of a kerosene lamp at midnight. I read it in a starched shirt and corduroys. I read it naked. I read it with prevailing moods of zeal, adoration, skepticism, all of which I whipped up beforehand in the hope that if I brought a definite bias with me into the book, then Lessing or her characters would have a little extra something to grab onto for the task of pulling me into their world. Nothing worked. In about six weeks I reached only as far as page 49, at which point someone named Molly laughs-but-from-politeness-because a-certain-nerve-has-been-touched-too-often and someone else says that this-isn't-the-point-because-the-letters-were-interchangeable, discounting-handwriting,-of-course. As soon as I read this I slammed the book shut for the last time. Letters interchangeable! Discounting handwriting! As though the sense of words could be transmitted without the formal articulation of the style of letter in which they were rendered! As though such complementary articulation could ever be discounted! I was outraged. I raced out to my linotype and wrote a scathing critique of contemporary typographical ignorance; I sold the piece to *The Letters Review* for $275, but I never returned to *The Golden Notebook*.

At first, Buzzy asked me how my reading was progressing; I always nodded and said something such as "Oh, I'm plugging away!" But after a couple of months, we began to develop our own intricacies of contention, and did not need Doris Lessing to provoke adult considerations for us. We did not have fights, or anything like them. Instead, we had peculiar moments, of disengaged concern, or misaligned enthusiasms, or misinterpretive emphasis. Enjoyments that we began together, we finished apart. Buzzy had particular trouble with laughter. Almost every time we were together for more than ten minutes, we reached some moment of shared amusement, and started laughing; but suddenly Buzzy would stop cold, with a wrinkle in her forehead, to think. The first few times this happened, she included me in her deliberation. It seems she has a perverse tendency to test what should be her best moments, by introducing a detached intellectual challenge to her happiness at the height of its spin: *Stop*, she thinks to herself, *and consider: are you really enjoying this?* Almost always, the act of challenging the fun is enough to spoil it, and she has to answer *No*. Nevertheless, she persists in her cold scrutiny, sacrificing innocent gaieties for the sake of distinguishing between true and false happiness, for whatever such a distinction is worth.

I soon recognized that Buzzy's interior distinctions were beyond my ability to appreciate, and certainly beyond my ability to assist. Life is a cheerful business to me. Any attempt on my part to grow solemn and discuss self-imposed denials of mirth seemed unnatural and intrusive, however sincere my wishes for Buzzy's success in resolving her woe. So when Buzzy would start to puzzle over herself, I would hang around only long enough to ascertain that my presence was not useful, and I would leave, giving her a hopeful squeeze.

I decided that the best course for me was to provide Buzzy with enjoyments that might survive her challenges. Ignoring the irony that by amusing her I set the scene for despondency, I worked hard to make her happy, even for moments at a time. I took care of all the small chores Buzzy found annoying — watering the plants, sweeping the floors, washing the clothes. I closed my printery at four o'clock so that I could have a good dinner on the table every evening when Buzzy came home at five from the birth-control clinic where she worked as a counselor. I baked breads. I brewed beers. Outside, in my printery, I took on a dazzling rush of jobs, whipping through posters and stationery and business cards and pamphlets so that Buzzy and I could spend bright Saturdays in elegant Georgetown shops, buying good things for our home. We purchased two puce chairs from Denmark, three cerulean rugs from Pakistan, a clear glass teapot from France. Eleven Duke Ellington records, and a boxed set of Bach harpsichord partitas complete with scores. A food processor. A waterbed. But nothing helped; Buzzy kept sulking, and we continued our odd misfires, which we could never quite succeed in discussing.

This brings us up to the day before yesterday. I woke up in the morning and found Buzzy up a full hour earlier than usual. She was dressed. She even wore her overcoat. She said "Good morning," but I could not reply right away, because I was quite surprised to discover that she was packing a suitcase.

"I'm going to New York for a couple of days," she explained. I stared at the tangle of tights and underwear she pushed into her small valise. "I'm sorry, but I just have to think about my situation here, by myself. My mother is out of town up there, so I will have the house to myself. I just have to pin a few things down. About me; about you, too. I'm not altogether sure that our . . . system here is really *functioning*, you know? There never seems to be very much to show for our time spent, or something. . . . I think I expected more of a sense of *context*, more of a feeling that living together, a man and a woman, was a *muscular* sort of thing. I feel a little *treated*, maybe. I just want to think a few days. I hope you understand. I'll be back in a couple of days and we'll see what signs there are, okay? Maybe . . . perhaps, you could try to do some thinking too. Men, women, how they come together, us, you, me. . . ."

We kissed quickly and she left.

I had a lot of printing to do, so I was unable to devote my attention to Buzzy's proposal that I do some thinking, until late afternoon. I closed the shop, returned to the apartment, and tried to begin thinking while preparing a salmon loaf. No luck; if I am chopping celery, I have to be *chopping celery*, not musing upon the musculature of cohabitative contexts. Once the salmon was in the oven, I sat down and devoted myself to thinking. Nothing came. I changed chairs, put on a sweater, closed the curtains. Nothing. No engagement with the issues Buzzy had raised, no fascination with the mechanics of adult relationships, generic or specific. I could gain no entry into the matter — my mind was like one of the noble gases, refusing to mingle molecules with the substance of the problems. When the bell on the oven timer signalled that dinner was ready, I gave up in relief, thinking *This is as difficult as reading that novel Buzzy gave me.*

The thought stopped me in my tracks. *That novel Buzzy gave me.* I could not remember the title, but I remembered that it had been about muscular adult relationships. Fairly rippling with context. I spooned out some salmon loaf and thought about the book: where was it? If I located it, I might be able to read it by the time Buzzy returned. The prospect seemed easier at the moment than the analysis of Buzzy's points. Perhaps a careful assimilation of the book would accomplish what my analysis might have done — perhaps I could consider in the novel exactly the issues Buzzy wanted me to consider in our particular situation. Who knows? — perhaps if I had reached such considerations before, if I had read the book early enough, these problems might not have arisen. *The Golden Notebook* — that was the title. I got up from my salmon loaf after a couple of bites, and went to look for the book, with its trashy gold and black cover flashing in my mind's eye. I found it at the bottom of a stack of printing trade journals in an antique brass bucket beside one of the puce chairs. I sat down eagerly to read it.

It did not take me long to realize that the same impenetrability persisted from my earlier attempts. I simply could not keep the page and its depictions before me. But I was determined, and I had no time to experiment with sandalwood baths and cocoa and the light of dawn — I was down to my last forty or fifty hours, and I had to get 666 pages of print behind my eyes. How could I force myself to do it?

The answer was not long in coming: I simply had to set the whole novel in type.

Perfect! My problem with the novel was an inability to maintain concentration; so I would take it to my linotype, where I am professionally conditioned to concentrate *on every single letter* of the text I am typesetting. I am a wizard of concentration once my fingers start dancing over the feather-touch keys, once the brass matrices start clacking as they assemble at my command, once the galleys start filling up with bright inches of silvery type. Not one comma, not one apostrophe of Doris Lessing's masterpiece would escape me. I would see it all.

I ran out to the printery to check my supplies. I had plenty of lead, though I really did not need more than a couple of pigs — I could dump each galley back into the linotype crucible as soon as the galley was full, because I did not need to keep the type to print anything. Pure composing was all that mattered. I turned the crucible on and ran back to the apartment to gather supplies while the lead in the pot melted. From the bedroom I grabbed a sweater, from the living room I grabbed *The Golden Notebook*, and from the kitchen I grabbed a basket of fresh muffins, a slab of the salmon loaf, and a jar of instant coffee. I had a hotplate and water in the printery. I was all set for a long haul at the linotype, and I did not intend to stop composing until I reached page 666.

In two hours I whizzed through 79 pages, filling six galleys. I went so rapidly and smoothly that I did not stop to recycle the lead, but shoved each galley onto a rack as I finished it. I was setting in six-point copperplate Gothic, in double columns of 30 picas each. The Gothic seems tiny at first glance, and many people complain that it is illegible; but they are simply weak readers with no ocular discernment or endurance. Every year, copperplate Gothic finishes at the top of the exhaustive tests run by the Institute of Foundries in Chicago, consistently outpointing other six-point faces in a dozen indices of technical readability. In copperplate Gothic, *The Golden Notebook* would be easier to *read* than it was to *read!*

When I stood up to stretch after the sixth galley, I found myself pulling a proof of the first page, out of habit. I had intended to slide the type directly back into the crucible, but before I really noticed my actions I had inked the form and taken an impression on my proof press. I glanced at it. That was when the entire idea came to me:

Why not pull proofs of every galley, and put together a special handmade copy of the book as a gift for Buzzy?

The pure beauties of the first galley proof inspired my enthusiasm. The Gothic characters stood out so clearly that the paragraphs seemed to *sing*, and the noble proportions of the double columns of 30 picas gave the text a legendary quality — suddenly, Toby Hutch's *The Golden Notebook* could have been William Caxton's *Morte d'Arthur!* I read the proofs of the first six galleys and corrected the few mistakes. Before pulling the final proofs I had an inspiration to add a double-hairline border to the margins. This was a stroke of genius — the border gave a contained bit of dash to the classicism of the print. I knew I had a very special project on my hands. This book was *really* going to "matter," as Buzzy had said eight months ago.

I had to hurry to execute. First, I needed some fine paper. I put on my sweater, locked the printery, and jogged four blocks to the shop of a papermaker with whom I do a good deal of business. He spent three years at a high guild school in Wessex, England. His small, varied lots of paper evoke in me the raptures that some people feel in the presence of exquisite silks and linens. I often buy odd packets of paper from him for no specific printing purpose, but rather for a sense of aesthetic collection; he has a similar appreciation of *my* craft, and has commissioned me several times to design and print unimportant or meaningless signs or slogans, simply so that he could appreciate the execution.

The shop was closed. He lived upstairs, so I rapped on his door. He opened it and told me that it was midnight. I told him I needed some precious folio stock. He took me downstairs and showed me exactly what I needed: a thirty-pound vellum the color of buttermilk, with a deckle edge like duck down. The opacity was unassailable, the life of the hue eternal. My friend had just made it during the week, so he had just enough for my project. I bought one hundred folios for one hundred dollars and returned to my printery.

The next few hours passed in a flurry of interdependent processes. My printery became an aviary of folio wings unfurled over clothesline for drying. I had a huge palette of inks spread out on the lockup stones, for I had started to augment the chromatic scheme: a little way into the text, I found out that *The Golden Notebook* is composed not of one but of five narrative strains — one straight descriptive narration, and four different texts representing the contents of four different notebooks written by one of the characters. Each of the notebooks is referred to by the color of its cover; there are red, yellow, blue, and black. Naturally, I leapt at this chance to lend a complementary typographical articulation to Lessing's text. I decided not to print the words of each notebook in an appropriate shade of ink, but rather to simply adjust the color of the borderline enclosing the text. So, the contents of the red notebook were now bordered by a double hairline of nazdarin crimson, the yellow notebook by a 70% cadmium, the blue by a deep indigo, and the black by a very pale blue that accentuates the ebony richness of the print's ink. The proofs of the notebook pages thus required two separate impressions, one for each ink, and this new intricacy slowed me down a bit. Nevertheless, I made good time in my progress through the book. In twelve hours I had blazed through 280 pages.

As I set the type and pulled the proofs, I grew increasingly excited at the prospect of presenting the book to Buzzy. The gift would mean so much to her! Here she had given me a flimsy, ill-printed, off-center pulp thing with a hyphen on the cover, and she was going to get it back as an aesthetic masterpiece composed precisely for her. If the shabby paperback had been an important book to her, certainly the new handmade edition would mean a thousand times more. I could envision her turning the pages slowly, scanning the graces of the copperplate Gothic, tracing with her delicate fingertips the neat impressions of the hairline rule, savoring the structural resonance of the double columns. With every new impression I realized that this book would be the apotheosis of my *giving* — it was composed of so many expressions of my particular insights, my private tendernesses, my unique inspirations, all mingling and reflecting in a layered richness that I offered to Buzzy for her patient exegesis.

In addition, Buzzy would have the knowledge, as soon as she saw the book, that I had labored over every letter of *The Golden Notebook*; she would know that I had read it, not once but *twice*, in setting and proofing it, and she would be able to enjoy the security that I had assimilated whatever it was she had wanted me to assimilate when she gave me the thing eight months earlier.

Such inspirations kept me going hour after hour. I fell asleep once, at page 422, for perhaps half an hour. When I woke up, I made a pot of coffee and ate some salmon smeared on a muffin. This refreshed me, and I raced through the next three galleys in record time. I was animated by the strange amphetamine of *pure productivity*, a vitality that is endemic to the processes of printing. I grew more exhilarated with every brassy clack of the mats. I burned with boosted zeal with every roll of the proof press. The folios dried, folded their wings, and nested on a clean stone. Others flew up in their places. The discarded pages of the paperback book (I tore off the sections I set, to reduce the bulk on my linotype's text-rest) filled a waste-basket. I sped on. And finally, after more than thirty hours, I tapped out the last word on page 666 — "separated" — and set the last period. I pulled the last proof and noted with satisfaction that I had finished with a string of five galleys without a single typographical error. It was done. *The Golden Notebook* (its final section bordered in metallic gold) was finished.

While the last set of folios dried, I planned my binding. I wanted to stitch the folios together and bind them in a stiff cover backed with some sort of rich gold *lamé* fabric. I got out my stitching press, my bindery glue, my stiffest chipboard. In a pan of water, ink, and varsol, I marbled endpapers to cover the inside covers. Now all I lacked was the gold fabric. A trip to Georgetown would provide that.

I locked the printery and set off briskly in the chilly night air. The moon sat high and white, the wind blew with the gentle force of breath. I was invigorated, giddy with accomplishment. But when I found the first fabric store dark and locked in Georgetown, and realized suddenly that it was about two o'clock in the morning, my zest puckered. I had forgotten about store hours in my haste to meet the deadline of Buzzy's return.

Without a proper binding, the whole book was severely devalued. A printing masterpiece must combine perfections — the magic of a great book depends on its uncanny consonance of all elements, all inks and papers and chipboards, all the limpness of riffling pages and the stiffness of covers swinging like gates, all the tiny designs of the thousands of characters contrasted with the huge monolithic face of color on the cover. I knew I had no dignified fabric at home; I did not even have any cheesecloth with which to bind the book. No stores were open. I looked around the dark streets, and faced the sudden cold fact that my project — perhaps my life with Buzzy! — was doomed.

Suddenly I was terribly tired. My sense of purpose, and my sense of direction, vanished; I wandered. From the looks I received from the few people I passed in the strange streets, I gathered that I must have been mumbling. I did not care to listen to myself, or to stop. I just walked, turned corners, lingered in alleys. I was adrift. My printery was forgotten.

As I said, I passed a few people now and then. I did not look at most of them very long, because they were dull and dark and ugly. But then, after I had wandered for perhaps an hour, I found my gaze lingering on a young blonde woman who crossed the street in front of me, passed beneath a streetlight, and entered a small bar. It took me a few seconds to focus on the aspect of her appearance that had attracted my unwitting attention, but by analyzing the memory of her passage through the pool of yellow light beneath the streetlamp, I isolated it:

She was wearing a gold *lamé* blouse. I had seen it flash between the lapels of her coat.

Immediately my lethargy and despondency left me. The book project started to click in my mind like a linotype suddenly switched on; my enthusiasm and determination tingled. I followed the path of the woman, and stepped into the bar.

It was a dark, quiet place, with only a dozen people inside. I had no trouble locating the young blonde. She was standing by herself, brow knitted sadly over a highball glass on the bar. I moved to a spot beside her, and quietly ordered a beer. She looked up at me. I smiled. She frowned at her glass, then looked back up at me. I smiled again. After a moment, she smiled too.

I do not remember what I said to her in the bar, probably because the words and actions were so unnatural to me that I am unable to reconstruct and apply them to my persona, in the intimate imagination that serves as memory. I do recall that we smiled quite a bit, and spoke in hushed tones, and laughed once; and I recall the satisfaction I felt when she signalled that my ploy had succeeded so far, by agreeing to take a walk with me.

We strolled in the night down dark streets. She took my arm. She began to squeeze it. We whispered, smiled, cooed. I grew warm and excited as I felt the culmination of my desires drawing closer. She pressed against me as we walked. I saw flashes of gold cloth covering the round breasts she rubbed against my arm. We walked, slowed, and finally stopped, on an empty street not far from a streetlamp. She moved to face me, and gazed into my face with a confused, tender look. I smiled, for the hundredth time, and lowered my gaze to her breasts. She moaned as though I had touched her, and rolled her shoulders slightly.

The cloth looked lovely. I was trembling with expectation. My only worries were that there was an insufficient amount, and that the fabric was too thick. I studied her shape: she was fairly plump, with a broad midsection. I tried to superimpose, in my mind's eye, the folio-sized chipboards on the breadth of her stomach and the corresponding expanse of her covered back — and I calculated that the blouse would suffice.

She whispered the name I had fabricated for myself, and inched closer to me. I smiled at her, stared again at her breasts, and slowly placed my right hand over the left one. She groaned, and pushed the soft flesh against my palm. I softly massaged the nipple, and felt it grow hot and hard beneath my fingers, beneath the cloth. The transference of texture and temperature through the fabric was almost immediate — I was certain that the *lamé* was thin enough to serve as the binding material. I grinned in anticipation.

"Yes," she moaned, "yes, you like it, don't you? Do you like it?"

"Oh, yes," I said, "certainly. It's perfect."

She smiled slyly and stepped closer. "Maybe you ought to try my other one."

"No thank you," I said, with a wink. "I only need this one, really."

She looked puzzled. I removed my hand.

"Do you . . . do you want . . ." she rubbed her hands tightly from her breasts to her waist, over the expanse of *lamé*.

"Yes," I said. "How much will it cost me?"

Her eyes widened, her jaw dropped, and she stepped back. "How much? How . . . What do you think I am? What do you . . . why do you think I . . ." she sputtered.

I had been afraid of this. Naturally, I had hoped that she was not fond of the blouse, and would sell it readily. But she seemed to be offended at the prospect of selling it, which meant that I needed to win her with unction or money. Money was easier. I offered her twenty dollars.

"*Twenty dollars!*" she yelled. Her eyes were blazing. I had not counted on such a fierce recalcitrance.

"I think twenty is generous," I said. "It's not as though the thing is new. It might even be worn out. Plus it probably smells, and I have no time to wash it."

She screamed and swung a fist at me. I blocked it, and she put her hands to her face and started sobbing. This was certainly more emotion than I had expected to encounter.

"Okay, look," I said, taking out a twenty-dollar bill and a ten. "Here's thirty. With that much, you can probably buy *two* new ones."

She jerked her head up and stopped sobbing. I held out the money. She stared at me queerly. "*New?* What . . . what are you talking about?"

I sighed. "Your blouse, of course."

She gawked at me, then looked down at her torso. "My . . . blouse?"

"That's it."

"You want to buy my *blouse?*"

"Desperately."

"You brought me all the way. . . . Is that . . . Is that why you smiled, why you picked me up in the bar? Why you asked me to come out with you? Is that . . . is that why you . . . felt me? My blouse?"

I nodded. "You see. . . ." I started to explain, but she began to laugh, almost hysterically, with sobbing and cackling, and I stopped. I was just as glad. It was getting on toward dawn, and I wanted to get the book finished.

Her laughter slowed for a second, and I said, "So do we have a deal?"

She stopped laughing and smiled at me as though I were an odd picture on a museum wall. She shook her head, then nodded. I held out the bills, but she ignored them. Instead, she slipped off her coat, and let it fall to the ground. Then, slowly, still smiling, she rolled her shoulders and reached behind her back with both hands. There was a long, tortuous sound of a zipper opening. I watched the tight cups of the blouse loosen over her breasts. Undulating slowly, she cupped her hands beneath her breasts and pulled the blouse away from them, toward me. The breasts bobbed and swayed in the moonlight. I reached for the blouse. She pulled it back for a moment. I looked at her face. She puckered her mouth, and shimmied her shoulders, sending her large breasts into jiggling gyrations. Then she threw the blouse at my feet, snatched the money, put on her coat, and walked away.

I pounced on the *lamé* — a blouse no longer! — and found my way home. On the way I examined the fabric, and found it sound. I had been correct about the odor — there was a stink of perspiration in the spots beneath the arms, and a whiff of cheap perfume in the breast cups, but I did not need these areas and hoped the patches across stomach and back were relatively clean.

It took me two hours to complete the stitching, gluing, snipping, and assembly. Just as the sun turned the printery windows pink, I held in my hands the marvelous object. *The Golden Notebook* was truly a masterpiece — it truly *mattered*. I knew that Buzzy would appreciate it in all of its manifestation of my ardor. I bore it into the house like a queen's crown.

I deliberated for a while on how to present it to her upon her return. I finally decided that it would be best to let her find it alone. If I gave it to her, the purity of her reactions would be tempered by her reactions to *me*; she would be too alert to my observation, and might miss some of the beauties that she would be free to examine if left alone with the volume. This was definitely best. I pulled a fine little cherrywood dropleaf table out from our living room and set it up in the hallway, so that it would be the first thing Buzzy saw after entering. I placed the book on the flat back cushion from one of the puce chairs. The gold fabric shone like a huge square coin on top of the berry color. The display was glorious.

It was daytime, and Buzzy might be back any moment. There was one last effect I wanted to apply. I went into the bedroom, and found a battered old anthology of ancient English poetry that Buzzy kept by her side of the bed. It was her favorite book, the only one she does not exhaust with a sequential reading. Inside the book, I knew, was a certain elegant bookmark that I had made for her, from a strip of French cotton paper and sterling foil. I had printed *Buzzy's Best Book* in 24-point Garamond italic across the pale blue paper, in mauve ink. This was the first gift I ever gave Buzzy, nearly a year ago. I took the bookmark out to the table, and propped it against a corner of the grand volume. *Buzzy's Best Book*; Toby's best gift.

I left the house. Since arranging the book, I have waited in my printery, passing the time at the linotype by composing this little description of things (in 10-point Cheltenham, a reliable face). A few hours have gone by. Buzzy has not come back. I have grown a bit sleepy. I have a cot in the corner of the printery here, and I think I might lie down for a while. I'm not worried about Buzzy. She'll come back, she'll see the book, she'll know where to find me. Most of all, she will see the book. She will see it, and she will apprehend all that I understand, about men, women, coming together, us. She will know: it's *all* in there.

ZEPHYR

Patricia Duncan

The ladies' noses were painted with one quick stroke, a slash, a brown line. And those noses were vital. For although they never looked much like real ones, they were the closest I'd been. If the brush was too wet and the color ran, if the curve began too soon, I threw the page away. For they were to be noses, not scars; noses, not misplaced ponytails.

That evening I made my slash and my moment of intensity was gone.

Putting aside the paints, I withdrew further into the raveling wicker chair.

It was here, in the garden daily at dusk, that I spred my feet among the phlox, weeds, and periwinkles to feel ashamed.

I heard her now, banging about the pots in the kitchen as she explained to the cat, Montgomery, why he could have no more milk today. I knew that Zephyr did not mind scrubbing macaroni from a pot while I hurried outside after dinner with my paints. In fact, Zephyr offered to do it; she handed me the watercolors and said: "You don't feel so hot, mama?" No, it wasn't feeling that my daughter resented taking over duties normally left to mothers that made me feel so guilty. Actually, Zephyr thought it great fun to collect rent from the roomers, telling them how to operate the air conditioners as she carefully printed their receipts. And it wasn't that Zephyr was the one who ran off for the plunger when the toilet was plugged up or that she held the raisin bread to the light to see if it was molding when she thought it should be. No, it was none of that.

It was the fact that the girl was ten years old and painted artifical eyes soaking in glass teacups and unicorns wearing sandals while I continued to paint the same ladies I had done for twenty years. It was the fact that Zephyr could amuse herself indefinitely with a magnet and a tiny metal Chevrolet, alone.

It was, after all, the fact that Zephyr raised herself which caused me to dribble colors on typing paper each evening. And it was a look a woman had given me in a grocery store that morning that made me feel especially disgusting as I wiggled my brush in the violet. Zephyr had been asking the stock boy where the cat food was. "The dry cat food," she had emphasized, "the mackerel and salmon actually," as I stood behind the cart gazing at my cuticles. The woman, who came speeding toward me from the detergent aisle, had shot me a glare clearly asking: "Why can't you do it?" And so I had rather meekly approached Zephyr and self-consciously taken her hand.

I sat staring now at my nails with their chipped polish and thought how easy it was to paint Zephyr's, who was, by the way, partial to an obnoxious orchid shade. I would dip the brush once and touch each little nail, making only a slight squiggle, and then she would do mine, biting her lower lip in concentration. At that moment, Zephyr came out with our Japanese roomer.

"Mama, Schozo's going to stay another month," she said, smiling and patting his hand. She seemed fragile as a fawn beside him, a cat's whisker, a shimmering chandelier prism. She had recently cut her own dark bangs and not done such a bad job, except that they dipped in the center in a vaguely vampish way.

"You are?" I said as Schozo bent his huge torso forward in a bow. "Well, we're happy to have you. Is there anything you need?" He cocked his head uncertainly; Zephyr cleared her throat and faced him.

"Do you need towels?" she said slowly, making a rectangle in the air.

"Towel? Oh, no, have three," he answered. "Have everything."

"What are you painting, mama?" Zephyr looked at the paper with that same gentle curiosity she always had, a curiosity I was sure had to be pretended, and I reacted with my same guilty shrug.

"Oh, you know, another lady."

"What's this one's name?" she asked quickly, for that was the only use for the pictures, this choosing of names.

"Hmm, well, I thought she would be . . . Mildred."

"Mildred!" Zephyr laughed. "Mildred! How about Mildew?" And she chuckled and hopped about with her joke.

"Mildew, okay, I guess that might fit her with that dingy gray dress." Zephyr took the brush and painted "MILDEW" in black, making spider webs droop from each letter. Schozo laughed, too, nodding and pointing at the picture.

"She make bugs by lady's head," he said.

"Schozo's going to be on TV again Saturday," Zephyr said. "I told him we'd watch."

Schozo approached me, motioning for me to look at his little finger. "In ring," he said, making a circle, "jump on finger." He stomped a few times. "Hurt finger."

I told him I was sorry, but it was an occupational hazard, a rather minor one, and he should expect such things. None of which he understood. So I asked him if some ice might help.

"Ice, yes, later."

"You don't have to wrestle tonight?" He shook his head. "I was thinking of some wine. Would you care for a glass?" He leaned forward in confusion and looked at Zephyr.

"Wine," she said. "It's kind of like beer."

"Beer? Oh, yes, thank you."

"No, wine, it's—"

"I'll just get some," I said, starting to rise. But Zephyr was already on her way to the kitchen.

Schozo sat and fondled his finger. I felt his uneasiness in Zephyr's absence and knew, with a private little pain, that my daughter communicated with him better than I, that her eagerness and efficiency smoothed the edges. For children can be better than adults with foreigners, the acquisition of language having not yet completely left their memories.

We sat silently as the light dimmed and a stray breeze knocked about the garden's petals, pistils, and stamens, and I wondered how Schozo could be so gentle by day when at night, wearing a black mask and greased with sweat, he beat people up for a living. "But I've heard that the fights aren't for real," Zephyr had told me. And she would know.

"It was too hot," Schozo said, wiping his chin.

"Yes," I answered, although I hadn't noticed, not even in the silk robe

I wore that was tangled in the vines and soil. Zephyr came out with a tray, a bottle of Chablis, and three wineglasses, hers filled with Hawaiian Punch. She handed a glass to Schozo, who in his thirst downed it before I had tasted mine.

"Where is father?" he suddenly blurted. I instinctively threw Zephyr a somewhat panicked glance.

"Gone," was her reply between pursed-lipped sips of punch.

"Ah," he breathed, swabbing his forehead with his shirt sleeve.

"Are you ever hurt badly in your work?" Zephyr asked him, doing a rather beautiful job of subject changing, as she mustered up a look of extreme interest which obviously flattered him. Yes, a much better job than I could have done, for I had urgently snatched up the hem of my dress to pointlessly inspect the stitching.

"Hurt bad? Oh, no, but one time. One time cut head pretty bad."

"I don't see a scar," Zephyr said, going forward to examine his forehead. "Well, just a little one." With a sigh, Zephyr picked up her glass and said she was going inside to do some chores, meaning she might brush the cat, check on the pregnant guppy, or wash her hair. "Call me if you need me," she shouted as she closed the door, and I wondered when she would tire of looking after mother.

"Most people would never worry about the well-being of such a child," I said suddenly. I immediately retreated into my chair, hoping Schozo would ignore the remark, one I thought terribly foolish. I tried never to discuss my worrying about Zephyr, my own lethargy, or, more important, my ten-year-old astonishment over being someone's mother. I poured us more wine.

"You worry about your little girl?"

"Oh, a little," I said with a casual shrug that came off more phonily than I had hoped.

"She sick?"

"No, she's very healthy."

"She is happy little girl."

"You think so?" I asked quickly.

"Why worry?"

"Well, I do," I murmured, and a new wave of it filled me. There were days when I spent hours agonizing over the name I had given her. You can take chances when you name a pet or a racehorse or a boat; you can be as bizarre as you like. But not with your own child. Zephyr and I often laughed about the names we christened my watercolored ladies and I wondered if my daughter had been named, say, Jane, would we laugh at Zephyr? But there had been a reason for it, a good one at the time.

"Do you think she has a strange name? Weird name? Bad name?"

"No, very pretty."

But then, to a Japanese, Mary would be as odd as Zephyr, wouldn't it?

"Well, her father was a meteorologist." Schozo grinned and nodded which meant he did not understand. "A weatherman . . . on television like you, says if it will rain, talks about weather."

"Oh, yes," he said loudly with a long nod, meaning he got it.

"Or if there will be a west wind, westerly wind, or a soft breeze. And, well, she wasn't a common thing and couldn't have a common name and that was all of him she would have, you know?"

Schozo nodded and grinned. I gave us each another dollop of wine.

"I see him on television?"

"Not here."

"He on trip?"

"I don't know where he is. She doesn't really mind not having him, I don't think. But then I don't know what she does mind. A few things, she hates liver, wool blankets, and cards. She likes board games with dice and fake money and all that. She likes winter more than summer; she was born in February, so that might have something to do with it. . . ." I saw that Schozo was leaning forward with that look I'd seen on faces in the language lab when people were frantically thinking, Can't you slow these damn tapes down, or do those people always gab like that?

"You not married to man on television now?"

"We were never married."

"Not married?" he asked loudly with a very long nod.

"We didn't know each other very well, about three weeks. In another city. And he knows nothing of Zephyr, but I've told her as much about him as I remember." I was rambling, but it was okay because of the wine and the translation problem. And he could barely see me in the near-dark, although I caught his face quite clearly in some street light or another, even his scar.

"I worry because it's been ten years and I still have to convince myself that I have this child. I had trouble bearing the responsibility of a cat before her, wondering if it had worms or needed a rabies booster. But a cat meows when it needs something, and Zephyr just gets it for herself. This makes no sense, does it?"

"Father not know he have Zephyr?" he asked, worrying a little himself now.

"No. I didn't know about her myself for quite a while, being just as sort of irresponsible then as now. Only when she let me know that coffee and cigarettes were against her principles about, I guess, three months along."

"You not get lonely sometime?"

"I have some friends." And that was another thing. Perhaps it was going a bit too far when Zephyr welcomed the few stray males who stayed the night. If there was anything she resented about them, it was not their hours in my room, but their premeditated smiling, their offering to play jacks with her. She did not like jacks and let them know by hauling out Monopoly, which they hated because that meant a good two hours.

"Why you never tell father?" Schozo asked, helping himself to the wine. I was annoyed suddenly with his preoccupation with the father. That was eleven years ago; he had merely been there. He had, like the rest of them, sperm and the habit of leaving the toilet seat up. While pointing at the temperatures in Tucson and Phoenix, his teeth and shirt looked white and well cared for; he read mysteries and had a fetish for lettuce-and-mustard sandwiches. I did not recall him looking anything like Zephyr. That was all I remembered, I couldn't help it, that was all there was.

"It's not as though it's such an original case," I told him. "Maybe another woman would have gone back after him, I don't know. But it's more than the fact that she's fatherless; I don't want her to be motherless, too. She'll never have anything to remember about her father and what's to make her *want* to remember how I sat around painting ladies and being childish while she was always so grown-up?"

I could tell that by now Schozo had wearied of translating, that he wanted to walk the wooden, blue-lanterned corridor to his room. Most likely he would look at his mail with its beautiful Japanese stamps, full of lacy moths and delicate networked trees, all in indigo and rose, before he lay down with snatches of odd American sounds.

"Good luck with the wrestling tomorrow," I told him. "I hope you win."

"Oh, I win. Tomorrow Tuesday, they tell me I win," he answered, bowing.

Zephyr was cutting pictures from *National Geographic* in her bedroom, filing them meticulously in a long cardboard box.

"Hi, I put some ice in Schozo's room for his finger," she mumbled, scissoring carefully along a page and then bending over the box.

I flopped into one of her beanbag chairs. "Why are you filing that alligator under C? Oh, I guess it's a crocodile."

"No, it's a caiman, a kind of alligator in South America."

I seemed to wither into the chair and, sighing, could not remember outsmarting my own mother very often, surely not at ten. Look, it's bad enough to be put down by your peers: by a woman in the supermarket, hairnetted and hurrying, by even the Avon lady last week who told me that the lipstick I stared at was not pink, as I thought, but Champagne Pink Frosté instead.

"I suppose," I said quietly as I flipped through the *Us*: Urals, Uxmal, Uzbek, "I suppose you don't think I'm very bright."

"Well, most people would think it was an alligator, mama. It *is* an alligator, just a special kind."

"But you knew it was a caiman."

"I just read that it was right here. See?" She flashed the magazine at me and removed it before I saw anything.

"Does it ever bother you that you know all these things and I don't?"

"Maybe if you read more —"

"I don't need you to tell me to read!" I snapped.

"Sorry," Zephyr said, studiously involved with Ks. She put a pencil behind her ear and sat tapping her foot in concentration. I was amazed, as usual, at her ability to fall so easily into seriousness, to ignore distraction, to be, somehow, important in everything she did. And to ignore me at that moment was something, for I was shamefully greedy for her attention; I hummed and sighed, I uncapped her perfumes, I switched on the aquarium light and startled the neon tetras.

"I do read, but there are other things that I have to do."

"What do you have to do?" she asked.

"What's that remark?" I said fairly insolently.

"I asked you what you had to do," Zephyr repeated, flipping through the magazine and stroking her chin pompously.

"So why aren't you a professor?" I asked her, extremely annoyed. I lit a cigarette, although she forbade them in her room.

"I'd have to go to college first," she replied, looking up for the first time. "And if you're going to smoke, would you please get an ashtray? I don't want my room to burn down."

"I can take care of my own ashes." We'd been through the cigarette debate before; last week she'd brought home a package of little filter gadgets that you attach to the end of the cigarette. "It's supposed to filter out 89.2 percent of the tar and nicotine on your brand," she had told me. And I obediently used them.

"Do you know what your lungs must look like by now?" she asked me. "Here, let me show you," and she hopped off the bed in search of some book.

"I know, black and hideous. Quit being such a know-it-all."

"Here," she said, coming at me with a picture of a horrible exposed lung.

"Would you get it away from me?" I shouted. "Now knock it off, Zephyr. Just sit down and cut out your pictures like a normal kid."

"Okay," she answered indifferently, jumping back on the bed.

Why didn't Zephyr ever get really angry, I wanted to know. And why was I so worried about her? After all, she was actually a godsend; she could have gone around letting air out of people's tires, spilling nail polish on carpets, or swearing. She could have been like the children I had babysat for long ago, the ones I had given fifty cents to go to bed, the ones who had inspired me to invent games in which the rules were: "Let's pretend we're deaf-mutes so we can see how good we have it now."

"You know, Zephyr, that sometimes you sort of, well, make me feel inferior."

"Inferior? How come?"

"Maybe I don't mean inferior. Maybe I mean that I'm just not much help to you."

Zephyr did not reply to this; she was thinking about it, very carefully, winding her hair around a finger, biting her lower lip.

"I admit I haven't been the most *normal* mother."

To this, Zephyr tilted her head and squinted at me.

"I actually hadn't planned to be a mother, you know," I told her. "You were sort of a surprise package."

"A good surprise?"

"Zephyr, what do you really think about me?" I decided to ask before answering her; for it was something I now needed to know, something I wanted out of her, quickly, and to the point.

"What, mama? Well, I think you're pretty," and she came forward to take a handful of my hair.

"No, come on, what do you think?"

"You're a lot better than *he* is, my *father*," she said shortly, wrinkling her nose and returning to the bed.

"You don't know him."

"He doesn't care about me."

"He doesn't *know* about you. I had to."

"Aren't you glad you know about me?" And there was some sort of look in her eyes I didn't recognize, that had never been there, an odd little stare which deepened the blue. It was not a pleasant look. It might even have been a frightened look or, in Zephyr, something as rare.

"Of course I'm glad."

Zephyr sat still a moment more, then loosened partially. She then began something quite uncharacteristic; she fidgeted. She picked at the bedspread, scratched her ear, cleared her throat.

"I just don't think you need me, that's all," I said. And there it was, out finally.

"But . . . but what would I do if —"

"You're wondering where you would live? You'd have your choice; anybody would want you."

"I know, but . . . things might not be the same," she said softly. And now she was obviously unsettled. I was startled at my cruelty, for I had her sitting as straight as a victim of charm school; I had her swallowing and blinking, and she was pressing her little orchid nails into her knees. And yet there was a satisfaction in this as well, a twinge of perverse pride that I was now the one delivering a bit of uneasiness.

"You think those ladies I paint are stupid, don't you?" I asked belligerently. "Really stupid."

"Stupid? No, mama. I — I like them."

"Oh, come on! They're all the same. You do better yourself. Now be honest with me."

Zephyr suddenly widened her eyes and pushed back her bangs. In a very smooth tone, she said: "I *am* being honest."

She might mean that, I thought. And bending closer to my daughter who had, above all, a need for truth, who had been told nothing but that all her life, who at ten wanted no fakery about the facts of her father and faced, rather gallantly, the phobias of her mother, I saw that she did mean it.

We settled to stare at each other, eyes blue to blue, huddled in Zephyr's room of tropical fish and dictionaries and exotic snapshots. Her hand came to my face, and with her thumb she traced my nose, just once, a slash, a very even line.

INDEX

ACKNOWLEDGMENTS (continued from page iv): *Quotations*

Margaret Atwood. Excerpts from *Lady Oracle* by Margaret Atwood. Copyright © 1976 by Margaret Atwood. Reprinted by permission of Simon & Schuster, a Division of Gulf & Western Corporation.

Robert Coover. Excerpts from *Pricksongs and Descants* by Robert Coover, copyright © 1969 by Robert Coover, as follows: from "The Gingerbread House," p. 61; from "Panel Game," pp. 79–80 and p. 80; from "The Babysitter," p. 206. Reprinted by permission of the publisher, E. P. Dutton.

Joan Didion. Excerpt from *A Book of Common Prayer* by Joan Didion. Copyright © 1977 by Joan Didion. Reprinted by permission of Simon & Schuster, a Division of Gulf & Western Corporation.

Laurence Gonzalez. Excerpt from *The New York Times Book Review*, Vol. LXXXV, No. 6, p. 13. © 1980 by The New York Times Company. Reprinted by permission.

Ernest Hemingway. Excerpt from Ernest Hemingway, *The Old Man and the Sea*. Copyright 1952 by Ernest Hemingway; copyright renewed. Reprinted with the permission of Charles Scribner's Sons.

Maxine Hong Kingston. Excerpt from Maxine Hong Kingston, *China Men*. Copyright © 1977, 1978, 1979, 1980 by Maxine Hong Kingston. Reprinted by permission of Alfred A. Knopf, Inc.

Flannery O'Connor. Excerpts from "The Life You Save May Be Your Own" from *A Good Man Is Hard to Find and Other Stories* by Flannery O'Connor. Copyright 1948, 1953, 1954, © 1955 by Flannery O'Connor. Copyright © 1976 by Regina O'Connor. Reprinted by permission of the publisher, Harcourt Brace Jovanovich, Inc.

Tom Robbins. Excerpts from *Even Cowgirls Get the Blues* by Tom Robbins. Copyright © 1976 by Tom Robbins. By permission of Bantam Books, Inc.

Diane Roberts. Excerpt from "Lamia" by Diane Roberts. Copyright © 1982 by Diane Roberts. Used by permission of the author.

Paul Simon. Excerpt from Paul Simon, "Still Crazy After All These Years," © 1974, 1975 by Paul Simon. Used by permission.